A Practical Guide
to Understanding and Serving
Students with Behavioral Impairments
in the Public Schools

Beyond Time Out

Second Edition

*An Introduction to Insights and Interventions from the
Field of Developmental Psychopathology*

John Stewart, Ph.D.

This book is dedicated to the memory of
Katie
A young friend whose short life was lived with courage,
grace, and most of all, spirit.

Acknowledgements

I wish to thank the following individuals for their help and support in writing this book:

My wife, Janet, for her ongoing support and thoughtful feedback as she read and reread many versions of this text.

Dr. Rachel Avery, for her friendship, encouragement and generosity in sharing a remarkable knowledge of children.

My sister, Marcia Breckenridge, for her help with proofreading.

Dr. Cynthia Sortwell, for her support in reviewing the section on medication.

Sandra Wilson, for her patience and good judgment in proofreading.

Kara Hanson, for her administrative support.

Brenda Chandler, for her generous spirit and wise editing.

Jim and Janice Boyko, for friendship and support in reading.

My kids, Sam and Anna, for teaching me at least as much as I have taught them.

My Mom and Dad, for their unyielding support.

The many kids, families and schools that have allowed me to be a part of their lives.

Table of Contents

Every thing that is done in the world is done by hope.
— Martin Luther

Preface

The manuscript that follows is largely derived from the content of a training seminar entitled Understanding and Managing the Aggressive and Acting-Out Child in the Public School. I have presented this seminar on more than ninety occasions to audiences composed of teachers, special educators, school administrators and public-school-based mental-health providers, all of whom share the difficult task of serving students with behavioral impairments in the public schools. The central message offered in this seminar is that, prior to establishing specialized programs for behaviorally impaired students, public schools must develop a coherent and compassionate understanding of these children.

For the reader with a limited mental-health background, this book provides a point of departure for understanding these complicated students; for the reader with considerable mental-health experience, it is offered as a model for consultation and training in the public schools. By way of disclaimer let me state that there is virtually nothing in this text that is not more extensively and more eloquently presented by other authors and, with the exception of the diagnostic categorization model, there is nothing that I can claim as original. Additionally, I have no doubt that, in my effort to present a somewhat simplified introduction to the central concepts of developmental psychopathology, I have diluted some of the complex theoretical concepts from which I have drawn. In light of this, it is my hope that the curious reader will investigate these theories and concepts further through additional reading and study.

Mental-Health Services in the Public Schools

This text represents my evolving thoughts and observations concerning services for children with emotional and behavioral impairments within the public schools. My experience working with this population has entailed a number of roles, ranging from employment as a special-education teacher in a self-contained classroom for adolescents with behavioral and emotional handicaps, to my current position as a psychologist consulting to the public schools. In many respects, my early experience as a special-education teacher has significantly informed my approach to school consultation. I remember well the considerable stress and responsibility I felt in that role, a stress associated not with high expectations on the part of my supervisors that I "fix," "heal," or even teach my students, but rather with the awesome responsibility simply to contain them. My administrative supervision in this role seemed to be characterized by three implicit objectives: contain the bodies, voices and energies of my students so that they not contaminate the broader community; do this without putting the school or myself at risk for criminal charges or civil litigation; and, lastly, each morning, no matter how difficult the preceding day, return to this classroom and try again. For two years I did relatively well at meeting these criteria, but ultimately I felt compelled to seek an easier means to make a living: I joined the Peace Corps and moved to an outpost near Antarctica to work with post-Allende Chilean political exiles.

Since my return to the public schools as a psychological consultant, I have generally seen the administrators with whom I work make a genuine effort to offer effective programming for their students with behavioral and emotional impairments. Unfortunately, I have also seen the vast majority of programs designed to serve this difficult population flounder and eventually fail. For this reason I will attempt to identify both the origins of problems and solutions to dilemmas in the public schools' effort to serve the increasing numbers of children with behavioral and emotional impairments.

Where Are We and How Did We Get Here?

It is beyond the scope of this work to address comprehensively why there appears to be a dramatic increase in the number of troubled and behaviorally handicapped children entering our schools. However, from my perspective, this increase is linked to two central issues: the stress associated with the rapid pace of technological advancement, and improved medical treatment that results in an increased survival rate for neurobiologically fragile children. Due to an unprecedented pace in technological advancement and the extraordinary demands of adaptation in a world that is constantly and rapidly changing, an ever-increasing number of individuals find themselves unable to establish a secure niche within contemporary culture. Effective adaptation to an ever-changing environment demands both the neurocognitive skills to understand and respond quickly to change, as well as access to education or retraining to support the development of new competencies. Consequently, individuals who do not possess these resources are often unable to establish an essential sense of competency and security.

Past generations faced a world characterized by gradual change, which allowed those with weaker adaptive resources to establish a narrow, but stable niche of competency in which they could develop both a livelihood and a sense of purpose. Because of recent advances in technology and automation, many of these niches no longer exist, and an ever-increasing portion of the population despairs of their ability to secure a valued place within the workforce and community. Unable to ride the wave of change, they experience a hopelessness that leads them to a shortsighted and volatile approach to life and behavior driven by the belief that long-term commitment rarely pays off. This promotes a lifestyle characterized by disposable relationships, inability to delay gratification, and reliance upon drugs and alcohol for relief from despair. Children raised by parents caught in this dilemma experience immeasurable insecurity and a deep sense of hopelessness. These children are limited in their ability to invest in endeavors—such as education—which entail delaying gratification for the promise of the future.

The second major force increasing the number of children with behavioral impairments entering our schools may be linked to medical advances in prenatal and postnatal care. As a result of these advances, the lives of children who are the product of complicated pregnancies and deliveries are more frequently preserved, increasing the number of children who enter the world neurologically vulnerable to adaptive struggle. This is not to lament the saving of these children's lives, but rather to underscore that work in serving this group goes well beyond addressing the medical needs of early life.

If these causal factors are valid, educators are forced to recognize that behavioral problems within our schools will improve neither quickly nor independently. Our culture has changed dramatically, and the gap between those who possess the skills to ride the wave of change and those without such skills is widening. If educators choose to define public education as the domain of those who possess the ability to ride the wave, a smaller and smaller percentage of children will fit this criterion, and public education will play a central role in perpetuating, as opposed to addressing, this situation.

SPECIALIZATION: "I'M A TEACHER NOT A THERAPIST!"

As the technological revolution has raced forward—creating an explosion in the amount of information needed to manage the many tools upon which we rely—we have rapidly moved towards an increased reliance upon specialists. With this evolving dependence on specialists to help us manage technology there has been a parallel shift towards a reliance upon specialists within non-technological and relationship-based endeavors. This carry-over is problematic, since a pattern of deferring to specialists leads to a reduction in the personal sense of investment and of obligation to address challenges outside one's perceived scope of expertise. As a result of this dynamic, individuals within our culture are increasingly reticent to accept responsibility for situations over which they feel a limited sense of mastery or competency.

Unfortunately, this reticence has serious implications for the willingness of educators to embrace the responsibility of meeting the often ambiguous and confusing needs of our most difficult and complex students. Inherent in the work with such students—regardless of one's background or training—are frequent feelings of inadequacy, frustration and limited competency. Consequently, contemporary teachers too readily defer to so-called experts, and thereby create several significant problems.

First among these potential problems is the student's feeling of abandonment as his teacher abdicates responsibility to the expert. The process is often experienced by the child as a fumbling transition from a teacher whom he experiences as anxious or fearful to an "expert" whom he neither knows nor trusts. This awkward transition has significant potential to further compromise an already insecure child's sense of security by undermining his belief that others will be able to understand and adequately meet his needs (see Chapter II, on socialization and relationship formation).

An additional problem associated with overreliance upon specialists is its tendency to undermine the teacher's personal obligation to develop a coherent, empathic understanding of a troubled child's needs. In my role as a school consultant, I am too infrequently asked to help teachers understand the behavior they are confronting and all too often asked simply to provide an intervention strategy or clinical rationale for moving the child out of the classroom. It is my sense that the common failure of teachers to attempt to understand aberrant behavior is largely a reflection of an inadequacy in teacher-training programs that do not prepare them to work with troubled students. I am not suggesting that teachers should receive the same training as mental-health clinicians. However, I do believe that if they are working with students with significant behavioral issues, it is imperative that they have extensive exposure to models that can help them understand the behaviors that they are obligated to manage.

Much of the following text will attempt to provide a useful and comprehensive (yet relatively simple) model for understanding children who present with behavioral impairments. In providing this information my intent is not to eliminate the use of psychological consultants or specialists, but to support the transformation of the process of consultation into one of collaboration between two parties who share a responsibility to understand first, and to intervene second. This two-step process is essential, not only because understanding of the child's behavior will direct intervention, but also because our most powerful intervention often lies in the commitment, hope and caring that are expressed in a committed effort to understand a troubled child.

WHERE DO WE GO?

There is no single factor more predictive of poor long-term adjustment than severe acting-out and aggressive behaviors during childhood. These behaviors often serve as a prelude to life-long patterns of maladaptation and institutional care (e.g., prison, psychiatric institutions, and welfare support). Because life-long institutional care incurs extraordinary emotional and financial costs, we are obligated, out of both compassion and pragmatism, to aggressively seek effective intervention for children exhibiting behavioral maladaptation. Unfortunately, limited consensus exists concerning the attributes of effective intervention for these children—with the exception of a universal recognition that the earlier the intervention occurs within a child's life the greater the hope for significant change or healing.

A significant aspect of the public schools' difficulty in effectively addressing the needs of students with behavioral and emotional impairments is linked to the fact that our schools generally function in a highly reactive mode and only direct resources to the most immediate sources of concern. This pattern is particularly unfortunate because it often means that resources are allocated to those older, more dangerous, and frightening students who are generally less affected by intervention. Too often, behavior-intervention resources are limited during the first years of a child's education. This is not to suggest that school personnel are unaware of the fact that many of their younger students are struggling with emotional and behavioral issues. However, during those early years, these students do not provoke the fear that they do at a later point in development when they gain physical strength. The young child with a behavioral handicap is generally thought of as a source of worry, but extensive efforts to organize a response to his needs are not typically mobilized merely out of a sense of concern. Within a few years, when this same child becomes more physically powerful, increasingly disruptive, and potentially dangerous, he becomes the object of considerable attention. This attention is often too late to be optimally effective, and takes the form of labeling the child as a criminal who needs to be served by juvenile corrections (effectively saying, "He is no longer our problem; get him out of here") or of writing an enormous check to any institution that is willing to accept responsibility for the student. It is my deepest belief that if our schools are to address the needs of their behaviorally handicapped students, they must abandon the philosophy of not doing today what they can put off doing (or paying for) until tomorrow.

Early intervention should ideally begin with prenatal care, but the public-school system's goal and mandated responsibility is to seek and serve special-needs children from birth to age twenty-one. In public education's process of identifying very young children with behavioral impairments, considerable focus will need to be directed toward collecting thorough developmental histories and assessing the children's neurocognitive skills, as well as their capacities to manage affect and use relationships (issues discussed extensively in Chapter II). Certainly by kindergarten and first grade, children who act out, exhibiting aggressive or other deviant social behavior, should be identified for special-education support services. As part of a commitment to pragmatism and to compassionate treatment of our most vulnerable children, I believe that the response to behaviorally impaired students must be characterized by both early and aggressive (broad, multi-modal) intervention.

The importance of early and aggressive intervention can be illustrated in an analogy between the treatment of child psychopathology and the treatment of a bacterial infection. In serving the child with behavioral handicaps—as in the treatment of an infection—it is imperative that intervention occur as early as possible to avoid allowing the pathology to spread and deepen. Clearly—as in the treatment of infection—the earlier we are able to identify and address the underlying pathology, the greater the likelihood of full recovery; and, conversely, the longer we wait to intervene, the less likely that intervention will truly be effective. Taking this analogy one step further, it is imperative not only that intervention occur as early as possible, but also that it be adequately aggressive. As with the use of antibiotics, inadequate treatment with too limited a dose or too short a period of intervention exposure is not only ineffective but also undermines future intervention efforts. Inadequate intervention partially masks symptoms that would have signaled the need for more-aggressive treatment, thus delaying the child's access to necessary intervention.

It has been my experience too often that the special-education directive, which requires that all students be served in the least restrictive setting, has been put into practice in a manner that systematically underserves the needs of many students with behavioral impairments. I believe that these students are frequently placed in programs which focus on the containment of their behavior, not on treatment of underlying pathology. This strategy often partially masks developmental psychopathology, thus promoting future adaptive failure and decreasing the potential efficacy of future intervention.

I am convinced that we must address the needs of emotionally and behaviorally vulnerable children through aggressive, multi-modal intervention during the primary-school years of their lives. This is not to say that every child who exhibits a degree of behavioral difficulty must be placed within a specialized program, but rather that we must become more effective in identifying those children who require this level of intervention and assure that public schools have ready access to necessary resources. And, for those students with evolving or less severe emotional and behavioral problems, we must ensure that teachers have adequate training and support to allow them to serve the students effectively.

In response to the stress associated with our rapidly changing culture, practicality demands a significant broadening of the public school's role in supporting the family—moving from a perspective that has focused on what the family can do to help the school, to a perspective that asks what the schools can do to support the family. If the public schools are truly to embrace the challenge of effectively addressing the needs of high-risk students, the school-based team will assume increased responsibility in supporting both the child and the family. Unfortunately, at present, our response to a troubled child is often similar to building a protective fence around a young plant (the child), while ignoring the eroding soil in which it grows (the family). Too often this strategy results in the plant becoming so compromised that we intervene by pulling it out at its roots and attempting to place it within new soils—a process which is neither effective nor humane.

POINT OF DEPARTURE

As indicated earlier, this text is organized around the belief that the first step in addressing problem behavior entails employing a useful model for understanding it—where "useful" is defined as the model's ability to explain the origin and character of the problem behavior, and to prescribe intervention. Consistent with this position, the following presentation on school-based intervention for the behaviorally impaired opens by providing a developmental model for understanding the origin and function of problematic behavior. In seeking a useful model for this task we must select a structure for understanding the child and his behavior that is eloquent (comprehensive and internally consistent), empirically validated, humane (excluding beliefs such as: "he is demon-possessed" or "from a bad seed"), and pragmatic (identifying appropriate strategies for intervention). As stated earlier, my experience within the public-school setting has led me to believe that we have woefully under-addressed our responsibility to provide educators with useful models for understanding these complex children. Adding to this problem is the fact that mental-health consultants often ignore the adage "Give a man a fish and he will eat for a day, but teach him to fish and he will eat for a lifetime." We have too readily handed out advice on behavior management to the "starving" educators seeking immediate relief from the ravages of problem behavior, but we have frequently ignored the far more important task of "teaching them to fish" by providing them the means to make sense out of their students' more complex and confusing behaviors.

Due to the complexity of work with students with behavioral handicaps, and the frequent feelings of frustration and hopelessness associated with teaching these children, I believe there are two fundamental realities public schools must embrace if we are to do this work well:

1. This work cannot be done by an individual working in relative isolation.

Intensive work with emotionally troubled children potentially elicits, between the helping professional and the child, a debilitating parallel experience of hopelessness, anxiety, fear and anger. These potentially debilitating emotions must be effectively managed if intervention is to be successful. The most effective means to manage them is through collaboration and sharing of this work with others. The emotionally taxing impact of this work must be dissipated through a sense of community, humor and shared responsibility.

2. Real change in a child's psychological profile occurs slowly and is often difficult to see on a day-to-day basis.

The importance of our ability to recognize and accept small increments of change as evidence of the child's capacity to heal and grow cannot be overstated. If we expect to see a child make dramatic improvements over a short period of time we will quickly become cynical and hopeless; as a result, we will define both the child and ourselves as failures. We must accept that our responsibility is to plant a seed that often requires a great deal of time to develop, and that, although we may not stay in his life long enough to observe the sprouting of that seed, our effort has not been worthless.

Section I

Understanding
the Children We Serve

Do not mistake a child for his symptom.
— Erik Erikson

I

Common Needs of All Children

Often overlooked in work with behaviorally impaired children is the fact that their fundamental needs are neither more complicated nor more confusing than those of their less challenging counterparts, even though the process of meeting those needs may be far more complex. In light of this, I will begin my discussion of school-based services to the behaviorally impaired with discussion of the broad developmental needs of all children. In this discussion three essential requirements for healthy emotional development are outlined:

1) a fundamental and pervasive sense of safety;

2) a sense of belonging;

3) frequent and expanding experiences of competency.

The section which follows will explain these needs and suggest guidelines for assessing the quality and nature of a child's school experience. Through careful attention to these three critical variables, we can assess the appropriateness and adequacy of the services we provide to both typical and special-needs students. If, in looking critically at the character of a student's experience, we determine that one or more of these variables is significantly lacking, we must not only question whether we are effectively serving him, but also face the unsettling possibility that we are actually harming his development.

Psychological Needs of All Children

Safety

Belonging

Competency

Fig. 1

SAFETY, BELONGING AND COMPETENCY

As stated above, the requisite experiences for healthy emotional development can be divided into three basic areas: safety, belonging and competency. The essence of each of these requisite experiences is its capacity to increase the child's fundamental sense of security and minimize his experience of potentially debilitating anxiety (see Chapter IV).

The following section will define and briefly discuss each of these fundamental experiences as they relate to the caretaker's role in the child's life. Please note that the term caretaker is used in a generic sense to refer to any individual within the child's life who supervises or cares for the child. Implicit in the use of this broad term is the belief that the fundamental responsibilities for any adult serving a caretaker role within a child's life is essentially the same—whether those responsibilities are carried out by a teacher, parent, therapist or neighbor.

Safety: Assurance that one's fundamental physical needs will be understood and met.

Safety is understood as the child's experiencing of his caretaker as having both the resources and commitment to understand and meet his fundamental needs. Adequate and consistent provision of safety results in the child's secure belief that he will have his basic needs for food, shelter and protection from harm met while under the supervision of the caretaker.

Meeting these needs allows the child to develop an adaptive faith in the caretaker's capacity to keep him safe, thus reducing his fundamental anxiety concerning survival. Unfortunately, should the child experience the caretaker as either incompetent or anxiously questioning his own capacity to assure the child's safety, the child's fundamental sense of security will be undermined and anxiety-related problematic behavior will result.

Belonging: A sense that one is not wholly unique and that others are empathically attuned (i.e. possess the capacity to know and understand one's needs, wants and fears).

A sense of belonging depends upon two distinct but related experiences: first, the child's belief that there are others within his life who are similar; and second, a sense that his caretakers are able to recognize and respond to his needs, independently from the child's capacity to understand or articulate these needs.

The first of these issues, the need to sense commonality with others, is clearly exhibited in most stages of development and is associated with the strong draw between same-age peers. In finding a "twin" as described by Kohut (1977, 1984) or a "chum" in Sullivan's terms (1953), the child experiences an important affirmation of self that supports a sense of camaraderie, adequacy and associated security. Unfortunately, for those children who significantly deviate from the developmental norm and exhibit inappropriate behavior, the process of gaining a relative sense of adequacy through a perception of themselves as similar to others is often unavailable. Children with inappropriate behavior not only lack the comfort of a sense of similarity with their peers, but also spend much of their time looking into the faces of startled and anxious caretakers, whose expressions communicate the message, "What's wrong with you? Why aren't you like everyone else?" The net result of these experiences is an evolving and debilitating sense of deformity, isolation and heightened anxiety.

The second of the requisite experiences for the healthy development of a sense of belonging is the child's perception of the caretaker as empathically attuned. Attunement is the caretaker's competency in understanding the child's inner experience and needs, regardless of the child's capacity to express or even recognize these needs himself. The child's experience of an empathetic and competent caretaker directly translates into a sense of security, reduced anxiety, and more effective adaptive functioning. Through trusting the caretaker's competency to understand and meet his needs, the child is released from a great deal of potentially debilitating anxiety. The absence of this attunement on the part of the caretaker—often associated with a caretaker who finds the child confusing and difficult to understand—directly results in the child's increased anxiety and decreased capacity for adaptive functioning.

Competency: Multiple and frequent experiences that support an expanding sense of one's own capabilities.

This developmental need demands a variety of skills from the caretaker that relate directly to the child's capacity to develop a fundamental faith in his own ability to manage life's demands. The qualities required of the caretaker to provide a sense of competency for the child include: a clear commitment to supporting the child's movement towards autonomy, accurate assessment of the child's abilities, and insight concerning the incremental and sequential nature of the learning process. If the caretaker lacks any of these requisite skills, his capacity to support the child in the development of an evolving sense of competency will suffer.

The process of supporting a child's movement towards a greater sense of competency requires the consistent provision of experiences, delicately balanced between overchallenging and underchallenging the child (see Chapter III on optimal frustration). Unfortunately, accurate reading of a child's cues (so as to discern the range between overchallenge and underchallenge) is often difficult and demands a high degree of empathetic attunement. Each child is different in his ability to confront the frustration inherent in challenge. Effective parenting and teaching require developing an accurate empathetic understanding of the child's individual abilities, limitations, emotional style, fears and needs.

DISCUSSION

It is my perspective that public education is frequently successful in providing its less-challenging students the essential experiences of safety, belonging and competency. However, in serving more-challenging students our schools often fall far short in providing these experiences, resulting in the behaviorally impaired child experiencing school as simply another setting where his needs are neither recognized nor met.

The failure of our schools to provide necessary and healing experiences for our most complex students is neither surprising nor difficult to understand, since a number of factors complicate this task. Key factors inhibiting the public schools' effectiveness in serving these complicated students include: limited understanding and empathetic insight on the part of the teachers, delayed intervention, limited intervention resources, and a sense of both ambivalence and hopelessness concerning work with this population.

As stated earlier, a core issue is the typical educator's lack of background or training with models to support him in understanding the behaviors presented by these students. In the absence of such models, the teacher may perceive the difficult and unusual behaviors as fully volitional and malevolent. This perception elicits a pattern of response (intervention) dominated by punishment rather than by consideration of the child's problem behaviors as a reaction to unmet needs.

A second factor that dramatically impacts the public schools' ability to meet the needs of behaviorally impaired students relates to the issue of delayed (versus early) intervention and the provision of the experience of safety. The inability of the behaviorally impaired child to monitor and control his own behavior in a manner that supports a fundamental sense of safety is characteristic of many of these children. These students frequently engage in impulsive and affectively driven behaviors that compromise both their perceived and their actual safety. In light of this fact, the task of affording these students the necessary and healing experience of safety entails an exaggerated responsibility on the part of their caretakers. The capacity of the caretaker to provide the appropriate level of support to assure safety (at least while the child is in the caretaker's presence) is essential. Ultimately, this responsibility demands that the caretaker be able to direct the child to safety and to provide physical containment when necessary as a part of assuring the child's well-being. The provision of compassionate, non-injurious physical containment becomes a complicated issue within the public school, particularly as the student matures and becomes more physically powerful. When appropriately trained through programs such as *Therapeutic Crisis Intervention*, teachers can effectively meet the physically aggressive behaviorally impaired child's periodic need for containment during his early school years. However, expecting public schools to meet this need in late middle school and high school is unrealistic. Ironically, it is too often the case that behaviorally impaired students (particularly those with antisocial characteristics) are not identified for the special services which would meet their needs for physical containment until they have reached a point in their development when the school is unable to do so.

A third factor undermining the effectiveness of public education for behaviorally impaired students is a general sense of hopelessness about the prospects of these students. In the absence of hope, teachers rarely expend the energy and creativity needed for this difficult work. Common factors eliciting a sense of despair among caretakers include: the slow rate of change for these students (even when needs are effectively met); the existence of biological/neurological limitations which are not correctable (e.g., severe learning disabilities, ADHD); home lives characterized by chaos, neglect or abuse; and, last but not least, the child's own, often deep and pervasive sense of hopelessness. If public education is to overcome the impact of hopelessness as it relates to work with this population, it will be through multi-modal intervention centered on providing training and ongoing technical and personal support to educators (see Chapter VII on supervision and consultation).

If public education fully embraces its responsibility to meet the needs of the behaviorally impaired student through providing their teaching staff with adequate background, training and support, this institution has tremendous potential to effect significant positive change for these vulnerable children. Unquestionably, if our schools become skilled in providing behaviorally impaired students the necessary experiences of *safety, belonging* and *competency*, no institution holds greater hope for supporting these children in their movement toward healing and optimal adjustment. However, it is additionally clear that, should the public schools fail to move toward a more enlightened management of these students, the population of troubled children will continue to grow, not only *within* the schools, but *as a reaction to* the schools. It is imperative that we not allow students with behavioral handicaps to flounder in school settings where they feel unsafe, alone and incompetent—ultimately resulting in behavior so unmanageable that the school is unable to meet their needs and proclaims, "We are done. You are now someone else's problem."

II

Understanding Individual Differences

In the section which follows I present two central developmental variables to support understanding of the wide range of behaviors exhibited by children within the public schools: *relational capacity* and *the capacity to organize.* By assessing a child's development with respect to these two capacities we can place him in one of four categories (Normal, and diagnostic categories A, B, and C) that can be used to better understand his behavior and direct intervention.

RELATIONAL CAPACITY

The first of the two broad developmental variables presented in this section is a child's capacity to form and utilize relationships. Discussion of this critical developmental variable will draw from the field of developmental psychology with particular focus upon Object Relations Theory and Attachment Theory.

The normal, healthy capacity to form and utilize relationships entails two sequential steps of development, each with the common function of supporting the child in the management of potentially debilitating anxiety. The initial stage of this development involves the child's capacity to experience a sense of calm and security when in the presence of the caretaker. This ability is contingent upon the child's developing a powerful association between the presence of the caretaker and experiences of safety and well-being. When this association is well formed the mere presence of the caretaker serves to calm the child and alleviate the anxiety. However, when this association does not evolve (as will be discussed at later point) the child finds little comfort or value in the caretaker's presence and is far more frequently plagued by problematic anxiety.

The second stage of development in using relationships to manage anxiety entails the child's ability to access a soothing emotional memory of the caretaker (positive introject) which may be employed as a means of managing anxiety in the caretaker's absence. Theoretical support for the presence and importance of this second stage of relationship development is abundant, but it is perhaps nowhere more clear than in the works of Margaret Mahler (1974) and D.W. Winnicott (1956, 1958, 1972, 1975).

Mahler, a developmental theorist who spent considerable time observing the interaction between healthy young children and their mothers, made a number of observations concerning the nature and function of mother-child bonds. In her observations, Mahler noted a common pattern of marked behavioral quiescence in preschool children functioning within somewhat novel situations immediately following separation from their mothers. She observed that children in these situations will initially shift to an internal focus and, for a period, appear disconnected from their surroundings. However, after a few moments they will emerge from this trance-like state and slowly return to an effective engagement with their environment. Mahler concluded that this brief period of "low-keyed" behavior reflected a highly focused internal or psychological process. This process was understood as involving disengagement from a sense of security based upon the physical presence of the mother and engagement of the child's emotional memory of the mother as a source of support. In this process, the child shifts his full attention away from the external environment and directs it toward the evocation of the soothing "mother memory."

The second theoretical concept useful in our understanding of the nature and purpose of the second stage of relationship formation (the use of emotional memories of the competent caretaker) is Winnicott's concept of "transitional objects." This term refers to an activity or object used in a ritualistic manner by a child to support himself in invoking the soothing emotional memory of the caretaker. Common examples of these objects include a child's security blanket, stuffed animal or his own thumb. These objects gain their power to calm the child (reduce anxiety) from their association with the caretaker. In the case of the blanket or stuffed animal, this occurs as a paired association process in which the caretaker supplies the child with the blanket or stuffed animal and then structures experiences which imbue the object with the power to soothe. By consistently offering the child the object and communicating its power to soothe, the caretaker essentially communicates, "Take this in remembrance of me." In the case of the child who sucks his thumb or rocks back and forth, these behaviors are soothing because they provide evocative kinesthetic cues to memories of shared experiences with his caretaker, such as breast feeding and being rocked to sleep—or perhaps the gentle movement experienced *in utero*. The following story, involving my daughter Anna, is a good illustration of this concept.

Anna

Between the ages of eighteen months and four years, my daughter Anna enjoyed a wonderful, although somewhat exclusive, relationship with my wife. Anna, periodically fond of her dad, clearly placed most of her emotional needs in the able hands of her mom. This reliance upon her mother translated into a pattern of regularly checking in with her whenever in need of a bit of support.

Because of this relationship, each day would begin with Anna methodically making her way down the long hallway from her bedroom into our room, dragging both her feet and blanket along the way. Arriving in our room barely awake, she would walk around our bed, ignoring her dad as she passed en route to her mother's side, where she would climb in for her morning dose of Mom. This routine was completely predictable, with the exception of those mornings on which, to her great disappointment, she would find that Mom had already left for work. These times were relatively infrequent—since her mom was a per-diem nurse who worked one or two days a week—yet frequent enough that Anna was forced to come up with an adaptive strategy to manage them.

As her dad, it was my mistaken assumption that I might be a logical substitute for Mom in these situations. On a number of occasions, I unsuccessfully attempted to assert myself in that role. However, it quickly became clear that this was not helpful for Anna. In my inadequate effort to function in a Mom-like way, I simply amplified Anna's experience of Mom's absence and her longing for Mom's presence. After several unsuccessful efforts at being Mom, I chose to allow Anna to lead the way in getting us through this morning ritual. To Anna's adaptive credit, she quickly came upon a strategy that worked quite well. This substitute routine, which I watched from bed with some degree of amusement, entailed a pattern similar to what happened when Mom was present. It included the walk down the hall, entry into our bedroom, and total disregard of Dad. Anna would walk around to Mom's side of the bed; arriving at the point where Mom would usually help her up into the bed, Anna would notice her absence, breath a deep sigh and pull her way up into her mom's spot. Once in the bed (continuing to ignore her dad) she would wrap her arms around her mom's pillow, bury her face within it and deeply inhale, searching for Mom's scent. Having completed this ritual, effectively using the pillow to bring up a clear emotional memory of Mom's presence, she would roll over to me and acknowledge my existence, in some manner expressing, "Mom's on board. Dad, I'm now ready for your marginally competent parenting."

Recognizing the profoundly detrimental impact of a weakness in the capacity to form and use soothing emotional memories of one's caretakers in the management of anxiety, we are obligated to attempt to understand and respond to the dynamics that contribute to this limitation. To this end I will present three critical relationship variables, each of which might occur either in isolation or in combination with the others. The first of these is the capacity of the child's caretaker to both understand and respond to the child's needs. The second is the child's neurocognitive capacity to develop a clear and well-organized perception (schema/memory) of the caretaker, and the third is the caretaker's ability to relate to the child in a manner which serves to promote an evolving sense of competency and faith in the child's own abilities.

Caretaker Competency

The initial, or foundation, variable impacting a child's ability to form and utilize relationships effectively is that of the caretaker's competency in understanding and meeting the child's needs. Competency in this arena is measured by the caretaker's ability to demonstrate consistently adequate empathic attunement to the child's needs, as well as the motivation, ability and resources to meet these needs. Many factors control the success a caretaker has in addressing this variable, ranging from his degree of empathic skill in accurately understanding the child's needs, to the nature and extent of those needs, to the availability of resources to fulfill those needs.

A caretaker's empathic attunement or awareness of a child's needs is controlled by many factors, including both the temperamental match between child and caretaker and the extent to which the child provides cues concerning his needs. When caretaker and child possess highly distinct temperaments the task of empathic attunement on the part of the caretaker is greatly complicated. This complication is linked to the fact that caretakers tend to view the child through the lens of their own perspective. Therefore, when fundamental temperament is quite distinct, caretakers frequently misinterpret cues, resulting in a pattern of consistent under- or over-response to the child's needs. Similarly, when a child is relatively non-expressive or consistently hyper-expressive the caretaker is at a great disadvantage in discerning the child's true needs, and once again at risk of both under- and over-response.

Further complicating the child's development of faith in the caretaker's competency is the fact that a child's perception of his caretaker is a wholly subjective variable and not an objective measure of the caretaker's skills. As a result of this fact a caretaker may prove quite competent with one child, yet grossly incompetent in the care of another. The child's experience of the caretaker is in no way tied to an objective assessment of the caretaker's competency, but rather to a simple association between the caretaker's presence and the child's wholly subjective experience. Therefore, it follows that more-complicated children with difficult-to-meet physical or emotional needs are more likely to experience their caretakers as incompetent, and thus will potentially develop problematic relationship skills. This is not to say that all children who experience early-life physical trauma (e.g., serious asthma, cancer treatment or traumatic injury) or emotional trauma (e.g., loss of a parent, exposure to violence) are doomed to problematic relationship skills, but rather that these experiences present challenges that require sensitive management. Effective management of this potential problem is largely centered upon the caretaker's ability to remain emotionally connected (empathically attuned) to the traumatized child, while at the same time not being undone or overwhelmed by the power of the child's affect. The ability to remain emotionally available to a child through a difficult experience, as described by Winicott (1955, 1972) in the concept of *emotional holding*, serves as our best hope to mitigate the detrimental impact upon relationship skills associated with early-life emotional or physical trauma.

As illustration of some of the problem dynamics outlined above, I present two case studies.

Katie

Katie, an eight-year-old girl born as the second child to an intact marriage between thirty-four-year-old, college-educated, professionals, entered life through a normal pregnancy and delivery. However, shortly after birth she developed serious respiratory difficulties and was eventually diagnosed with severe asthma.

Throughout infancy and early childhood, Katie consistently struggled with frightening asthma attacks, and as a result was significantly limited in her ability to participate in a number of activities. In response, Katie directed much of her energy towards sedentary and solitary activities. She became an avid reader, developed a mild to moderate weight problem, and had an extremely quiet and introspective social presentation.

Unfortunately, Katie's style of adjustment (temperament) turned out to be quite different from that of the rest of her family. In contrast, her thirteen-year-old brother, Sam, was an extremely committed and talented athlete. He participated in many team sports, and excelled in track and cross-country. Sam's abilities were not unexpected since both of his parents had been serious athletes throughout childhood and into their adult lives. As a result, a great deal of the family's energy and resources were directed towards athletics—including family trips to cities where Katie's parents and brother would participate in competitive long-distance running.

In addition to the fact that Katie's interests, activities, and energy level were quite different from those of the rest of her family, so too were other aspects of her temperament. Katie was clearly the least expressive, most quiet in her family. When her parents or her brother were upset or hurt, they were quick to express these sentiments and would frequently engage in brief, yet intense, expressions of agitation or anger at one another. The fact that Katie was not overtly expressive with her thoughts and feelings was openly recognized but not easily accepted by her family; they perceived her quiet manner as arrogant self-containment and saw her as having a tendency to sulk and feel sorry for herself. Although it was unspoken, a rule had developed in which there was a joint family effort to "support" Katie in being more assertive and expressive by passively ignoring her whenever she communicated in a subtle or indirect manner.

The fact that Katie's family's general temperament was quite different from hers set the stage for their consistent misinterpretation of her actions and motives—greatly complicating the management of her severe asthma. A common scenario around one of Katie's frequent asthma attacks involved her parents not noticing, or semi-consciously ignoring, her quiet, subtle cues concerning an initial breathing problem. This would be followed by a response of considerable anxiety and frustration as the attack progressed and Katie frantically expressed a marked inability to breathe. These episodes generally concluded with Katie feeling angry and frightened, and her mother express-

ing frustration and irritation with what she perceived as Katie's lack of communication concerning the initial symptoms of an asthma attack.

This presentation of Katie's story is clearly an oversimplification of a complex developmental drama. However, in this history we find a useful illustration of the non-abusive, non-neglectful causal dynamics which can inhibit a child's ability to form and use soothing emotional memories of his caretakers. In Katie's story we see two central dynamics that significantly undermine her experience of her caretakers as competent to keep her safe and secure. First, Katie experiences her parents as unable to protect her from the anxiety and trauma of her severe asthma. Second, the temperamental differences between Katie and her family impair their empathetic attunement to her needs and their related capacity to respond effectively. Clearly, from Katie's subjective perspective her parents are neither competent to assure her safety and security (they are unable to protect her from the impact of her asthma), nor do they know how or when to soothe her. Therefore, for Katie the emotional memory or (introject) of her parents offers little support in the management of anxiety. Although Katie's family certainly would not qualify as abusive or neglectful, her experience within the home environment provides an inadequate sense of parental attunement and security. Ultimately, Katie's parents were unable to protect her from the impact of her asthma attacks and, due to their frustration with her style of relating, unable to remain emotionally available to support her in managing these frightening episodes. In light of this background, it is likely that Katie will experience pervasive difficulty managing anxiety, as well as some degree of ambivalence concerning the role of past and future relationships within her life.

Josh

Josh, age ten, is a young boy who was born to an impoverished, fifteen-year-old, single mother who had limited prenatal care and drank alcohol moderately during her pregnancy. After his birth, Josh's mother returned to her mother's home with plans to remain there and raise her son. This home was a small, two-bedroom apartment on the third floor of a run-down tenement in a ghetto of a large, east-coast city. The number of persons sharing this home ranged from one to eleven, depending upon a multitude of variables. However, all the regular and periodic residents shared the experience of poverty and a common involvement with drugs, alcohol, crime and violence. Clearly, the home was unstable, a setting in which it was difficult to predict what would happen next.

*Josh's care during infancy and early childhood was managed by many dif-
ferent caretakers, who changed from day to day. By the time Josh was twelve
months old his mother was no longer living with him in the home. His grandmother, who reluctantly and by default became his guardian, loosely managed
his care. Although it went long unnoticed by his family, Josh needed medical
care at age two and a half for what turned out to be a serious ear infection.
When he was seen in the emergency room the doctors expressed concern that
Josh was demonstrating significant developmental delays in language. A later
follow-up, which resulted from an emergency-room doctor referring Josh to
Head Start, revealed several mild to moderate areas of developmental delay, all
of which were associated with poor nutrition, chronic untreated ear infections,
and stimulus deprivation.*

*As Josh grew into early childhood his interactions with his caretakers
became increasingly conflicted, and his overall experience of the environment
went from one of fundamental neglect to one of both neglect and abuse.
Throughout Josh's early childhood his grandmother's despair concerning her
life and the life of her family translated into severe alcoholism. The character
of Josh's interactions with his grandmother ranged from periods in which she
would express her infinite affection for him and use him as her sole confi-
dant, to periods when she would respond to his very presence with violence
and abuse. To her, Josh symbolically represented the many ways in which her
life had been limited by the need to care for others.*

*Aside from Josh's unpredictable experiences with his grandmother, his
encounters with other adults within his home and neighborhood were often
frightening and painful. At home, Josh had the sad reality of regular
encounters with an uncle who was a sadistic pedophile and who often had
easy, unsupervised access to him. By the age of eight, Josh had also faced
many difficulties outside the home. He had witnessed two shootings and
been subjected to a number of threats and aggressive acts from gang members
attempting to indoctrinate him to the rules of the street.*

Clearly, Josh experienced his caretakers as fundamentally incompetent in their capacity to assure his safety and security. Little discussion is
needed to illuminate why Josh would have established limited or no
"soothing introjects" for use in the management of anxiety—or why he
grew to value relationships only in the context of their capacity to meet
an immediate need or desire.

Neurocognitive Capacity to Develop a Clear and Well-Organized Perception (schema/memory) of the Caretaker

A second important variable impacting the child's capacity to form relationships that are useful in the management of anxiety, relates to his general neurocognitive ability to organize (see Chapter II on organizational capacity). When a child has a general weakness in accurately perceiving and organizing his environment, a parallel weakness is likely to exist in the development of organized and useful perceptions, or emotional memories, of his caretakers. This weakness results in a limitation in the child's ability to develop an organized sense of faith in the caretaker's capacity to meet needs and assure safety, and an associated limited capacity to use well developed emotional memories of the caretaker to soothe himself in the caretaker's absence. This is not to suggest that children with mild weaknesses in the capacity to organize will be significantly less able to form and use relationships, but simply that this ability to organize does potentially impact relationship skills. Children with moderate to severe limitations in the capacity to organize (e.g., Autism, P.D.D., Childhood Schizophrenia, severe A.D.H.D.) will consequently exhibit limitation in the ability to form and utilize relationships.

As illustration of this dynamic I offer the following case study.

Matthew

Matthew, an eight-year-old boy with moderate autism, has been raised in a stable, highly supportive home composed of both biological parents and a ten-year-old sister. His parents and sister understand his disability well and have provided him a great deal of structure and support throughout his childhood. Although Matt is generally apprehensive concerning new situations, particularly when functioning outside his home, he has developed a comfortable adjustment within both the home and his self-contained classroom at school.

Although Matt's family is quite competent at meeting his needs, the stress of constant vigilance in their effort to protect him from the unexpected is taxing and set the stage for the family to plan a brief vacation without Matt. Much thought went into how to make this departure from Matt's routine and separation from his family as workable for him as possible. Eventually it was decided that while the rest of the family was on vacation, Matt would be cared for by his Aunt Sue. In preparation Aunt Sue, an individual whom Matt knew well but did not rely upon for direction, began to spend a great deal of time in the home learning to understand and meet Matt's needs. Sue watched Matt's family members carefully and began to mimic their style in interacting with Matt. This process went relatively well and resulted in the setting of a date for the family vacation. They repeatedly reminded Matt about the upcoming vacation and the plans for him to stay with his Aunt Sue.

By the time Matt's family finally left on vacation, Sue had spent many hours with Matt and had provided a great deal of caretaking under his family's supervision. Unfortunately, however, the transition of Matt's care to Sue went poorly. Even though Sue was well attuned to Matt and had spent considerable time caring for him prior to their departure, due to his autism he was ultimately unable to use an organized memory of his family or Aunt Sue's presence to afford him a sense of security. With Matt's failure to find comfort in either of these resources his anxiety escalated and he began to function in a highly agitated and confused manner, ultimately requiring the resources of a hospital setting to assure his safety.

Matt's story represents a situation where a child's limitation in the ability to organize a useful emotional memory of his competent caretakers undermined his core relationship skills. Even though every effort was made to support Matt in using his Aunt Sue as a source of security based upon her demonstrated skills in caring for him, Matt was not able to employ her presence effectively as a means of security and management of anxiety.

(Note: this illustration is in no way meant to discourage parents of children such as Matt from seeking respite time. As a matter of fact, to do their job well parents must use respite both to maintain their own emotional health and to support their child in developing a broader group of caretakers in whom they have faith.)

Evolving Sense of Competency

The last of the critical variables associated with a child's ability to form and utilize relationships is the capacity of the caretaker to create or facilitate experiences that increase the child's faith in his own competency. This topic will be discussed in great detail under the heading of "Optimal Frustration," but here I present a brief introduction to this issue. This aspect of the caretaker-child relationship is primarily related to the child's ability to move from the first step of relationship skills (security based upon the physical presence of the caretaker) to the second stage of relationship skills, involving the child's ability to use the emotional memory of the caretaker to support him in the management of anxiety. This second step involves the child's capacity to use the memory of the caretaker to elicit feelings of competency which serve to mitigate anxiety.

This process entails the child's consistent exposure to caretakers who are attuned to the child's capabilities, and who provide or structure experiences which are challenging yet ultimately result in the child's own experience of success and competency. Through the association of these experiences with the caretaker who structured or provided them, the memory of this caretaker elicits in the child feelings of anxiety-mitigating competency. Therefore, caretakers who are not only competent in meeting a child's needs but also skillful in helping the child discover his own evolving competency are the most effective in supporting the development of broad relationship skills as they relate to anxiety management. Conversely, a caretaker who does not effectively support a child in an evolving awareness of his competency (as a function of either over- or underchallenging them) promotes relationship skills which are fixed at stage one, where the child must depend upon the caretaker's direct presence and intervention, as opposed to promoting growth to stage two, where the memory of the caretaker (through association) serves to elicit a soothing sense of faith in one's own competency.

In summary, the primary psychological function of relationship development is that of supporting the child in managing potentially debilitating anxiety. This developmental capacity to form and use relationships unfolds through a two-step process. The initial stage of this process entails the child's development of a sense of security based upon faith in the caretaker's ability to meet his basic needs. The second stage of this development involves the child's ability to use an emotional memory of the caretaker as a means of managing potentially debilitating anxiety.

The child who does not achieve competency in either stage of relationship development will not value or seek interpersonal connections. For these individuals, clinically referred to as schizoid, indifference and mistrust will be the hallmark of their interactions with others. For the child who achieves the initial stage of development but is unable to pass to the second, relationships will be valued only when others function directly in service to a want or need. For these individuals, more-subtle aspects of relating, associated with emotions such as compassion and empathy, will be limited. For the child who makes his way to the second stage of development, relationships will become his central resource in managing anxiety. This child will develop a rich inner world of useful emotional memories of others and will value and care for his connection with others through both compassion and empathy.

CAPACITY TO ORGANIZE

The second of the two central developmental variables to be considered within this text is the capacity to organize. Ultimately, this variable (together with the child's capacity to form and utilize relationships) will be used to construct a diagnostic framework that places all children into one of four categories.

The capacity to organize is a child's ability to develop accurate and useful perceptions (organizational schemas or models) of his environment. The process of organization (or schema formation) occurs as a basic human drive to make sense of one's environment and functions as an important developmental variable, controlled by neurocognitive factors and experiential background. Recognition of the role this variable plays in both adaptation and anxiety management is central to understanding why many children exhibit problematic behavior. The capacity to make sense of (or organize) one's environment entails the ability to separate essential from non-essential detail, and to perceive the dynamic of cause and effect, thus allowing for the accurate interpretation and prediction of environmental events. If the child is unable to separate the important from the unimportant and, in turn, recognize causal, sequential patterns in environmental variables, then his world is subjectively experienced as wholly unpredictable and governed by randomness. Unfortunately, the experience of one's environment as random or chaotic creates a dramatic challenge to both adaptation and the critical process of anxiety management. The individual who experiences his environment as unpredictable has little choice but to adopt a highly anxious, consistent state of readiness for the assumption of the fight-or-flight response (see Chapter IV). Many of the children who exhibit significant behavioral problems in school do so largely out of an anxious sense that the world is highly or wholly unpredictable.

Factors Affecting a Child's Capacity to Organize

Neurocognitive Profile

As we attempt to understand the origin of a child's capacity to develop accurate and useful organizational schemas of his environment, we must look at the roles of both nature (neurological variables) and nurture (the character of the child's past experiences). From a neurological perspective, the inability to organize is often linked to higher-order, executive cognitive weaknesses such as those experienced by children with moderate to severe learning disabilities, attention deficit disorder, and autistic spectrum disorders. Children with these disorders are less competent than the general population in their ability to form accurate, useful models of their environments. These children are far more likely to experience the world as governed by randomness, and to respond to this perception by adopting a highly anxious, ever-present readiness for the unexpected.

Unfortunately, a child's weakness in the capacity to organize not only occurs with respect to events in the external world, but also affects his ability to understand and anticipate his own inner world of perception, affect and emotions, and this further complicates the adaptive functioning. To varying degrees, these children experience life as a constant encounter with unpredictable and threatening forces that originate from both outside and within.

As discussed in the preceding chapter, the caretaker's ability for empathetic attunement is an important factor in a child's ability to understand and manage his own emotions. For a child with weak organizational capacities, the importance of the caretaker's consistent, empathetic attunement and emotional support cannot be overstated. The impact upon a child of functioning in emotional isolation while trying to manage the stress of a world (both internal and external) experienced as unpredictable is unquestionably devastating.

It is imperative that the poorly organized child experience his caretaker as able to structure and make predictable as much of his world as possible. This fact has powerful implications for intervention with such children; it underscores the need for a highly predictable environment with clear expectations and consequences delivered in a manner which offers emotional support and is informed by an empathic awareness of the child's emotional state and needs.

Experiential Variables

As we attempt to understand the possible experiential origins of a child's inability to form effective models, or schemas, we will focus on a child's experience of growing up in a highly inconsistent or chaotic environment. It is both intuitively sound and empirically demonstrated that considerable time spent in highly unpredictable or chaotic environments produces a child who is negatively affected in three central respects.

First, due to limited success and benefit from the effort to compre-
hend patterns within a chaotic environment, the motivation to seek
order eventually ceases and results in the child exerting minimal effort to
understand (form an organized perception of) his environment.
Unfortunately, this "surrender to chaos" often becomes generalized and,
regardless of the structure or consistency that might be available within a
distinct environment, the child will fail to seek a sense of order.

Second, a limited opportunity to practice (particularly during early
life) in the cognitive domain associated with organizational ability is
likely to result in greater neurocognitive weakness. In other words,
although a child may enter the world with adequate neurocognitive
resources to allow for the development of effective models of his environment, if the environment does not lend itself to organization, the
child's organizational skills will likely atrophy. By analogy, an animal
born with normal sight but raised in total darkness eventually loses
much of its capacity for vision due to the fact that the neural channels
for sight have remained understimulated.

The final negative aspect associated with development within a chaotic environment is that the vulnerability associated with such an
environment directly translates into elevated anxiety and an associated
drop in cognitive efficiency. Unfortunately, anxiety creates a self-reinforcing process (to the detriment of the child's development of organizational
abilities), in which heightened anxiety undermines the child's cognitive
efficiency and capacity to organize, and in turn increases anxiety.

Common situations or dynamics that are rife with the potential to be
experienced as impossible to organize include: life with an alcoholic or
drug-addicted parent, where the parent's response to the child is contingent upon variables such as the parent's level of intoxication or
withdrawal that the child cannot understand or assess; life with a mentally ill parent, where non-observable, intrapsychic factors within the parent
change dramatically, without explanation or notice, and profoundly
impact parent-child interaction; a life of poverty, in which families must
respond to basic needs and cannot attend to higher-level issues of security
or stability (e.g., a child may find himself living in a shelter with dangerous or unstable adults to avoid freezing to death on the street). Clearly,
unstable living arrangements become a critical variable, as multiple or
rapid changes in environment result in the child not having adequate
opportunity to develop a coherent understanding of his environment.

Sadly, a great many children experience both the organic and non-
organic dynamics outlined above and, as a result, are profoundly

disabled in their ability to make sense out of their worlds. They experience life as fundamentally unpredictable—perilous, without safe harbors and promoting debilitating anxiety.

Program Challenges In Work with Children with Weak Organizational Capacity

Effective work with children who possess weak organizational ability is significantly complicated by the inherent challenge of developing a clear and accurate understanding of the child's experience, perception and needs. Two central factors seem to account for this challenge. First, due to their weak capacity for organization, these children are often limited in their ability to form an organized sense of their own needs—and are equally limited in their ability to effectively communicate these needs to others. This fact too often sets the stage for a situation where a confused caretaker looks to a confused child to tell him what the child needs. Unfortunately, almost without exception the net result of this is increased anxiety, frustration, sense of isolation and hopelessness for both the caretaker and child.

The second central factor is the challenge in achieving empathetic attunement when dealing with an individual whose ability and temperament is quite different from one's own. It follows logically that those with good ability to organize, including most educators and mental-health professionals, will experience difficulty in accurately perceiving and understanding the experience and perceptions of a child with significant weakness in this area.

Through my experience as a public-school consultant, I have observed that one of the greatest obstacles to effective work with this vulnerable group of children is misinterpretation of the fundamental needs and motivations presented by children with weak organizational skills. This is not to suggest that educators are indifferent to the needs of these children, but rather that their personal range of experience often leaves them with a limited framework within which to understand or share the child's perspective. This limitation often results in an *empathetic miss* in which educators provide for the student what they themselves would want or need, because they interpret the student's behavior as meaning what it would if the educators themselves were to engage in these behaviors.

The most common way in which children with weak organizational skills are misunderstood is by an underestimate of their need for *explicit* guidelines and structure. Frequently, teachers will establish a *relatively* clear structure within their classroom, resulting in a positive response on the part of most of their students, and then will misinterpret the poor behavior of the weakly organized child as oppositional. This is not to suggest that opposition is never a factor in a child's non-compliance, but rather that, more often than not, at the core of his behavior is the child's effort to gain a sense of control in a world he experiences as random or chaotic.

It is also important to recognize that children with weak organizational skills initially respond to an environment with clear structure and boundaries by stumbling into those boundaries and defensively challenging their existence and legitimacy. This fact often misleads caretakers to believe that the organizationally weak child rebels against structure and boundaries, when in reality it simply takes him longer to recognize and respond to structure. With time to understand and master an environmental structure, the organizationally weak child ultimately finds great security and comfort in it.

In an effort to support educators in the development of a clearer empathic understanding of children weak in organizational skills, I often suggest the following exercise.

Empathy Training Exercise for Working with Children with Weak Organizational Skills

Situation 1: Analogous to the experience of an individual with strong organizational ability

A large group of teachers have gathered to participate in a day-long training designed to help them in their work with students with behavioral handicaps. Early in the day, after requesting that two participants remain behind, the conference leader directs the rest of the group to a large, empty room adjacent to the meeting space. Once in the room, the leader places eight to ten volleyballs on the floor, with instructions that the participants spread themselves evenly around the perimeter of the room and distribute the balls among themselves. The leader then provides the group with instructions to be followed when he brings the first of the two remaining participants to rejoin the group. The group is instructed to stand quietly as the leader places the first participant, subject A, in the center of the room and walks back to the perimeter. Then, upon the leader's command, "GO!" group members who have a ball are to call out

"HERE!" and one at a time throw the ball at subject A and continue this process until instructed to stop.

As subject A, for no reason comprehensible to him, finds himself in the center of a room, surrounded by strangers who are calling out and throwing balls at him, he undoubtedly will experience heightened anxiety. However, in all likelihood, he will quickly begin to form an organized perception of the situation: he will recognize the people surrounding him as fellow conference-attendees and as relatively non-threatening, identify the objects being thrown at him as volleyballs, and realize a pattern in which someone calls his attention and then throws a ball in his direction. As a result of his ability to develop an accurate and organized sense of this situation, subject A's anxiety level will remain relatively low, allowing him to think clearly and respond adaptively. This adaptive response is likely to entail turning to catch the balls as they come his way while attempting to establish a rapport with the group through the use of eye contact, humorous comments and friendly facial expressions. Eventually, either by collecting the balls as they are thrown or through establishing a rapport that alters the behavior of the group subjecting him to this treatment, subject A will effectively manage his dilemma.

In this situation, subject A's ability to rapidly develop an understanding of this situation allows his anxiety level to remain low and enables him to think clearly and develop an effective response. As a result, subject A not only manages this situation effectively, but gains reinforcement for his general sense of competency. This affirmation of subject A's sense of competency will, in turn, serve him in future encounters with challenging situations by providing a positive expectation for his ability to manage difficult dilemmas.

Situation 2: Analogous to the experience of a child with poor or limited organizational capacity

This exercise unfolds in much the same way as the first, but involves the second of the pre-selected participants, subject B, who is placed in the center of the large room after the leader has made two significant changes in his directives to the group participants. Unlike subject A, subject B will not be given a warning before balls are thrown in his direction, and, more importantly, the lights in the room are to be turned off, making vision impossible.

After being led to the center of the room, subject B stands blind, hears the directive, "Go!" and immediately confronts a series of flying objects. Unlike subject A, who had both sight and sequential auditory cues to support him in quickly and accurately developing an organized sense of his situation, subject B is unable to develop a useful model of his experience. Subject B's experience is characterized by an inability to determine who is *surrounding him, what is being thrown, and when or from where the next projectile will come. This inability to develop a model for understanding his situation results in subject B experiencing his environment as wholly unpredictable and elicits a highly anxious sense of vulnerability that activates a fight-or-flight response and the assumption of a fetal position on the floor in order to escape from harm.*

Subject B's response, although understandable, does little or nothing to affect his situation directly and sets the stage for him simply to endure his plight until some external factor intervenes. Unlike subject A, who actively adapted and ultimately gained affirmation of his competency through his experience, subject B must simply suffer his dilemma and is likely to experience increased generalized anxiety about his adaptive skills.

Ultimately, as the large group continues to pelt subject B with balls, it is likely that one of the participants will begin to feel uncomfortable with this situation. Judging the group's actions to be unfair (if not sadistic), he might attempt to protect or help subject B. However, as he approaches in total darkness and touches subject B on the shoulder in an effort to find and support him, subject B's reaction to his gesture is not likely to be an immediate expression of gratitude. Rather, it is more likely to be one of defensive aggression—striking in the direction of the very individual who has committed to help and protect him. Although this compassionate participant's motivation is to help subject B, it is experienced or perceived by him as simply another unpredictable threat to which he must respond defensively.

Now further complicating subject B's situation is the reaction of his potential rescuer, who set out to be helpful and in the process got whacked for his effort. If the rescuer responds with anger (an understandable yet unfortunate reaction) and either abandons the effort to help or retaliates, the plight of subject B becomes even more difficult.

Many of the children with behavioral handicaps spend their lives in a state similar to that of subject B. They are unable to understand or predict much of what happens to them and around them. They are constantly, anxiously poised on the threshold of fight or flight, and struggle against the often confusing efforts of those who attempt to give them support.

III

Diagnostic Categorization

As a school consultant serving children with special needs, too often I have seen educators embrace policies and practices which are intuitively sound yet, upon deeper analysis, are not in the child's best interest. Most significant among these problematic policies is the frequent reluctance to use diagnostic labels in categorizing and selecting programs for students with behavioral impairments.

Special education often supports its avoidance of diagnostic categories by asserting a distinct delineation between clinical and educational responsibilities, with diagnostic categorization assigned to the clinical domain. However, if special education does not avail itself of the body of knowledge organized by diagnostic categories to predict behavior and select appropriate intervention, the children it serves will be at a significant disadvantage. This is in no way to suggest that the clinical world "has it all figured out," but rather that when meaningful diagnostic groupings have been developed and effective intervention has been identified for these groups, special education has an obligation to access and use this information.

Other common explanations for special education's avoidance of diagnostic categorization is linked to concern about self-fulfilling prophecy, as well as the assertion that a label might in some way undermine the schools' obligation to develop highly individualized programs. Although I do not doubt that those who offer these explanations are sincere, it is my belief that in their commitment to avoid labeling a child they are often ignoring pathology in a manner which precludes earlier, more effective intervention. The simple process of avoiding clinical terminology or labels does not change the child's reality. It does, however, frequently contribute to program decisions that do not take into consideration an extremely useful, available body of knowledge.

Another factor that undermines special education's ability to make use of established clinical knowledge is the fact that most special-education consultants have relatively limited clinical training and experience. For reasons related to politics, cost containment, and efforts at specialization, the training and experience of those who do the majority of school-based psychoeducational evaluations and consultation are very different from those providing child-psychodiagnostic services outside the school. The fact that school-based psychological service providers often lack experience with more severe child psychopathology too frequently results in their being unable to effectively identify psychopathology and support educators to understand the emotionally disturbed child's condition and needs.

In making this observation, in no way do I wish to criticize school-based providers, or paint all such providers with the same brush. There are a great many competent, school-focused clinicians in the public schools who effectively and compassionately serve millions of children. My observation is simply that the majority of school-focused providers have had limited training, supervision and experience within the clinical model of diagnosis and treatment of emotionally and behaviorally impaired children. Conversely, most outside clinicians with strong training and background in the clinical model have a limited understanding and experience of the reality of the public schools. Both disciplines have much to offer one another and greater collaboration is needed.

Public schools are at best ambivalent concerning the assumption of clinical responsibilities, and clinical consultation in this setting is often challenging. However, it is my belief that if special education is to be effective, it must embrace the clinical task and the associated pragmatic use of diagnostic categories to identify, and create programs for, behaviorally impaired students. If special education maintains an artificial delineation between clinical and educational tasks and disregards the use of diagnostic categorization, it will promote a sense that children with behavioral handicaps are either all essentially the same or are beyond understanding. *This conclusion is neither true nor useful.*

SIMPLE DIAGNOSTIC FRAMEWORK

As a point of departure for understanding the behaviorally impaired child, the following section will present a framework for separating children with behavioral impairments into one of three broad, diagnostic categories—each with distinct origins and needs. This system of categorization focuses on the interaction between the two critical developmental variables discussed in the previous chapter: the *capacity to form and use relationships*, and the *capacity to organize*. The relationship between these variables as they are revealed within an individual child will be depicted through use of a chart where the capacity to form and use relationships is plotted along the horizontal axis and the capacity to form organized schemas or models of the environment is plotted along the vertical axis (see fig. 2).

A plotted position on the horizontal axis depicts the child's degree of development with respect to relationship capacity. Placement at the left margin represents weak capacity in this area, and placement to the right represents strength in this area. Similarly, on the vertical axis, the child's capacity to organize his environment effectively is represented by his relative placement from top to bottom. Placement at the bottom indicates a weakness in this ability and placement at the top indicates strength. Representation of an individual child's developmental profile can be found by plotting the intersecting point of a child's development in relational capacity and their capacity to organize. Thus, each child's categorization, reflecting their broad adaptive profile, will be defined by a single point of intersection between their abilities in these two, critical developmental areas.

The outer configuration of this chart is asymmetrical—to represent the capacity to organize (vertical axis) as a controlling, limiting factor on relational capacity (horizontal axis). This representation reflects a theoretical perspective which conceptualizes the ability to form clear, useful memories of significant others (introjects) as a specialized form of organizational schema. Therefore, children who are significantly limited in their capacity to organize in a general sense will be limited in their capacity to form and use organized emotional memories (introjects) of caring others.

With a clear understanding of the manner in which this framework represents a child's developmental status, let's now turn our attention to the way in which it can be used to create useful groupings, or diagnostic categories. For this purpose, the chart includes areas designated as nor-

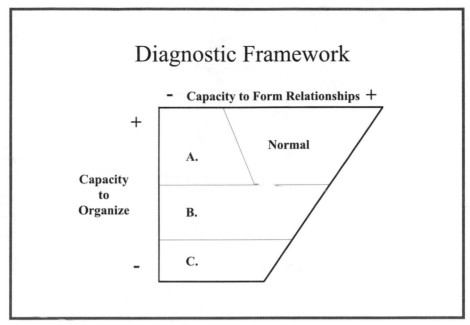

Diagnostic Framework

− Capacity to Form Relationships +

Capacity to Organize

+

A.

Normal

B.

C.

−

Fig. 2

mal, A, B and C. These categories serve as our point of departure in creating useful diagnostic groupings for the children whose development would fit within them. The nature of each of these diagnostic categories (A, B, C) will be described and discussed next.

CATEGORY A

Children who fall within Category A characteristically have an average to above-average ability to form organized perceptions of their environments (organizational schemas), yet have limited to virtually no capacity to form strong and useful relationships (see fig. 3). These children typically have average to superior general intellectual ability and processing capacities, but have developed problematic relational patterns associated with growing up with neglectful, abusive, or poorly attuned caretakers. Although children in Category A are mildly to severely limited in their ability to form strong interpersonal connections, they may be competent in the expression of superficial social skills, allowing for the manipulation of others. In other words, these children may be able to access and use excellent interpersonal insight in their relationships, accompanied by limited empathy or compassion.

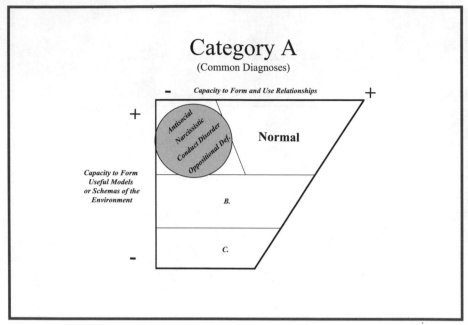

Fig. 3

Children who fall into this category would such carry psychiatric labels as Conduct Disordered, Antisocial, Sociopathic, and Narcissistic-Personality Disordered. Within the non-clinical culture the terms con-artist, criminal, self-centered, and manipulative might be used to describe these children.

It is both impossible and unwise to attempt to simplify the multitude of variables that impact the course of child development and to pinpoint a single factor as responsible for a child's limited capacity to form relationships. However, if we are to be helpful to these children, we must have an available model for understanding their developmental failure and to direct our interventions. Beyond what has been presented in the section on relational capacity, Heinz Kohut's (1978, 1984) concept of optimal frustration is helpful in understanding this group of children's developmental failures. The following section will present a brief overview of this concept and its application.

Kohut's Optimal-Frustration Model

The concept of optimal frustration was first presented by Heinz Kohut, the originator of self-psychological theory, in his discussion of the conditions necessary for a child to establish a stable, secure experience of self. To understand this concept it is helpful first to define

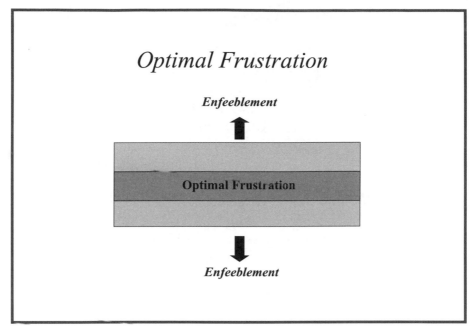

Fig. 4

Kohut's notion of frustration and then the conditions under which this emotional reaction might be optimal to the child's development. For this purpose, the concept of frustration is understood as a child's reaction to a situation in which he confronts an unmet want or need. However, the adjective "optimal" implies that the child's experience of this frustration ultimately serves to motivate and support him in discovering his own capacity to successfully acquire the unmet want or need. Critical to the caretaker's ability to provide experiences of optimal frustration is his possession of empathic attunement both to the level of frustration which a child can tolerate without a debilitating emotional reaction, and to the child's available resources to acquire the unmet need or want.

It is intuitively obvious how optimal frustration would serve to promote feelings of competency, but its connection to the development of relationship capacity might seem less clear. This connection occurs in the context of the second stage of relationship skills (the ability to utilize an emotional memory of the caretaker to help manage anxiety) in that the paired association of the caretaker with the child's experiences of evolving competency and self-sufficiency afford to the "emotional memory" of the caretaker the power to soothe fear and anxiety. In other words, the memory of this competent caretaker supports the child in accessing faith in his own competency and adaptive skills and mitigates anxiety.

To illustrate the concept of optimal frustration, Kohut offers the example of the game of peek-a-boo played between a mother and an infant. He describes this game as involving an infant who, joyfully basking in the comfort of his mother's loving gaze, is confronted with frustration when she hides her face. The mother's withdrawal of the desired attention creates frustration for the child, exacerbated by the child's limited developmental skills in object consistency. At this point, the mother's capacity for attunement and her response to her child's frustration will determine the developmental impact of the experience. The following are possible outcomes, which result in either growth-promoting optimal frustration or enfeebling underfrustration or overfrustration.

Optimal Frustration

Optimal frustration in the game of peek-a-boo is achieved when the infant's mother hides her face, yet effectively monitors and responds to her child's frustration in the game. When the game is played well the child's mother accurately reads his cues in a manner that allows her to rejoin him at a point just prior to his becoming overwhelmed and upset. By reading the child's cues and allowing him to experience frustration at a degree that he is ultimately able to manage, his mother has allowed the child an opportunity to increase both his own sense of competency and his faith in his caretaker's ability to meet his needs. He also gains a positive association between the memory of his mother and experiences of competency.

Too Much Frustration

Should the infant's mother lack empathetic attunement and the ability to attend to the child's escalating frustration, the outcome will be negative. He will move from an initial sense of mild frustration to a state of high anxiety and feelings of being overwhelmed—as evidenced by tears and emotional distress. Since he has been overly frustrated and unable to effectively manage this experience it will negatively impact his faith in both himself and his caretaker as well as his ability to utilize the emotional memory (introject) of the mother to soothe himself. Experiential backgrounds with consistent patterns of overfrustration are characterized by poor attunement, deprivation, neglect and abuse, and may include any of the following:

- Severe poverty, where the lack of basic resources often overwhelms the child with the fact that his primary needs (e.g., food, shelter, protection from danger) are not addressed.

- Parental incompetence due to mental retardation or mental illness, where the incompetence negatively impacts both the parents' attunement and ability to meet needs.

- The parents' need for the child to demonstrate consistently high achievement and autonomy, resulting in limited attunement and ability to respond appropriately to the child's vulnerability.

- Indifferent, neglectful, abusive or sadistic parenting, where attunement to and investment in the child's development and well-being are significantly limited.

- Extremely insecure, anxious, egocentric or narcissistic parents who are limited in their perception beyond their own overwhelming sense of need. Their child's needs are attended to only when he is meeting the needs of the parents in some manner.

Too Little Frustration

It is easy to understand intuitively how the pattern of being consistently overfrustrated, and the consequent insecurity, would decrease a child's ability to form trusting, useful relationships. It is less intuitive, though just as true, that a child who is consistently underfrustrated is subject to the same negative outcome. Underfrustration occurs with a child who is developing within an environment that is hyperalert and overresponsive to his frustration. In such an environment, the child is ultimately enfeebled by the lack of opportunity to grow in his sense of competency through managing appropriately measured challenges. A child raised within an over-attentive environment does not have the opportunity to develop an association between his caretaker and feelings of his own competency, therefore is unable to use the emotional memory of the caretaker to elicit a soothing faith in his own competency or adaptive skills.

Common backgrounds wherein a child experiences over-attunement or too little frustration include:

- A child with serious and/or chronic medical conditions (e.g., asthma, cancer), where the caretaker overcompensates for the child's difficult reality by over-attending to virtually any expression of frustration.

- A child raised by a caretaker who cannot tolerate the child's expression of frustration in that it triggers the caretaker's own painful affect, therefore the caretaker works diligently to protect both the child and himself from the pain associated with the child's frustration (co-dependency).

- A child whose caretaker has a special investment in the child's life that demands that the child not experience any negative emotion. A common example of this situation is the profound commitment of a caretaker from an abusive childhood who attempts to work through his own early experience by providing a totally distinct experience for his child—hyper-vigilantly protecting him from any degree of negative emotion.

- A child who is raised by a caretaker who, for a multitude of possible reasons, is afraid of the child's anger, therefore setting the stage for the caretaker to over-attend to the child in the hope of avoiding any disappointment or frustration that might elicit anger from the child.

Too Much *and* Too Little Frustration

Unfortunately, it is a common pattern of parenting to alternate between overfrustrating and underfrustrating the child, a pattern just as debilitating to the child as is consistent over- or underfrustration. His general sense of competency and development of useful relationships are compromised by the added anxiety of the unpredictability of the parental response.

Common backgrounds associated with unpredictable alternation between overfrustration and underfrustration include:

- An alcoholic or drug-dependent caretaker whose interactive style is inconsistent and contingent upon the level of intoxication, withdrawal or sense of remorse for previous behavior.

- Parents who have a highly contentious relationship, which often results in a split in which one parent consistently overfrustrates and the other consistently underfrustrates the child.

- Parents who are generally unavailable, yet periodically provide brief, highly focused periods of overindulgence (underfrustration).

Unfortunately, regardless of whether a child is subjected to extensive experiences of underfrustration, overfrustration or vacillation between the two, the outcome is largely negative. The result of this inadequate exposure to "optimal frustration" is a child whose insecurities are linked to a lack of faith in the competency of both his caretaker and himself. This experience directly compromises the child's relational skills, impeding development at either the initial step (the development of faith in the caretaker's capacity to meet one's needs) or the second step (the capacity to use the emotional memory of one's caretakers to soothe or calm oneself).

The life of the Category A child is characterized by anxiety, insecurity and mistrust in others. As a result, these children vigilantly monitor and guard against vulnerability and are limited in their concern for others. For these children emotions such as empathy and compassion are restricted, and the value of a relationship is controlled by the question, "What have you done for me lately?" As a result of this psychological adjustment these children are prone to self-serving behaviors with limited or no regard for the impact of their behavior upon others.

As we understand the origin of the Category A child's relative indifference towards the welfare of others, it must move us beyond a simple punitive response to his troubled and troubling behaviors. Through the use of this model we recognize the fact that *children value relationships with others only when relationships with others have been of value.* Therefore, in work with these children we must discover ways to minimize the impact of their problem behavior upon others, while at the same time providing healing experiences of optimal frustration.

CATEGORY B

As we shift our discussion to children in categories B and C, it is important to realize that many of the same dynamics which apply to the Category A child apply to these children as well. However, the development of children in categories B and C is additionally impacted by their lower-than-average ability to develop organized and accurate perceptions (schemas) of their environments.

Children in Category B range from above average to slightly below average in general intellectual ability, but they experience some degree of adaptive struggle associated with mild to moderate, neurocognitively based weakness in the capacity to organize. More often than not, these children are initially identified in school as language disabled or learning disabled, and over time develop more-problematic behavioral concerns.

The evolution of a Category B developmental profile involves some degree of underlying, organically based weakness in the capacity to organize. However, the extent to which this weakness unfolds as a limitation on the child's adaptational skills depends upon the level and consistency of structure and support in the environment in which he is raised. Clearly, a child with weak, organically based organizational skills who grows up within a chaotic setting will exhibit a greater adaptive disability than a child with the same weakness raised within an organized, structured environment. Aside from the relational issues associated with a caretaker who does not provide an environment well-suited to his needs, the negative impact of life in a chaotic environment on a Category B child is twofold. First, due to the chaotic and inconsistent environment, the child lacks opportunities to gain competence at creating useful schemas, or organized perceptions. Second, this child will often develop a sense of hopelessness concerning his ability to understand his world, which in turn further inhibits his effort and ability to make sense of his environment.

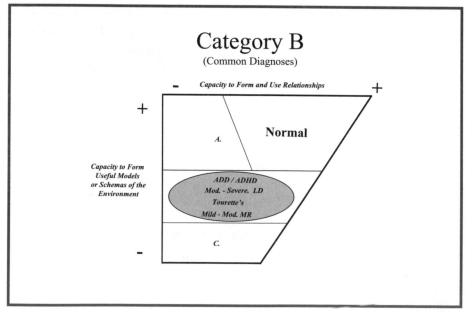

Fig. 5

Further affecting the degree of adaptive struggle experienced by a child with a mild to moderate weakness in the capacity to organize is the impact of this limitation upon the child's ability to form and utilize relationships. As stated before, the fact that the Category B child has a broad weakness in organizational skills may translate into a weaker ability to accurately perceive his caretakers and develop and use relationships in the management of potentially debilitating anxiety.

Within the clinical diagnostic terminology, children who fall into this category would carry such labels as Attention Deficit Disorder, Learning Disabled, Bipolar Disorder, Tourette's Disorder, and Borderline Mental Retardation. Unfortunately, should their environments not respond well to their special needs, over time these children may develop deeper, broader psychopathology, characterized by decreased relational skills.

CATEGORY C

Category C children are clearly the most overtly disabled of the three diagnostic groups. These children experience developmental deficits that are almost entirely linked to organic limitations in the capacity to organize. The extent of their weakness in developing organized and accurate perceptions (external and internal) results in both a highly anxious sense of the world as largely unpredictable and a limited ability to form clear

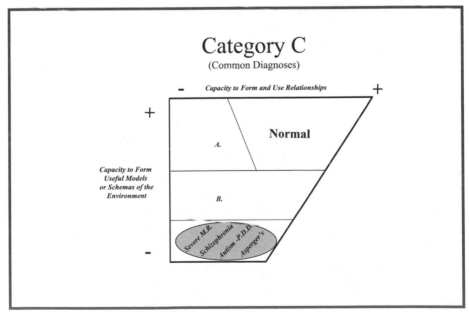

Fig. 6

and well organized (soothing) perceptions of their caretakers (see fig. 6). The extent of their limitation in the ability to organize is illustrated in their difficulty sorting out their experience and determining whether an event is happening in the world around them or simply within their thoughts or imagination. In other words, a common aspect of the profile of the Category C child is a weakness in the ability to discern reality and a vulnerability to psychotic symptoms such as hallucinations, delusions and magical thoughts.

As mentioned above, for the Category C child the world of relationships in many respects is simply another unpredictable aspect of one's life, from which little support is consistently derived. The inherent complexity and confusing nature of human behavior and emotion results in the Category C child experiencing relationships as not only limited in their power to comfort, but as a powerful source of anxiety. This results in a general pattern of withdrawal from relationships and a resistance to allowing others adequate intimacy to be supportive.

When we take into consideration the fact that the Category C child lives in a world which he experiences as largely unpredictable and in which relationships create, rather than soothe, anxiety, we gain a clearer empathic understanding of their lives. The dynamic associated with desperately needing the support of others, while at the same time experiencing relationships as potentially threatening, captures much of the complexity of either being or helping a Category C child.

Within the clinical diagnostic terminology, children who fall into this category would carry such labels as Autism, Asperger's, P.D.D., Childhood Schizophrenia and moderate to severe Mental Retardation.

SUMMARY

The categorization system presented above is offered as a point of departure in developing an easily understood means of classifying children with significant behavioral problems into useful groupings. The purpose (or usefulness) of this categorization or diagnostic process is to support school-based caretakers (teachers, social workers, counselors, psychologists and administrators) in better understanding both the origin and nature of a child's behavioral problems and the development of interventions based upon this understanding.

The requisite insight concerning a child's development within each of the two critical areas of functioning (*capacity to organize* and *capacity to form and use relationships*) necessary to place him within a category can be drawn from many sources. These may include everything from formal clinical evaluation (e.g., WISC-III scores) to observation and simple empathic and intuitive appraisal. Although useful as a starting point in understanding and serving these complex children, this system must be recognized as creating broad categories in which children within the same category may maintain significant differences from one another. However, these differences will be reflected more in the degree of pathology than in the fundamental form or pattern of their developmental weakness. For example, children within Category A all struggle with a primary disability associated with a limitation in the capacity to form and use relationships. However, the extent of this disability might range from that of a child with a severe antisocial personality who is completely unable to form relationships (extreme left-hand side of the diagram) to that of a child with moderately oppositional behavior who forms relationships easily, yet struggles to fully trust within these relationships (charted toward the horizontal midline of the chart).

It is important that this diagnostic model, as is true with any such model, be used simply as a framework for understanding and that we not become rigid or overconfident in our assessments of a child with regard to their diagnostic categorization. In the use of this tool it is imperative that we hold onto the idea that children can, and do, develop and heal and that in the context of this model it is our job as caretakers to help children move up (gain organization skills) and to the right (gain relational skills) in their placement within the diagnostic chart.

Section II

Responding to Problem Behavior

Kindness in words creates confidence. Kindness in thinking creates profoundness. Kindness in giving creates love.
— Lao Tsu

Following an initial discussion of the nature and impact of anxiety with respect to all children, this section is organized around each of the three diagnostic categories (A, B, C) and will:

1) provide a framework for understanding the origin and function of many of the problem behaviors presented by these students;

2) outline a point of departure for developing effective strategies and programs to serve children within each category.

IV

Anxiety

In our effort to understand problem behavior, there is no more important focus than the issue of anxiety. What follows is a simple definition of this important psychological variable and discussion of its origin, impact and management, with respect to all children.

Anxiety: A Psychophysiological Response to a Sense of Threat

The term psychophysiological as used here implies an impact on both the physiological and psychological level of functioning and is critical to understanding the effect anxiety has on behavior. On the physiological level, an anxiety reaction causes changes within both the endocrine system (i.e. release of adrenaline and cortisol) and the central nervous system (i.e. shifts in neurotransmitter release, and binding within specific regions of the brain). These shifts move the body towards a state of readiness for a defensive response, assuring the availability of the necessary resources for fight or flight. On the psychological level, the response to a perceived threat entails a shift of attention towards the immediate concerns of safety and away from long-term concerns and broader management of the environment. Mild to moderate anxiety generally serves to heighten cognitive efficiency by increasing motivation and focused thinking. Highly elevated levels of anxiety, however, inhibit cognitive efficiency, as all of the individual's available resources are directed towards readiness for the fight-or-flight response. With the loss of cognitive efficiency and the associated, higher-order cognitive skills (e.g., split attention, problem analysis skills), the individual becomes unable to access more-sophisticated, adaptive skills and is locked into the primitive fight-or-flight response pattern.

The concept of the fight-or-flight response is central to understanding much of the problem behavior exhibited by children in the public-school setting. Often, the nature of the underlying threat or the source of anxiety is unclear, frequently setting the stage for problem behavior to be misinterpreted as intentional or malicious, rather than as involuntary and self-defensive.

DIMENSIONS OF ANXIETY

To understand the relationship between anxiety and aggression, this text will present anxiety as having two broad dimensions: *baseline anxiety* and *rate of anxiety escalation*, both of which relate to a child's potential for aggression with movement into a fight-or-flight posture. To assist in understanding these dimensions, an automotive analogy will be used, in which *baseline anxiety* is analogous to the engine's idle speed, and the *rate of anxiety escalation* is analogous to the engine's rate of acceleration.

BASELINE ANXIETY

Baseline anxiety is the child's typical resting level of anxiety, and is a critical controlling variable in determining how readily a child is moved up to and across the fight-or-flight threshold. A child who is fortunate enough to have a relatively low baseline anxiety is far less likely to have experiences that move him across the threshold. He is less prone to exhibit problematic behavior, or to encounter anxiety at levels that undermine the cognitive efficiency necessary for him to generate an effective response to a real or perceived threat (see fig. 7).

However, a level of stress that is easily managed by a child with low baseline anxiety may well elicit the fight-or-flight response in a behaviorally impaired child who lives his life at a much higher level of baseline anxiety. The movement across the fight-or-flight threshold is easily triggered and activates both a problematic behavioral response and an inability to access the higher-order cognitive skills that are necessary for adaptive responding and learning (fig. 8). Sadly, this dynamic creates a pattern in which a child with high baseline anxiety consistently finds himself least able to think clearly in those moments when he is feeling most threatened. As a result, the child moves quickly towards a problematic, potentially aggressive fight-or-flight response. As is explained below, this reaction further reinforces a higher baseline anxiety, due to repeated experiences of being overwhelmed, unable to think clearly, and engaged in maladaptive fight-or-flight behaviors.

DETERMINANTS OF BASELINE ANXIETY

The factors controlling a child's anxiety baseline can be divided into three broad categories: genetic predisposition, neurocognitive-based factors impacting adaptive competency, and the degree of security and predictability of the child's earlier experiences.

With respect to a child's baseline anxiety, the issue of genetic or family linked predisposition is relatively well established through clinical observation and biogenetic research. This factor is essentially beyond the scope of direct school-based intervention but is useful to recognize in that it may direct treatment toward inclusion of medication-based intervention.

The issue of neurocognitively based competency is an additional critical factor in understanding and intervening with many of the children who exhibit aggressive behavior within the school setting. This issue is

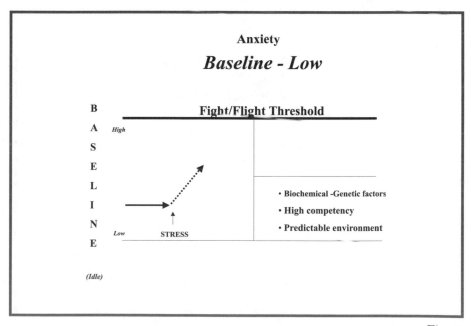

Fig. 7

central to understanding aggressive behavior, since many children who exhibit problematic or aggressive behavior are limited in their ability to organize, interpret and learn effectively with respect to both environmental and internal psychological events and dynamics. This limitation results in these children having frequent experiences of incompetence with respect to the ability to foresee potential sources of threat. This experience and the resulting self-perception of incompetence lead them to establish a consistent high degree of readiness for response to the demands of a seemingly dangerous and unpredictable world. This elevated baseline anxiety readies the child to respond to the unexpected at all times, thus chronically staging him on the threshold of a potentially problematic fight-or-flight response.

The third variable affecting a child's baseline anxiety is the child's personal history, specifically the safety, security and predictability of the environment in which he has grown up. Logically, a child fortunate enough to have grown up within a safe and predictable environment will have only a limited need to maintain a high degree of readiness for the management of unpredictable peril. However, a less fortunate child, growing up within an unpredictable and dangerous environment must adapt to this environment by maintaining a persistent state of readiness, expecting the unexpected. The maintenance of a vigilant state of readiness carries with it an associated

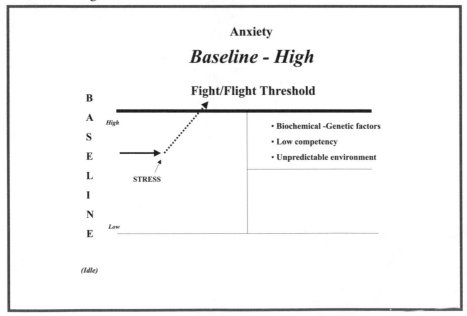

Fig. 8

vulnerability to rapid and frequent movement to an often maladaptive fight-or-flight response. Common factors which promote a pervasive perception of life as both unpredictable and unsafe include: poverty; a caretaker addicted to substances; a mentally ill parent; significant exposure to violence; and chronic or serious childhood medical conditions such as asthma or cancer.

In summary, the majority of the children who exhibit significant aggression have come to this behavioral maladjustment as a result of living their lives chronically on the threshold of the fight-or-flight response. The combination of a genetic predisposition to anxiety, multiple experiences of adaptive incompetence, and life within an environment experienced as unsafe and unpredictable set the stage for these children to maintain an elevated "idle" (baseline anxiety). They are therefore ready, in response to relatively limited stress, to escalate up and through the fight-or-flight threshold and exhibit problematic and potentially aggressive behavior. Unfortunately each encounter that results in a maladaptive fight-or-flight response serves to increase the child's sense of incompetence, in turn further raising his baseline anxiety.

RATE OF ANXIETY ESCALATION

The second critical dimension of anxiety as it relates to aggressive or problematic behavior is its rate of escalation, which might be thought of as analogous to an automobile's acceleration. For many reasons, individuals exhibit wide variability in their regulation of anxiety reactions. Fortunately, the majority of us are blessed with central nervous systems that seem to respond in a measured manner to initial indications of threat and adaptively, but not exclusively, focus energy and attention towards the management of the perceived threat. Most individuals are able to experience an anxiety-triggering event and yet remain capable of thinking clearly and effectively (see fig. 7). In response to a perceived threat they are able to develop strategies to calm or soothe themselves, while at the same time organizing an adaptive response to the source of threat. However, others, particularly those who exhibit aggressive behavior, often respond to a perceived threat in an unmodulated or labile manner (see fig. 9). They move rapidly from a state of relative calm to one of panic, in which all available resources are frantically and inefficiently shifted to the immediate concern or threat. This pattern often

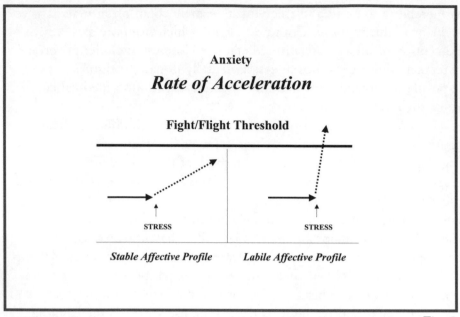

Fig. 9

results in a disastrous outcome associated with the inability to consider broader concerns related to long-term well-being.

Much of the aggressive behavior exhibited by children within the school setting is best understood as a function of the child's limited capacity to regulate affect in the face of a perceived or real threat, leading to the rapid unfolding of a fight-or-flight response. Fred Pine (1974), a distinguished child psychiatrist who collaborated extensively with Margaret Mahler, used the concept of "signal anxiety" (Tolpin, 1971) to help explain the aggressive behaviors of many troubled children. Pine believed that their lack of an effective self-monitoring capacity limited their ability to detect early signs of anxiety escalation and precluded the time and opportunity to soothe or calm themselves and maintain stronger adaptive skills. Pine believed this inability to self-monitor and the associated impact of being "blindsided" by extremely high levels of anxiety create in these children generalized anxiety and patterns of persistent adaptive failure associated with anxiety.

Unfortunately, many children who exhibit aggressive behavior experience not only elevated baseline anxiety (high idles), but also rapid affective escalation (acceleration) (see fig. 10). For these children, experiences of even minor stress or threat move them to a psychological

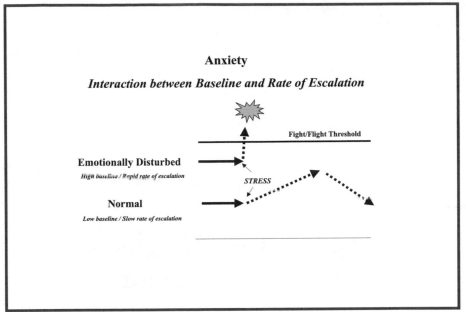

Fig. 10

state in which their ability to think clearly and adaptively, as well as learn from past experience, is dramatically compromised and propels them towards the repetitive employment of a maladaptive fight-or-flight response.

V

Category A — Origins of Problem Behavior

Children who fall within this category are often the most diffi-cult special-needs students to understand and manage within the public-school setting. Students within this group typically exhibit the most strategic and sophisticated forms of misbehavior, and are frequently clever in their avoidance of consequences, skillful in staging vulnerable others to take the blame for their actions, and competent at orchestrating conflict among those in authority. Additionally, these students are particularly difficult to manage within the school setting since their behavior often elicits from school personnel considerable ambivalence concerning the appropriateness of their participation in public school, let alone their entitlement to special consideration. Sentiment of this nature is frequently expressed in such statements as: "These kids don't belong in public schools — they gain nothing and disrupt much," and "These kids are criminals and should be managed by the criminal justice system, not the public schools!" Unfortunately, this ambivalence dramatically undermines much of what could be done to serve these children, as the time spent struggling with the question of who should have responsibility for these students is time not spent learning to serve them effectively.

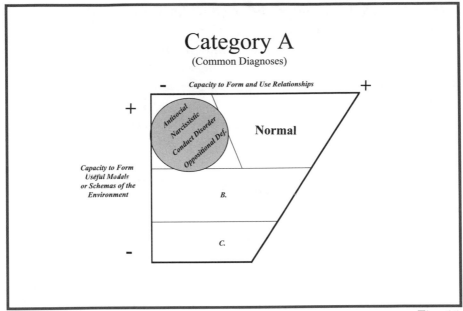

Fig. 11

PROBLEM BEHAVIORS ASSOCIATED
WITH CATEGORY A STUDENTS

The following section attempts to provide information helpful in both predicting and explaining some of the more common situations or dynamics associated with aggressive or problematic behavior in the Category A student. These dynamics do not represent the full range of possible difficulties for these children, but rather serve as an entry point in understanding their needs, predicting their behavior, and developing effective strategies to manage and support them in the school setting. Clearly, many children within this category will not exhibit all identified dynamics; however, from a theoretical perspective, all children within this category are vulnerable to these dynamics. Additionally, it is important to realize that no matter how aware one is of a child's vulnerability, it is not always possible or even advisable to avoid a potentially provocative dynamic. Unfortunately, many of the social dynamics that are most difficult for the Category A child to manage are the very same dynamics that their behavior seems consistently to elicit, causing work with these students to be both frustrating and too often seemingly hopeless. Even when graced by insight concerning an evolving dynamic or behavior, we may often feel we have no choice but to play out the script which the

Category A child has provided, although we know well in advance that the result will be undesirable, or at least unpleasant.

For the purpose of this introduction, I will discuss five critical dynamics and their potential to elicit aggressive or problematic behavior from the Category A child: 1) acting out; 2) narcissistic injury; 3) reestablishment of the central schema; 4) identification with the aggressor; and 5) avoidance of profound feelings of emptiness. Following the discussion of each of the activating dynamics I offer recommendations for their management.

Acting Out

Acting out is an unconscious psychological process that allows for the avoidance of debilitating conscious awareness of powerful anxiety-laden unconscious thoughts or feelings by diverting this then directly into behavioral expression.

A basic understanding of acting out, a psychoanalytic concept, can be extremely useful in school-based work with aggressive students, as it explains and predicts a great many problem behaviors and directs our response to these behaviors. Within psychoanalytic theory, "acting out" is conceptualized as an unconscious psychological defense used to manage potentially debilitating anxiety. Through the unconscious

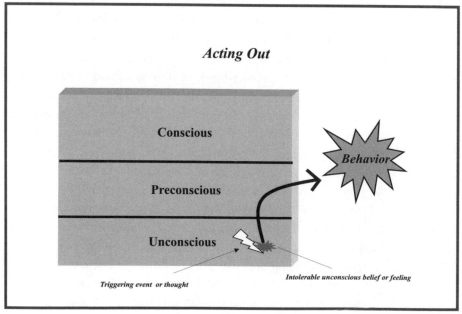

Acting Out

Conscious

Preconscious

Unconscious

Behavior

Triggering event or thought

Intolerable unconscious belief or feeling

Fig. 12

employment of this defense, painful underlying (unconscious) psycho-logical content, threatening to erupt into consciousness (often triggered by events within the environment) is diverted directly into behavior before conscious awareness can occur.

Within the psychoanalytic model there are three levels of psychologi-cal content: the unconscious, the preconscious and the conscious, each of which can be associated with overt behavior. The unconscious level of psychological functioning, the hidden but core experience of ourselves, is that part of the human psyche which is not readily accessible to lan-guage-based awareness, yet which significantly impacts emotions, perceptions and reactions. Its effects can be seen, for example, when we meet someone for the first time and without knowing him have a strong emotional reaction of like or dislike. Only later do we perhaps find that, in some unknown manner, this individual reminded us of someone from our past about whom we had strong feelings. Within this model, the unconscious can store thoughts, beliefs or emotions that, if they were to reach full awareness (consciousness) would create a level of anxiety that could effectively undermine adaptive functioning.

In contrast to the unconscious, the conscious level of psychological functioning is that part of the human psyche for which we possess full language-based or mediated awareness and volitional control. Within this realm we know what we feel and believe and why we behave as we do and are generally able to tie our thoughts and feelings to coherent origins.

The third level of psychological thought, the preconscious, lies between the unconscious and conscious levels and functions as both boundary and gateway between these levels. At this level, non-language-based unconscious content begins to be consciously experienced as present yet is still unorganized into a language-based understanding. It is in this region of thought that "signal anxiety," a concept described earli-er, alerts the individual of anxiety-producing content erupting from the unconscious and spurs the employment of a psychological defense.

Within the psychoanalytic model, behavior originates from all three levels of thought, the deliberateness of the behavior being determined by the degree of consciousness. In contrast to the popular perspective within our culture, psychoanalytic theory does not promote the idea that all behavior is conscious and therefore within clear and complete control of the individual.

The concept of acting out entails the *unconscious* employment of a strategy to avoid potentially debilitating anxiety triggered by the surfac-ing (from unconscious to preconscious to conscious) of disturbing thoughts, beliefs or emotions. This strategy entails the rerouting of a sur-facing awareness of anxiety-producing content into behavior, thus avoiding its conscious awareness and its associated debilitating anxiety (see fig. 12). This response proves useful and adaptive in the avoidance of anxiety, yet creates its own significant cluster of problems, as is illus-trated in the following case study of James.

James

James, a bright five-year-old kindergartner, recently arrived in his new foster placement and quickly began the familiar process of settling into a new home and preparing to attend a new school. Unfortunately, this was not the first or even the second such placement for James. His story is a sadly com-mon one, involving birth to a young, impoverished mother who ultimately was unable to care for him, leading the state to remove him from her care to placement within a series of foster homes.

As James first entered foster care, his aunt, at the request of his mother and the state, accepted him into her home and care. However, after a year, the aunt became involved with a new boyfriend and eventually moved in with this man, who in a short period proved to be extremely jealous of and aggressive towards James. This situation deteriorated rapidly, and shortly after the boyfriend moved into James' home the state declared the situation unsafe and placed James in a state-run, short-term, emergency foster home.

At this point, James was two-years-old, and his Department of Human Services caseworker was not willing to run the risk of another failed place-ment within an extended family member's home. The D.H.S. caseworker sought to move James into a long-term, state-licensed foster home. However, there were no long-term homes available and the caseworker was forced to leave James in the short-term foster home until a long-term home became available.

As is often the case, the wait for a long-term home took over a year, so James was three-years-old when he moved into his new long-term foster home. This placement worked fine for James, and all was well for the first year. James stabilized in his new home and began to call his foster mother "Mom." However, a problem began to evolve when James' foster mother became preg-nant and developed a complicated pregnancy which ultimately required complete bed rest. During this period, she grew increasingly concerned about this long-hoped-for pregnancy, shifted her full attention and attachment to her unborn child and began to fear that the demands of caring for James might compromise her pregnancy. After much painful consideration, James' foster mother contacted the D.H.S. caseworker and informed her she was not willing to continue caring for him.

In response to the foster mother's sense of urgency to have James removed from her home, the state placed him in a short-term, emergency group home while waiting for a new long-term foster home. Due to the instability of his past placements and his young age, the state moved James to a priority position on the waiting list for a long-term foster home. This priority status allowed James to be placed in just under three months. He arrived at his new home in time to enter kindergarten in a class that had just begun a week earlier.

As a result of his many truncated relationships, James confronts the psychological need to develop a means (a schema or model) by which to understand his many losses, as well as manage their associated emotions. For James, as for most children, the process of understanding one's life experiences is primarily focused upon the question: "Why did these things happen?" Unfortunately, because of immature ego functioning and limited cognitive development, children generally develop answers to this question which are highly egocentric. This egocentricity, combined with an innate psychological need to preserve their perception of the "goodness" of the parental figure, generally translates into an understanding of painful or difficult life experiences as wholly attributable to an innate negative quality of the child himself. In light of this dynamic, James is well en route to establishing a clear sense of himself as someone who does not elicit enduring nurturance, or in other words someone who is fundamentally unlovable.

As if this conclusion concerning himself were not bad enough, we must additionally take into account the fact that his age carries with it an inherent and psychologically immature view of the world as governed by "magical forces," which deliver rewards and punishments based upon one's worthiness. The culmination of these variables (egocentricity and magical perspective) results in James embracing the disastrous and profoundly anxiety-producing conclusion: "I am not lovable, and I deserve to have bad things happen to me."

If James is to function adaptively without overwhelming and debilitating anxiety, he must have strategies available to manage the profound emotions associated with both his many losses (i.e. sadness, anger, disappointment), and his belief that he is unlovable and deserving of bad things. For most children the dominant strategies used in managing profoundly painful and anxiety-provoking emotions are denial, repression (the maintenance of painful thoughts or feelings within the unconscious) and acting out.

Repression and denial involve the management of problematic psychological content by keeping it within the unconscious. However, when factors within the environment trigger increased awareness of profoundly painful and disturbing unconscious psychological content, *acting out* becomes a secondary line of defense. With the unconscious employment of acting out, the child effectively avoids painful psychological content and associated anxiety through channeling this content into behavior, unaccompanied by conscious awareness of its underlying origin.

(James' story continues)

It was James' first day in kindergarten and his new foster mother brought him to school a little early to meet his teacher. Introductions went well, and James immediately began to ask his teacher relevant questions concerning the school and the organization of the day. After saying goodbye to his foster mother, James very quickly become comfortable with his new teacher and immediately began to explore the classroom.

As the day progressed James continued to do well, up to and through the morning recess, during which he organized several of his classmates into a game of hide-and-seek. After recess, James returned to the classroom and quickly followed the lead of the other students, who had picked up their backpacks and were laying out napkins and food on their desks for snack time. However, as James reached into his bag he quickly realized that, unlike the others, he had no snack. Clearly this situation resulted from his foster mother's not realizing that she was to pack him a snack, not from indifference. However, as James saw his classmates with their snacks, the experience of feeling not as well cared for as others, associated with finding no snack in his bag, was more than he could manage. Instantly and without warning, James jumped to his feet and ran around the classroom knocking over desks and pushing his classmates' food onto the floor. As his teacher desperately attempted to reach him, James made his way to the door and ran down the hallway yelling, "I hate you!" As he passed the principal's office he was intercepted, but he foiled his potential capture by soundly kicking the principal in the shins, running down the hall, and ducking into the janitor's closet.

Once reinforcements had been gathered and pulse rates slowed, the principal and James' teacher slowly opened the janitor's closet to find James sitting quietly on the floor next to a mop bucket. At this point the principal began his post-crisis interview with the completely reasonable and understandable question: "James, why did you get so upset and why did you kick me?" To which James, in time, responded with the expected, but most unsat-isfying, "I don't know."

This scenario offers an all-too-typical illustration of the central features of an episode of acting out. The underlying dynamics associated with this episode include: 1) a child with an experiential background that has result-ed in feelings which, if brought into consciousness, could elicit overwhelming or debilitating anxiety; 2) management of this potentially anxiety-producing psychological content by containing it within the unconscious (repression); and 3) a triggering event, generally an occur-rence in the environment which directly or symbolically pulls the child's attention towards the repressed content. With these factors in mind, it is easy to see how the stage is set for James, and others like him, to exhibit disturbing behavior about which they have limited awareness, let alone insight or understanding, and why, when asked the reasons behind their behavior, they honestly report, "I don't know." Ironically, the very purpose of the behavior we are asking the child to explain is to *avoid* awareness of the intolerable underlying thoughts or feelings which we wish him to share with us.

Guidelines for Identifying Acting-Out Behavior

Although it is ultimately impossible to provide simple, clear guide-lines to differentiate acting-out behavior from volitional behavior, several criteria for making this distinction prove helpful. If the answer to each of the following three questions is affirmative, it is likely that the child's behavior is driven by the acting out dynamic and that management of this behavior will be most effective if the guidelines in the next section are followed.

1) Is the power of the child's affective response disproportionate to the apparent precipitating event?

2) Does there appear to be no overt benefit from the behavior? (Caution is offered against employing simplistic definitions of benefit, i.e. attention seeking, if the child's affect is truly inappro-priate.)

3) Does the child demonstrate little or no insight into his own behavior? (Caution is offered against accepting a child's simplistic explanation if it seems to neatly fit into the child's "I'm a bad per-son identity," i.e. "I broke the window because I felt like it, and I hate this place.")

Responding to Acting-Out Behavior

If we accept the analytic model's concept of acting out and look within it for insight to support us in our effort to work effectively with children who exhibit such behavior, a number of guidelines are available. The presentation of these guidelines will be broken into two categories: 1) interventions to avoid and 2) interventions to apply.

Interventions to Avoid

Because effective management of acting-out behavior often entails the employment of counterintuitive strategies (linked to the understanding that these behaviors are driven by the unconscious), discussion will begin with a focus upon common avenues of intervention which are ineffective or contraindicated.

Forced Accountability

Among the most common and ineffective strategies employed in managing acting-out behavior is the insistence that the child provide an explanation for his behavior. Unfortunately, in an era when accountability has become a mantra for many of those who are concerned with society's current direction, tremendous effort is often directed towards coercing the acting-out child into explaining his behavior as though it were the result of a conscious decision. Ironically, if one accepts the analytic understanding of acting out, the very purpose of the child's behavior is to avoid the understanding of its origin. Therefore, efforts to extract an accurate explanation for the problematic behavior are destined to fail. Often, however, the child will respond compassionately to the adult's need for an explanation by fabricating an inaccurate representation of the behavior as volitionally aimed to achieve a particular outcome. With the young child this fabrication often results in an explanation which is wholly absurd: for example, "When I came into the room Jenny called me a name," even though Jenny is a little girl who has not looked up from her desk since the first of the year, let alone spoken out loud. However, with the older child, who has had much more exposure to the way in which others understand his behavior, it is much more likely that the fabricated explanation will have greater surface validity: for example, "I swore at Mr. Jones because I wanted out of class so I wouldn't have to take the math test we were going to have today."

If the child does not experience himself as consciously choosing to engage in problem behavior, the use of punishment as the primary intervention will be misguided and generally ineffective. An adult's misunder-standing of the unconscious origin of acting-out behavior and insistence that the child knows why he did what he did and that he had clear control over the decision to engage in the inappropriate behavior has a profoundly negative impact. First, the misperception confirms to the anxious child that his caretaker understands him no better than he understands himself, a belief which significantly undermines a child's core sense of safety and security. Second, since the child has no sense of the origin of his behavior, attributions of intention around negative behavior are experienced as undeserved attacks or criticism. Third, this misperception conveys to the child that there is something inherently bad or wrong with him, leading to a negative sense of self which will play a significant part in directing future behavior.

Not holding the child fully responsible for identifying the motivation behind his inappropriate behavior is in no way to suggest that a child should never be held accountable for his acting out. Rather, it is important to utilize logical consequences in an enlightened, non-punitive manner that neither undermines the child's sense of security and hope, nor promotes in the child a problematic negative identity. A later chapter will discuss strategies for presenting the consequences of acting out in a way that avoids these negative outcomes. However, in simple terms, consequences should be presented with compassion and as an expression of the caretaker's commitment to help the child address and overcome problem behaviors. The caretaker should align himself beside the child, simultaneously communicating the logical consequences for inappropriate behavior and expressing empathic attunement and both hope and belief in the child's ability to grow beyond his current struggles (i.e. "James, I'm sorry but we have a rule in our school that if you strike someone you must go home for the balance of the day. But I know that when you kicked me you didn't know what else to do and that you were feeling really angry and confused. When you come back to school tomorrow we will talk and find some good ways to help you manage those times when you feel that way in the future. I know this is a tough start in a new school, but lots of kids have a tough time at first and I know this is going to be a good school for you. I'll see you tomorrow and we will start over.")

Psychological Interpretation

A second common problematic style of response to the acting-out child is to offer him a psychological interpretation of the origins of his behavior. This strategy is often applied by well-meaning adults who, in the face of the child's obvious pain or sadness, attempt to support him by interpreting or bringing into consciousness the unconscious content that is being acted out. The problem with this strategy lies in the fact that the child has access neither to the necessary developmental skills (i.e. the ability to "self-observe") nor to interpersonal dynamics that would allow him to hear and effectively manage the caretaker's interpretive observations.

Interpretation, a cornerstone of traditional psychodynamic psychological intervention, is based upon the belief that in the context of a safe and secure relationship with a therapist the patient will be able to delve slowly into the painful or anxiety-producing unconscious content. The purpose of this process is to bring unconsciously held painful emotions and thoughts into consciousness, thereby reducing the need to engage in potentially problematic defenses such as acting out. An example of this process can be illustrated in the dynamic that might occur in a teenage female who has grown up with a neglectful and abusive alcoholic father. She, like all children, must on a conscious level maintain to some extent an idealized perception of her father. This perception allows her to avoid the potentially debilitating anxiety associated with recognizing that he is not willing or able to care for her and the pain of believing that she is unlovable. In light of this need, recognition of her father's neglect and abuse are relegated to her unconscious. However, within her social life she is periodically exposed to men with a character similar to her father's. The behavior of such men serves to trigger her negative unconscious memories of her father, thus activating a need to act out to avoid their conscious awareness. Sadly, this acting out often takes the form of establishing a relationship with such a man, recreating many of the painful experiences of her relationship with her father.

In psychodynamic psychotherapy, treatment for this young woman would begin by supporting her in developing a trusting relationship with the therapist and then using this relationship to help her manage the sadness and anxiety associated with bringing the awareness of her father's abuse and neglect into consciousness. Once these memories and the attached emotions are mastered (allowed to be a conscious part of her) her need to act them out will no longer be present. This process of bringing painful content into consciousness provides insight into the reason why, as they go further through the therapeutic process, patients in psychodynamic therapy often become increasingly distressed prior to experiencing relief.

The necessary conditions for the effective use of psychological interpretation include:

1) the child having a strong trusting relationship with the individual providing the interpretation;

2) the child sensing adequate control over the process and the rate at which psychological content is explored;

3) the child having a clear sense that the motive of the individual making the interpretation is supportive and useful;

4) adequate time for the child to integrate painful content once it is brought up; and

5) accurate empathic attunement to allow the individual making the interpretation to be relatively "on target" concerning the unconscious content behind the acting-out behavior.

Unfortunately, these conditions are rarely present within the school setting, and so psychological interpretation is rarely useful within the school. When inappropriate efforts at interpretation are applied, they typically elicit one of two problematic responses. First, interpretation serves to reactivate acting out, as the child remains unable to tolerate conscious awareness of the content being interpreted. Second, the child shuts down emotionally and employs an equally problematic process of withdrawing from his feelings (dissociation from his affective state) which causes him to appear, and in fact experience himself as, completely shut off from his emotions and relationships.

Although it is rare that the use of interpretation is appropriate in the public school, periodically there are situations in which the conditions above do exist. When this is the case, we can generally determine that interpretation has been useful by the child's expression of appropriate affect (sadness or pain) and willingness to allow the individual making the interpretation to support him. This might take the form of the child breaking into tears and then turning to the adult, seeking the comfort of being held.

Useful Interventions

Critical to the management of acting-out behavior is a recognition that this behavior is not a function of a simple conscious choice or volition, but rather a complex, unconscious response generally experienced by a child as outside his control. In light of this fact, compassionate and effective management of acting out will entail: 1) supporting the child in avoiding or more effectively managing similar situations in the future;

2) supporting the child in "undoing" the damage associated with his acting out behavior; and 3) supporting the child in accepting and managing the natural and logical consequences of his behavior.

Obviously missing in the management options listed above is reliance upon punishment as a primary mode of intervention for acting-out behavior. Punishment is indicated and useful in promoting social and emotional development only when the behavior it targets is experienced by the child as under his conscious control. In no manner is this meant to suggest that a child's acting-out behavior be passively endured, but rather that the response to this behavior must be both pragmatic and compassionate. It is essential that those working with the acting-out child recognize the distinction between the contraindicated application of punishment and the effective provision of behavioral support and logical consequences. As indicated above, this process typically entails three points of focus: supporting the child in avoiding or more effectively managing similar situations or dynamics in the future, supporting the child in "undoing" the damage associated with his acting-out behavior, and supporting the child in accepting and managing the natural and logical consequences of his behavior. Illustration of these three aspects of intervention with respect to James' blow up after he found he had no snack might involve:
1) checking James' bag prior to snack time to assure that he has a snack (changing the environment to avoid situations which he is unable to manage); 2) allowing James to pass out cookies to his classmates at lunch time the next day, as a means of "undoing" the fact that he knocked their snacks on to the floor (helping him undo the damage associated with his behavior); and 3) arranging and communicating to James, in a non-punitive manner, that for a period of time he is to be in constant and direct adult supervision, stating, for example, "James you are so important to us that until we are certain that you won't do something in which you or someone else might get hurt, you will have a teacher close by to help you if you need him" (employing logical consequences to assure effective management of the student's potential to act out).

If in our understanding of acting out behavior we recognize its origin in anxiety or pain, so that the child exhibits a behavior which he neither understands nor senses as volitional, our response to this child must then be that of providing appropriate support. However, too often, out of lack of understanding of the child's experience, we respond to this overwhelmed and anxious child with threats and rejection, which unfortunately serve to increase his anxiety and further promote the likelihood of acting out.

Narcissistic Injury

Another dynamic to be considered with respect to the Category A child is that of narcissistic injury and the broader issue of the narcissistic self-esteem. For the sake of our current discussion, sense of self (a cognitively organized structure) and self-esteem (an affectively based structure) will be understood as developmental variables measuring the degree and nature of an individual's unconsciously organized experience of himself. In other words, "self" or "identity" evolves as a function of both the child's experiences within his environment and the character and nature of his unconscious organization of these experiences. For example, the child who is cognitively intact (able to organize effectively) and grows up within an environment in which his caretakers are able, most of the time, to meet his needs and affirm his evolving competencies is likely to develop a general sense that he is both lovable and competent. Conversely, a child lacking either the ability to organize his experience effectively or a caretaker who is able to consistently meet his needs is likely to develop a poorly defined and predominately negative sense of himself.

As we consider the dynamics presented in the earlier chapter on anxiety, particularly with respect to the issue of baseline anxiety and the negative impact of elevated anxiety upon adaptive functioning, the importance of a well-developed and positive sense of self comes into focus. As discussed in the chapter on anxiety, a well-established and positive sense of self, characterized by a child's fundamental belief in his own competency, as well as the safety and security of his environment (as assured by his caretaker's ability and commitment to meet his needs) are central factors in the effective management of anxiety. In light of the importance of a well-developed and positive sense of self in the management of potentially debilitating anxiety, it follows that those children who have not established this critical developmental variable must develop a means by which to compensate. Clearly, should a child not develop a means by which to manage a profoundly negative sense of self, the outcome will be unchecked anxiety, poorly organized behavior and dramatically compromised functioning.

Fortunately, the human psyche has developed a means by which to manage a negative sense of self and, for the most part, shield the individual from the potentially debilitating anxiety associated with negative self-assessment. This psychological process involves the unconscious employment of an inflated or grandiose sense of self, referred to as a "narcissistic sense of self." As illustrated in fig. 13, the narcissistic or

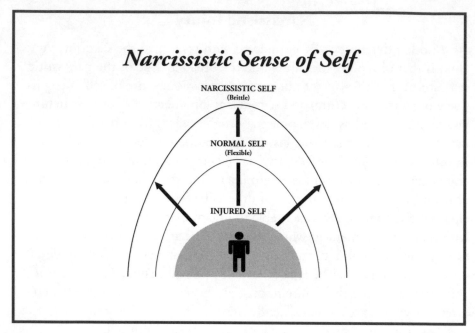

Narcissistic Sense of Self

NARCISSISTIC SELF
(Brittle)

NORMAL SELF
(Flexible)

INJURED SELF

Fig. 13

grandiose sense of self (depicted by the larger of the three arcs) springs from the underlying negative sense of self and serves as a substitute or pseudo-self, defending the individual from the debilitating impact of this underlying negative sense of self.

This false, narcissistic sense of self, although effective in protecting the individual from the profound underlying insecurity associated with his negative experience of self, does not do so by simply substituting the functional belief, "I'm as good as everyone else," but rather by imposing a grandiose or inflated self-perception which asserts, "I'm better, bigger, smarter, more important than everyone else." In the following section, narcissism or narcissistic self-esteem will be discussed in greater detail by comparing and contrasting it with normal or healthy self-esteem. This discussion will begin with a brief presentation on the nature and function of normal or healthy self-esteem.

Normal Self-Esteem

Normal or positive self-esteem serves to mitigate anxiety triggered by frustration, failure or rejection. Central to the functional quality of positive self-esteem is the attribute of flexibility, defined by the capacity to: 1) endure injury to one's self-esteem in a limited or circumscribed manner (e.g., fail a math test without succumbing to profound sense of general incompetence); 2) employ self-soothing strategies for self-esteem stabilization and recovery (following failure on a math test, be able to recall other tests where you have done better and take comfort in the recognition of the relationships in which you are loved and cared about); 3) learn from experiences which have challenged one's self-esteem (in response to failing the math test, accept the need to study more prior to the next exam). For individuals with normal or positive self-esteem, difficult dynamics such as the experience of criticism, rejection or failure result in decreased self-value for a brief period and within a circumscribed aspect of the individual's sense of self. With time and perspective, the individual with positive self-esteem is able to integrate and learn from these experiences, without threat to his fundamental positive sense of self. The character of normal or positive self-esteem is illustrated in the vignette that follows. (The reader is asked to accept that, for the sake of illustration, I represent myself in this vignette as an individual with positive self-esteem, regardless of moments within my marriage in which my wife would suggest that I serve as a far better illustration of narcissism.)

The Training Conference

Having presented a lecture at a day-long training conference for school psychologists, I was approached by a conference participant who shared with me that she had enjoyed my presentation but felt compelled to offer an unflattering fashion critique concerning my choice of ties. In response to this comment I, being a bit more vain than I would like to admit, experienced a slight, but noticeable, drop in my self-esteem, associated with painful introspective questions such as, "Could it be that my sense of color coordination is weak?" and "Could my taste in ties be deeply flawed?"

Rapidly, my consciousness was flooded with painful self-doubt, which mercifully ended quickly as I began to stabilize and employ strategies of self-soothing by evoking memories of those whom I know love and value me. I began to think to myself, "My wife likes this tie. My daughter said this tie looked nice with this shirt. The dog loves me." My self-esteem begins to stabilize, and I set about the process of containing the damage associated with this cruel attack on my fashion sense. Ultimately, I calmed enough to activate a secondary line of coping skills which involved discrediting the critic by finding some aspect of her presentation to assess negatively and therefore dismiss her observation as wholly irrelevant (e.g., "With those shoes, she's speaking to me about fashion?"). However, as painful as this experience may have been, if I truly have positive self-

esteem it will not preclude my learning from it and next time I choose the same tie and shirt combination, before wearing it I will seek consultation from others.

As illustrated, a central quality of positive self-esteem is that of flexibility, which allows the individual to experience criticism, failure or rejection without being completely overwhelmed by a powerfully negative shift in self-assessment. The flexible character of positive self-esteem allows the initial impact of negative feedback or failure to activate soothing strategies and ultimately supports containment of negative experiences to a limited aspect of the individual's sense of self. Clearly, the experience of failure, criticism or rejection is unpleasant no matter what the character of one's self-esteem. However, if one possesses the ability to tolerate these experiences without being overwhelmed, such experiences can be instructive for avoiding similar situations in the future. Conversely, if one's self-esteem is not capable of tolerating and integrating these painful events without activating a broad and profoundly negative self-assessment, each such experience generates greater intolerance for failure and dramatically reduces one's capacity to learn from such experiences.

Narcissistic Self-Esteem

Unlike normal or positive self-esteem, narcissistic self-esteem, which protects the individual from profound underlying feelings of inadequacy, is characterized by an all-or-nothing quality of brittleness. This quality, if we compare it to the brittle quality of glass, results in a pattern in which threats to self-esteem (i.e. criticism, rejection and failure) elicit either no reaction (as if a rock were to bounce off a pane of glass and leave no impact) or a devastating impact (as if shattering the pane of glass). In other words, in some incidences the narcissistic individual will appear indifferent to criticism or failure and show virtually no response (fig. 14), while in other situations he may be highly reactive and express a profound sense of injury and anger, referred to as "narcissistic rage" (fig. 15). The potential power of this rage directed at whomever the child perceives as shattering his defense cannot be overstated and is driven by a motivation to retaliate for the pain and vulnerability unleashed on the child as a result of the failed narcissistic defense.

In understanding the power of narcissistic rage, it is important to realize the child's response is linked to his momentary exposure to the full thrust of pain and vulnerability accumulated over a lifetime, not simply a

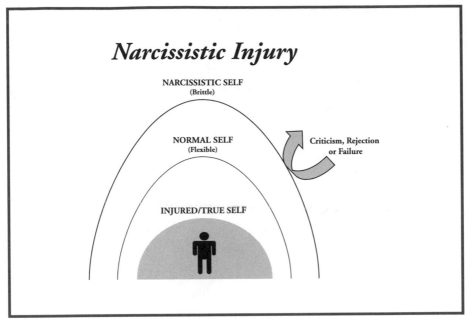

Narcissistic Injury

NARCISSISTIC SELF
(Brittle)

NORMAL SELF
(Flexible)

Criticism, Rejection
or Failure

INJURED/TRUE SELF

Fig. 14

reaction to the triggering dynamics or event. Those who have been the object of narcissistic rage from a five- or six-year-old respect it. Those who have been the object of such rage in an older, more sophisticated and powerful individual fear it. The nature of the narcissistically defended individual's response to threats to self-esteem, although often experienced by others as unpredictable, is generally related to four interactive dynamics:

1) The child's degree of vulnerability with regard to a particular area of functioning.

Most narcissistic individuals have areas of functioning in which they are more vulnerable and others in which they are less vulnerable. A narcissistically defended child who has experienced a good deal of academic success is likely to be less reactive to a frustrating learning experience than a child with a learning disability who has experienced a great deal of academic failure.

2) The context in which the threat to self-esteem occurs.

The narcissistic child's experience of threat to self-esteem is significantly increased when it occurs within a public context. This child's feelings of exposure to others as vulnerable or incompetent are significantly more intolerable than those felt by a child with positive self-esteem. For most narcissistically defended children "saving face"

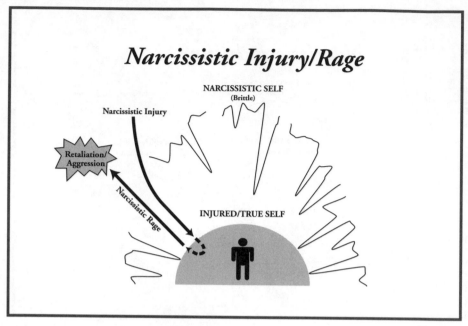

Narcissistic Injury/Rage

NARCISSISTIC SELF
(Brittle)

Narcissistic Injury

Retaliation/
Aggression

Narcissistic Rage

INJURED/TRUE SELF

Fig. 15

within the public arena is as imperative as their need for oxygen. Those working with these children must keep this fact in mind.

3) The cumulative impact of recent or current threats to self-esteem.

Take, for example, a narcissistic child who plays on a baseball team and generally behaves in an appropriate manner. He may have a game in which he strikes out twice and then misses a catch in the field. After overthrowing the catcher on a play to home, he then has a tantrum and walks off the field, throwing his glove and telling the coach that he's an idiot and doesn't know how to coach.

4) The nature of the relationship between the child and the individual delivering the injury to self-esteem.

Interestingly, this dynamic generally entails an exaggerated response to narcissistic injury when linked to individuals at both ends of the relationship spectrum: those whom the child significantly devalues and those whom he idealizes. In most situations the narcissistic child is far more likely to exhibit a negative reaction to an individual he perceives as having low status, particularly when that individual is in a position of authority (e.g., hall or bus monitor). In dealing with the exercise of authority from such an individual the demand to subordinate himself to a devalued other is a threat to the narcissistic child's self-esteem which is not easily managed. However, at the other end of the spectrum, within a relationship with someone whom he idealizes, the narcissistic child may also be highly reactive. In this situation the child's value of this individual's approval may be so exaggerated that minor criticism or rejection is experienced as devastating to the narcissistic defense.

The following dialogue provides an illustration of the dysfunctional, brittle quality of the narcissistic defense.

Benny

*Benny, a thirteen-year-old eighth grader growing up in poverty with an alcoholic single mother, sets off for a day at school. It is early in the morning and his mother was up late drinking the night before and has awakened with a hangover. (**Bold print** represents Benny's thoughts, not his comments.)*

Benny:	*"Bye, Mom, I'm going to school."*
Mom:	*"What? Would you stop screaming. Benny, did you clean your room like I told you last night?"*
Benny:	*"I'll do it later. I've got to go."*
Mom:	*"You little bastard. You never do anything I tell you. I swear to God every day you become more like your father, and if you don't watch it you'll turn out to be a loser just like that S.O.B."*
Benny:	*"You old drunk. I don't blame him for leaving you. I don't give a damn what you say." (Criticism bounces off, see fig. 11)*

Benny walks to the bus stop and waits for the bus, which quickly arrives.

Bus Driver:	*"Benny, someone carved in the upholstery back where you were sitting on the bus last night. I think it was you. So I can keep an eye on you, from now on you need to sit up here in the front seat."*
Benny:	**You stupid old bastard, I didn't do it, but I wish I did. I'll sit up here, not because you told me to, but because the kids at the back of the bus are all jerks and I can't stand to listen to them talk about their pathetic, moronic lives!** *(Criticism bounces off.)*

Benny arrives at school, walks into his homeroom and is greeted by his teacher, with whom he has a good relationship. His teacher notices that Benny is wearing a new ball cap and the following exchange occurs.

Teacher:	*"Good morning, Benny. How are you doing today?"*
Benny:	*"Okay."*

Teacher:	"Hey, is that a new Cubs hat?"
Benny:	"Yeah."
Teacher:	"I like it. I respect that you are a loyal fan. Even though the poor Cubs can't win a game to save themselves, you stand behind them."
Benny:	"I don't care about the Cubs, I just like the hat."
Teacher:	"Okay, but I tell you the Cubs could use some loyal supporters. Hey, remember the new rule on hats and be sure to take it off when the bell rings, okay?"
Benny:	**My hair looks like hell ever since my mom tried to cut it. I am not taking this hat off and having other kids give me crap about my hair.**
Teacher:	"Benny, did you hear me about the hat? Look it's not my rule but I do have to enforce it. So please take it off and stick it in your pocket."
Benny:	(Ignoring the teacher and sitting quietly at his desk.) **I am not taking this hat off. I take enough crap from everyone and I am just not doing it.**
Teacher:	(Walking back to Benny's desk, attempting not to draw much attention to himself or the exchange with Benny.) "Benny, you really do have to take your hat off. I'm sorry, but it's the rule." (The teacher then gently reaches over and removes Benny's hat by the bill.) (CRASH! The defense shatters, see fig. 12)
Benny:	(Grabs a chair raises it over his head.) "Give me back my hat you S.O.B. or I swear I'll kill you!"

Within this scenario, the origin of Benny's violent rage is not the injury associated with his well-meaning teacher's request that he remove his hat. Rather, this incident illustrates a common dynamic in which aggressive behavior is associated with the failure of the narcissistic defense in the face of a combination or serial impact of minor injuries to the child's self-esteem (i.e. the comments from his mother and the bus driver, together with the prospect of public humiliation concerning his hair). With his teacher's removal of his hat Benny became flooded by his profoundly painful, underlying insecurities, triggering a retaliation for the full sum of this pain against a teacher who inadvertently pushed his brittle defense beyond its breaking point.

Unfortunately, a heavy reliance upon a narcissistic defense for the management of underlying insecurity not only explodes in episodes of narcissistic rage, but also entails a number of less dramatic but equally difficult dynamics. First among these is the fact that the brittle nature of this defended sense of self results in a limited ability to learn from criticism, since negative feedback is generally disregarded or deflected. If one's profound need to preserve an inflated sense of self results in a psychological process which shields one from awareness of life's more subtle failures and automatically projects blame for such failures upon others, the critical process of trial-and-error learning is dramatically undermined. Second, the social ramifications of this defense are highly significant and extremely complicated, particularly in light of the fact that one of the primary dynamics promoting the need for this defense relates to insecurity concerning the quality of one's relationships and the ability to elicit caring responses from others. Socially, the individual who relies heavily upon a narcissistic defense needs and demands from others a great deal of affirmation of his grandiosity. In many respects, he values relationships with others only when they serve to reflect back his inflated sense of self, resulting in an interpersonal style that reflects a sense of entitlement and is limited in compassionate attunement to the needs of others. This style of relating, unless performed with tremendous sophistication and skill (as in narcissistic charismatic leaders), draws or elicits considerable resentment and criticism from others, thus further supporting the individual's underlying sense that others will not find him worthy of caring or love.

Helping the Narcissistic Child or Adolescent

At the core of effective work with the narcissistic child is the balance between one's use of authority and compassionate understanding of the child's underlying vulnerability. The child's grandiosity should be challenged in a manner which does not precipitate the complete failure of the narcissistic defense. Effective intervention demands a careful attunement to the child's range of optimal frustration with respect to challenges to self-esteem, while remembering that to the narcissistic child preservation of this defense is as essential as oxygen.

In many respects the use of a primitive psychological defense such as a narcissism is analogous to the biological process involved in the body's response of raising its temperature to thwart infection. However, in both biology and psychology, our adaptive response to threats may use a strategy that is effective in solving one problem yet creates another. When the body attempts to defeat infection by raising its temperature to a point at which the infection can not survive, it also creates a situation that is intolerable for its own delicate organs, such as the brain. If we are to support the reestablishment of health, whether within a biological or psychological model, we must not define the "problem" too narrowly. We must remain focused on both primary and secondary dynamics or, as in the illustration above, focus on both the fever (or narcissistic defense) as well as the underlying infection (or negative sense of self).

Understanding narcissism dictates an intervention process which addresses both the underlying negative self-beliefs (infection) and the narcissistic attitudes and sense of entitlement (fever). To this end, the following intervention insights and guidelines are offered:

- A narcissistic defense is never taken away from a child. The child will give it up when he no longer needs it.

- The child will no longer need his narcissistic defense when his underlying negative self-assessments are replaced by feelings of worth and competence.

- The goal in management of the narcissistic child's behavior is to bend, but not break, his defense and to recognize an approximation of appropriate response as a step towards healthier functioning (optimal frustration).

These few statements provide the framework for understanding and guiding intervention with narcissistic children. As stated above, effective work with these children demands a delicate balance in which their sense of entitlement is challenged, but not in such a powerful manner that their defenses fail completely. Unfortunately, conceptualizing this balance is far easier than actually achieving it. Work with these youngsters is often profoundly frustrating. To be in the presence of a child who has an extremely limited ability to honor our basic right to be treated as an equal, let alone to defer to our authority as adults, is for most of us an unpleasant experience. These children often overtly disregard the needs and wants of others, and so elicit indignation. Management of our own frustration and natural desire to retaliate against the narcissistic child's sense of entitlement and inability to defer to authority is truly one of the most difficult aspects of work with this population. Ultimately, the ability to work effectively with these children is significantly predicated upon our ability to manage the inherent assault on our own self-esteem produced by work with a child whose esteem is based on the negation of our worth.

There is an adage in the world of psychology that if one questions whether a patient is narcissistic, simply place him in a room with someone who has already been identified as such. If only one emerges from the room alive, the diagnosis is confirmed. The profound struggle for supremacy that plays out between two individuals with narcissistic personalities is not a foreign occurrence within the public school. As a matter of fact, the most frequent dynamic in which profoundly aggressive behavior erupts from the narcissistic child involves negative interactions with significantly narcissistic adults. Adults with significant narcissistic vulnerabilities themselves may voice such folksy attitudes as: "That kid needs to be brought down a notch!" or "That kid has a chip on his shoulder that I plan to knock off for him!" We must recognize that if an intervention program for this population is to be effective, we must identify staff who have an effective interpersonal style for work with narcissistically vulnerable children. It has been my experience that in the absence of attention to this variable, regardless of the quality of a school's behavior-management program, effective intervention will not occur.

The process of challenging, without destroying, a narcissistic child's defense demands tremendous attunement to the child's inner state, as well as a patient long-term perspective. We must remember that real change for these children occurs over time, not as a result of winning an individual battle or power struggle. However, effective intervention is equally predicated upon the adult's absolute clarity concerning both the child's need for the adult to be in charge and the adult's capacity to be so. The issue of power is an ever-present focus in the world of the narcissistic child, particularly with respect to his sense of power relative to others. Effective work with these children requires that the caretaker have both an innate sense of his personal power and clear empathic attunement to the child's need to preserve self-esteem. The narcissistic child's perception of the caretaker as powerful reduces the narcissistic injury associated with subordination to the caretaker. When the narcissistic child subordinates himself to someone perceived as having great power, he experiences relatively limited threat to his own grandiosity; however, subordination to someone perceived as weak or incompetent is a significant threat to his self-esteem. The caretaker who is perceived as both powerful and compassionate lowers the child's general level of anxiety and increases the potential for those healing challenges to narcissism that fall within the range of optimal frustration.

Achieving a compassionate and balanced use of power with the narcissistic child is not a simple task. Therefore, the following guidelines are offered:

- Honor approximations of subordination. Do not demand that the child comply exactly as directed, allow for some degree of resistance, and do not require that the child carry out his compliance with a pleasant attitude.

- Avoid bringing your own charged emotion to confrontational interactions. Stay calm.

- Exhibit patience, avoid moving too quickly to threatening consequences for non-compliance. Don't expect or demand immediate or complete compliance. Give him time to comply and let him use his slow pace to save face.

- Do not lecture or moralize. Simply state your directive clearly and, when necessary, outline the logical consequence for non-compliance. Say what you need to say but then keep quiet.

- Do not express a desperate need for the child to comply. Again, stay calm. If the child senses in the adult a desperate need for him to comply, the weakened position associated with this need may well elicit resistance.

- After a difficult encounter with a student, find a private opportunity to acknowledge your sense of remorse that the problem occurred and your appreciation that he ultimately complied with your directive.

- Attempt to identify together a plan that would avoid a recurrence of this situation.

The following vignette illustrates effective employment of these principles.

Sam

Sam, a difficult fifteen-year-old high-school student, has come into his third-period class in an upbeat mood, laughing and talking with friends. The bell rings and the instruction begins. However, Sam's exuberant mood persists and he continues to talk during the lecture. In the first moments of class, Sam receives two requests from his teacher to quiet down and a warning that if he continues to make it difficult to teach he will be asked to leave the classroom. Approximately ten minutes into the period, Sam is still talking openly and disrupting the lecture. At this point the teacher quietly states, "Sam, I can see you're having a hard time quieting down, which is making it hard for me to teach. I'd like you to leave the classroom and go to the office for the rest of the hour." Sam sits quietly, appearing to contemplate his options, not gathering his things in preparation to leave. In response, his teacher returns to his lecture, ignoring Sam for approximately the next thirty seconds, and then he quietly, but clearly, states, "Sam, I've asked you to leave the classroom. You are welcome back tomorrow, but I want you to leave for the rest of the hour." The teacher returns to instruction for approximately sixty seconds, then turns to Sam and states, "Sam, I don't want to struggle about this, but I have asked you to leave." The teacher then sits down at his desk and ceases instruction while he quietly waits for Sam to leave. Sam then asks, "What are you waiting for?" The teacher does not respond. Ultimately, Sam asks, "What are you going to do if I don't leave?" The teacher calmly responds, "I'm not certain, Sam. I hope that you'll do what I am asking, because if you don't I won't be able to teach and I will need to come up with some consequence for your interfering with my ability to do so."

At this point several of the other students indicate to Sam that he should go and he angrily gathers his belongings and proclaims, "This class is bullshit and you are an asshole. No problem, I'm out of here!" Sam knocks his desk around as he gets up to leave and he walks out the door with the parting offering, "See you later, chumps. I need a cigarette and Professor Asshole wants me to go have one."

Once Sam has left the classroom the teacher calmly states to the rest of the class, "I'm sorry this had to play out this way. I enjoy having Sam as part of our class and hope we can work things out so he can come back and remain with us." Then he returns to his lecture with no further comment concerning Sam or the incident.

Up to this point the teacher has handled this situation with skill and grace. He has remained calm, avoided threats, refused to argue, given Sam time to respond, and avoided backing Sam into a corner; however, effective work with Sam now requires that his teacher attempt to reestablish contact with him prior to their next class period. This takes the form of an interaction similar to the one that follows:

Later in the day Sam's teacher finds a means to speak with him alone in the hallway. He opens his exchange with the statement, "I'm sorry class didn't go well for us today." Sam, still angry, responds, "It would have gone fine if you had just relaxed and not been into your teacher power thing." To this, his teacher responds, "Sam, I know it seems to you that I was unreasonable. I'm sorry that you can't understand the way the situation felt to me, but I did what I thought I needed to do. But that's not really what I wanted to talk to you about. I have two things to say. First, I know that the situation in class was hard for you today, and I appreciate that you did leave when I asked you to, and second, I want to see if we can find some way to avoid putting each other in that situation again. Do you have any ideas?"

At this point the student is often unable to offer much in the way of a constructive suggestion and will generally express either indifference or rejection of the idea of a plan. The adult will need to tolerate the child's apparent indifference to his empathetic response. The responsibility to generate a plan that would be useful to both the teacher and student will in most situations fall almost exclusively upon the adult.

Effective work with narcissistically defended children is among the most challenging of the clinical education tasks. These children demand from their caregivers tremendous patience, self-restraint and capacity for forgiveness, couched within a clear sense of security and comfort in their capacity to use authority compassionately yet effectively. Unquestionably, this constellation of needs is far easier to meet when supporting a younger child than when working with a more powerful, sophisticated and potentially dangerous adolescent. Work with these children and adolescents calls for the adult to develop an adaptive delusion of omnipotence, which empowers the adult with both a profound sense of authority and a capacity to guarantee the child's safety and security.

Reestablishment of the Central Organizational Schema

The third dynamic I will present to explain the Category A child's most problematic and aggressive behaviors is this population's often discouraging pattern of behavioral improvement followed by dramatic regression. Those working with these children generally recognize this pattern but often have a limited model for understanding its origin or function. Unfortunately, this pattern is extremely problematic in that it promotes a pronounced and debilitating sense of hopelessness within both the child and his caretakers. In light of this, it is imperative that those responsible for supporting behaviorally impaired children possess an understanding of this pattern that provides some degree of inoculation from its potential to elicit feelings of hopelessness.

Key to understanding this frustrating pattern of improvement followed by regression is an appreciation of the central importance of preserving one's fundamental organizational schema or belief system (i.e. one's understanding of the nature of humanity, religious and moral convictions). Beliefs or fundamental assumptions about the nature of life serve to organize experience so that life can be experienced as coherent and orderly, not disorganized and incomprehensible. Belief systems provide us a point of departure in understanding and responding to life's demands. Experiences that seem to challenge the validity of our organizing beliefs generally provoke anxiety and are unwelcome.

The importance of an individual's fundamental belief system as a way to make sense of life and avoid the anxiety-producing perception of randomness means that these beliefs will not be given up readily, even if the individual encounters considerable data or experience challenging the validity of his belief. In the case of the Category A child, to varying degrees depending on the child's history or experience, the dominant schema or belief system concerning life and relationships is essentially: "People don't help or care; therefore, it doesn't matter what I do to people in the process of acquiring my wants and needs." The range of behaviors that can arise from such a perspective will have grave implications for the Category A child's social adjustment, since it allows him to engage in unsocialized behavior to meet his perceived needs, which generally cluster around the acquisition of power and possessions. Had this child's early life experience allowed him to discover the value of relationships, both his dominant belief system and perceived set of needs would have unfolded very differently. In the case of a child who has grown up in relative security with a parent who has provided adequate experience of optimal frustration, his dominant belief system will be: "People keep me safe, give me what I need and help me feel good about myself. All good things come through people." This perspective is profoundly distinct from that of the Category A youngster's and is associated with a very different pattern of behavior, one characterized by a socialized, primary focus upon the development and maintenance of relationships.

By recognizing the importance of faith in one's central schema, we gain considerable insight into the complicated experience of the Category A child who finds himself in a relationship with an adult who is both supportive and empathically attuned. It is this experience of being well cared for by an attuned adult that will allow the Category A child to move towards modification of his fundamental schema and towards socialization. However, this transition will not occur smoothly. Although we may perceive a change in the child towards valuing relationships, this process will elicit considerable anxiety and struggle for the Category A child, who must simultaneously recognize the inadequacy of his current belief system while making the transition to one that is new and untested. Generally, this transformation occurs over considerable time and is characterized by an erratic pattern of behavior as the child vacillates between the eroding and the evolving schemas.

The complicated process of supporting a child in redefining the role of relationships within his life is often characterized by moments of significant relational breakthrough followed by seemingly unprovoked hostility or aggression directed at the individual with whom he has the evolving relationship. Individuals working with these students must be prepared for the demoralizing pattern of progress almost always followed by setback. In the more benign playing out of this dynamic, these setbacks take the form of the child's pulling away from the relationship, e.g., not attending school after a significant success or not attending the next therapy session after a particularly helpful or powerful earlier session. In the more extreme form of this dynamic, the child engages in overtly hostile acts towards the individual with whom he has the evolving relationship.

Ultimately, the child's ability to amend his relational schema will be contingent upon two factors. The first is our ability to structure the child's experience such that when in our presence he is afforded a sense of security and competency, at least most of the time. The second is our ability to manage his efforts to challenge or invalidate his newly evolving schema with respect to relationships. Central to this is the need to monitor our own emotional tolerances: we should guard against giving ourselves to such an extent that when the child inevitably violates the relationship we are left without the emotional resources to forgive and to continue our attempt to meet his needs. In the final analysis, effective work with these children demands that we have the capacity to ride out their need to sabotage and test the evolving relationship until the point at which they no longer need to do so. In other words, we must be careful never to go so far out on limb for a child that when he inevitably needs to saw the limb off (with us on it) we are too injured to climb back up and try again. Although I am uncertain of the origin of the adage, "The only thing that therapists do which is truly 'healing' is the fact that they just keep showing up," I hold it to be at least partially true.

In summary, the fact that positive interpersonal dynamics often provoke difficult or aggressive behavior is clearly understandable and predictable when they are recognized as a threat to the validity of the Category A child's central schema with respect to relationships. These children, as a function of their history, have core belief systems in which relationships are held to be of limited value. Because of this perception they pursue the acquisition of power and possessions without the limiting impact of concern for the well-being of others. This indifference concerning relationships often affords these children their most successful avenues for pursuing and satisfying wants and needs. Therefore the Category A child will experience the evolution of a sense of connection to a competent caretaker as a source of threat, to which he responds by either pulling away from or sabotaging the evolving relationship. If the caretaker has the capacity to reengage and tolerate the child's resistance to the relationship, the child's schema will begin slowly to shift. However, if in the child's effort to affirm his negative perception of relationships, the child successfully sabotages the adult's commitment or ability to remain available, his negative schema will be affirmed and his relational pathology will deepen.

The process of supporting a child in the changing of his central schema for relationships is gradual and slow. Typically, this process begins with what I refer to as "the one-exception rule." This rule allows the child to amend rather than remake his central schema. Such amendments often take the form of: "People don't matter, except for my sainted seventh-grade English teacher or my kind old Aunt Bell." In this amendment lies hope, for with this exception we have opened the door for the child to experience potential within relationships. The process of providing a child with an experience that challenges his lack of value for relationships is often one in which we play the role of preparing the soil for the next sturdy seed that should fall upon it. Unfortunately, the process of moving from the single exception to generalization and to a point at which the Category A child routinely expects his relationships to be positive is an extremely slow transition in which some will succeed and others will not. However, each relationship within the child's life that is characterized by attunement and caring opens him further to valuing others.

Identification with the Aggressor

The fourth of the five dynamics that explain the Category A child's most problematic or aggressive behaviors is the psychological defense of identification with the aggressor. This dynamic is a critical factor in explaining the tragic cycle in which children who have been abused may frequently develop patterns of abuse towards others. The link between a history of victimization and abusive behavior towards others is often thought of in relatively simple terms, wherein abusive behavior is understood as a learned or modeled behavior. However, there is considerable evidence to suggest that the transformation from victim to perpetrator involves a far more complex process.

As an initial step in understanding the complex concept of identification with the aggressor, it is important to recognize this dynamic as a psychological defense. As with all such defenses, it functions as an unconscious mechanism to protect the individual from the experience of potentially overwhelming anxiety. In addition, it is important to understand that identification with the aggressor is a subcategory of a broader defense referred to as dissociation. In light of this fact, we will open our discussion of identification with the aggressor with an explanation of the concept of dissociation.

Dissociation, like most psychological defenses, is adaptive in that it addresses the need to manage anxiety, and in limited or targeted application has great utility and few drawbacks. In simple terms, dissociation entails the temporary disconnection between one's emotional or affective state and conscious awareness. As a result of this process the individual is partially shielded from the potentially debilitating impact of powerful emotions.

A common adaptive application of dissociation occurs in crisis situations (e.g., one's arrival upon an accident scene), where the images (blood and suffering) and demands (the need to provide care that is beyond one's knowledge) have tremendous potential to elicit overwhelming anxiety. At such times, it is adaptive to employ a dissociative strategy that allows access to cognitive resources without interference from anxiety or emotion. This process allows us to function in a highly effective, albeit emotionally disconnected, manner during the immediate crisis. However, as time passes and the demand for effective reaction lessens we will generally, and with varying degrees of delay, experience much of the affect which had been excluded from awareness: after we have effectively managed the crisis, we become an emotional mess.

The dissociative response is a useful unconscious strategy for the management of potentially overwhelming affect, yet, as with all psychological defenses, it has the potential to be maladaptively employed. This is often observable in the functioning of children who have been exposed to repeated trauma or who have had a single, highly traumatic episode processed in a manner that results in frequent experiences of its reenactment. The negative impact of the maladaptive employment of the dissociative defense is complex. Key problems associated with the frequent activation of the dissociative state include: 1) the inability to consistently and effectively access and utilize affect to assess issues of safety within the environment (analogous to turning off the warning lights in an automobile's electrical system); 2) the inability to learn, for the benefit of future functioning, from experiences which occur while within a dissociative state (analogous to losing one's memory of past experience); and 3) the promotion of a fragmented, chaotic and highly anxious sense of self (analogous to discovering that while sleeping you are regularly performing out-of-character and potentially dangerous acts).

It is important to note that a child's reliance upon dissociation as a means of managing difficult experiences or feelings is problematic in that it is highly self-reinforcing. With each employment of this strategy, the likelihood of its future employment increases. This dynamic is linked with the fact that the threshold for activating the dissociative response seems to drop with each episode. In addition, although employment of this coping strategy is initially unconscious, over time the traumatized individual will often learn highly destructive means by which consciously to activate dissociation, using them as a strategy to buffer himself from non-traumatic, yet sad or painful emotions. Both of these dynamics are further explained in the following paragraphs.

A pattern of escalating reliance upon dissociation for the management of difficult experiences and emotions leads to the lowering of the threshold for the activation of the dissociative state. The connection of affect to awareness can be compared to a nail within a piece of wood. The initial effort required to pull the nail from the wood is great. However, once pulled, if the nail is returned to the same hole, each subsequent removal will require less force, and eventually the nail will fall from the hole under the minimal stress of its own weight. Similarly, a child who has had multiple experiences of trauma and associated episodes of dissociation is likely to struggle with a problematic pattern in which he dissociates under minimal stress.

The second of the dynamics associated with a pattern of maladaptive dissociation involves the traumatized individual's eventual discovery of the volitional use of dissociation as a means for managing or escaping painful emotion. This discovery, which generally does not occur until adolescence and is more prevalent in females than in males, entails stumbling onto the realization that self-injury (i.e. self-mutilation, cutting) can serve to activate the dissociative process and provide relief from painful affect. This discovery too often leads to a pattern of self-injury as a means of stress management. Unfortunately, the use of self-mutilation as a means of managing stress is highly addictive and carries with it all the associated problems of addiction, as well as several other problems unique to this particular addiction.

The problems associated with addiction to self-mutilation are highly complex and play out on both psychological and psychosocial levels. Psychologically, the process of self-mutilation as a means to activate dissociation is destructive in two central respects: 1) it lowers the threshold for dissociation, self-induced or otherwise (whether you pull the nail out yourself or someone else does it for you, the strength of the bond between the wood and the nail weakens with each separation); and 2) it promotes a devalued sense of self and an associated reduced commitment to self-protection. The individual looks at his scarred body, recognizes what he has done to himself, and experiences profound feelings of shame, disgust, repulsion and an associated sense that he deserves whatever negative experiences might come his way. Interpersonally, self-mutilating behavior often activates a number of complicated dynamics. Foremost among these is the potential for acts of self-mutilation to be misperceived as suicidal behavior. This misperception often results in a great many problems including: 1) enhancement of the traumatized individual's sense of being misunderstood and alone with his reality; 2) employment of treatment interventions designed to assure safety as opposed to helping the individual develop alternative soothing strategies; and 3) the traumatized individual's eventual discovery that threats of suicide result in considerable positive attention and support, promoting a maladaptive pattern in which less-than-genuine threats of suicide are used as a means of gaining much-needed support. Unfortunately, after multiple threats of suicide and acts of self-injury, others often begin to experience this behavior as manipulative and respond with reduced empathic attunement and concern which in turn promotes a greater sense of isolation and desperation on the part of the traumatized individual.

With this basic understanding of the concept of dissociation and some of the dynamics with which it is associated, I will now discuss the specific nature and function of one of its subcategories, *identification with the aggressor*. This complicated, yet relatively common, psychological defense begins with the child's dissociation from the pain of physical or sexual abuse. Yet this goes a step beyond simple dissociation from the pain and trauma of abuse and helps the child manage the intolerable sense of powerlessness associated with abuse. This strange, although functional, psychological process entails the adoption of an empathically derived sense of the abuser's perspective of the child and the abuse. In other words, in order to avoid the intolerable experience of profound powerlessness, identification with the aggressor allows the child to experience his abuse through the empathically derived perspective of the abuser.

The child's transition in psychological perspective from that of the victim (experiencing the associated pain and powerlessness) to that of the perpetrator (in control and acting in accordance with distorted reason — "the child deserves the abuse") is for many a difficult concept to understand and accept. It is often perceived as just too theoretical. However, there are significant data which suggest that this process does indeed occur. These data provide a useful understanding of why and how it is that abused children often grow into abusive adults. As mentioned in the introduction to this section, the relationship between growing up as an abused child and developing into an abusive parent appears to be linked to a far more complex process then simple mimicking of parental behavior.

A common experience within my clinical practice, supporting my acceptance of the validity of the identification with the aggressor has occurred in my work with parents suspected of abusive behavior towards their children. In the course of assessing the presence of abuse, the interview with parents suspected of abuse will eventually involve exploration of childhood memories and questions concerning abuse to which they might have been exposed. It has been my experience that an extraordinary percentage of those parents who are ultimately identified as abusive acknowledge early-life experiences of abuse, yet relay their memories of this abuse in a manner suggesting they deserved their maltreatment or that it really was not that bad. Common statements in these interviews include such comments as: "Yeah, my dad was tough, but the truth is I deserved most of it," or "Sure, my mom would beat the tar out of me, but I would really ask for it. I was a real monster. I guess I needed it. After all I didn't turn out so bad." What is striking in these statements is the fact that the child has ultimately adopted his abusive parent's position and now sincerely believes that the abuse he experienced was both warranted and perhaps even helpful. Additionally, these parents, when pushed to remember their experience of the abuse, are generally unable to access any emotional content. Most frequently, they will make vague, emotionally unattached statements about their memories such as, "I guess I didn't mind it or I would have changed my attitude," or "I don't think kids really think about what they feel; they just go from moment to moment."

In the cycle of moving from victim to perpetrator, a victim who has managed the pain and powerlessness of the abuse through identification with the aggressor will, when the environment triggers memories (conscious or unconscious) of powerlessness and vulnerability, unwittingly adopt the perspective of his perpetrator. The abused child, now a parent who experiences his own child in a manner that calls up an intolerable memory of abuse, activates identification with the aggressor and tragically acts this role out upon his own child.

Further support for the validity of the concept of identification with the aggressor is found in the research and clinical trials addressing the transformation from victim to perpetrator. This research has demonstrated that one of the most effective means to break this cycle is through the use of individual and group therapies in which the previously abused parent is supported in accessing the emotional memory of his own victimization. When adults who have experienced abuse in childhood have the opportunity, within the context of a supportive relationship, to reconnect or access the disturbing memories of their victimization and powerlessness, the evolution from victim to perpetrator is often halted. Within the psychodynamic model of treatment, the healing or curative dynamic associated with the process of bringing these painful memories into consciousness is couched in the belief that, once managed or tolerated within the individual's conscious awareness, identification with the aggressor is no longer needed as a defense.

Within the school setting, our awareness of this troubling dynamic commands considerable sensitivity to our management of children we know or suspect to have a history of abuse. Foremost among the obligations associated with this awareness is the need to protect both the abused child and his potential victims. This requires of school personnel an awareness that abused children are essentially "programmed" to abuse others, and therefore must be carefully, but compassionately, monitored. Since abuse of others is theoretically triggered by the abused child's memories of powerlessness and vulnerability and the consequent identification with the aggressor, it is particularly important to monitor these children in their interaction with less powerful or vulnerable children. This fact has implications of significant concern when considering the common public-school practice of managing all children with behavioral problems within a "non-categorical behavioral intervention classroom." In these classrooms, Category A students with histories of abuse and an associated vulnerability for abusive behavior towards those perceived as powerless, are too often placed in ready contact with both Category B and C students, who often exude vulnerability.

As we work with children who have been victims of abuse and understand how their abusive experiences have programmed them to move unconsciously into the role of abuser, we experience a breakdown in the distinction between perpetrator and victim. A model which directs compassion towards the victim and disdain towards the perpetrator is far from enlightened. I believe it is our responsibility to attempt to break out of this simple "good vs. bad" mode of thought and embrace a more progressive perspective of addressing the complex issues associated with a history of abuse. As a point of departure, it would seem that we must: 1) assume a highly vigilant role in monitoring for potential abuse, both from parent to child, and from child to child, and when abuse is identified, act in a compassionate but clear manner to address this issue; and 2) work to help abused adults and children gain access to therapeutic support in the process of recapturing and working through the emotional memories of their abusive experiences, in hopes of breaking the cycle in which victims evolve into victimizers.

Avoidance of Intolerable Feelings of Emptiness

The last of the five triggering dynamics for problem behavior in the Category A child is chronic vulnerability to, and intolerance for, the experience of boredom. To understand these children's propensity for boredom, as well as their inability to tolerate this experience, it is first necessary to clarify or define boredom as it relates to the Category A child child's experience. To this end, the following section will compare and contrast the Category A child's experience of "downtime" (a period of time during which there is no compelling adaptive demand or external source of distraction) to that of a healthier, well-adjusted youngster.

In understanding the contrast between the more typical child's experience of boredom and that of the Category A child it is useful to begin with a discussion of the distinct internal worlds of thought and emotion of each of these groups of children. The internal world of the emotionally healthy child or adolescent is organized around a sense of evolving competencies and a rich constellation of emotional memories of those to whom they have a sense of relationship or attachment (see Chapter II, Relational Capacity). As a function of these psychological resources, when confronting downtime, the emotionally healthy child is generally able to engage in stimulating or comforting thought linked to aspirations and emotional relatedness. For these children, encounters with downtime and the experience of boredom are not particularly pleasant but are nonetheless tolerable. These children possess internal diversions and the capacity to soothe themselves, allowing for a tolerance of boredom without significant emotional upheaval. In contrast to the well-adjusted child's relatively rich internal world, the Category A child, lacking a well-defined sense of self and with only limited attachments, lives with an internal world that is often strikingly empty. For this child, downtime results in exposure to an inner landscape devoid of sustaining resources. The experience of boredom casts these children towards an intolerable encounter with emptiness and results in their desperate need to generate external distractions as a means of escape. The Category A child often dedicates a considerable portion of his psychological energy attempting to avoid boredom and its associated intolerable affect. This drive sets the stage for the Category A child or adolescent to frequently engage in thrill-seeking behavior, with little concern for risks or consequences.

Too often within the school setting the distinct nature of the experience of boredom for the Category A child is both misunderstood and disregarded. Ironically, with this population of children, we often attempt to use exposure to boredom (i.e. detentions and in-house suspension) as punishment for behavior that may well have been generated by their inability to tolerate boredom. It is additionally common to attribute the Category A child's willingness to employ extreme behaviors (in an effort to avoid or manage the experience of boredom) to their absolute "moral bankruptcy." Those working with these children have an experience of boredom which is so fundamentally different that it is difficult to see its avoidance as understandable motivation for many of the difficult behaviors exhibited by these children. This incomprehension of the Category A child's inability to tolerate boredom often undermines effective behavior management and compromises compassionate support on the part of school staff. Unfortunately, those who enjoy a fundamentally healthy internal or emotional world often find it extremely difficult to imagine that an experience of boredom could be so distinct from their own experience.

As an illustration of this dynamic I offer the following vignette, in which disruptive behavior evolves out of a Category A student's inability to tolerate boredom. Included in this vignette are two possible outcomes for the exchange between the student and teacher. The second of these is offered not as a likely or realistic scenario, but what might be if the

Category A child had the capacity to understand and express his inner experience.

Ben

Ben, a particularly difficult eighth-grade student, has been within his current math class for approximately six months, where, due to his non-completion of homework, he fell further and further behind as the year progressed. At present, Ben is completely lost in this class and has given up on the course's content. With this abdication, Ben's classroom behavior has deteriorated to the point that his teacher, in desperation, has offered him the following (all-too-common) contract:

Teacher: *"Ben, it's clear that you don't care about my class or about learning. So this is the deal: You can come to class and do absolutely nothing. You can sit there with your head on your desk or looking out the window, I really couldn't care less! I promise I won't bother you by attempting to teach you. However, I do not plan to waste my time addressing your behavior. Do you understand this, Ben? I am giving you what you want, you can sit and do nothing, BUT DO NOT DISRUPT MY CLASS! Do we have an understanding?"*

Ben: *"Whatever."*

For the next several class periods, Ben attempts to comply with this contract and during math period sits quietly sleeping, looking out the window, or drawing pictures on his notebook. However, Ben eventually becomes overwhelmed by his experience of boredom (in addition to feelings of incompetence and rejection) and responds by throwing a pencil across the room in the direction of one of his friends, an event which unfortunately catches his teacher's attention.

Teacher: *"DAMN IT, BEN! WHAT DID I TELL YOU? I let you sit and do nothing, which I would not tolerate from any other student, with the one requirement that you not disrupt my classroom. BUT, YOU WON'T EVEN DO THAT! I'VE HAD IT!"*

The teacher now walks back to Ben's seat.

Teacher: *"Why did you throw that pencil? I want you to help me understand why you would disrupt my classroom and potentially harm someone by doing something childish like throwing a pencil across the room."*

Real-world response:

Ben   *"BECAUSE I WAS BORED AND FELT LIKE IT."*

Teacher: *"BECAUSE YOU WERE BORED! THIS IS YOUR*
EXCUSE? A LITTLE BOREDOM JUSTIFIES DESTROY-
ING MY CLASSROOM AND POTENTIALLY
HARMING SOMEONE? GET THE HELL OUT OF
HERE! THERE IS NO PLACE HERE FOR SOMEONE
LIKE YOU!"

Insightful response:

Teacher: *"Why did you throw the pencil?"*

Ben: *"Mr. Jones, I was sitting here, lost and uninvolved in the les-*
son you were teaching. I was feeling bored and trying to pass
the time by looking out the window. Suddenly, I was over-
whelmed by immeasurable feelings of emptiness and existential
void. I felt as if I was falling off the universe, alone with no
one even noticing my descent into the abyss of nothingness. I
was spiraling down, deeper and deeper, into a feeling of
absolute isolation! Finally, in desperation, and with no
thought for the profound impact of my behavior on others, I
found myself grabbing my pencil and hurling it towards the
outside world in a panicked effort to escape these intolerable
feelings. I threw the pencil as a flare to alert the outside world
of my desperate situation. I threw the pencil as a lifeline, to
pull myself back to the world of others, and away from my
implosion into nothingness."

Teacher: *Without words, the teacher steps forward, offers Ben a handful*
of pencils, and gestures his support to throw at will.

Clearly, the dialogue above will not occur and perhaps the Category A child's experience of downtime and associated boredom is not always quite the existential crisis indicated. However, there seems no doubt that those blessed with both a well-established network of internalized relationships and a stable sense of self experience boredom quite differently than do those lacking these resources.

The implications of the Category A child's inability to tolerate boredom are relatively broad and demand sensitivity with respect to both the character of the general classroom and the choice of options in behavior management. Clearly, this child will do best within a learning environment that is highly stimulating and limited in its reliance upon self-directed activities or rote learning. It follows that strategies used to support him in self-soothing or as consequence for inappropriate behavior must take into account his limited ability to tolerate boredom. These factors generally dictate a classroom characterized by considerable "active learning," the availability of resources to allow the agitated student opportunity to soothe himself through action-oriented strategies (e.g., shooting baskets, listening to music), and the avoidance of a heavy reliance upon traditional consequences such as in-school suspension and detention.

VI

Programming for the Category A Student

As we turn our attention to school-based intervention with the Category A child/adolescent, Dr. Efram Bleiburg of the Menniger Clinic offers an extremely useful framework in his article "The Yogi and the Commissar" (1992). In this article Bleiburg outlines the role for the caretaker (parent, teacher, clinician, probation officer, administrator) working with narcissistic and antisocial children and adolescents as promoting change from both the inside-out, through "Yogi"-like empathic understanding and relationship formation, and from the outside-in, through "Commissar"-like restructuring of the child's environment, so that pro-social behaviors are rewarded and anti-social behaviors are contained and punished.

Unfortunately, in many respects Bleiburg's assertion serves as an indictment of much of what is done in our current efforts to serve this population, as we separate the roles of Yogi and Commissar through assignment of their respective responsibilities to distinct institutions or professions. Generally, we assign Yogi responsibilities to mental-health and educational institutions and professionals, while the work of the Commissar is relegated to law enforcement and correctional institutions and their professionals. Thus, the child is volleyed between distinct professions and institutions, each with distinct roles as the Yogi or the

Commissar. Rarely does he find the integration of the two roles that is necessary for healing.

WORK OF THE YOGI

The work or function of the Yogi is to empathically experience, understand and competently manage the full range of the child's inner world. The character of this yogi-like healing relationship with the caretaker is essentially consistent with D.W. Winnicott's notion of the therapeutic "holding environment" and the provision of "emotional holding" (1986). Winnicott asserts that the child's process of learning to manage powerful or disturbing affect centers upon the opportunity to experience these emotions in the context of an empathically attuned adult able to share this experience without activating debilitating anxiety, within the adult.

As has been discussed, for the Category A child the content of underlying emotions or affect is often deeply disturbing and is the root of most behavioral difficulties. In view of this fact, intervention for this population must provide the child an effective means for managing these underlying emotions. Fulfillment of this responsibility demands that the caretaker be capable of both understanding and tolerating the child's inner world. When the child senses that the caretaker is able to empathically experience, understand and tolerate his powerful underlying thoughts and affect without being overwhelmed or needing to detach or distance himself from the child, he experiences a much-needed sense of security and hope regarding his potential to not be alone with, and ultimately controlled by, his disturbing inner world.

By definition, children who fall within Category A do not expect emotional support and understanding from others and accordingly respond to the initial efforts of others to establish trusting relations as an intrusion or threat from which they must defend themselves. Ironically, much of the initial work with the Category A child involves managing his organized effort to thwart the development of potentially healing relationships. Often, the child's effort to protect himself from the risk associated with forming relationships involves an unconscious pattern of provocation, intimidation and physical aggression. To manage these dynamics, it is imperative that the caretaker have the empathic skills and resources that allow him to understand the child's emotional experience, the physical resources to contain the child's behaviors safely, calmly and compassionately, and the patience to wait for the child to "open the door" slowly, inter-mittently, to the formation of a functional trusting relationship.

WORK OF THE COMMISSAR

The role of the Commissar is to set and uphold clear behavioral lim-its. As we turn our attention to this role, we confront the need for the public schools to adopt a policy of early intervention in serving the Category A student. This necessity (although linked to other variables as well) stems from the fact that as the Category A child grows to physical maturity, the public schools' ability to fulfill the role of the Commissar and provide behavioral containment safely and effectively decreases sig-nificantly. The older Category A student, now more physically powerful and potentially influenced by some combination of hormones, violent youth culture, drugs and alcohol, often presents with behavior beyond the schools' ability to contain or manage it. Unfortunately, the Category A student, although easily identified in the elementary years, often receives little or no specialized services during this period. Too often this neglect results in a pattern in which public schools postpone the neces-sary focus upon these children until adolescence, at which point they assess themselves as unable to manage their behavior and abdicate responsibility through suspension and expulsion.

Further complicating the public schools' management of the Category A student, particularly the older, more powerful student, is the fact that the reluctance or inability to fulfill the role of the Commissar often serves to dramatically undermine their capacity to function within the Yogi role. In the face of threats or acts of aggression, the caretaker who senses himself to be unequipped to contain a child's physical behav-ior is generally unable to maintain a calm, empathic attunement to the child's inner experience. Unfortunately, the anxiety and agitation associ-ated with an overwhelmed or frightened caretaker responding to a violent or aggressive child serves to increase the child's anxiety and the potential for an aggressive fight-or-flight response. This results in a pat-tern in which the child and the caretaker unwittingly drive each other towards greater and greater anxiety and increase the risk of problematic, dangerous or aggressive behavior.

Given these dynamics, it is imperative that schools serving this diffi-cult population of children (i.e. most public schools) provide their staff with adequate training in crisis intervention and de-escalation strategies. Fortunately, there are a number of programs available to provide this essential training. In many respects, the most effective outcome associated with training staff in crisis management is the fact that the associated sense of competency reduces staff anxiety when approaching such situations. This allows staff to support and calm an agitated child without inadvertently increasing the child's anxiety through exposure to a frightened or agitated adult.

Although the public schools must develop effective means to serve the older Category A student, the first step in addressing the growing number of these children within secondary schools is early intervention. By directing our attention to the identification and treatment of Category A students in early childhood, we far more readily have available the necessary tools to provide truly effective intervention, and in doing so avoid the problems associated with later more difficult and less effective intervention.

The Category A child represents society's most problematic and potentially dangerous group of children. If we do not develop more-effective strategies for their management, the price will be both financially costly and emotionally painful. Unfortunately, due to the complexity of both their presentation and needs, this group of children has not been well served by public education. However, I believe that—if they can move beyond their resistance, beyond disclaiming responsibility for meeting the needs of this population, beyond simply consigning them to mental-health or law-enforcement professionals—our public schools hold the greatest promise of providing truly effective intervention.

SPECIALIZED PROGRAMMING RESOURCES

The following section provides a brief overview of what I believe to be the most important considerations and resources for effective public-school-based work with the Category A child. The information serves as a broad brushstroke of program-design considerations for the Category A student and is no way an exhaustive list of useful strategies or interventions.

It is critical to remember that the perceived need to obtain and maintain power and control (as means to assure safety) is a central motivating force for Category A children. Their limited ability to trust in others and use relationships as a source of comfort and security results in an associated need to seize and maintain control. This is quite distinct from the reality of more-typical children, who, by virtue of their history of fundamentally positive and supportive relationships, value a sense of connection with others and are motivated to form and use relationships as a means of emotional and physical security. The distinction between these two perspectives on the nature and value of relationships is dramatic, and significantly impacts each group's interpersonal style and behavior. In many respects, work with the Category A child must be based upon a clear understanding that these children generally perceive interpersonal relationships as valueless or potentially threatening.

The awareness of the Category A child's negative perspective and expectations with respect to relationships, when accompanied by a compassionate and empathic sense of the origin of this perspective, is critical to the development of an effective treatment milieu. With this insight, program development for the Category A child shifts away from a typical teaching model, with its heavy reliance upon social reinforcement (which is of little value to these children), to a model which reinforces desired behavior through the awarding of concrete reinforcement or sanctioned power. A management strategy that relies upon social reinforcement to motivate behavioral compliance and pro-social behavior commonly undermines work with Category A students. This strategy is analogous to trying to reinforce a hearing-impaired child's behavior by playing soothing music. Efforts to shape a Category A child's behavior through use of social reinforcement often serve as yet further evidence to the child that the caretaker neither understands nor has the capacity to help him. This is not to suggest that treatment of this child should be predicated upon the acceptance that he will never value relationships, but rather that treatment be organized to support the child in moving toward the valuing of relationships. This process demands that we first understand or accept the child's perspective on relationships, but discover means of interaction that will help the child gratify his needs or wants in a socially appropriate way. If the caretaker is successful in this, the child will eventually begin to associate the relationship with a caretaker with positive outcome, and in doing so will slowly move toward valuing this relationship.

I offer the following story as an allegory, to illustrate the often difficult and counterintuitive process of developing and maintaining effective intervention programs for a Category A child. Central to this story is the delicate balance needed between power and empathy, a balance needed in work with the Category A student.

The Chronicles of "Different-1"

Far away in a distant ocean on an uncharted volcanic island there lived a small population of descendants of a hunting party who, many generations earlier, had drifted by raft to this remote spot. In their cognitive abilities and physical attributes, the inhabitants of this island (subsequently named Different-1 and its residents the Different-ones) were very similar to those who lived off the island. However, similar though they were, so too were they different, particularly in their patterns of social behavior and child rearing. These differences originated from the fact that the Different-ones practiced a form of child rearing that largely left the young to raise themselves in relative isolation. As a function of evolution the young Different-ones now began life with many more basic survival skills than their mainland counterparts, and so were self-sufficient at an earlier age.

Because of this evolution and the remoteness of their island the Different-ones lived highly isolated lives both from one another and from the surrounding world. However, one day an extraordinary event occurred. On this day, an enormous cruise ship, battered and disabled by a storm and carrying a thousand passengers, drifted ashore on Different-1. As would be expected, with the arrival of the ship's passengers Different-1 would forever be changed and serious problems of coexistence arose for both the islanders and the stranded tourists. Because the tourists were (by nature) quite egocentric and far outnumbered the Different-ones, it quickly became their objective to "socialize" their new hosts. (The reader is encouraged to disregard any and all aspects of this story which lack realism, i.e. the fact that rescue from the island is never mentioned as of any interest to the tourists). So the tourists hoped to develop programs or treatments to transform the Different-ones from beings of social isolation and indifference concerning the welfare of others into beings who value social contact and seek to form and maintain relationships. Unfortunately, this task proved to be far from simple and created significant difficulties for both the tourists and the Different-ones, and early "treatment" efforts failed miserably.

The initial "treatment" attempted to "civilize" the Different-ones by demonstrating to them that tourists were to be trusted and not feared. This effort involved a strategy in which one member of each group would share a small comfortable living space. Those tourists who participated in the treatment dyads were chosen for their outstandingly gentle and compassionate nature.

Unfortunately, while the impact of this initial socialization effort upon the Different-ones was minimal, its impact upon the tourists was significant and led to a dramatic reduction in the number of kind-hearted tourists within the colony, as the tourist members of the treatment dyad were quickly and indifferently murdered by the Different-ones (and in most cases enjoyed as snack food). Understandably horrified by this outcome, the discouraged and frustrated tourists quickly abandoned this treatment model and set about attempting to develop a new "socialization program."

The next effort involved a very distinct strategy. This treatment entailed placing the Different-ones in the same living arrangement as in the initial program, but this time the tourist roommates were well armed and selected for their brutality and "take-no-prisoner" attitude towards life. Sadly, this strategy proved to be no more successful than the first and resulted in two significantly problematic outcomes. First, the population of Different-ones dropped significantly, since over half of those placed within this program were killed within a short period by their intolerant counterparts. Second, those Different-ones who survived this treatment shifted from a relative sense of indifference concerning the tourists (aside from their periodic enjoyment of a tourist as snack food) to what appeared to be a deep hatred of the tourists, prompting several brutal, senseless attacks against the tourists.

With these two failed efforts behind them, the tourists moved toward a far more balanced effort at "socializing" the Different-ones. This effort, once again, involved placing a tourist and a Different-one in a small comfortable living area. However, the tourists who were selected for this role were chosen for their even tempers and their comfort in asserting power. To assure the safety of the tourists, each was equipped with a non-deadly, paralyzing spray (which just happened to be in ready supply aboard the ship) to use if their roommate should become troublesome. Ultimately, this strategy proved relatively effective. The living arrangement became conflict-free and the Different-ones seemed to have their taste for tourists curtailed by the fact that each attempt to enjoy this delicacy resulted in the strange experience of being temporarily frozen.

Although this treatment model promoted a sense of peaceful coexistence (as long as the tourists had access to the paralyzing spray), it did little to help the Different-ones develop caring and valued relationships with the tourists. As time went on, it became increasingly clear that Different-ones subjected to this treatment remained absolutely indifferent to tourist welfare. Tourists could not count on the Different-ones for the smallest degree of empathy, support or courtesy. As a result the tourists were treated with both the caution and indifference afforded a thorny bush along a path.

Given the disappointing results of the early treatment efforts, the tourists redoubled their energy to design a treatment model that would more effectively help the Different-ones develop socialized characteristics such as compassion and empathy for others. With this goal in mind, the tourists were challenged to think about the Different-ones from an entirely different perspective and they began to ask themselves questions such as: "Why are the

Different-ones so different?" and "How does their behavior make sense in the context of their experience and perspective?" Much thought went into these questions, and ultimately the best minds among the tourists came to the consensus that the Different-ones, unlike tourists, did not value relationships because they had never had a consistent experience in which another individual was found to be truly useful. Informed by this insight, the tourists set about designing a different kind of treatment condition. They incorporated what they had already found to be useful (a balance of compassion and power) with a design in which the tourists consistently and effectively helped the Different-ones satisfy their wants and needs.

The initial efforts to move the Different-ones in the direction of developing a genuine desire to relate with the tourists was only marginally successful, and left most of the tourists frustrated and confused about what to try next. This confusion was linked to the fact that in their effort to win a place in the heart of the Different-ones the tourists had done everything they could imagine to help them acquire life's "good things." Yet the Different-ones continued to be unmotivated to relate to the tourists and remained indifferent to tourist welfare. The tourists spent considerable time sharing ideas among themselves in an effort to identify what could be done to please the Different-ones and lure them into a desire to connect or relate. In this effort, the tourists repeatedly returned to that central tenet of relational wisdom, "Do unto others as you would have them do unto you." So they tried to win over the Different-ones with everything from words of encouragement and physical affection to small nuggets of gold (which were generally quickly ingested by the Different-ones). Unfortunately, none of these generous offerings seemed to have an impact on the Different-ones, even though the tourists certainly thought they should have. Sadly, as the tourists observed the Different-ones' lack of appreciation for their significant generosity, many tourists grew increasingly angry and resentful towards them.

A movement quickly developed advocating the abandonment of reform efforts in favor of building large detention centers and applying a policy of "three strikes and into the volcano you go."

Eventually, after many years of frustration and limited success at "socializing" the Different-ones, an unusual tourist, who happened to share many common characteristics with the Different-ones, came forward and made the following radical observation: "Though our objective is to make the Different-ones more like us, at this point they lack a number of our qualities. This being true, it may follow that the experiences and material objects enjoyed or appreciated by us may not be appreciated by the Different-ones. Therefore, these things may be ineffective when used as an incentive to move the Different-ones towards valuing their tourist counterparts." This observation was found to be both annoying and unhelpful by many of the tourists, particularly those who were frustrated with the Different-ones and had decided it was time to stop trying to help them. They felt the Different-ones should "just get over it and shape up" and begin to act like tourists or face "becoming one with the volcano." However, other more pragmatic tourists began to question if these radical observations might have validity and should be considered. A small group of tourists began to step back from efforts to change the Different-ones and choose first to observe, study and attempt to make sense of their behavior. With this distinct focus, they discovered new insights concerning the psychological make-up and course of development of the Different-ones.

Some of the important observations included: 1) the young of this species seemed to adapt to environmental change much more easily than older individuals; 2) Different-ones seemed to most enjoy activities which are immediately gratifying, such as eating a snack or taking a rest in the shade; and 3) Different-ones seemed to grow quickly uncomfortable and anxious when approached or placed in situations in which they felt limited control.

Informed by these new insights, several of the tourists began the process of testing new treatment models. These centered around an effort to intervene as early as possible in the Different-ones' life cycle and reinforce the value of relating to tourists by linking tourist contact with outcomes and activities inherently appreciated and enjoyed by the Different-ones. The tourists eventually discovered that the most powerful incentives for getting the Different-ones to approach and relate to them were those activities the Different-ones preferred in their natural environment. These included counterintuitive strategies such as rewarding pro-social behavior with food and offering opportunity for self-directed activity, even though the Different-ones consistently challenged authority when functioning under close supervision.

With the implementation and refinement of these innovative strategies, the tourists began to observe slow but significant progress in their efforts to move the Different-ones toward a greater appreciation for tourists and socialized behavior. Yet, even though the majority of the Different-ones seemed to respond well to these new programs, the treatment continued to have little effect on those entering treatment later in their life cycle. In time it was noted that some tourists seemed to be far more effective in creating change in the Different-ones than others. In an effort to understand this fact, the tourists who had the most positive impact on the Different-ones were questioned and observed, and the following guidelines and recommendations were established for the "Different-one Treatment Programs."

Policy and Procedure for Different-one Treatment Programs:

Central to effective Different-one intervention is recognition of the fact that Different-ones do not value social relationships because they have experienced contact with others as both anxiety-producing (others have been experienced as unpredictable and often threatening) and of no demonstrated value. Therefore, the cornerstone of the treatment process to socialize the Different-ones is an organized effort to demonstrate the predictability and value of tourist contact (while at the same time minimizing the number of tourists who are enjoyed as snacks along the way).

To this end we offer the following intervention guidelines:

- *Never attempt to address a Different-one's problem behavior without first developing an understanding of the behavior's origin and purpose, as well as identifying an alternative and acceptable means by which to meet the associated need or want.*

- *Exercise caution in the application of the Golden Rule ("do unto others as you would have them do unto you"). This guideline is contraindicated when the other individual is significantly different from you.*

- *Always approach the Different-ones with a balance of compassion and authority. Express a clear sense of respect for both others and yourself.*

- *Recognize that real change occurs slowly and is often marked by two steps forward and one step back.*

- *Since real change occurs only over time, carefully safeguard your ability to remain committed to the long-term relationship with the Different-ones. Never place yourself in a position that allows them to take more from you than you can afford to give.*

- *Avoid cornering or aggressively pursuing a Different-one when he is in a highly anxious or agitated state. Give him space to calm down or seek support to provide physical containment safely and compassionately.*

- *Above all else, attempt to intervene early in the Different-ones' life cycle.*

In this allegorical treatment of the complex dynamics that arise in work with the Category A child, fiction was used to exemplify a more objective and thoughtful consideration of these vulnerable children and our approach to supporting them. I have tried to emphasize that

Category A children (like Different-ones) are no less human than the rest of us but that their experience has been distinct and results in a very different approach and perception of others.

WHAT DO THEY NEED?

I have consistently emphasized that behavioral intervention must begin with an effort to understand the motivation and purpose of the behaviors targeted for change. Such an effort demands consideration of the problem behavior within multiple temporal frames and environments, as well as through multiple levels of perception. The multiple temporal contexts in which behavior must be understood includes the child's present environment and the environment in which the problematic behavior originated. The levels of perception affecting behavior include both the external widely held perception of the environment, and the child's often distinct, egocentric and idiosyncratic perceptions.

Understanding a child's behavior by taking into account the role of past experiences in the evolution of current behavioral patterns is, for the most part, a relatively simple and intuitive process. Most people understand that a child who has grown up in a war zone will exhibit highly apprehensive perceptions and guarded behaviors, even after being removed from exposure to combat. However, the behaviorally handicapped child's capacity to perceive and remember events in a manner dramatically different from the perception of others is often far less easily accepted. Too frequently the caretaker's reaction to a troubled child's misperceptions or misattribution is characterized by a personal sense of indignation about the child's distinct perception of a shared experience. For example, a student who has been gently requested to stop tapping his finger on his desk may report that he was yelled at to stop, or a student who clearly provoked another student into an assault may insist that she did nothing to elicit the attack. To understand this phenomenon, an analogy from photography is useful: the child, like the lens of the camera, may see what is seen by others, but the resulting record of that moment (the child's perception and memory) may differ dramatically due to the quality and nature of the film. In photography the resulting picture may be represented in black-and-white images, or may miss critical detail due to lighting variables, or might be superimposed on an earlier picture; or there might be total failure of the film to react to the exposure. Similarly, within a child's perception of the environment, experiences may be processed and remembered in a highly egocentric and distorted manner, or not remembered at all, depending on the character of the psychological tools employed (unconsciously) to manage and organize the experience.

As noted above, clarity concerning behavior linked to a child's idiosyncratic perceptions and needs is not easily obtained through direct observation. It must evolve over time as a result of empathic understanding. Therefore, our efforts at behavioral intervention must take into account that the problematic behaviors we target for change are in some manner functional or adaptive within the context of the child's experience and perception. With this fact in mind, school-based intervention, designed to promote behavioral change, is dependent upon our ability to structure the classroom or treatment environments to promote the child's employment of safer, and more socially acceptable, alternative strategies for adaptation. In other words, as discussed in the allegory of the Different-ones, our initial efforts to effect change must provide socially appropriate means for the Category A child to acquire not only what we feel he needs and wants (such as praise and acceptance), but also what he feels he needs and wants (autonomy, power and control).

When operating with limited understanding of the motivation or purpose of a child's problematic behavior, it is common to ignore the need to provide the child an alternative means by which he can meet the needs associated with his problem behavior. This often results in an intervention model which almost exclusively uses punishment to extinguish undesirable behavior and does not reinforce or teach the child new, more appropriate, behaviors to acquire or meet his perceived needs. This punitive posture translates into an effort to structure the environment so that the cost associated with a problem behavior is far greater than the gain. However, the child's limited reaction to punishment demonstrates that, for him, the need or gains associated with the targeted behavior greatly outweigh the cost of enduring even severe punishment. Therefore, attempts to use punishment as the primary means of behavior modification often result in profound frustration (for both the caretaker and the child) and intervention failure. Clearly, the child's fear of potential punishment, regardless of its severity, will not modify his behavior if he perceives the targeted behavior as essential to survival. Just as a person on the verge of starvation will not respond to threats of punishment for stealing food, these children will not give up behaviors they experience as linked to physical or emotional survival.

Through observation of Category A children, I have identified four common factors that seem to drive much of their behavior:

- the pursuit of power and control within interpersonal relationships;

- the need for high levels of stimulation;

- limited ability to regulate emotions; and

- problematic peer-group affiliations.

Effective interventions must in some manner provide and promote socially acceptable means by which to address these issues. With this focus in mind, I present below a more in-depth discussion of means by which to draw on these insights to develop intervention strategies.

Power and Control

As a function of the Category A child's limited capacity to trust in the goodwill and competency of others (particularly caretakers), much of his behavior is organized around the pursuit and maintenance of power and control as a means of assuring safety and security. In view of this fact, it is imperative that school programming for this population avoid overreliance upon authority-centered structures in which students are expected to comply readily with autocratic directives. In my experience, many of the most difficult and unworkable dynamics confronted by the public school occur in situations in which a Category A student is placed under the supervision of an adult who operates fairly exclusively from an authority-centered model and who becomes increasing authoritarian in response to the child's inability to subordinate himself. This dynamic generally plays out in a pattern of increasing tension and challenge between the teacher and the student, and often results in the student's expression of aggression or an absolute refusal on the part of the student and/or the teacher to attempt cooperation.

Fortunately, the majority of educators do not approach behavior management exclusively from an authority-centered model, but instead use a management style which is at least partially rule-centered, in which the teacher functions as both a committed subject and guardian of the rules. In the application of an effective rule-centered model for behavior management, there must exist a clearly outlined and well-understood network of expectations (rules), rewards and consequences, as well as legitimate, sanctioned avenues for gaining power and control. This structure provides the child opportunity to defer to the "authority" of the rules instead of subordinating himself to a mistrusted authority figure, and is significantly less likely to elicit a struggle from and within the Category A student. In the implementation of an effective rule-centered classroom, the character of the teacher's administration of the rules remains critical. Consistency in applying the rules and the teacher's ability to represent himself as both compassionate toward the child yet a committed functionary of the rules requires careful attention.

The importance of consistency in a rule-centered environment cannot be overstated as a controlling variable in work with the Category A student. As much as any other factor, it is the supervising adult's ability to function strictly within the dictates of the rules which will determine the effectiveness of this model in mitigating the Category A child's need to struggle for power and control. When the classroom rules are administered in a manner experienced by the child as both predictable and consistent, the student is released from the demand to simply subordinate to the supervising adult, in exchange for subordination to the less-threatening network of rules. However, should the rules be applied erratically, the "power of the rules" becomes diluted, and the child reverts to perceiving the teacher's authority as the center of control in the classroom, a perception that activates a greater need to struggle for power and control.

The use of a rule-centered classroom structure does not result in loss of the teacher's prerogative to address the needs of a student, but rather demands that the nature and breadth of the teacher's prerogative be clearly defined within the rules. For example, it is imperative that the rules define the teacher as the appropriate source of judgment concerning the adequacy of a child's compliance, as well as outline the range of options available for rule enforcement and consequences for non-compliance. When the teacher is able to represent himself as both supported and bound by the rules, as is the student, it greatly facilitates the Category A child's capacity for rule compliance. However, when, out of frustration or ignorance, the teacher operates outside the prescribed rules, the impact upon the child's perception of the sanctity of the rules is profoundly negative, often leading to a power struggle with the teacher, whom the child now perceives as having shifted into an autocratic mode.

In addition to applying the rules consistently, it is imperative that the teacher working with the Category A student express a compassionate attunement to the child's experience. This position demands that the caretaker set clear, firm limits and assign consequences for non-compliance, without presenting a personalized sense of retribution, anger, disappointment or frustration. In the management of the student's difficult behavior it is imperative that the caretaker express his own acceptance of the authority of the rules. This means that if the rules prescribe a particular response from the adult he must carry it out. In doing so, the caretaker is able to show adherence to the boundaries and directives of the classroom structure, while expressing empathy for the child's displeasure. He might offer such statements as, "Ben, I'm sorry you have to lose your recess because you didn't complete your homework. I suspect there was a pretty good reason why you didn't get it done, but you know we don't have a choice. The rules say you can't go out for free time." In short, the caretaker's use of the rules as the source of authority effectively avoids many of the power struggles activated by a demand for subordination to an authority figure. Their joint subordination to rules also allows the caretaker to empathize with the child's frustration with the prescribed consequences and thus help him tolerate them.

One of the most common mistakes made by teachers in work with the Category A student is to revert rapidly to an autocratic position in managing difficult behavior. Two factors that seem to lead to this common mistake are: 1) It feels good. Work with this population is not easy and from time to time we all feel a compelling need to unload on these kids, essentially acting out our own frustration; and 2) It sometimes works. It is true that placing a child "off balance" by responding to him in an emotionally charged (intimidating) manner that is inconsistent with our standard mode of relating can provide the teacher a momentary sense of empowerment. However, the cost of this moment is generally not worth the brief sense of empowerment it affords, because it will ultimately erode the power of the rules and propel the child back into a pattern of power struggle with the caretaker.

From time to time, there may well be situations in which the prudent use of intimidation is warranted, but it should be limited to those situations when the use of a less expedient strategy could potentially result in a disastrous outcome. Examples of such situations might include raising one's voice at a child as he is about to unwittingly make a comment that would elicit an assault from another child, or when a child is about to flip a switch on a computer and cause the loss of a significant amount of work. However, whether a situation merited the use of intimidation or not, following its use it is important to process the experience with the child and attempt to help him understand why this dynamic occurred. For example, the teacher should relay that this is not how he wishes to relate to the child and apologize for the invalidation the child might feel as a result of the interaction. If the use of intimidation was linked to the teacher's frustration or misunderstanding, rather than avoidance of imminent disaster, it is important that the teacher acknowledge his mistake and seek forgiveness from the student (e.g., "I'm sorry I raised my voice just then. I didn't understand that you and Ben were only playing.")

Narcissism and the Rule-Centered Classroom

In creating and employing a rule-centered classroom structure with the Category A student, the teacher must not only address the child's limited capacity to trust authority, but also mitigate the risk to the student's narcissistic self-esteem. For this student, one of the most challenging aspects of functioning within the school setting is the threat to self-esteem associated with the demand to fully subordinate himself to authority. This requirement often serves as a powerful triggering dynamic for the failure of the narcissistic defense and the unleashing of aggressive retaliation (see section on narcissistic injury). Fortunately, the establishment of a well-defined set of expectations and consequences can minimize the potential for the Category A student to experience narcissistic injury. This is particularly true when teachers are able to present the rules as a fact of life, something beyond question and larger than any individual or group governed by them; in doing so, teachers can frame their own authority simply as a function of the rules.

Although the use of a rule-centered classroom structure minimizes the student's experience of narcissistic injury associated with compliance with authority, students with narcissistic features will not respond well to an authority figure perceived as impotent or anxious. In fact, the supervising adult's ability to present himself as confident and secure (but not arrogant) in his enforcement of the rules is a critical variable in effective behavior management for the narcissistic child. In simple terms, it is less threatening to the fragile self-esteem of the narcissistic child to subordinate himself to a powerful and competent authority figure than to one perceived as weak or incompetent. Unfortunately, almost all social contacts for these children occur in the context of a competitive struggle for control. As is true for competition in general, it is far easier to lose to an opponent who is perceived as both formidable in skills and gracious in victory than to an opponent of questionable skill who gloats in victory. This dynamic is evident from the disastrous outcome that generally occurs when an anxious, disempowered and narcissistic adult is placed in the position of supervising and managing the behavior of a narcissistic child.

Again, one of the most useful aspects of the rule-centered classroom structure is that it provides the opportunity to uphold the rules while maintaining empathic attunement to the child's struggle with compliance. This double focus is a critical skill in effective work with the narcissistic child and requires the capacity to set clear and firm behavioral limits while simultaneously providing emotional support to the child as he responds to these limits and consequences. What follows is a dialogue between a Category A student and a teacher, illustrating the use of the rule-centered structure in achieving both of these goals.

Chuck

Chuck, a ninth-grade Category A student, is entering his second-period class after the bell has rung.

Teacher: *"Chuck, the bell rang about fifteen seconds ago. I'm sorry, but you know the rules, so head to the office to get a pass and hurry back. I'll wait to start class until you're back so you don't miss anything."*

Chuck: *"That's stupid! They don't give us enough time between classes and then we get detentions for being late."*

Teacher: *"Chuck, I know there isn't much time to get around, but the rules are absolutely clear that when someone arrives late I must see his pass. I'm sorry, I hate some of the rules too, but I don't have a choice. I have to require a pass from you. Please go quickly, so you can come back and join us."*

Chuck: *"Okay, I'm going, but this rule sucks and you're a chump to enforce a rule that you know is stupid."*

Teacher: *"I understand how you feel. Maybe we can try to do something to change the rule, but for right now I don't have a choice."*

This style of interaction is in no way guaranteed to succeed each time and result in a happily compliant student. However, it is far less likely to result in a behavioral explosion than a more personalized representation of authority in which the teacher fully assumes the cloak of authority and responds to the student's late arrival with a sense of indignation.

In the enforcement of behavioral limits, it is tremendously important to be consistent, powerful and clear while at the same time avoiding unduly harsh and provocative interactions. The distinction between clear, effective and non-provocative strategies for setting limits and those which are unduly harsh and provocative can be compared to the distinction between a wrestler being taken down on a cushioned wrestling mat and a wrestler being slammed onto an unprotected cement floor. In neither of these instances does the limit (the floor) yield significantly; however, in experiencing the gentler resistance of the mat the child is far less likely to experience the limit as a hostile force eliciting a powerful defensive reflex and desire for retaliation.

In work with this population of children it is important to remember that beyond our effort to control a child's immediate behavior lies our intent to facilitate his internalization (acceptance) of the value of relationships and the associated wisdom of societal rules and expectations. Through the process of internalization, the child evolves into an autonomous individual who possesses both a clear understanding and acceptance of societal expectations, as well as a capacity to monitor and regulate his own behavior. Unfortunately, helping the Category A child accept behavioral limits and value relationships is easily undermined through the inconsistent application of limits or a pattern of unduly painful and humiliating consequences for inappropriate behavior. Although it is intuitively easy to understand how a pattern of inconsistent limit-setting can result in a child's ineffective internalization of the desired code of conduct, the negative impact of unduly harsh (provocative) limit-setting may not be as evident or easily understood.

Problems Associated with Unduly Harsh Child Management

Although a lengthy discussion of the impact of unduly harsh behavior management is beyond the scope of this text, I do consider it important to discuss this issue briefly. Unduly harsh methods of management or limit-setting often seem to result in rapid, short-term positive behavioral change that can reinforce the perceived effectiveness of such management. However, what is not easily observed is the impact of the psychological process activated within the child to manage the fear and anxiety associated with harsh, punitive treatment. This process often involves a developmental fixation in which the child's motivation for compliance with rules and expectations is associated with the avoidance of negative consequences or punishment, rather than with the development of a well-established set of values and motivation to monitor and regulate his own behavior.

Effective Limit-Setting

Effective work with the Category A child is largely contingent upon the caretaker's ability to manifest confidence in his authority, while simultaneously exercising power in a manner sensitive to the inherent challenge to the child's brittle self-esteem (narcissism). To achieve this objective, the caretaker must pay careful attention both to the manner in which he delivers a limit-setting directive and to providing support for compliance. In many respects, effective limit-setting demands of the caretaker the ability to state and enforce limits in a calm, clear, firm and supportive manner. Each of these qualities is equally important; however, managing a difficult moment with a challenging Category A child, one can easily lose sight of any or all of these requirements. In the section that follows, I present an illustration of both effective and ineffective limit-setting.

Alex

Alex, a seventh-grade student dismissed from the resource classroom several minutes prior to lunch as a reward for completing his homework, found himself unsupervised in the cafeteria, where he began to entertain himself by removing empty milk cartons from the trash and stomping on them, making a loud noise. Startled by this sound, the assistant principal, Ms. Jones, walked into the lunchroom and found Alex surrounded by smashed milk cartons and a small amount of milk distributed on the floor, walls and tables around him. At the moment when the assistant principal entered the room Alex was about to stomp on a partially full carton of milk and splatter much of the surrounding area.

The following scenario is an illustration of a positive or effective limit setting response:

Assistant Principal:	*"ALEX!" [Said in a loud voice to get his attention before he stomps on the next carton.] "Alex, you've made a mess here, and you need to go to the maintenance closet and get a mop to clean it up."*
Alex:	*"You're always waiting around to get on my case about something. Anyway, most of these cartons were smashed before I got here."*
Assistant Principal:	*"Alex, I don't want to make a big deal out of this. As kids often do, you kind of got carried away with this milk carton thing, and all I am asking you to do is clean it up."*

Alex:	"Like I said, most of this stuff was here when I came in, so I don't think cleaning it up is my job. After all that's why we have janitors."
Assistant Principal:	"Well Alex, that is your choice. But you need to understand that if you don't clean it up, there will be a consequence for the fact that you created a mess and left it for someone else to deal with."
Alex:	"So, what's your plan? Maybe you'll call the police, have me arrested or expelled? All because I stomped on a few milk cartons?"
Assistant Principal:	"No Alex. However, if you refuse to clean up your mess I will give you a detention and talk to your fourth-period teacher to make certain that she no longer lets you out of class before there is someone here to supervise you."
Alex:	"That's stupid! All because I stomped on a milk carton!"
Assistant Principal:	"Alex, I'm going to count to three, and if you start to pick this stuff up by the time I get to three, I'll help you clean up. We'll get a mop and be done with it. However, if you choose not to, I will clean it up alone, and you will owe a detention and will not be able to leave class even a minute early to come to lunch. That's how it is. One—two—three."

In this illustration the assistant principal has remained calm, avoided making provocative statements critical of the student's character, provided a clear and firm directive, communicated an appropriate consequence for non-compliance and supported the student in tolerating the directive by offering to help clean up. Critical to the assistant principal's success in managing this situation was her care to not attack Alex's core sense of self by suggesting that he is dramatically out of the norm or that there must be something wrong with him to have caused him to do what he has done. Nor has the assistant principal allowed herself to be pulled off focus by responding to Alex's provocative statements. In the management of difficult students, we must remember to govern our interventions by what supports both short-term and long-term behavioral change, not by our need to vent frustration, assert authority or express our position as protectors of the broader community. Even if the Category A student's behavior is dramatically out of line from the norm, statements forcefully pronouncing this fact (e.g., "This is not acceptable! This is ridiculous! Who do you think you are creating a mess like this and leaving it for someone else to clean up!") are not useful, since they prove provocative and do not support compliance. In effect, the assistant principal in this illustration has helped Alex maintain perspective on this situation in a way that does not prompt him to sense that his fundamental character is under attack, yet at the same time holds him responsible for his behavior.

The following dialogue illustrates a negative or ineffective limit setting interaction within the same situation:

Assistant Principal:	*"ALEX!" [Said in a loud voice to get his attention before he stomps on the next carton]. "Alex, this is ridiculous. It is clear that you cannot go two minutes without supervision and not do something destructive. Now clean up this mess."*
Alex:	*"If you want it cleaned up, why don't you do it?"*
Assistant Principal:	*"You heard me Alex. I am not asking you to clean this up, I am telling you to clean it up. If you don't, you will suffer the consequences."*
Alex:	*"Go to hell, you loser."*
Assistant Principal:	*"I will not be spoken to in that manner. I am going to count to three and if you haven't started to clean this mess up by the time I reach three, you are coming to the office with me, and I am sending you home for the rest of the day."*
Alex:	*"Oh no, not that, Ms. Jones! [Said sarcastically.] And what if I refuse to come? Maybe you'll call the police, have me arrested or expelled? All because I stomped on a few milk cartons?"*
Assistant Principal:	*"Alex, I have a responsibility to the rest of the students and staff to keep this school a safe place, and I am very serious about that responsibility. So yes, Alex, if you refuse to respect my authority, I will do whatever I need to assure the safety of the school. If that includes calling the police, so be it."*
Alex:	*"That's stupid! All because I stomped on a milk carton!"*
Assistant Principal:	*"STOMPED ON A MILK CARTON AND DISRUPTED THE LEARNING ENVIRONMENT FOR OTHERS, AS WELL AS DEFACING OUR SCHOOL BUILDING! I'm going to count to three, and when I get to three, if you have not started to clean this mess up, I will have Officer Rogers escort you to my office."*
Alex:	*"Go ahead, you BITCH! That's what you've wanted to do all year, so here's your big chance. But, you now have to figure out how to catch me, WHICH ISN'T GOING TO HAPPEN!"*

(Alex runs off down the hallway yelling "Ms. Jones is a ########".)

In this illustration, the assistant principal has failed to manage the situation effectively with respect to all four of the critical limit-setting variables (calm, clear, firm and supportive). In her initial encounter with Alex, she offers an agitated proclamation or judgment ("this is ridiculous..."), thus violating the directive to remain calm. Next, she offers a non-specific directive to "clean up the mess" and a non-specific description of the consequences for non-compliance, violating the directive to be clear. Following these provocative actions, she moves to a process of offering statements to convince Alex of her authority and her responsibility to the school community, an impotent strategy which negates the directive concerning the importance of a firm and powerful presentation. Finally, this assistant principal offers Alex virtually no support that might make the process of compliance less threatening to his brittle narcissistic self-esteem; she instead backs Alex into a corner from which there is no escape but a fight-or-flight response. In this illustration the inability to simultaneously confront and support Alex ultimately results in dramatic behavioral escalation, as is often the case in such situations.

Managing Emotional Volatility in the Limit-Setting Process

Since the Category A child's response to behavioral limits is often one of frustration and anger, an important aspect of limit-setting for this child is the caretaker's capacity to provide what has earlier been described as "emotional holding or containment." In D.W. Winnicott's model, from which the concept of emotional holding is derived, it is through the child's attachment to an empathically attuned caretaker, able to effectively contain or manage the child's disturbing affect, that children ultimately develop the capacity to tolerate and regulate their emotions independently. To understand this process, it is helpful to think of an agitated child as a bell vibrating at a high frequency. In this state, the agitated child experiences both a profound sense of vulnerability and volatility, as well as a compromised capacity for clear, logical thought. At this point he is essentially dependent upon the caretaker to provide emotional dampening. Should this emotional holding (dampening) not be available, the child will experience the impact of unchecked anxiety, generally resulting in the employment of less appropriate anxiety-management strategies such as dissociation or acting out. However, should the child experience the caretaker as both empathically attuned and competent (able to remain calm in the presence of his disturbing emotions), he will draw comfort from the caretaker and ultimately learn to rely upon relationships as an important aspect of anxiety management.

It cannot be overemphasized that "emotional holding" requires an accurate empathic attunement to the child. Thus, the adult's sense of calm in the presence of the child's agitated affect is not associated with being out of touch with the power of the child's emotions, but rather in touch with, yet able to tolerate and contain, this affect. This distinction is essential, for an agitated child's experience of a calm but emotionally disengaged or detached adult is not only unhelpful but frequently provocative. Conversely, when the caretaker's response to a child's agitation is to respond as emotionally as the child, it typically increases the child's anxiety, pushing him closer to the fight-or-flight response and undermining his capacity to think and respond adaptively.

This process of asserting one's authority in setting clear and firm limits, while simultaneously supporting the child in managing his negative reaction to limit-setting, is not an easy balance. The inability to establish this difficult balance is often associated with one of two issues: 1) the caretaker's frustration or anger (narcissistic injury) in reaction to the child's challenge to authority; and 2) the caretaker's anxiety concerning losing control of the child and the potential negative outcomes. Unfortunately, none of us is entirely immune to either of these dynamics, and their management is rarely simple or easy.

In light of the importance of providing the Category A child the balanced experience described here, programs serving this population must address this critical issue from a number of angles. The initial, and in many respects most important, of these angles relates to staff selection. In my experience, there is no single factor more closely linked to a program's success or failure than that of the teaching staff's temperament. Too often overlooked in the development of programs for the Category A child is the fact that the effectiveness of the school-based program is largely dependent upon the character of the teaching and support staff. When those not temperamentally suited to work with this population are employed to do so, disaster is often close at hand (regardless of training). Personalities which tend to be problematic in caretakers working with the Category A child include individuals who are emotionally highly reactive, rigid in their adaptive style, narcissistic, emotionally detached, or weak in organizational ability.

In recognition of both the importance of and difficulty in establishing this balanced approach to behavior management, the school must also provide adequate clinical support and supervision for those working with this difficult and volatile population of students. The supports generally found to be effective for those working with this population within the public school include:

- crisis-management training and support (i.e. Therapeutic Crisis Intervention, or T.C.I.);

- training in child psychopathology (e.g., this text, workshops, courses in child psychopathology);

- ongoing clinical supervision and support; and

- team development (consultation to promote a sense of shared responsibility and mutual support among the educational team members serving this group of children).

THE NEED FOR STIMULATION

Because of the Category A child's propensity for chronic feelings of boredom and debilitating emptiness, this group of students has distinct programming needs. For these students, the diversion from intolerable emotion (i.e. pain and emptiness) found in stimulating activity serves as a central strategy for managing their difficult inner worlds. In light of this fact, effective programming for these students must offer extensive opportunity for engaging in stimulating, socially acceptable activities — or we will confront the reality that in the absence of such opportunity these students will readily move to socially unacceptable and problematic avenues for stimulation. Unfortunately, within our current culture, a child seeking distraction from his inner emotional life needs to look no farther than his front yard to access powerful yet destructive diversions such as drugs, alcohol, promiscuous sex, violence and crime.

School-based programming for the Category A student, using empathic sensitivity to his inability to tolerate boredom, must incorporate stimulating activities as an integral part of the school day. These activities should not, as is too often the case, be a small, adjunct component to the classroom, used exclusively as a reward for appropriate behavior. (In many respects, offering highly stimulating activities to the Category A child as a reward for appropriate behavior is analogous to the use of aspirin to reward a feverish child's ability to drop their body temperature.)

The following section provides a point of departure in identifying viable options for creating necessary stimulation within a school-based program. Programming options have been organized into five categories of positive diversion or stimulation: 1) physical (kinesthetic); 2) artistic (creative); 3) competitive; 4) competency or mastery; and 5) intellectual. The reader is encouraged to think of these options as simply a list of possibilities, not as a definitive or exhaustive list of programming options. It is also important to keep in mind that no single activity will be effective in engaging all students; what might be highly stimulating for one child might hold no potential for engaging another.

Suggestions for Engagement and Stimulation

1. **Physical:** These activities will usually involve some form of physical risk-taking (potential for physical injury), entailing exposure to such variables as speed, height and impact.
   Activities: skiing, /snowboarding, skateboarding, mountain biking, rock climbing, surfing, go-carting, dirt-bike racing, rugby, marathons, triathlons, and all forms of what are referred to as extreme sports.

2. **Artistic:** These activities might be useful to a slightly smaller group of students than the physical activities listed above. However, for those students who are able to identify "creative expression" as an avenue for diversion and stimulation, this channel can be extremely rich and promising as an alternative to socially inappropriate behavior. Unfortunately, special-education programming often seems to exclude the Category A child from participation in music and art curricula because these students struggle with the structure of the traditional art and music class. In addition, the instructors of these content areas, due to less frequent contact, generally do not know the students as well as do their academic teachers. Therefore, the situation within these classes is ripe for serious behavioral problems. Exploration of creative channels for diversion and stimulation must take place on an individual basis before being ruled out as a useful programming option.
   Activities: painting, drawing, cartooning, sculpture, graffiti, poetry, short-story writing, screenplay writing, film production, song writing, musical performance (e.g., guitar and drums, singing), record

spinning/D.J.-ing (I still don't get this stuff, but folks I trust tell me it is an expressive art), dance, and customizing automobiles.

3. **Competition:** Participation in competitive activities often serves as a useful form of both stimulation and affirmation for the Category A child. However, in providing opportunities for competition, problems related to brittle self-esteem when losing frequently arise. Although the Category A student is often volatile in his reaction to failure, it is critical that our programming provide opportunities for the practice and mastery of emotions associated with the competitive experience. Often undermining these students' development of competition-based social and emotional skills is their volatility in response to frustration and failure, frequently causing them to be excluded from participation in traditional sports and recreation programs. Although it is understandable that the Category A child's volatility often results in their exclusion from these activities. By excluding them we are excluding the very children who most need the opportunity to practice the skills of emotional regulation from the opportunity to do so within the context of a structured and supervised activity. (See Addressing Skills for Affective Regulation.)
   Activities: board games, touch football, basketball, track events, volleyball, hockey, tetherball, four square, golf, skiing, card games, pool, bowling and debate.

4. **Competency and mastery:** This category of activity entails considerable overlap with other categories but seems to have enough of its own character to merit separate mention. It is comprised of activities in which the core motive for participating seems to be the pursuit of affirming competency.
   Activities: auto mechanics, yo-yo tricks, tagging (street calligraphy), skateboarding, magic tricks, card tricks and juggling.

5. **Intellectual:** This category of activity can be one of the most effective, yet most difficult, avenues through which to engage the Category A child. Resistance to this channel of activity is often linked to a negative association with academics that results in conscious resistance to activities having a typical "intellectual" or "academic" character. However, when it avoids triggering established patterns of "academic resistance," intellectual stimulation can be a highly effective avenue for socially appropriate diversion.
   Activities: solving puzzles, creative problem-solving linked to

logistical challenges (e.g., how do we move this large desk from one room to the next through a small door?), abstract social challenges (e.g., how do we help a new student feel welcome?), and last, but certainly not least, academic work.

ADDRESSING SKILLS FOR AFFECTIVE REGULATION

Gaining mastery over one's emotions is generally linked to the experience of growing up with an attuned and competent caretaker who is able to provide effective support in understanding and containing powerful emotion. However, other useful avenues for the development of this ability do exist. For the Category A child who has not had the benefit of adequate experiences of emotional containment, an alternative by which to achieve a degree of mastery over powerful underlying emotion is the structured practice of emotional regulation. One of the most readily available opportunities for practice of emotional regulation (particularly of aggression) is participation in sporting activities. However, due to the Category A child's struggle with subordination to the coach or team, difficulty maintaining athletic eligibility due to failing grades, and propensity for poorly modulated emotional reactions during competition (e.g., punching an opposing team member in the face when tackled), this group of students is often unable to participate in structured athletics.

The Category A child's need for structured practice of emotional regulation is a fact of which these children are frequently intuitively aware. An often ironic and interesting manifestation of this is that many Category A adolescents report vocational interest in the armed forces, particularly the Marines (known for both their fighting intensity and discipline) or law enforcement. I believe that the draw of these vocations for this group of young people is largely associated with their desire for power, preference for an explicit network of rules, need for stimulation and extensive opportunity for the practice of emotional regulation. These vocations provide much the same opportunity to utilize external structure in learning to engage and manage powerful emotion as participation in athletics.

In the absence of the opportunity to participate in traditional organized sports, the Category A adolescent may gravitate towards less-socialized activities: gang wars, fighting and crime. In light of the obvious problems associated with these alternatives, it is incumbent upon those who work with this population to create and support socially acceptable alternative avenues for practicing and mastering the regulation of aggressive affect. This responsibility is not easily fulfilled, since the Category A child's weak skills in managing aggressive feelings will initially entail significant behavioral problems within the context of competition (e.g., regularly attempting to "punch out" opponents). Nonetheless, if we embrace the responsibility to support these children in learning to manage their aggressive affect, we must provide them opportunity to practice these skills. Programming for the Category A child should include structured and supervised opportunities for aggressive competition, while recognizing that (as with all learning) "failure will precede mastery." These experiences must be structured in a manner that responds to the Category A child's weak affective regulation skills and propensity for inappropriate acts of aggression within these activities. The result should neither exclude the child from the activity nor manage expected and necessary failures by punishing and shaming him.

Activities designed to provide a learning experience for anger control or affective regulation must be carefully monitored but not over-controlled by the supervising adult; in managing these activities the principles of optimal frustration must apply. In other words, it is necessary for the learning experience to push the child beyond his comfort and place him in the position of being challenged with respect to behavioral control. This optimal learning opportunity requires careful attunement, as well as a relative degree of tolerance for aggressive affect, by the supervising adult. Ultimately, the effectiveness of this form of intervention is important not only in providing opportunity for the practice of affective regulation, but also as an experience of the supervising adult as a source of "emotional holding," able to experience the child's powerful aggressive affect and still manage these emotions.

In providing programs that allow practice of emotional regulation or anger control, it is clear that tight supervision must assure adequate safety of both the staff and students. It is imperative that careful attention be paid to monitoring staff reactions to the student's inappropriate behavior, in that inappropriate expression of aggression can easily trigger a strong affective reaction within the supervising adult. For example, the student, in anger, may lash out verbally or physically at the supervisor or victimize another, less powerful student. This dynamic can easily elicit a highly punitive response driven by the moral indignation of the supervising adult. While the need to oversee and support the staff monitoring these activities requires some explanation, the need for careful supervision of the volatile Category A student does not. Clearly, in structuring learning experiences, which involve the placement of highly volatile children and adolescents into situations designed to trigger anger, little needs to be said about the need for careful supervision. Vigilant monitoring of competitive activities, with careful attunement to the participants' affective state, is essential, as is readiness on the part of the caretaker to intervene in whatever manner necessary—from offering a suggestion for a time out, to physically restraining an enraged and assaultive child.

Participation in competitive sports, with adequate supervision and realistic expectations, can serve as an excellent opportunity for the emotionally volatile child to practice and gain mastery in affective regulation. In the use of competitive athletics for this purpose, it is often helpful to build support into the game for both the child's self-monitoring of his emotional state, as well as a non-punitive strategy to allow for the soothing or "cooling down" of an agitated participant. What follows are ideas for the modification of two sports activities to allow them to better meet the needs of this group of children. Although only two options are presented, it is important to realize that, with a bit of creativity, any number of activities might be modified to provide the same opportunity.

1. Modified Wrestling (offered jointly by the Physical Education and Special Education Departments)

This activity provides the typical introduction and instruction for the sport of wrestling, as well as participation in a modified tournament. Modifications that would be useful for the Category A student entail both a structure that supports the wrestlers in assessing their own level of affective agitation, as well as the availability of support in calming or soothing themselves when overly agitated. These modifications might include the use of a large poster illustrating a thermometer with gradients marked by colors depicting varying states of agitation (i.e. blue = calm, pink = "OK," green = beginning to get upset, and red = about to explode). This chart could be used as a tool to help students monitor and report their current emotional state at both predetermined and referee-designated points throughout the wrestling match. The modification from standard wrestling rules might involve the referee blowing his whistle every twenty seconds, at which point the competition would pause for each wrestler to report on his emotional state by quickly indicating the point on the thermometer that reflected his current level of agitation. If both wrestlers report an acceptable level, the match would proceed; if either or both of the wrestlers express extreme agitation or limited emotional control, the match would "hold" until both reported a readiness to proceed. During this holding period, each wrestler would employ some form of soothing activity which he had previously identified as useful (e.g., counting to ten or envisioning himself on a quiet beach).

In further modifying this activity, it might be useful to create a code word such as "red," which a student could yell out, should he find himself overly agitated. The match would then be paused, giving the participants the opportunity to calm down. To encourage and support the use of these strategies, it would be helpful to tie the scoring for each match to typical wrestling points, as well as to the effectiveness of the wrestler's anger management and use of the modified program. It might be useful to award points for a student's ability to pause the match when necessary, as well as points for the opponent's ability to quickly give the agitated wrestler the necessary space to calm down. To further encourage the student's participation, it would be useful to connect the points within the match to some form of token economy or reward.

2. Modified Touch Football

This activity would consist of a typical game of touch football with several modifications to promote better regulation of affect or anger. These modifications may be as simple as requiring a brief handshake, or some other civil interaction between the opponents, prior to the beginning of each play. Use of a penalty box model (like hockey), which would result in a team playing with one less player if a player were placed in the box for a rule infraction, could also be incorporated. However, distinct from hockey, the referee would have the responsibility to monitor the affective state of the players, not just their behavior; should a player become overly agitated, he would be placed in the "calming box" until he regained composure. This would be done without a punitive connotation. When a player is placed in the box the game will be held for thirty seconds to give him a chance to calm. Should he succeed in regaining composure in this time, his team would not be forced to play with one less player. If unsuccessful, however, his team would play without him until he demonstrated a calmer state of mind.

Clearly, the actual programming of activities such as those offered above will require considerable fine-tuning, and at first is not likely to work smoothly. However, this form of programming, if done with creativity and patience, is both possible and necessary.

PEER-GROUP AFFILIATION

In our effort to understand and meet the needs of the Category A student, it is useful to observe this group within the context of their natural environment and to note those situations and dynamics to which they seem drawn. Interestingly, if not paradoxically in light of this group's limited relational skills, within their natural environment they frequently develop highly committed delinquent peer-group affiliations such as gang membership. This phenomenon seems to have roots in two central psychological factors. The first of these factors is the Category A child's strong affinity for power, which is often readily accessible through gang membership. By joining forces, each member acquires increased power and authority within the community.

A second dynamic which seems to draw otherwise relationally detached Category A children into gang affiliation is that, unlike one-on-one relationships, gang membership offers a defined, or organized, identity. The Category A child's sense of self is generally fragmented and poorly organized, resulting in a deep sense of identity confusion and emptiness. In a gang, the disturbing existential experience of being lost, with its central questions such as, "Who am I?", is answered through the gang's concrete response: "You're a Jet, and when you're a Jet, you're a Jet all the way, from your first cigarette to your last dying day." (Tony, *West Side Story*)

With an understanding of the lure and function of the delinquent peer group, it is clear that if our response to gang involvement is to be effective it must be far more coherent than simply employing punitive consequences for gang participation. As we recognize the very real needs met through gang involvement, we confront the responsibility to shift our focus toward supporting the Category A child in developing alternative, socially acceptable means by which to meet these needs. Although this task is far from simple, if we can demonstrate the existence and availability of an effective, alternative avenue for accessing power and establishing an organized sense of self, it will often be taken.

Greatly complicating the task of identifying and developing positive and socially appropriate means for the acquisition of power is the fact that these young people often lack the requisite resources (i.e. skills, knowledge, experience, temperament) to gain power through more-traditional positive means. In other words, socially acceptable avenues for recognition and power as a function of accomplishment, special ability or social skill are often unavailable to the Category A student. However, as complex as this dilemma may be, a socially acceptable avenue for providing the Category A child much of what he derives from gang membership can be found in our culture's strong capitalistic/materialist roots and work ethic. Thus, in line with our culture's endorsement of the notion, "Money is power and power is money," an opportunity for socially acceptable access to power for the Category A student may lie in gainful employment.

Often undermining the Category A child's ability to gain power through legitimate financial accomplishment (employment) is a socioeconomic family background of poverty, which subverts any image of oneself as a likely candidate for empowering employment. In fact, most children raised in poverty foresee lives locked into financial disempowerment. Our schools must either address this issue or accept that many of these students will surrender to economic hopelessness or turn to crime as a means of income. One underutilized avenue for addressing this dynamic is for schools to develop positive employment experiences in which these students are both valued and well paid for their work effort.

The second factor that seems to draw the Category A child into gang involvement is the gang's ability to provide a clearly defined sense of identity. With creativity and effort this need, too, may be effectively addressed by gainful employment. Although many have discussed the relationship between employment and identity (e.g., Robert Kegan's early work *The Evolving Self*, a study of male identity development and its powerful link to employment or profession), it is my sense that this issue is often under-addressed in our work with the Category A student. If we accept that within our culture a significant degree of identity is derived through identification with an established or foreseen vocation, it is reasonable to assume that those who have no sense of vocational direction would be prone to adopt an alternative, possibly problematic or unsocialized identity. However, it is also reasonable to assume that if a vocational opportunity is readily available and affords the Category A student both a sense of power and an organizing sense of self, he would be likely to embrace it.

In developing an employment opportunity to provide the benefits described above, the Category A child's cynicism and need for immediate gratification are significant impediments. The typical model of lengthy vocational training prior to employment, which demands a delay in gratification, must be substituted with vocational options both immediately financially rewarding and easily accessible.

An interesting, recent development within the culture of the inner city, particularly East Los Angeles, has been the arrival of an alternative to gang involvement in the form of group participation in business-like entities referred to as "party crews." These groups function essentially as for-profit service agencies, organizing and publicizing all night parties, or "raves." The crew is an organized group of young people from the same background as gang members who work together to promote and manage parties for which they charge admission and share in the profits. Clearly, these groups are a far cry from Junior Achievement and create significant difficulties for their communities, due to the inherent problems associated with raves (i.e. drug use, limited supervision). However, in the pursuit of profit as a means of acquiring power these "crews" are less prone to raw violence and intimidation than the traditional gangs they replace.

There are many options for developing opportunities to engage the Category A student in therapeutically beneficial employment. However, in considering these options it is important to realize that the pay-off for the student's participation in the activity must be significant and relatively immediate. Unfortunately, the typical path for entry-level employment involves a process of starting at the bottom, earning very little, and often waiting several weeks for the first paycheck, none of which is easily tolerated by the Category A child. Therefore, in work with these students we are faced with the responsibility of creating a contrived employment situation which alleviates these obstacles. This effort requires creativity and initiative on the part of the school but is not impossible. One possible avenue for such employment opportunities entails creating school-based businesses based on such activities as lawn care, snow removal, window cleaning, automobile reconditioning, house painting, temporary services, moving services and mail handling (envelope stuffing).

School-Based Business

Once a viable business venture is identified, the next task is the development of an employment agreement which explicitly describes the (significant and immediate) benefits of employment, the structure of the business (e.g., a shareholder model) and exact expectations for employees, with specific details as to the consequences for non-compliance with employment rules. The following section will present an example of a school-based therapeutic business or employment opportunity for the Category A student.

Evergreen High School Lawn-Care Services

Employment Agreement: All employees, hereafter referred to as associates, of the Evergreen High School Lawn-Care Service will enter employment through the establishment of an individually tailored "associate agreement." This agreement will detail all work-related rules, as well as the associate's number of hours for employment and schedule (including work-release time from school), job description, rate of pay and schedule for payment.

Employment Options: Work release: One half day to five half days weekly (with conditions of academic eligibility determined on an individual basis).

Employment Structure: The business offers employees two levels of participation: Associate and Vested Associate. All employees enter employment as an Associate and at the end of thirty days of satisfactory performance become Vested Associates. Vested Associates are eligible for monthly profit-sharing bonuses. When a Vested Associate leaves the business with two weeks' notice, he receives a prorated profit-sharing bonus for the month of termination and may return to employment at the Vested level if openings exist; if, however, he leaves without two weeks notice, profit sharing for that month is forfeited and his return to employment would be at the Associate level.

Positions: Direct lawn care, sales, equipment maintenance, job supervisor (Vested Associate only), administrator (Vested Associate from the junior or senior class.)

Payment: Rate of pay will be based upon a base rate (equal for all employees), plus or minus a percentage of that rate linked to the payment option chosen and bonuses and penalties incurred:

Payment options: Daily Payment = base rate

Weekly Payment = base rate + 10%

Bi-weekly Payment = base rate + 15%

Bonus options: 1% bonus (per pay period) for each week of satisfactory work history, up to 20 weeks; 5% bonus (per pay period) for each week beyond the second week in which the Associate shows up for work on time, does not have an absence and is evaluated as having worked in a satisfactory manner during that week.

Expectations: Associates will arrive at work on time and when scheduled. The business offers no distinction between approved and unapproved absences; any employee sent home by the job supervisor due to behavioral difficulties will forfeit his pay for that day. Any employee suspected of drug or alcohol use on the job will be sent home without pay for that day. Relatively minor infractions of work rules or expectations will result in a formal warning. If an employee receives two warnings in one week, he forfeits all bonus payment for that week. Serious infractions will result in a period of probation (work without bonus), suspension and/or loss of all employment seniority benefits (vested status, etc.) The replacement cost of any intentional destruction of property caused by an associate will be deducted from his paycheck.

Group Benefits: All students who have participated in the program during the previous two weeks will have supervised school release time for a group activity such as skiing, lunch out or a movie, paid for by the business.

The development and running of a business such as the one described involves considerable commitment and cost to the supervising school, as well as community support. However, in maintaining perspective on the cost of such a program we must consider the long-term expense associated with a young person who perceives the employment world as holding no promise. Through programs such as this we may direct 50 percent of the participating students towards a belief that employment holds real promise. If so, the long-term savings to society will be extraordinary. In the absence of such a belief, these young people will cost society dearly, as they will require institutional care (juvenile and adult corrections, psychiatric care) or turn to crime and welfare as a way of life.

SUMMARY

In summary, more than any other group of students, Category A children challenge and stress our public schools, which often therefore demonstrate marked ambivalence toward responsibility to serve this challenging population. However, as we increasingly encounter a society burdened by criminal behavior from undersocialized children who grow into undersocialized adults, it is clear we can no longer afford a marginal commitment to these children. We can no longer afford our public schools' ambivalence concerning this responsibility. It is imperative that our schools retool their efforts at cooperation with mental-health providers and obtain the resources required to address the needs of these children and move beyond our current pattern of passing the responsibility from one institution to the next. Public schools, more than any other institution, have early and prolonged contact with virtually all children, and play a central role in identifying and treating the growing number of troubled and troubling children who fit within the Category A group.

VII

Category B — Origins of Problem Behavior

As we turn our attention to those children who fall within Category B, it is again important to note that not all children will fit neatly within a single category and exhibit only those behaviors, vulnerabilities and needs defined by that category. However, it is my belief that this system of categorization can be a useful first step in understanding children who present with significant behavioral impairments.

The character of the Category B child's behavioral difficulties is distinct from that of the Category A child in that the intensity of the behavior associated with the Category A child is exchanged for the Category B child's broader range of difficulty. This distinction is a function of the fact that the neurocognitive weaknesses (i.e. L.D., A.D.H.D., mild Mental Retardation) of the Category B child cause these children to be generally less competent than the Category A child. Therefore, it is far more common for the Category B child to misperceive environmental cues and to exhibit inappropriate behavior as a result of these misperceptions. Unfortunately, this pattern of inaccurate perception and adaptational failure results in a debilitating impact upon the child's fundamental sense of competency and security, and promotes within the Category B child significant anxiety and feelings of hopelessness and discouragement. Comparatively, the many misperceptions of the Category

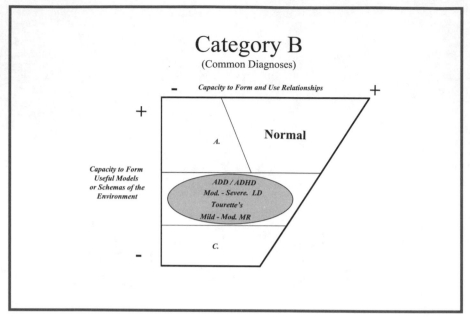

B child result in more-frequent behavior problems, where the Category A child's profile results in more strategic, directed or intense behavioral issues. Those working or living with a difficult Category B child are most likely to be stressed by the relentless task of managing inappropriate behavior, whereas life with the Category A child is marked more by the profound power of the child's affect and relative disregard for the well-being of others.

It is important to note that most of the problem behaviors exhibited by Category B children are a simple function of their misperceptions of environmental demands. Too often, however, due to the caretaker's poor understanding of the Category B child's organizational weaknesses, problem behavior is interpreted as oppositional and manipulative, instead of being more accurately attributed to confusion and fear. (At this point the reader is encouraged to review the earlier presentation on the capacity to organize in Chapter II.)

In an effort to organize the dynamics associated with the more pervasive problematic behavior of Category B children, I will present three triggering dynamics. Two of the three involve revisiting the concept of optimal frustration as it relates to acting-out behavior, and the third will focus on neurobiological issues, which are relatively common in the Category B child.

OPTIMAL FRUSTRATION AND PROBLEM BEHAVIOR IN THE CATEGORY B CHILD

To explain and predict why and when the Category B child is most likely to exhibit severely problematic behavior it is helpful to return to Kohut's (1978) concept of optimal frustration in combination with the concept of acting out. As we use the optimal-frustration paradigm to predict and understand the Category B child's tendency to act out, it is helpful to briefly restate our understanding of this concept. In short, acting out is inappropriate behavior unconsciously employed to avoid awareness (consciousness) of potentially debilitating underlying (unconscious) beliefs or emotions which have been propelled towards consciousness by some event or experience (for more detail see the discussion of acting out in Chapter V).

For the Category B child, whose fundamental competency is limited, acting out is most often associated with experiences that trigger awareness of these limitations. It is in this context that the optimal-frustration paradigm is helpful in understanding and predicting acting out behavior in the Category B child, since for this group of children experiences that are either over- or underfrustrating often elicit acting out.

Understandably, when the Category B child is confronted by situations which are clearly beyond his capacity to manage, the associated experience of failure often elicits intolerable underlying feelings of incompetence, thus activating acting out. However, conversely, low expectations or demands (underfrustration), which communicate a lack of faith or belief in the child's competency, may elicit the same underlying vulnerabilities and serve as an equally powerful precipitant to acting out.

The Category B child's strong tendency to act out in response to both over- and underfrustration demands that our management of problematic behavior initially focus on carefully assessing the child's ability to manage the situation in which the acting out is occurring. In light this obligation, we must be careful to avoid moving too quickly to the use of punishment or positive consequences as a remedy to acting out. By focusing first on providing optimal frustration to address acting out, we are not only correcting the child's behavior but, more importantly, providing experiences which have the potential to increase his underlying sense of competency. This is not to suggest that punishment and rewards should never be used in our attempt to manage the behavior of the Category B child. Rather they should be used only after carefully assessing whether or not the environment within which the acting out occurs provides adequate experiences of optimal frustration.

NEUROBIOLOGICAL TRIGGERS TO AGGRESSIVE BEHAVIOR

A second factor sometimes associated with triggering aggressive behavior in the Category B child is the link between neurobiological events, such as seizures, and behavior. It is well established that children with neurobiologically based disorders such as learning disabilities, Tourette's Syndrome or ADHD are somewhat more prone to other forms of neuropathology (i.e. mood disorders, anxiety disorders or seizure disorders) than children without these disabilities. Thus, it is not infrequent for a Category B child to be identified with an additional neurobiologically based disorder at some point in his life. Two of the more common neurobiologically based disorders associated with aggressive behavior are cyclic or bipolar mood disorders and subtle seizure activity.

It is increasingly common for children who exhibit patterns of aggressive behavior to be diagnosed and treated for a cyclic affective disorder. A cyclic mood or affective disorder, often referred to as bipolar illness, can be defined as a chronic neurobiologically based illness which results in significant swings in affect, from highly energized mania or hypomania (less than full mania) to depression or dysthymia (mild depression). The affect associated with the upward swing (toward mania) often entails profound feelings of well-being, creativity, energy, inflated self-esteem and hopefulness, potentially escalating to a point of profound breakdown in adaptive functioning associated with delusions of grandeur and invulnerability. In contrast, the downward swing in the affective cycle includes profound feelings of worthlessness, hopelessness, isolation and vulnerability, potentially deteriorating to severe depression, involving suicidal ideation, paranoid delusions and a broad adaptive failure.

Although all cyclic mood disorders involve significant variation in mood, there is a variety of manifestations of this illness with respect to both the length of cycles and the height and depth of the associated affect. Individuals with cyclic mood disorders may show a range of symptoms, from gross impairment in adaptive functioning to normal functioning accompanied by a subjective affective instability. More-severe behaviors, such as aggressive outbursts, can be associated with either end of the cyclic swing. These more problematic behaviors are generally linked to a manic or hypomanic sense (or delusion) of entitlement and invulnerability, or to profound irritability, mistrust (to the point of paranoia) and desperation associated with the depressive pole of the cyclic swing.

Once diagnosed correctly, most individuals with cyclic mood disorders respond relatively well to medication such as Lithium and Depakote. However, early diagnosis is not common with this disorder, and individuals with this illness have often lived for years with the ravages of an ever-changing and erratic internal affective state and the associated pattern of maladaptive behavior. As a result, many individuals with cyclic mood disorders have been traumatized by this experience, which creates a problematic psychological profile secondary to their biologically based illness. Therefore, effective intervention with individuals suffering from cyclic mood disorders, particularly if they were diagnosed at a later age, generally requires both medication and psychologically based intervention.

A second biologically based factor associated with aggressive behavior is a subtle form of seizures, sometimes referred to as partial complex seizures. Unfortunately, unlike more-typical seizure disorders, which are diagnosed through use of EEG studies, the diagnostic process to identify these subtle seizures is relatively subjective, involving no definitive laboratory marker or diagnostic procedure from which to draw a clear conclusion. Therefore, the diagnostic process is often one of ruling out other possible explanations for the patient's symptoms, followed by a trial period on anticonvulsant medication (e.g., Depakote or Tegretol) and careful observation of the patient's behavior in response to these medications.

VIII

Programming for the Category B Student

Central to understanding the needs of the Category B child is recognition of his compromised (below-average) ability to form useful and accurate perceptions or schemas of his environment. This child functions with a mild to moderate limitation in his capacity to separate essential from non-essential environmental detail and to link these details into a pattern that explains the dynamics of cause and effect. This limitation can lead to considerable adaptive failure as the child is unable to make well-informed decisions by using an accurate cognitive model of his environment. Unfortunately, in addition to the Category B child's neuropsychologically based perceptual and organizational disability, his many experiences of adaptive failure promote a secondary disability of anxiety and poor self-esteem. This secondary, psychologically based disability is cyclical or self-reinforcing, as heightened anxiety undermines the child's cognitive abilities and further weakens his perceptual skills, in turn increasing adaptive failure, which in turn increases the child's underlying anxiety. In light of this devastating cycle in which failure promotes anxiety which promotes greater failure, our primary intervention for the Category B child is to provide experiences of environmental mastery and competence. These serve to mitigate the debilitating impact of pervasive anxiety and hopelessness, which is fueled by the child's sense of fundamental incompetence.

The following section addresses the needs of the Category B child with respect to his weak organizational abilities, as well as the management of associated anxiety.

STRUCTURE AND ENVIRONMENTAL MASTERY

The initial task in helping the Category B child develop an essential sense of competency centers on creating an explicit and consistently structured learning environment. The Category B child requires repeated interaction with stable environmental variables so that, despite his weak capacity to organize and perceive the environment accurately, he is able to develop an accurate and useful schema or model of this environment. Having established this accurate perception of the environment, the child is then able to employ this schema in a manner which promotes both adaptive functioning and a sense of competency, which in turn reduce the debilitating anxiety associated with the anticipation of adaptive failure.

Although we understand that a neurocognitive weakness in the capacity to organize is the primary or core disability for the Category B child, intervention with this population is focused largely on the management of anxiety, a secondary disability. This interventional focus on the secondary disability, as opposed to the primary, is linked to two central factors: 1) aside from neuro-maturation, very little can be expected to significantly change a child's neurocognitive profile, and 2) poorly managed anxiety, associated with a history of extensive adaptive failure and limited faith in his competency, greatly reduces the child's ability to persevere in practicing new skills, reduces cognitive efficiency and serves to trigger a number of psychological defenses linked to problematic behavior (e.g., acting out).

As stated above, if we understand the Category B child as having a core weakness in organizational ability, which results in extensive adaptive failure, we can create an effective school-based intervention for this population of children by developing a learning environment which affords a sense of adaptive competency. The optimal experience for the Category B child includes supervision by a caretaker who understands the child's abilities and limitations, who can effectively read his emotional state, and who provides an environment which is explicitly structured, consistent and predictable.

For most adults, the development of a highly structured learning environment is not an easy or intuitive task. The challenge in the creation of such an environment is linked both to our incomplete empathic understanding of the child's limitations and to the range and nature of our own organizational strengths relative to the child's weaknesses. The typical teacher, with his well-developed and deeply integrated organizational skills, unconsciously reads a wide range of explicit and implicit environmental cues, and often perceives that the learning environment is far more explicitly structured than is experienced by the organizationally limited child. Because of the inherent difficulty in recognizing, understanding and responding to the many elements of structure for which the Category B child is likely to need support, the following section will identify and discuss three primary dimensions as they relate to the school programming: time, space and interpersonal boundaries.

Time

The usefulness of time as a structure or boundary to help the Category B child gain a sense of mastery and security cannot be overstated. When we are able to help a Category B child perceive and use a temporal map (schedule) within his daily life the benefits are numerous. This task involves supporting the child in both understanding the "temporal map," as well as instructing him how to gain his bearings within that map (a watch or a checklist of events). The use of time as a supportive structure can be achieved in many ways, often entailing starting each day with a careful look at the calendar and schedule. This is best approached by initially orienting the child to his current place in time, through discussion of what happened yesterday or earlier that morning, and then moving on to the presentation of the schedule for today, and ending with a brief discussion of plans for tomorrow. The presentation of the day's events or schedule should be reviewed carefully, with as much detail as possible, paying particular attention to transition periods between activities and aspects of the schedule that fall outside of the ordinary. The schedule should be posted for all to see, as well as copied for the student to keep with him during the day.

Helpful strategies to help the student learn to rely upon his schedule include:

- When questioned by the child as to what is expected of him in a particular moment, gently refer him back to his daily schedule.

- When unexpected changes in the schedule occur, take the time to rewrite the balance of the day's schedule.

- Throughout the day make numerous references to the schedule, and establish a routine of providing regular notices orienting students to the schedule and preparing them for transition (e.g., "It's 10:30; we are halfway through our reading period." "We have five minutes until clean-up time." "We have one minute until the bell rings.").

- Once an activity has been completed, there should be a moment taken to cross this activity off and refer back to the schedule to determine what lies ahead.

- Whenever possible, scheduled activities should remain within the timeframes prescribed by the schedule. There is no better way to "undo" many children with organizational weaknesses than to create a schedule and then disregard it. A particularly effective means to transform an enjoyable activity into a miserable experience is to extend a designated time for an activity because it is "going well." Start and stop activities in accordance with the schedule.

Although these suggestions are somewhat counterintuitive in work with older students (in middle or high school), it is important to note that they are equally important and effective with this population.

Space

Structuring the Category B child's experience of the space within which he functions is an additional way to provide support. Structuring of the spatial dimension entails explicitly defining particular areas of the environment as associated with specific expectations and tasks. This structure provides two aspects of support to the child. First, it breaks the environment into smaller, clearly defined regions, each with an explicit set of rules. This releases the child from the often overwhelming responsibility to read and respond to complex or ambiguous environmental cues concerning behavioral expectations. Second, the clear defining of a set area of the environment for the performance of a specific task allows the child to develop an unconscious association between this location and the ability to perform this task.

Although structuring the child's space within the school setting can be approached from a number of different perspectives, what follows are several key considerations for this task:

- Boundary points between specific areas should be explicitly marked or designated, and might take the form of either physical or symbolic markers. Examples of physical boundaries include the use of room dividers placed between work areas or tapelines on the floor surrounding each student's desk designating personal space. Examples of symbolic boundaries include the teacher's announcement to the class, as they enter a neighboring classroom, "Remember, we are now guests," or when the class has an indoor recess, "When the bell rings, we will be back in class session and all rules of the classroom apply."

- Rules or expectations for each area should be made as explicit as possible and reviewed on a regular basis. Place these rules in writing and post them in the appropriate area. It is also helpful to use a formal assessment strategy to determine each child's awareness or understanding of the rules. Approach mastery of the rules as an academic assignment and assess mastery as you would any other content area.

- When possible, specifically designate areas for an exclusive, assigned purpose, and remove a child from an area if he is not appropriately engaged in that purpose. (If, after a reasonable effort to redirect an off-task student back on task, he is still unable to attend to the assigned work, excuse him from his work area to a time-out or neutral space until he is ready or able to return to the work area and function in accordance with this area's expectations.) This is done not as a form of punishment, but rather to preserve the power of the association between the specific area and the task with which it is associated. If a child spends as much time in his work area visiting with others as he does working, the power of that area to elicit working behaviors will be diminished.

Interpersonal Boundaries

Of the structural dimensions critical for supporting the Category B child, none is more important, nor more difficult to define and provide, than interpersonal structure or boundaries. Within this dimension lies a broad range of rules or variables which play out between the teacher and the student, as well as between student and student. These rules pertain to interpersonal issues of privacy, personal distance, respect, etc. Greatly complicating the child's management of this domain and our ability to provide a clear and consistent structure of rules and expectations within the interpersonal realm is the fact that rules differ significantly from person to person and depend upon a wide range of variables. The variables dictating the rules for interpersonal engagement include:

- well-defined, stable factors, such as each individual's role or position (teacher, student, parent, etc.);

- clearly defined but unstable factors, such as the setting of the interaction (the classroom, the playground or a store in the community);

- unclear, yet relatively stable factors, such as each individual's personality or temperament (shy, outgoing, cautious, serious, light-hearted);

- and relatively inconsistent and difficult-to-discern factors such as an individual's current affective state or mood (excited, frightened, frustrated, sad, happy).

When the wide range and unstable set of variables that dictate interpersonal expectations and boundaries are taken into account, it is no wonder that the child with weak organizational skills frequently misreads and violates the interpersonal boundaries or rules of others. With this in mind, as well as recognition of the impossibility of creating an absolutely clear or stable set of interpersonal dynamics and associated rules, it is the teacher's responsibility to provide as much support as possible to this child in his effort to make sense of the interpersonal world. The following suggestions are offered for the development of structure and clarity within the interpersonal realm:

- Be as explicit as possible. Define behavioral expectations as they apply to interactions between persons within distinct roles. For example, students are to refer to teachers as Mr., Miss, Ms. or Mrs., while students are referred to by their first names or by a nickname that they commonly use.

- Requests made by a teacher to a student are to be followed without significant challenge; however, once having complied with the teacher's directive the student may ask for an explanation of the rationale for the directive and (appropriately) challenge its wisdom.

- Both students and teachers are to greet one another appropriately as they enter the classroom in the morning and when passing each other in another part of the building.

- Effort should be made to allow the teacher and students to inform each other about their likes and dislikes with respect to interpersonal interactions. This may be approached by allowing each class member (including the teacher) to create a statement of "personal rules" to be posted on the side of their desk and up-dated and reviewed periodically with the class. This process might include some degree of group discussion and input regarding each class member's personal rules. It might be that others in the class have discovered a rule concerning a student, that the student has yet to realize consciously about himself and which might be helpful for both the student and others to know (e.g., When I am upset I do not like to have anyone touch me. In new situations I like to hold back and move in slowly. When feeling nervous or anxious, I like to use humor to make things feel less intense. I get really upset if I think someone is being treated unkindly.). Once each member in the class (including the teacher) has established a brief list of four or five statements, there is opportunity to discuss whether a particular rule is something the student likes or wants to change.

The issue of mood as it impacts the rules of interpersonal relating is important and complex because fluctuations in mood affect our attitude and behavior toward others. Category B children, although often quite intuitive once focused, frequently do not effectively read social cues regarding the affective state of those with whom they are interacting and therefore tend to misread the social demands related to another's mood. This demands that those working with these students either are considerably stable in mood or have the capacity to offer students clear warnings concerning a shift in mood. They should also draw up interpersonal rules for relating linked to each affective state. This might be approached by starting the day with opportunity for any class member who is in an unusual state of mind to describe his mood briefly. ("My dog ran away last night so I am kind of tired and worried today." "I couldn't get to sleep last night so I'm feeling sleepy this morning." "I'm going for a visit with my mom tonight so I am feeling excited.") This process is not intended to absolve class members from the responsibility to behave appropriately, but rather to allow others insight that might help them support one another.

CHALLENGES TO THE IMPLEMENTATION OF STRUCTURE

Complicating the processes of determining the adequacy of the structure within the Category B child's routine (at home or school) is the fact that his initial encounter with a highly structured environment is likely to entail considerable adaptive failure. Until he begins to recognize the new environment's patterns or structure, the child will inadvertently violate most expectations and boundaries. Only slowly does the child work his way through the learning curve. Ironically, due to this fact the Category B child's initial response to a poorly structured environment may, in many respects, be superior to his response to a highly structured setting. However, over time the highly structured and consistent environment (if administered with empathy and compassion) has great potential to increase the child's underlying sense of competency, but the poorly structured environment provides the child, at best, a sense of "getting by" and, at worst, yet another experience of being lost. It requires considerable time to determine the appropriateness of a particular environment for a child, and a determination cannot be made quickly in response to the child's initial inability to recognize and function within behavioral boundaries.

Although the development of a well-structured environment is a critical first step towards the meeting of the Category B child's needs, the manner in which this structure is administered will be as important as the structure itself. It is critical that the child receive empathic and compassionate support as he learns (often slowly) to recognize and use the structure of the environment. This well-attuned support is imperative to help the child through the often prolonged and frustrating learning process, which involves considerable failure prior to mastery. In light of this fact, one of the greatest responsibilities facing those working with these children is the effective management of their own (and the child's) feelings of frustration and hopelessness during the child's slow process of gaining mastery within the structured environment.

Empathic and Compassionate Behavioral Support

In order to assist in providing empathic and compassionate behavioral support, the following concepts or tools are offered and discussed:

1) padded boundaries;

2) therapeutic forgiveness;

3) realistic goals/recognition of goal approximation; and

4) effective use of supervision and consultation.

Padded Boundaries

As stated earlier in the discussion of Category A children, the effectiveness of behavioral limits depends on the caretaker's ability to be consistent, powerful and clear, while at the same time avoiding unduly harsh and provocative management strategies. Although both Category A and B children will respond poorly to unduly harsh limit-setting, the underlying emotions which are provoked by harsh management are somewhat different for these two groups. In the case of the Category A child, unduly harsh limit-setting will elicit strong emotions of anger, resentment, and possibly rage. However, for the Category B child, the response to the same management style will more frequently be intensification of underlying feelings of hopelessness.

The fundamental distinction between harsh limit-setting and supportive limit-setting lies largely in the attitude and manner in which the child is addressed. Again, the difference for a wrestler being "taken down" on a padded mat or being slammed into a concrete floor illustrates this concept. To support the assessment of the quality of our limit-setting skills, one can use the mnemonic acronym RESPECT, which suggests seven aspects of effective limit-setting. (Clearly, it is not possible or even necessary that all limit-setting encounters comply with all seven criteria; however, the basic concept and spirit of RESPECT for the child should inform all interactions. It is also likely that as the caretaker grows in his knowledge of a child, he will discover that each student is particularly supported by and sensitive to one or two specific components of the RESPECT model.)

R.E.S.P.E.C.T.

Relaxed: Address the child in a calm voice and manner. Avoid harsh or threatening statements. ("Joe, please sit back down until I have finished giving directions.")

Empathic: Express a degree of understanding concerning the child's behavior. ("Joe, I know it is difficult to sit through a long set of instructions, but I am almost done, so please sit down.")

Specific: Be as specific as possible concerning the behavior which needs to change and the alternative behavior you want the child to adopt. ("Joe, I would like you to sit back in your seat and face forward with your hands on your desk until I have finished.")

Patient: Recognize that compliance with a directive may take a moment. Give the child a chance to think about what has been said and, if necessary, offer clarification of the directive. Remember that behavioral transitions are difficult for this group of children, and they often process directives slowly and ineffectively.

Encouraging: Express your belief in the child's ability to meet behavioral expectations. Avoid the use of sarcasm. ("Joe, I know it is difficult to sit through a long set of instructions, but you did a great job listening in math this morning, and I bet you can get through this also. So please sit back down at your desk.")

Confident: Express a behavioral directive as if you are confident that the child both wants to comply and will comply. ("Joe, I know you want to do well on this assignment, and I am certain you will, so when you get back to your seat I will be over to help you get started.")

Timely: Try to find the balance between over-vigilant monitoring of a child and allowing the behavior to escalate to the point where it will be difficult to slow it down. The process of learning to accurately read a child's cues as to where he is in this continuum often requires considerable time and experimentation.

Therapeutic Forgiveness

The concept of therapeutic forgiveness is not easy to define. Nonetheless its presence and use within the classroom is essential for work with all children, particularly those within categories A and B. Forgiveness is an ethereal dynamic which occurs between two people following some form of perceived interpersonal transgression; it puts the transgression behind them through the expression of a sense of acceptance and caring. This process of healing between two or more persons additionally communicates the sense, "I judge and value you for something beyond your individual behaviors." The Category B child, in his frequent misreading of social cues and propensity for inappropriate behavior, needs affirming and healing expressions of forgiveness and acceptance. Without them he faces an ever-increasing backlog of transgressions that neither he nor others can leave behind in order to focus on the future.

Realistic Goals and Recognition of Goal Approximations

As has been noted throughout the discussion of the Category B child, one of the most difficult dynamics associated with this group is their vulnerability to extremely debilitating feelings of hopelessness. An organized effort to manage or mitigate this vulnerability requires careful attention to the establishment of realistic goals and an acknowledgment of approximation of these goals.

Serving as a school consultant, I have observed no single factor that more consistently undermines the effectiveness of school programming for this group of children than the establishment of unrealistic goals or expectations. Too often, I have observed both competent and committed teachers and well-motivated students become paralyzed by a sense of hopelessness linked to behavioral goals that are essentially unobtainable. Generally, the development of inappropriate behavioral goals is a function of an oversimplified perspective on the dynamics that underlie and drive problem behavior. The most common of these simplistic perspectives is the assumption that almost all behavior is volitional, resulting in the belief that if the appropriate motivation for change is established (through rewards and punishment) change will and should occur quickly. Unfortunately, this perspective often results in an endless and frustrating pursuit of the "magic combination" of rewards and punishments which will fully and rapidly correct a child's problem behavior, and detracts from attending to the factors within the child or the environment that are making success in the given situation impossible. In many respects this is analogous to seeking the right combination of rewards and punishments to spur a blind child toward mastery of a complex obstacle course without allowing for adaptive failure as part of the process.

This is not to suggest that realistic goal-setting is contingent upon the teacher's ability to develop a full understanding of the dynamics driving a child's problem behavior, but rather to emphasize the critical importance of the teacher's awareness of the fact that behavior is a result of a complex combination of variables, some of which are under the agency of volition and some of which are not, and that long-standing patterns of adaptation typically change slowly. With this awareness clearly in mind, we are far more likely to define progress as movement towards an ideal, not limited to achievement of the ideal.

We have come a long way in safeguarding the all-important commodity of hope when a teacher is able to define his responsibility as that of taking a student as far as possible, as opposed to that of healing or fixing him. From this perspective, we are able to find an essential sense of hope in small changes and to celebrate these changes, even when the child's behavior continues to fall far from the mark of appropriateness. As a result, a child's progress from a pattern of aggressively assaulting his peers ten times daily to striking them only six times daily can be defined as a cause for celebration.

An additional factor which encourages teachers to develop unrealistic goals for the behaviorally impaired student is an exaggerated fear that the consequences of a child's behavior are so disruptive, dangerous or otherwise unacceptable that they must be immediately and completely brought under control. Unfortunately, this anxious urgency is sensed by the child and serves to promote his anxiety and further precipitate problem behavior. A teacher experiencing this form of anxiety will often benefit from ongoing clinical consultation and supervision. These resources provide both additional tools (e.g., more-effective behavior-management strategies, additional staffing, medication intervention) to support better behavior control and can help redefine the consequences of the child's behavior as less catastrophic. They also affirm that the teacher is not alone in addressing the child's behavioral needs and does not have sole responsibility to solve what might be an unsolvable problem. In my experience, as much as any factor, effective consultation to teaching staff assuages the teacher's anxiety and isolation and allows him to return to the task of addressing the child's needs with a renewed sense of hope and capacity for creative thinking.

Supervision and Consultation

The importance of consultation and emotional support to teachers working with emotionally and behaviorally disabled students cannot be overstated. However, it is important to reassess the process and nature of consultation and supervision as they are typically approached in education. This reassessment is particularly relevant when recognizing the very distinct supervision model used within the clinical professions most strongly tied to serving children and adults with emotional handicaps. A comparison between the educational and clinical models for supervision yields a key distinction in the definition of the appropriate target and boundaries of the supervision process.

The traditional model for educational supervision has been primarily didactic in nature, involving training that results in mastering additional skills. This model involves a focus upon the supervisee's knowledge base, while maintaining significant interpersonal boundaries that preclude in-depth exploration of the emotions that accompany the supervisee's work. Competency is defined by both the supervisor and the supervisee as the supervisee's ability to master skills and autonomously obtain instructional objectives. Unfortunately, this model often serves to promote a work environment in which there is a negative connotation associated with the need for ongoing support or consultation, which limits the likelihood that teachers will seek out or comfortably accept support. Not surprisingly, this model produces an exaggerated sense of isolation and anxiety when difficulties arise related to working with behaviorally handicapped students, whose needs are extensive and complex.

In contrast to the supervision model generally used within school settings, the clinical model of supervision is distinct in both its definition of appropriate interpersonal boundaries and its implicit goal of promoting autonomous or independent functioning. Central to the clinical model is the recognition that effective intervention with emotionally handicapped individuals necessarily involves engagement within complex, powerful, emotional and relational dynamics. Recognizing this and the associated emotional intensity of this work, the clinical model for supervision openly addresses the highly personal aspects of the supervisee's emotional responses to these children. In doing so it supports the staff in clarifying and managing the complex and difficult emotions associated with this work. The power and nature of the emotional content present in work with emotionally and behaviorally impaired students can become "affectively toxic" to staff members and significantly impair their general sense of well-being and capacity to function effectively within their work. Therefore, this work demands regular opportunities for a "detoxification process" involving the open sharing of emotions, thoughts and concerns linked to this work. In the absence of ongoing support for the management of the difficult affective aspects of this work, the caretaker is highly vulnerable to emotional distress. Once in this emotionally off-balance posture, the teacher is far more likely to be ineffective in his work, if not potentially damaging to the child, as he unconsciously engages in behavior associated with his own problematic psychological defenses.

If service providers, teachers and clinicians working with these populations are to avoid becoming incapacitated by these complex dynamics, appropriate support and supervision must be available. Unfortunately, the process of converting from the traditional educational supervision model to a more psychologically open, "clinical" model is not a simple task. The obstacles in making this transition are resistance on the part of educational supervisors to fulfilling this distinct role, as well as getting teachers who are accustomed to less open and intimate supervision to feel safe in accepting this form of supervision. In light of these obstacles, incorporation of a "clinical-like" model of supervision for use in education, as it relates to work with behaviorally impaired students, may be best approached through the use of clinical consultants who offer regular access to individual and group supervision. This is preferable to attempting to retrain educational administrators, many of whom may be extremely competent in their current role, yet temperamentally not well suited for a more intimate form of supervision.

SUMMARY

In our work with the Category B student, it is imperative that we recognize that most of these children enter the classroom with not only neurocognitively based weaknesses but also psychological adjustments significantly impacted by years of failure, frustration and discouragement. In light of this, hope, a prerequisite to positive change for both the child and his caretaker, must be safeguarded and developed by setting realistic goals and expectations that can be reached, recognized and celebrated. For these children, marked growth or change does not occur over days or weeks, but over months and years. Therefore, the ability to recognize and reinforce incremental movement in the right direction is the key to nurturing hope and the potential for real change. Conversely, programming centered upon unrealistic and unobtainable goals serves to promote hopelessness, and not only perpetuates but also potentiates the struggles of the Category B child.

IX

Category C — Origins of Problem Behavior

As we approach the last of the three diagnostic categories, it is helpful to focus on the profound sense of vulnerability associated with the Category C child's inability to organize his environment into useful and accurate schemas. The lack of this skill results in the experience of his world (internal and external) as fundamentally random and unpredictable, promoting a generalized apprehension and anxiety associated with having a limited sense of what might happen next. For these children, a sense of security is found in either a familiar environment characterized by a limited number of variables, with explicit structure and predictability, or retreat from reality into isolated worlds of fantasy and/or soothing rituals.

Although it is always important to consider the possibility that an operant dynamic is driving a child's problem behavior, this is particularly true of the Category C child. However, in work with this population of children the underlying reinforcement associated with a particular behavior may be extremely difficult to identify. These children often perceive and experience life very differently than more-typical children and adults. An example of this difference lies in situations such as that presented by a Category C child who becomes agitated in response to gentle and supportive touch from others, while conversely experiencing self-injury (e.g., head banging) as a means of soothing. In light of the

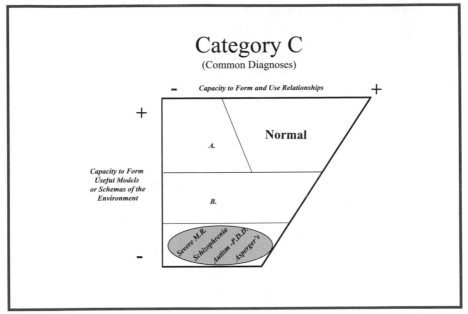

Fig. 17

often counterintuitive, highly idiosyncratic dynamics driving much of the more problematic behaviors exhibited by this group of children, it is imperative that we approach our efforts to understand these behaviors largely from an operant model, attempting to uncover the often hidden reinforcers promoting problem behavior.

As a function of the profound and pervasive sense of vulnerability associated with the Category C child's limitations, the vast majority of the aggressive behavior demonstrated by this population is best understood as an expression of the fight-or-flight dynamic. Typically, these children's lives are dominated by anxiety associated with not knowing what to expect next, which rarely allows them to move back from a state of readiness for fight-or-flight. For these children, security and the avoidance of the fight-or-flight response is almost wholly dependent upon the perception of the immediate environment as familiar, safe and predictable. The two most common events or dynamics which elicit the fight-or-flight response from the Category C child are exposure to unfamiliar settings or experiences, and experience of a familiar environment which is in some manner inconsistent with the child's expectation.

When facing an environment that is fundamentally unfamiliar, a child who has weak ability to organize and make sense of his surroundings will experience a high degree of anxiety. Further complicating the adaptive functioning of the Category C child is that their limited organizational skills often preclude generalization from one experience to the next. In other words, Category C children form extremely rigid models for understanding their environment, and when confronted by even a minor discrepancy between the established schema and the immediate environment the child's sense of familiarity and competency is negated, triggering an anxiety reaction often involving fight or flight.

Both the rigidity and associated vulnerability of this population with respect to established organizational schemas is often remarkable. For many children in this category an entire day can be ruined by unmanageable anxiety resulting from minor disturbances in routine, such as discovering that the teacher will arrive five minutes late, that the teacher's aide did not park his car in his regular spot, or that someone has hung his jacket on the hook that the child is accustomed to using. As illustrated in these examples, these children are often so rigid in their schema formation that even minor demands to generalize between two virtually identical situations may cause the child to experience their model as wholly invalid, resulting in a sense of being thrust into a completely unfamiliar and unpredictable environment.

In addition, the Category C child may have significant difficulty making the transition between environments, even when both environments are familiar and comfortable in isolation. An example of this dynamic is a family Christmas routine involving visits to several familiar homes in rapid succession; although each of the various stops is well known and comfortable, the need to move rapidly from one to another can become confusing and too often results in grossly inappropriate, anxiety-driven behavior.

Similarly, such behavior can result from simultaneous exposure to multiple familiar environmental factors. The need to use and integrate multiple schemas within the same moment, such as a visit by a teacher from a past year to the current classroom, may be experienced as highly confusing and anxiety provoking.

The last of the common dynamics that serve to elicit problematic, severe, or aggressive behavior in the Category C child is linked to this group's propensity for psychotic or psychotic-like thought processes. As noted earlier, psychosis, within this text, is understood as a dramatic breakdown in the fundamental ability to organize, ultimately resulting in an inability to make clear distinctions between one's internal world (thoughts and emotions) and external world (reality). The extreme confusion associated with the intermixing of reality-based and fantasy-based perception of psychosis may result in a wide range of unusual thoughts or perceptions, ranging from subtle magical beliefs (e.g., it is only safe to drink out of red cups), to gross misperceptions involving visual and auditory hallucinations. Unfortunately, it is often extremely difficult to determine the nature of the child's inner perceptions, particularly if he has limited language skills and is in a highly agitated state. In view of this, when a Category C child demonstrates highly unpredictable or unexplainable agitation or fear, it is reasonable to consider the possibility that he is lost within a frightening psychotic misperception and may require both comforting support and treatment with an anti-psychotic medication (see Chapter XI on medication intervention).

X

Programming for the Category C Child

As we shift our attention to the issue of school-based intervention for the Category C child, it is helpful to recognize that the primary distinction between these students and those in Category B is not in the character of their disabilities and needs but rather in the extent of their disabilities and needs. The material presented in the previous section on intervention with the Category B student is also true for the Category C child if employed with sensitivity to this group's more exaggerated need for predictable structure and support. This greater need is linked to the fact that, unlike anxiety driven by a fear of incompetence on the part of the Category B child, the anxiety of the Category C child is linked to a more profound and primitive fear of annihilation.

Supporting the Category C child's adaptive functioning requires extremely sensitive attunement to the student's affective state; once anxious, these children have very limited capacity to think or learn. In the language of Kohut's "optimal frustration" model, children within this category often seem to move directly from the experience of being underfrustrated (functioning within the range of mastery) to that of being overfrustrated (overwhelmed and incapacitated), with barely a perceptible passage through that critical range of optimal frustration. This fact demands that programming for these students be characterized by the presence of a highly predictable and structured environment which does not burden them with the responsibility to create structure through their own efforts or internal resources. For the most part, the Category C child will live his entire life within the supportive structure created by others. He will measure the quality of his life by his capacity to obtain security and the absence of fear, largely controlled by the ability to accept and trust in the support and structure created by others.

Given the similar needs between the Category B and Category C child, the discussion of programming for the latter will focus on the aspects of intervention which differ between these two groups. In addressing these distinctions, I will identify and discuss three central interventional focuses with respect to the Category C child:

1) the management of ritualized behavior;

2) support in social skills; and

3) the management of psychotic misperceptions.

RITUALIZED BEHAVIOR

One of the most common, problematic aspects of the Category C child's behavior is his propensity for potentially debilitating or socially inappropriate ritualized behavior (e.g., rocking, head banging, repeated verbal utterance or rigid adherence to idiosyncratic rules). The origin of these behaviors is best understood as linked to both a neurocognitively based tendency for perseveration (locking within a repetitive thought or behavior) and the self-reinforcing, soothing aspect of repetitive involvement of a familiar activity or thought which allows for a sense of mastery, safety and security.

Perseveration is best understood as a tendency to become "caught" in a loop of thought or behavior that repetitively cycles back upon itself, not unlike the way the needle repeatedly cycles back to the preceding groove on a scratched record album. The origin of this phenomenon is undoubtedly neurocognitive and is most likely a function of weakness in the frontal-lobe-based capacity for higher-level organization (executive functioning), resulting in a limited ability to link distinct thoughts into a fluent flow. However, although the origin of the perseverative thought pattern is neurocognitive, there is considerable evidence to suggest that over time perseverative patterns become reinforced by psychological factors. It is the point at which a perseverative thought or behavior begins to fulfill a psychological function that a behavior is considered ritualized. The psychological need met through the child's engagement in rituals is most frequently that of managing potentially overwhelming anxiety. Children prone to ritualized behavior often exhibit a significant increase in these behaviors during times of increased environmental stress.

Although it is impossible to know definitively how it is that repetitive thought or behavior supports this child's management of anxiety, there is an intuitive validity to the notion that ritualized behavior affords the child a comforting sense of familiarity and mastery.

As we consider the profound anxiety associated with being a child whose organizational abilities are as weak as those of the Category C child, the notion of being drawn to repetitive, highly familiar and predictable activity as a source of comfort is not difficult to understand. In many respects, the seeking of familiarity as a response to a stressful period in our lives is a common coping strategy for most of us, as evidenced in the common tendency to reread a book, watch a movie for the second time, or visit a familiar setting in response to stress.

In that the primary motivation for ritualized behavior is self-soothing, efforts to eliminate these behaviors are best directed towards reducing the child's exposure to stress or helping him establish a more appropriate tool for anxiety-management. However, because ritualized behaviors serve an important psychological function, before targeting such a behavior for intervention one must carefully consider whether the behavior is socially or functionally debilitating enough to justify denying the child this useful strategy. In making this judgment, it is important to consider that the Category C child has extremely limited adaptive capacity to manage anxiety and that the process of disallowing an established strategy is generally difficult, slow and, to some degree, traumatic. Therefore, a ritual that may carry relatively minor negative impact (e.g., rocking or repetitive phrases) should generally be tolerated despite the fact that it causes the child to be perceived as somewhat different. However, when a behavior carries a debilitating impact (e.g., self-abuse), there is little choice but to attempt intervention.

As noted, the initial step in addressing an inappropriate ritual is to identify and reduce sources of anxiety within the environment. This process begins with a general analysis of the child's environment, assessing its adequacy with respect to structure and predictability (discussed in the section on structure for the Category B student, Chapter VIII), and then proceeding to the careful observation of the child within this environment. Attempts should be made to correlate inappropriate ritualized behavior and specific events or environmental dynamics. Unfortunately, the highly idiosyncratic nature of this child's perceptions often makes it difficult to rely on conventional perception or empathic insight to determine the source of stress or anxiety. These sources can only be identified through an empirical process of looking for patterns in which environmental events or dynamics precede ritualized behavior. This process often results in the discovery of counterintuitive dynamics in which a child's anxiety is increased by a factor within the environment typically perceived by others as either benign or supportive.

After the environment has been carefully studied and modified to eliminate or reduce the factors that elicit ritualized behavior, interventional focus can be shifted to an analysis of the child's inner experience. This analysis is directed at gaining insight concerning both the quality and character of the child's thought process and affective profile, in order to determine whether medication might be appropriate. In this process, the focus is on determining the possible presence of an anxiety disorder, depressive disorder or psychotic thought process, each of which is a common cause of increased problematic ritualized behavior and may respond well to a medication. Although the issue of medication intervention is somewhat controversial, it is my experience that many children in this category are incapacitated by anxiety, and their adaptive functioning and general quality of life can frequently be significantly improved when they are provided appropriate psychopharmacological intervention. Considering the relatively limited range of organized coping strategies available to children within this category and their vulnerability to the frightening, often terrifying, experience of chaos associated with psychotic levels of confusion, I believe intervention with this population that does not consider the use of medication is irresponsible.

Once a problematic ritualized behavior has been addressed through reduction in the child's experience of anxiety and the provision of additional environmental structure and medication (when indicated), focus should turn to the task of training the child in alternative means of self-soothing or the development of more-appropriate ritualized behavior. This process requires an effort to understand the inappropriate ritual's soothing quality and in turn use this understanding to identify alternatives. New soothing behaviors may be taught and reinforced while attempting to reduce the inappropriate ritual through typical behavior-modification strategies (e.g., negative consequence, removal of reinforcement).

Full understanding of the manner in which a ritualized behavior functions to soothe a child is beyond our ability. However, it is often possible to make a relatively simple distinction between rituals which seem to soothe as a function of a kinesthetic quality (e.g., rocking) versus a more symbolic quality (e.g., the need to touch every doorknob in the room before sitting). Often, although not always, this distinction is related to the child's general level of functioning; lower-functioning children are far more likely to engage in kinetically soothing rituals, and higher-functioning children in symbolic rituals. This distinction can be useful as we attempt to identify and reinforce a new, more-appropriate substitute ritual, since the establishment of more-appropriate ritual will be somewhat easier if it offers the same mode of soothing (kinetic or symbolic).

Although ritualized behavior patterns are most often associated with their capacity to soothe and support the child in the management of anxiety, these patterns may also evolve as a function of the environment having provided a subtle and unintentional pattern of reinforcement of the behavior. Unfortunately, the process of identifying the nature of the reinforcement of a ritualized behavior, as well as the establishment of a means by which to control or eliminate this reinforcing dynamic, is often complex and difficult. This process demands careful analysis of the context of the ritualized behavior, with particular focus on the environment's response to its enactment. In my experience, my behaviorally oriented colleagues often have the best tools for conducting these analyses, and so they are frequently the best clinicians for providing services to the lower-functioning Category C child. Although I have serious concerns regarding the utility of a strictly behavior-focused "Functional Behavioral Analysis," (a behavioral-theory-based assessment required by special-education regulations in the evaluation of behaviorally handicapped students) for Category A and B children, I believe this structured assessment is extremely useful in work with the Category C children. In light of this fact, I refer the reader to the extensive body of literature available on this topic.

In short, the issue of how to understand and respond to problematic ritualized behavior has no simple answer. As with all intervention, we must first develop a working model (hypothesis) for understanding the origin and purpose of the problem behavior and then design and implement a coherent intervention. In this process we must remember not to take an adaptive tool from a child without providing him a replacement strategy, nor inadvertently reinforce behaviors we are attempting to extinguish.

SOCIAL SKILLS

Addressing the relationship skills of the Category C child involves looking at two dimensions of adaptive functioning. The first of these is the capacity for appropriate social behavior such as the ability to manage social anxiety, understand social convention and read social cues. The second dimension, which builds upon the first, is the capacity to use relationships as a source of emotional support. In the following section, these relational skills will be further outlined, as will ways to optimize the school environment to support the Category C child's capacity to form and utilize relationships.

The initial step in the development of the Category C child's social capacity is to facilitate his ability to establish and rely upon an accurate perception of social behavior. Once this has been established, promoting the child's effective use of this understanding to make decisions within the social arena can follow. As the core of the Category C child's disability is his significant weakness in the capacity to organize his experience, it follows logically that his basic understanding of social behavior will be contingent upon our capacity to provide him consistent and relatively simple patterns of social experiences from which to learn. Those serving the Category C child must create school environments in which social interaction is experienced as predictable, consistent and governed by explicit rules.

The creation of explicit classroom rules for social interaction requires the identification and formalization of basic interpersonal expectations followed by the translation of these expectations into a set of relatively simple rules. Once formalized into a written set of guidelines (see example below), these rules should be consistently applied and carefully reviewed with the child on a regular basis.

Classroom "People Rules":

1) *Students are not to touch one another, unless as part of an activity or game, or unless they have asked permission from the other student. ("Can I put my hand on your shoulder?")*

2) *Students are not to use nicknames or name calling under any circumstance.*

3) *Students are not to touch the belongings of others unless given permission by either the owner or the teacher.*

4) *Students may not share or trade food or objects without permission from the teacher.*

5) *Students are not to leave their desks without first raising their hands and asking permission.*

6) *Students who want to work on a project with another student must first ask permission from the teacher, and then ask the other student.*

7) If another student is having a difficult time and his behavior is inappropriate, students should inform the teacher and then allow the teacher to manage the situation.

8) If a student is feeling upset or angry, he is to inform the teacher and ask for a time out or the opportunity to discuss the problem.

Although the establishment of a set of clear classroom rules is essential, the Category C child's experience of his teacher as empathically attuned, stable and consistent is an equally important variable. To a large extent, a teacher's ability to provide this experience is far more a function of the teacher's adaptive style, temperament and empathic skill than of his training or knowledge. In other words, those working directly with the Category C child must be innately well suited for this work if they are to be effective. The requirement that intervention with the Category C child be approached with equal attention to content and process is linked to the highly brittle character of these children's adaptive functioning, their extremely limited ability to self-soothe, and their narrow window of opportunity for "optimal frustration." The notion that "Good teachers are born not trained" could not apply more than it does with respect to this student. However, an important caveat is that the definition of a good teacher may differ significantly for different groups of children. Clearly, the better a teacher's personal style of adaptation and coping matches that of his students, the easier it is for the teacher to understand and respond to the students' needs. In work with the Category C student, a personality style characterized by a highly stable affective profile, relatively low-key interpersonal style and appreciation for quiet and contemplative pastimes will likely be most effective.

The other aspect of relational-skill development involves the Category C child's ability to experience interpersonal contact as positive, supportive and soothing. It is important to note that for the more severely impaired Category C child this higher level of interpersonal relationship skill may not be possible; however, for the majority of the children in this group, this ability is both possible and essential to optimal adaptive functioning. Since the children within this category have significantly limited organizational skills, it is critical that they develop the capacity to accept, seek and use support from others. For many of these children, the capacity to trust in others and to accept direction and supervision comfortably becomes a central factor determining the quality of their life.

The school's ability to facilitate this child's development of a deeper level of trust and reliance upon relationships is to a large extent dependent upon the match between the child, his teacher, his classroom environment, and the length of time in which the child is exposed to this well-matched set of variables. In the typical academic system, organized around a nine-month placement, the child's ability to gain from this experience is often dramatically compromised by not remaining within a particular environment long enough to benefit optimally. Effective service to the Category C student involves multi-year, year-round (twelve-month) programming, with extensive transitional support when moving from one placement to the next.

In summary, the Category C child's ability to form and use relationships is complicated by his significant weakness in the capacity to organize. Intervention must occur within a highly structured and predictable social context and be administered with an extraordinary empathic attunement to the child's anxiety and coping strategies. When functioning within an environment characterized by considerable structure and attunement, the Category C child can learn to accept and use the support of others, an essential skill in light of this population's significantly limited ability for independent adaptation.

PSYCHOTIC LEVELS OF CONFUSION

As stated, the Category C child's limited capacity to effectively organize his experience results in a propensity to perceive the environment as governed by randomness. In reaction to this perception, problematic adaptive patterns of anxious hyper-arousal (perpetual readiness for the unexpected) or avoidance of anxiety through retreat into fantasy are common coping strategies for Category C children. Unfortunately, the interaction between a weak capacity to organize, elevated anxiety and lack of social relatedness often sets the stage for these children to develop gross perceptional and cognitive distortions, referred to as psychotic or psychotic-like symptoms.

The term "psychotic" refers to a profound breakdown in the capacity to organize one's perceptions. This breakdown manifests itself in the child's inability to determine which experiences and perceptions are within his thoughts and which come from the external environment. This dramatic breakdown in cognitive functioning is generally associated with the interaction between an organically compromised central nervous system and profound levels of psychological stress (anxiety). The process of "psychotic decompensation," a term used to describe the deterioration from a non-psychotic state to that of psychosis, often involves three central factors: 1) a neurocognitive predisposition to profound levels of disorganization (a characteristic common among all Category C children); 2) profound or debilitating anxiety which significantly undermines cognitive efficiency and is linked to a highly reactive affective profile or pronounced stress within the environment; and 3) social isolation, often sought in order to minimize confusion and vulnerability but resulting in a greater propensity for the development of egocentric, non-reality-based perceptions.

Although most of us are fortunate enough to have never had the experience of significantly losing the capacity to know what is real, with little effort we can imagine the vulnerability and fear, if not terror, associated with such an experience. Given the traumatic nature of psychosis, an effort to support the Category C child in avoiding psychotic levels of anxiety and disorganization through whatever means available is critical to maintain our commitment to humane treatment. Therefore, in work with Category C children, a group highly vulnerable to psychotic thought, we must remain carefully attuned to the quality of the child's thought and affective state in order to recognize and intervene in the process of psychotic decompensation as early as possible. Further supporting the importance of early and aggressive intervention with psychotic decompensation is a body of evidence suggesting that long-term adjustment and quality of life for individuals vulnerable to psychosis is significantly improved when the individual is protected from ever experiencing a full decompensation leading to a florid psychotic state. Although it is beyond the scope of this text to discuss this issue in detail, it may be useful to think of the terrifying experience of psychosis as profound trauma that can result in a trauma-based psychopathology (i.e. post-traumatic stress disorder), as an overlay to the child's existing constellation of developmental struggles.

Given the inherent vulnerability of the Category C child to psychotic levels of anxiety and confusion, we now turn our attention to both the identification of psychotic symptoms and strategies for intervention.

Identifying Psychotic Symptoms

The following outline presents the symptoms most often associated with psychosis. In using this outline, the reader is encouraged to recognize that it is neither an exhaustive list of possible symptoms, nor a list of factors the presence of one or more of which definitively indicates a psychotic thought process. The process of assessing a child for an evolving psychotic decompensation, particularly early in the decompensation process, is not a simple task. This assessment requires a significant knowledge of the child's current and past patterns of thought and behavior, and may ultimately require psychological testing to carefully survey and measure the nature of the child's thought process.

Common Psychotic Symptoms

Social isolation: Withdrawal from social contact, marked avoidance of interpersonal interaction (e.g., unwillingness to respond verbally, refusal of eye contact).

Inappropriate affect: The expression of inappropriate affective responses or a highly idiosyncratic sense of humor (e.g., finding humor in benign, insignificant events, the expression of an irrational or generalized sense of fear or anger).

Confusion: Inability to understand and perform simple tasks, particularly those related to social behavior (e.g., trouble understanding how to select an item for purchase and take it to the cashier).

Unusual language: Problems linked to a highly concrete or overly symbolic interpretation of language and the invention of words or strange word combinations (e.g., confusion resulting from the literal interpretation of metaphors such as "Don't let the cat out of the bag," unusual use of pronouns, neologisms such as "Doggybird").

Unusual rituals: A compulsion to perform unusual rituals (e.g., touching objects a set number of times, refusal to sit facing in a particular direction).

Magical thinking: Irrational belief in the existence of causal relationships between unrelated dynamics and events within the environment, particularly related to the power of thoughts to control factors in the environment (e.g., belief that wishing harm to another will cause ill fate, belief that random events have special meaning, highly idiosyncratic superstitions).

Paranoid beliefs: Belief that there is some organized, malevolent effort to harm or intrude within one's thoughts or life (e.g., a delusion that others are able to read or control thoughts, belief that one's family is conspiring to harm him).

Hallucination: Gross sensory misperception, involving auditory, visual, olfactory or tactile experiences which are not real (e.g., hearing laughter or ridicule from persons who are not present, hearing commands or directives from persons not present, seeing frightening imagery). These perceptions may or may not be accompanied by overt behavior indicating their presence (i.e. the child may or may not move his eyes in response to a visual hallucination or acknowledge hearing voices).

Intervention with the Psychotic Child

Unfortunately, the options for intervention with a child struggling with the profound breakdown in his thought processes characteristic of psychotic decompensation are relatively narrow. These options may be broken into three broad categories: reduction of stress and confusion within the environment, disallowing social withdrawal or isolation, and the use of antipsychotic medications.

Reducing stress

When a child's thought process is suspected to be deteriorating or decompensating, the initial intervention should be a careful analysis of the sources of stress within the child's environment. The goal is to identify factors that might be contributing to the child's increased anxiety, with particular attention to factors within the child's life that may have changed at the time of, or just prior to, the deterioration in his adaptive functioning. Factors commonly associated with increased stress and anxiety may involve such issues as change in family structure (e.g., the divorce or remarriage of parents), movement to a new classroom, arrival of a new teacher, the broad range of changes associated with transition from childhood into adolescence. In light of the potentially negative and overwhelming impact of transition or change for this child, effective intervention demands both an effort to minimize exposure to change and the development of means by which to support transition. Supporting this child demands the thoughtful, well-organized anticipatory guidance that will help the child understand what the upcoming change will entail and create a specific plan for its management.

The following example offers an illustration of anticipatory guidance used to support a student in an upcoming field trip involving a bus ride.

Preparation for a Field Trip to the Fire Station:

1) Mark the field trip on the school calendar seven days in advance. Each day prior to the trip identify how many days until the outing.

2) Show the child photos of the firehouse and ask him to draw a picture of how he thinks it will appear when he visits.

3) Meet the bus driver who will be taking the group to the firehouse and visit the bus the day prior to the trip. Select a seat for the student on the bus and practice sitting in that seat for a minute or two. Describe where the teacher will sit and where several other students will sit.

4) Look at a map of the route you will be taking and identify the things you are likely to see on the trip to and from the firehouse. Have the student draw pictures of some of the things he might see en route.

5) Describe what he will probably see once at the firehouse. Discuss the rules for behavior in an unfamiliar setting.

6) Describe events that might occur while at the firehouse and how he might respond to these events (e.g., what if the firefighters receive a fire call?).

7) Discuss what the student is going to do if he begins to feel worried or anxious, including whom he is going to tell and how he is going to express it.

8) Review the plan several times prior to the day of the trip and once again just prior to leaving. Write the plan out and have the student carry a copy of the plan in his pocket during the field trip.

Once again, the general adaptive skills of a child vulnerable to psychotic decompensation are best thought of as "brittle," since there is little warning prior to a relatively dramatic breakdown in adaptive functioning. This brittle quality often results in a pattern in which the child provides little or no indication of increased confusion or anxiety until the point at which he exhibits dramatic symptomology. Further evidence of the brittle nature of these children's adaptive skills is the fact that once agitated or confused it is very difficult for them to calm or reorient. Therefore, the caretaker must carefully monitor the environment for potential sources of change or stress, to allow for a preemptive intervention prior to the point at which the child becomes overwhelmed and shatters.

Generally the most effective means to reestablish a lower level of anxiety, increased security and reduced psychotic symptomology is to create supportive structure and reduce the complexity of the child's environment. Within the school setting this might include pulling the child out of the mainstream and into a self-contained classroom, isolating the child from highly energized and unpredictable peers, or implementing a highly predictable schedule involving a limited number of encounters with unfamiliar people.

Discouraging withdrawal

A second area of focus, relevant to mitigating the impact of vulnerability to psychosis, includes addressing the Category C child's common pattern of social withdrawal in response to anxiety and confusion. Unfortunately, the decompensating child's retreat from social contact as a means of avoiding confusion and anxiety creates two dynamics that are problematic and must be addressed. First, pronounced social withdrawal undermines the caretaker's ability to access information from the child that would help him understand and intervene in the dynamics that are being experienced as overwhelming. Second, isolation sets the stage for the child to ruminate in his own confused thoughts, without benefit of input from others to offer him a clearer perception of reality (reality testing).

The process of responding to a child's use of social withdrawal as a means of managing anxiety is far from simple, since it entails drawing the socially anxious child into social contact without eliciting further anxiety. This balancing act is generally achieved by slowly increasing the child's social contact through structured and highly predictable encounters with familiar others.

Medication

The class of medicines generally associated with the treatment of psychosis or psychotic levels of anxiety and confusion is referred to as neuroleptics, and primarily impact the neurotransmitter dopamine. This category of medication has evolved significantly over the last forty years, yet remains plagued by side effects which must be monitored carefully. The first of these medications widely prescribed was Thorazine, followed by similar compounds such as Haldol and Mellaril, and more recently developed medications such as Risperdal, Zyprexa and Clozaril. Psychopharmacological research in this area is advancing rapidly and the potential for the development of newer and more-effective antipsychotic medicines with fewer side effects is great. However, the use of these medicines generally entails a period of acclimation involving mild to significant drowsiness, as well as the slight risk for the serious and potentially irreversible long-term side effect of Tardive Dyskinesia (TD). Responsible use of these important and often dramatically helpful medications demands that they be carefully monitored by a physician with a good working knowledge of both their effectiveness and potential side effects.

The benefits generally realized through use of antipsychotic medication involve a marked drop in anxiety and an associated increased cognitive efficiency (improved reality testing). As with virtually all psychiatric medications, the process of identifying the most effective medication and most beneficial dose requires medication trials and assessment (see Chapter XI on medication). As a rule, some benefit from these medications is noted almost immediately (within twenty minutes of ingestion). However, the full impact on the thought process (referred to as "clearing") can take up to several weeks. In treating children with chronic vulnerability to psychotic decompensation, it is not uncommon to place them on an antipsychotic medication during periods of stress, and to manage the potentially negative side effects by reducing or discontinuing these medications as the environmental stress remits.

Conclusion

Due to the Category C child's profound reliance upon others to support him in organizing and understanding his world, work with these children demands careful attention to the structure and consistency of the school environment, as well as attunement to the child's brittle affective profile. The central aspect to effective work with this population is the ability to create an environment in which the child experiences himself as competent and secure, thus consistently able to use his cognitive capacities without the debilitating impact of profound anxiety.

XI

Psychiatric Medication and the Public School

I believe that the thoughtful, well-informed approach to serving children with severe behavioral and emotional impairments must include consideration of psychopharmacological intervention. However, my position is not shared by all, thus demanding a careful analysis of the concerns expressed by those resistant to the use of psychiatric medications with children. Common concerns have included:

- fear regarding the long-term physiological impact of psychiatric medications;

- concern that medication simply conceals a child's symptoms and does not address the "real" issues or deficits;

- the belief that placing children on a chronic medication regime will increase their comfort with the use of artificial agents and promote future substance abuse;

- the concern that medication is used to make the school's work easier, not to meet the child's needs;

- concern that when medication is an available option, teachers consider themselves absolved of the responsibility to think creatively and make necessary adaptations to the classroom; and

- fear that the use of medication will cause the child to perceive himself as "sick" or "broken," resulting in a devastating impact upon self-esteem.

Unquestionably there is a degree of relevance in each of these concerns. However, it is imperative that in assessing the appropriate role of medication, we contrast the risk factors associated with the use of medication against risk factors associated with the child's continued pattern of adaptive failure. It is my experience that, in attempting to determine or assess the appropriateness of medical intervention, too often a great deal of attention is focused upon the potential negative impact of this intervention, while the risks associated with a child's prolonged exposure to profoundly disturbing levels of anxiety, failure and social rejection are disregarded. Clearly, all medication regimes, whether psychiatric or other, carry risk and some form of negative side effect. Nonetheless, a medication's utility is not determined exclusively by assessing its side effects or negative potential, but rather by taking a balanced perspective which includes its potential cost and benefit. Based upon my observation of hundreds of children treated with psychiatric medication over prolonged periods, I have absolutely no doubt that a large percentage of the Category B and C children are dramatically helped by these medications. My conviction is so strong with respect to this issue that I believe the refusal to consider this treatment option constitutes clinical neglect.

Accompanying the obligation to consider medication intervention is the responsibility to do so in an organized and effective manner, focusing on a number of important variables. Although decision making concerning medication intervention is ultimately the responsibility of the treating physician, the importance of the physician's access to a well-informed team's observations and insights cannot be overstated.

The following information provides the non-physician with basic information concerning major issues that must be taken into account when considering the use of medication in the treatment of children with behavioral handicaps. This information is organized around several key questions: When should an evaluation for medication be recommended? How should an evaluation for medication be recommended? Who should provide medication services? What should be expected in the course of utilizing a medication intervention? What is the appropriate role for the school in ongoing treatment with medication?

WHEN SHOULD AN EVALUATION FOR MEDICATION BE RECOMMENDED?

The question of determining when to refer a child for a psychiatric medication evaluation is relatively complex, involving a carefully balanced appraisal of three fundamental issues: 1) the severity of the child's presenting problems; 2) the demonstrated effectiveness of medication in the treatment of children with similar diagnostic profiles; and 3) the adequacy and effectiveness of previous non-medication-based or behavioral intervention. Unfortunately, the effective evaluation of these variables is significantly subjective and often involves an intuitive albeit well-informed judgment on the part of the prescribing clinician or treatment team.

In assessing the severity of a child's presenting behavior, "severity" is defined by several variables. First among these is the child's fundamental and immediate physical safety. Clearly, a child whose behavior is highly erratic, explosive or otherwise dangerous to himself or others must be the focus of aggressive intervention, and behavioral support through the use of medication must be considered. However, severity as it relates to less overt forms of risks (i.e. psychological risks) must also be taken into account in assessing the appropriateness of medication intervention. It is common that an emotionally handicapped child's overt behavior will remain relatively well controlled, if not over-controlled, while under the surface the child is enduring prolonged exposure to psychologically traumatizing experiences. These experiences might include the terrifying impact of psychotic confusion, debilitating anxiety and the destructive impact of profound isolation, hopelessness and depression. In view of this, the assessment of a child's psychological safety demands careful and insightful consideration, which goes well beyond simply observing overt behavior. The assessment of the child's underlying psychological reality demands a thoughtful evaluation by a well-informed and empathically attuned clinician and may require competently administered and interpreted psychological testing.

In my experience, one of the most disturbing aspects of school-based psychological services is that both the school staff and the evaluated child's family often inaccurately believe the school's psychoeducational assessment is a broad-based screening of the student's psychological health, comparable to a doctor's physical or check-up. However, in actuality these evaluations are often extremely narrow in focus and address only those questions directly posed by the referral source, and they neither attempt to develop a comprehensive diagnostic understanding nor identify the full range of appropriate treatment options (including referral for medication evaluation). It is not uncommon for significantly impaired children to undergo a school-based "psychoeducational evaluation," which essentially ignores assessment or screening for a wide range of psychopathologies not directly linked to the referral question. Too often parents and teachers believe that these assessments have evaluated the child's broad mental health and that the lack of discussion or concern regarding mental-health issues within the evaluation report means there were no findings concerning psychopathology. This misinterpretation often results in parents and schools under-responding to the child's mental health needs because they believe that psychiatric illness has been ruled out by the evaluation.

Following consideration of the severity of the child's mental-health needs, the next issue in determining the appropriateness of a medication trial is that of the demonstrated effectiveness of medication in the treatment of a child's particular presenting problems. Consideration of this factor demands both a relatively clear diagnostic understanding of the child and knowledge concerning the effectiveness of medication in the treatment of specific disorders. For example, when a clinical evaluation results in the diagnosis of a bipolar illness, the established effectiveness of mood stabilizers (e.g., Lithium, Tegretol, Depakote) in reducing the destructive impact of this illness strongly supports a medication trial. However, in addressing other pathologies such as antisocial or narcissistic personality disorders, the demonstrated ineffectiveness of medication for these diagnoses would significantly reduce the appropriateness of a medication trial. In light of the importance of medication in helping a large number of children recover from or manage psychiatric illness, it is imperative that schools have staff or consultants available who have both well-developed diagnostic skills to competently identify psychiatric illnesses, as well as a basic working knowledge of psychiatric medication intervention, so that they will know when a referral for a medication consultation is appropriate.

In addition to these critical factors, the initial step in considering a medication intervention must include a careful assessment of the availability and adequacy of non-medication-based intervention. When it is possible to meet a child's needs without medication, this option should always be elected. The process of exploring the utility of non-medication-based interventions (as is true of medication intervention) entails informed experimentation (trial and error), which involves developing a hypothesis concerning the child's psychopathology and related needs and implementing an intervention designed to address these issues. However, following an adequate trial period when a child's response to a well-designed and implemented behavioral intervention is limited, augmentation of this intervention with a medication trial must be considered.

Having made the decision to explore a medication intervention, it remains incumbent upon those serving the child to continue to bring energy and creativity to non-medication intervention efforts and not be sidetracked by a belief that medication is "the answer."

Although medication is often a useful part of an effective school-based program serving children with emotional handicaps, it must be accepted that for some of these children medication will not be a treatment option. The lack of this option is linked to a number of variables, ranging from the nature of the child's psychopathology to parental unwillingness to consider medication. Regardless of the availability of medication intervention, the responsibility of the school staff working with these students remains that of developing and implementing effective behavioral programs which optimally serve the student. Thus, it is extremely important that school staff not become too focused upon medication and, in the process, neglect the interventions within their domain and control.

HOW SHOULD PARENTS BE APPROACHED REGARDING A MEDICATION EVALUATION?

The issues that determine the effectiveness of the school's approach in recommending psychiatric medication consultation to a child's parents are relatively simple, yet critical. Most important of these issues is the parents' perception of the individual making the recommendation as someone who is competent, motivated by interest in their child's well-being and personally knowledgeable of the child. In addition, the individual making this recommendation must be able to communicate a balanced sense of the benefits and drawbacks associated with the use of medication, while at the same time expressing that the choice to use medication is both difficult and absolutely a parental prerogative.

It is extremely important that those discussing the possibility of a medical intervention with parents remain aware of the range of issues brought to the forefront when psychiatric medication is suggested. For many parents, the process of accepting that a child requires medication for emotional or behavioral issues pushes them across a psychological threshold, propelling them into the painful acceptance of their child's disability as a reality. Crossing of this threshold is always painful, and more often than not some aspect of the associated pain will be acted out in anger and resistance against the messenger. We must carefully maintain perspective concerning a parent's reaction to the initial recommendation for medication, and not overreact or personalize an angry or resistant initial response. Often, when given the time and support to gain acceptance of the child's disability, the same parent who initially responded negatively will later exhibit a cooperative and appreciative attitude toward the treatment team. However, this process often takes considerable time and can be significantly slowed by too persistent or forceful a recommendation concerning the need for a medication evaluation.

Typically, it is best that a recommendation for a medication evaluation come from a clinically trained staff member or consultant (psychologist, social worker, counselor or nurse) who is able to convey both a personal knowledge of the child and a working knowledge of psychiatric medication. In approaching the parents for this discussion, it is important to schedule a private meeting allowing enough time for questions and answers. The staff member's agenda should be simply to start the process of talking about the possible need and benefit of medication, not to arrive at a decision. After this initial meeting, a follow-up meeting should be scheduled to allow the parents time to process this new information. It is helpful to let the parents know that they are not expected to have made a decision by the next meeting, and that if they would like to have someone else (e.g., a grandparent, friend) join them, they are welcome to do so. We must realize that it is much easier to decide to place someone else's child on medication than our own. Coming to this difficult decision is a process, not a discrete event.

An additional strategy that is useful in helping resistant parents consider the possibility of seeking a medication evaluation involves the development of a parent-to-parent support system. For a number of reasons, it is not uncommon for parents to approach information provided by school or clinical personnel with a significant degree of mistrust or cynicism. Many parents fear school personnel are primarily interested in bringing the child's behavior under control in order to make their own job easier, not to safeguard the child's well-being. School or clinical personnel may inadvertently discuss the issue of medication in a manner that promotes this perception through statements about issues such as the school's responsibility to shield the child's classmates from his behavior or the need for order within the school setting. Although these statements may be true, they are not the concern or responsibility of the child's parents and often serve to promote the notion that medication is being recommended, not because it is in the child's best interest, but because it is in the school's best interest. In response to this dynamic, and because human nature is such that we tend to trust those we perceive as most similar to ourselves, the development of a parent-to-parent support information network for medication and psychiatric services is often extremely useful.

A parent-to-parent network is relatively easy to establish and generally involves little more than asking several parents within a school community who have children who were successfully treated with medication if they would be willing to speak with parents who are confronting this issue for the first time. The school personnel can indicate to parents facing this issue that, should they wish, they will be provided with the names and telephone numbers of other parents who have had to deal with similar issues and who are willing to share their thoughts and experiences. It has been my experience that parents generally refuse this support on their initial visit but often seek these contacts at a later time.

To support parents in accepting the need for a medication evaluation we must clarify why we feel it is in the child's best interest to be considered for treatment with medication and how we believe it might help. It is important that the individual making the recommendation not only have adequate knowledge of the child and medication, but also have a relatively clear manner of sharing this knowledge. What follows is a metaphor I have found useful in addressing medication intervention with parents. (Note: It is important to tailor one's choice of metaphors to one's audience. In my home state of Maine, where much of life centers around duct tape and WD-40, a machine lubricant, this metaphor may be more applicable than in southern California where rust is not a way of life.)

WD-40 Analogy

As I think of the options available in work with children with behavioral handicaps, I often draw a parallel between this work and automotive repair, particularly those challenging moments in a mechanic's work when he encounters a bolt or a nut rusted or frozen in place. The parallel between the two very different tasks of loosening a stubborn bolt and helping a child with a behavioral impairment begins with approaching the frozen bolt (child) as one would any other and expecting it to simply unscrew (behave) when leveraged to do so. However, as it becomes apparent that the bolt is not loosening, the first step is to carefully inspect both the bolt and the tool selected to identify or define "the problem" (diagnosis). As a result of this inspection, one may reconsider the choice of tool (non-medication behavioral intervention) and change it if appropriate, and then apply greater torque to the bolt. Unfortunately, at this moment, the mechanic often experiences movement of the wrench, only to find not that the bolt has not loosened, but rather that the wrench has rounded off a corner of the bolt's head. It is common then to make one more effort at simply unscrewing the bolt, with perhaps a yet more powerful tool, such as a pair of vise grips (increasing the behavior program's rewards and punishments even further). However, in time it becomes clear that the bolt is not only not loosening, but that with each effort of the wrench the head of the bolt is becoming more compromised and less likely ever to be useful in loosening the bolt (the child develops an increased sense of anger, frustration and discouragement in response to a behavior-management system which is not able to provide adequate support to allow for success). It is at this point that the wise mechanic turns to the WD-40 (psychiatric medication), rather than run the risk of continued failure and increased damage to the bolt, potentially making its removal impossible without use of dramatic measures (more-restrictive options such as hospitalization, incarceration or long-term residential placement). However, in electing to use WD-40, the mechanic's work with the appropriate tools does not end; as matter of fact, the application of WD-40 alone, without reapplication of the appropriate tools, does nothing to remove the bolt. However, after applying the WD-40 and allowing a period for the oil to penetrate (the time necessary for the medication to reach a clinical level in the child's system, a period that differs dramatically from medication to medication and child to child) and then employing the same tools as before (a well-designed behavior-management program), the bolt loosens! (The child begins to experience success!)

Key points:

1) Don't look to WD-40 until you are certain you are using the right-sized tool.

2) Don't continue to employ a tool even though you are aware that it is not working and may well be destroying the bolt.

3) After applying WD-40, be certain to allow it enough time to work.

Who Should Provide Behavioral Medication Services?

The initial step in making a referral for a behavioral medication consultation involves choosing which medical specialty is most appropriate for a specific child and family (e.g., pediatrics, family practice, neurology, general psychiatry, child psychiatry). This choice is often complicated both by clinical issues (i.e. which specialty has the greatest expertise relevant to a particular child's needs) and by non-clinical factors, ranging from the availability of medical specialists within a geographical area to finances, insurance constraints, and parental attitudes concerning health and mental-health providers. These limitations notwithstanding, it is my belief that the preferred point of departure in seeking a child's behavioral medication consultation is a child psychiatrist. Clinicians within this specialty have broad training in the interaction between the biological and psychological basis of child behavior, allowing them optimal competency in approaching medication to address emotional and behavioral issues in children. Training in child psychiatry provides critical skills in psychodiagnostics and medication intervention, including symptom targeting, dosing, poly-pharmacy (medication combinations) and the management of side effects. Although it is beyond the scope of this text to delve into these medical management issues in depth, I hope that greater understanding will facilitate more-effective cooperation and coordination between medical and educational service providers, and offer the following overview of each of these concerns.

Symptom Targeting

The process of psychopharmacological "symptom targeting" involves two important steps. First, it entails forming a diagnostic hypothesis that identifies the child's core or underlying neuropsychiatric pathology, supporting a targeted intervention that avoids a focus on individual or secondary-level symptoms. This approach is analogous to the treatment of a child's ear infection (core pathology) with an antibiotic, as opposed to an intervention with a medication simply aimed at reducing the child's temperature (secondary symptom). Second, the process involves determination of which aspects of the child's behavioral profile are likely to be responsive to medication and which aspects will require an alternative intervention.

MEDICATION SELECTION

Selecting the appropriate psychiatric medication is a critical and complex task, demanding strong diagnostic skills and up-to-date knowledge concerning the rapidly changing field of psychopharmacology. The complexity of this task, particularly in serving highly impaired children, generally requires the use of a specialist (i.e. child psychiatrist), since remaining current with the relevant literature requires a significant commitment unlikely to be found in a provider who is rarely involved in this area of treatment. Further necessitating the skills of a psychopharmacology specialist is that many of the most effective medications for addressing psychiatric issues in children are used "off label," meaning that, although they may be widely used in work with children, they do not have formal F.D.A. recognition for this purpose. Therefore, it is even more imperative that the prescribing clinician have adequate knowledge of the full range of medical options with respect to their potential benefits, contraindications and side effects.

Greatly complicating the issue of medication selection is the fact that, although there are clear guidelines suggesting the use of particular medication regimes for particular diagnoses or problem behaviors, actual responses to medication are often highly idiosyncratic. This being the case, the prescribing physician must approach the identification of the optimal medication regimen through a careful process of medication trials. It is imperative that parents recognize that they are entering a process of seeking an effective medication intervention that may well involve a number of trials. It has been my experience that when parents understand the likelihood of multiple medication trials the process proceeds far more effectively and is less encumbered by a loss of faith in the physician each time a change is made in the child's medication regimen.

DOSING

Because of significant variability in response from child to child, there are relatively few clear guidelines for identifying optimal dosing or medication levels. The choice and regulation of dosage is yet another complex issue, requiring a careful process of trial and assessment. Related to the obligation to introduce as little medication into a child's system as necessary to gain adequate benefit and minimize side effects, children are generally started at a low dose on all psychiatric medications.

Unfortunately, one of the most common problems associated with non-specialized physicians prescribing psychiatric medications to children is their overly prudent or cautious dosing practices. In their effort to "do no harm" in prescribing medications with which they have limited familiarity, non-specialists are prone to prescribe psychiatric medications to children at sub-clinical doses, providing little or no benefit.

POLY-PHARMACY

The term "poly-pharmacy" refers to a treatment regimen involving the simultaneous use of more than one medication. Due to a fundamental treatment principle requiring the trial of simpler medication regimes prior to employing more-complicated pharmacological strategies, poly-pharmacy is rarely the point of departure in psychiatric intervention. However, when simpler treatment regimens result in less-than-optimal outcome, the current norm in psychiatry is to move into the far more complex practice of poly-pharmacy.

The common practice of poly-pharmacy often results in more-effective treatment outcomes than the use of a single medication regimen, as it allows for broader targeting of psychiatric symptoms and the use of secondary medications to reduce negative side effects associated with a primary medication. However, when a poly-pharmacy strategy is used there is often a more protracted process of medication trial as the prescribing clinician attempts to fine-tune the interaction between multiple medications and doses.

ASSESSMENT OF MEDICATION EFFICACY

Determining the effectiveness of a medical regimen is a process of timely assessment of the child's adaptive functioning, thought, and mood following the initiation of treatment. This process must include significant knowledge concerning the child's psychological profile, the range of possible reactions to the prescribed medication, and the latency period between starting a medication and the realization of a treatment benefit. This process of assessing a medication's efficacy is complicated not only by the wide variability in the impact of medications from child to child, but also by the need to sift out the impact of non-medical environmental factors which may be affecting the child's psychological functioning and behavior.

Unfortunately, the process of determining the effectiveness of a medication never occurs within a vacuum. Rather, it takes place in the context of the child's interaction with a wide range of environmental events, both positive and negative, and so considerable clinical judgment is necessary to determine accurately the effectiveness of a medication intervention. Factors to be considered as an alternative explanation for change in a child's presentation include variations in the child's physical health, increased stress within the environment (e.g., parental separation, increased work load at school), decreased stress (e.g., school vacation), placebo effect (the positive impact of the child's expectation that things will improve with medication) and the "halo effect" (the positive impact of the expectation of others that behavior will improve with medication).

Management of Side Effects

As all medications carry some form and degree of side effect, assessing and managing a medication's side effects is a critical aspect of intervention. Side effects associated with psychiatric medication range from common and relatively minor anticholinergic effects, involving symptoms such as a dry mouth and slightly blurred vision, to more-severe or life-threatening symptoms, such as cardiac or liver damage. The management of less-severe side effects entails patient and parent education and careful physician monitoring through interviews with the child and his parents. Management of potentially dangerous side effects often requires medical clearance (e.g., cardiac assessment involving an E.K.G.) prior to starting a medication and ongoing medical testing (e.g., E.K.G., liver function test) over the course of treatment. Effective management with psychiatric medication is largely dependent upon careful and well-focused assessment and response to potential problematic side effects. Fortunately, many of the most common side effects associated with psychiatric medication are most significant during the initial period of treatment but remit after several weeks, while the intended or positive response to the medication remains. Unfortunately, the pattern of negative side effects at the onset of treatment, prior to any experience of benefit or symptom relief, often results in the patient developing a negative attitude concerning a medication and refusal to complete the medication trial. Careful patient and parent education concerning this pattern often avoids the premature conclusion that a particular medication is not beneficial. Although most medications have common side effects, the process of predicting or assessing side effects with a particular patient is greatly complicated by a high degree of variability among individuals.

Once side effects have been assessed as severe enough to require intervention, the physician's response may take several directions, some of which may seem counterintuitive. The physician may increase or decrease dosing of the current medication, change the time of day when the medication is taken, discontinue the medication, prescribe an additional medication to target or treat the side effect, change to a different medication within the same family of medicines, or switch to a medication with a completely distinct focus or action. The determination of which of these options to employ is based upon a wide range of variables and, once again, requires some degree of experimentation.

What to Expect in the
Medication Intervention Process

For the many issues outlined above, the decision to employ psychiatric medication in treating a child's behavioral or emotional impairments is not a simple or single-step choice. Rather it entails a decision to enter a careful process of experimentation, informed by the treating physician's personal experience and knowledge of clinical research, to eventually identify a medication or combination of medications that significantly improve a child's quality of life. Based upon my experience in the treatment of children with more-complicated behavioral issues, this process typically unfolds over the course of six months to a year and is often accompanied by an ever-increasing uneasiness on the part of all parties with its experimental nature. Fortunately, it has also been my experience that as a result of this careful process a positive medication regime, effective in supporting the child in the management of problematic emotions and behavior, is eventually established.

The School's Role in the Ongoing
Treatment with Medication

Once a child has begun treatment with medication, school staff become an important source of feedback and information about the effectiveness of the treatment. However, the politics and logistics of establishing and maintaining this line of communication are often complicated by a number of factors. Issues such as parental resistance to open communication between the treating clinician and the school, as well as difficulty on the part of the school in establishing contact with the treating clinician, become involved. Effective management of these obstacles generally requires persistence and sensitivity.

In approaching a child's parents concerning the establishment of direct communication between the school and the treating physician, it is generally best to propose an ongoing written observation log, providing daily or weekly reports regarding the child's functioning at school. For many parents, the sense that the school might be communicating information to the physician of which they are not aware requires greater trust in the school than the parents are able to offer. The process of producing a written observation log to be shared with the physician allows the parents to see exactly what is being communicated, and also allows for discussion between the parents and school concerning these observations. The use of a written log, particularly if observations are relatively short and objective, is also effective in reducing the likelihood of difficulty in contacting the treating physician. It also precludes the need to obtain a release-of-information form (since the parents themselves pass the log on to the physician).

One of the common drawbacks associated with school involvement in the assessment of medication effectiveness is a tendency for school personnel to become overfocused on the issue of medication at the expense of more-appropriate attention to optimizing the child's experience within the school setting. Since much of the work with this population of children is slow and difficult, it is relatively easy to focus on medication intervention as the answer; yet, although medication is frequently helpful, it is virtually never the primary or central factor in effective intervention. With this in mind, it is imperative that the full force and creativity of the school team remain directed towards optimizing the effectiveness of the school program, and not be diluted by a shift in focus towards finding a magic bullet in the medication intervention.

In summary, medication intervention is an important and often critical aspect in effectively supporting children with emotional and behavioral impairments. However, it is imperative that we not view medication intervention as "the answer," but as a tool that supports the child in more effectively accessing and benefiting from the healing structure and relationships available within their school environment.

XII

Final Thoughts

The intent of this text has been to provide educators with a useful point of departure in understanding and responding to their most complex and challenging students. In addressing this topic I have presented a developmental model which organizes children with behavioral impairments into three diagnostic categories (A, B, and C) delineated by their capacity to organize and their ability to form and use relationships.

As is true of any effort to explain and simplify complex dynamics, the model I have presented is not perfect; not all children will fit neatly into an individual category, nor will origins of pathology or strategies for intervention suggested for each category prove uniformly accurate or useful. However, if used with empathy, compassion and common sense, this model provides a useful structure to guide our work with this vulnerable population of children.

In the final analysis, what is demanded of us in serving children with behavioral impairments, as is true for all children, is caretaking characterized by the consistent expression of both wisdom and love.

References

Bleiberg, E. (1992). The Yogi and the Commissar: Integrating individual and family approaches to the treatment of narcissistic children and adolescents. Residential Treatment for Children and Youth, 9, 5–27.

Kegan, R. (1982). The Evolving Self. Boston: Harvard University Press.

Kohut, H. (1977). The Restoration of the Self. New York: International University Press.

Kohut, H. (1978). The Search for the Self. New York: International University Press.

Kohut, H. (1984). How Does Analysis Cure? Chicago: University of Chicago Press.

Mahler, M. (1974). Symbiosis and individuation: The psychological birth of the human infant. The Psychoanalytic Study of the Child, 29, 89–106.

Pine, F. (1974). On the concept of "borderline in children": A clinical essay. The Psychoanalytic Study of the Child, 29, 341–368.

Sullivan, H.S. (1953). The Interpersonal Theory of Psychiatry. New York: W.W. Norton.

Tolpin, M. (1971). On the beginnings of a cohesive self. The Psychoanalytic Study of the Child, 26, 316–354.

Winnicott, D.W. (1956/1958) Primary maternal preoccupation. Through Paediatrics to Psychoanalysis. New York: Basic Books

Winnicott, D.W. (1956/1958). The antisocial tendency. Through Paediatrics to Psychoanalysis. New York: Basic Books.

Winnicott, D.W. (1956/1958). The capacity to be alone. The Maturational Process and the Facilitating Environment (pp. 29–36). New York: International University Press.

Winnicott, D.W. (1986). Holding and Interpretation. London: Hogarth Press.

Glossary

Acting out

An unconsciously employed process of diverting potentially overwhelming thoughts or feelings into active behavior as a means of avoiding their conscious awareness and the debilitating anxiety associated with such awareness. A psychoanalytic defense mechanism.

Adaptive failure

An effort to respond to the demands of the environment that proves ineffective.

Affective disorder

Mental illness associated with poor regulation of emotions, generally involving either depression or unduly elevated mood. When associated with swings in mood it is often referred to as a cyclic or bipolar affective disorder.

Anxiety

Both a psychological and physiological response to a sense of threat that readies the individual for defensive reaction. This response occurs within a gradient between simple heightened alertness and the primitive fight-or-flight response.

Attunement

Intuitive awareness of another's motivation, needs, thoughts and feelings.

Cognitive ability

The mental processes associated with problem-solving and memory.

Dissociation

An unconsciously employed process entailing the disconnection between one's conscious awareness of both the immediate reality and one's internal emotional state. A psychoanalytic defense mechanism.

Emotional regulation

The process of managing or modulating emotional reactions.

Empathic miss

An ineffective effort at attunement.

Empathy

Understanding so innate that the feelings, thoughts and motivation of another are readily comprehended.

Fight or flight

The extreme end of the anxiety reaction. A state in which all psychological and physiological resources are channeled toward self-preservation, resulting in powerful, often primitive behaviors organized around either an aggressive or avoidance response to perceived threat.

Internalization

The process of transforming a value, belief or relationship such that it is experienced by the individual as a core aspect of self.

Narcissism

An unconscious psychological process involving the establishment of a grandiose sense of self as a means of avoiding anxiety-producing underlying feelings of inadequacy and vulnerability.

Narcissistic injury

An experience of failure, criticism or rejection which threatens one's narcissism or defended sense of grandiosity.

Neurocognitive

Pertaining to an individual's biologically based capacity for the mental processes associated with problem-solving and memory.

Object relations

A psychodynamic branch of psychology focused on the way in which relationships are formed and used.

Optimal frustration

A concept from Self Psychology concerning the developmental importance of caretaking in a manner which does not consistently over- or under-challenge a child's adaptive skills.

Psychodynamic

Pertaining to an understanding of motivation, thought and emotion based upon the interaction between conscious and unconscious factors within the individual.

Psychological defense

An unconsciously employed strategy to manage or avoid potentially debilitating anxiety.

Psychosis

A profound breakdown in the capacity to discern reality accurately.

Psychotic-like

A circumscribed or limited aspect of functioning characterized by a near-psychotic level of confusion.

Suicidal ideation

Thoughts, often obsessive in nature, concerning suicide.

Temperament

An individual's innate style or pattern of perception and reaction.

Table of Figures

About the Author

John Stewart, Ph.D. is a licensed psychologist, nationally certified school psychologist and has over 20 years of experience working with behaviorally handicapped children in rural and urban public schools. At present he serves as clinical director of Hastings Clinical Associates, clinical director of the Maine Special Education / Mental Health Collaborative, training supervisor for the Department of Psychiatry - Child Psychiatry Residency at Maine Medical Center and as a consultant to many public-school systems. In addition to Dr. Stewart's role as a training and clinical consultant, he maintains an active private practice, providing psychological services to children, adolescents, adults and families.

Dr. Stewart welcomes feedback and may be contacted at jstewart@server.nlbbs.com or Hastings Clinical Associates, P.O. Box 884, Gorham, ME 04038-0884.

JESSE YATES

Acknowledgments

This project began in 1992 at Indiana University as a dissertation idea. I walked into the office of a new faculty member I had never met and babbled something about my unfocused desire to write about water, the West, and literature. After we talked for a while, he leaned back in his chair and said: "It sounds like you're interested in water as a privileged signifier." "Yes," I thought. "Yes, that's it exactly." Cary Wolfe was that faculty member, and he proved equally instrumental at every phase of this project, lending erudition, support, and mentoring. Lee Sterrenburg directed the dissertation. Through his guidance, the project took form and came into its own as scholarship. Scott Sanders and James Justus also helped me refine my ideas into a workable thesis.

Many other people and entities bear prominent mention. I am grateful to the Indiana University School of Public and Environmental Affairs, which supported my graduate work though my degree was in English; to Dan Willard, my advisor at SPEA, who cheerfully believed in my work and in me before I gave him reason to do so; and to the National Endowment for the Humanities, which gave me a summer fellowship to work with N. Katherine Hayles—a privilege beyond reckoning. A number of my colleagues at the NEH seminar also offered invaluable guidance and criticism. I single out for special mention Stephanie Strickland and Joe Tabbi, whose insights and criticisms pushed me to say what I meant and to have what I meant to say mean something. I am also very grateful to Rob Dawson, whose photographs lend meaning to my words, no doubt because they say more about the region than words ever could. In addition, Julie Anderson spent many a precious summertime hour in the University of California, Berkeley, library sifting through photographs and helping me choose the images that enrich this book. Others deserving of special mention include J. D. Scrimgeour, Arthur Haubenstock, Carol Mitchell, and Ann Ronald, who gave generously of their time and insight. In addition, the chapters on Steinbeck and Abbey have appeared in different forms in *Papers on Langauge and Literature* and *ISLE,* respectively, and I am grateful to those journals for allowing their reproduction here.

I turn now to my loved ones. I come from a family of writers and editors. My brother Lenny and my parents Ike and Tobby Cassuto have been invaluable to this project. Each of them read, critiqued, and read again; never doubting but always questioning. My mother, a historian, also lent me her formidable research skills as well as her enthusiasm. There are no words for the kind of thankful I am.

Finally, my dear one, Elizabeth Downes, gets her own paragraph. It is not just for the clarity and incisiveness of her criticism and the generosity of spirit with which she offers it, but also for all the other things that, in attempting to describe, I could never do justice. Through two books now, she has been there for me in every possible way. During the home stretch of this one, she also carried our beautiful son, Jesse, to term.

I am many times blessed.

Contents

Introduction

Touch water and you touch everything.
John Gunther

More than any other single characteristic, aridity defines the American West. It has shaped the land west of the hundredth meridian, the components of the social contract enacted among its inhabitants, and the compact between the inhabitants and the land.[1] Water's scarcity and its biologically critical function have also molded the regional literature. Using novels by Mary Austin (*The Ford*, 1917), John Steinbeck (*The Grapes of Wrath*, 1939), Edward Abbey (*The Monkey Wrench Gang*, 1975), and Barbara Kingsolver (*Animal Dreams*, 1990) this study aims to demonstrate how the myths pervading the regional literature interact with the myths that shape water policy, each helping to create the other, and both growing out of a limiting material condition.

The tensions and contradictions presented by these four novels underscore the compelling need for an ecocritique of the cultural symbiosis that exists between literature and politics. They further show that the need becomes especially urgent with regard to western water issues. *Dripping Dry* has two overarching aims: (1) to demonstrate the relationship between literature and politics with respect to the myth structure and policy choices involving water use in the West; and (2) to document the social consequences resulting from that relationship. More specifically, *Dripping Dry* focuses on the implications—both literary and ecological—of the Reclamation myth in the American West, as well as that of Restoration, its recent ideological rival.[2] A third myth, that of Sustainability, is explored in the concluding chapter.

Taken together, Austin, Steinbeck, Abbey, and Kingsolver traverse almost the entire twentieth century and therefore the entire Reclamation era (beginning in 1902, with the establishment of the Bureau of

Reclamation, and lasting till the present). Their works offer distinct versions of the conflict between the creations of an expanding, hydraulic
society (i.e., dams, reservoirs, and other diversionary structures as well
as energy and technology-intensive factory farm apparatuses) and the
ecological realities of an arid region. In *The Ford,* Austin fictionalized
the appropriation of the Owens River by Los Angeles, an event that
came to symbolize the monopolistic water-grabbing that typified the
Reclamation era. The novels of Steinbeck and Abbey explicitly participate in the dialogue over the efficacy of Reclamation policies. Kingsolver's integration of ecofeminism and Native American spirituality
represents a compelling attempt to create a new vocabulary and system
to supplant the extractive paradigm.

Examined collectively, the four works present a composite portrait of
Reclamation. And Reclamation, I will argue, is one of the most important
cultural and ecological phenomena in this nation's history. Born of the
desire to graft the American yeoman ideal onto a sere western landscape,
Reclamation eventually took on a life of its own. The supposed beneficiaries of massive water diversion projects became secondary to the projects
themselves as a need for Reclamation for its own sake became ingrained
in the national consciousness. Today, as the Reclamation era draws to an
end, it leaves a cultural and ecological legacy that, for better or for worse,
will remain with us for centuries.

Reclamation implies prior ownership (the root word is "*reclaim*") and, in
this context, also suggests a time when the land and its inhabitants
enjoyed bountiful water resources rather than a water-scarce desert
ecosystem. The underlying metaphor posits a contest between the forces
of nature that illicitly appropriated the West's water, and human ingenuity, which seeks to reclaim it. John Wesley Powell, principal architect of
the notion of Reclamation, spoke of "rescuing" and "redeeming" western
rivers. Maintaining that "conquered rivers are better servants than wild
clouds," he stressed the necessity of an ongoing war with the West's river
systems ("Irrigable Lands" 767) and counseled that, for the arid lands,
irrigation is "an absolute condition of continued prosperity" (776).

But Powell also advocated a pragmatic approach to irrigation that acknowledged the innate aridity of the western lands and the high cost of hydraulic projects. This cautious aspect of his philosophy was lost in the flood of enthusiasm for reclaiming the desert and making it bloom. By the turn of the century, the conservationist dogma propounded by the Roosevelt administration proclaimed that all the nation's assets (including the "reclaimed" West) should and could be put to human use. Americans fell back upon the rhetorical principles of their Puritan forebears, embracing Cotton Mather's doctrine, "That which is not useful, is vicious."

Mather's aphorism was reworked for the twentieth century by Gifford Pinchot, architect of the philosophy of conservation propounded by the Roosevelt administration. Pinchot advocated judicious stewardship of natural resources and attention to ecological realities, but only so that humans might better regulate nature and shape it to their aims. "The first duty of the human race is to control the earth it lives on," Pinchot declared (qtd. in Evernden 131). The central tenet of conservationism and its accompanying progressive ethic lay in the greatest good for the greatest number. Natural resources could and should maximize benefit to the populace.[3] Though mining and forestry also posed major concerns, water's use and control reigned as the West's most important issue. Powell's assessment of the region's hydrology, as well as his recommendations for the development of the land, forced decisions about the allocation and conservation of water resources.

Paramount among the desert's uses was, of course, enabling human habitability. Standards of comfort and habitability that depended on the climate and geography of the eastern United States were grafted on to the West. The idea that the arid region could be redesigned to meet eastern expectations of beauty and utility became an integral component of American myth.[4] It spurred the construction of many ecologically destructive dams and agricultural policies as its adherents strove to create a neo-Baconian Eden in a region with an average annual rainfall of less than twenty inches.[5]

By contrast, Restoration, a comparative newcomer to American mythology, looks to reconstruct ecosystems rather than subordinate them to human aims. As Carolyn Merchant describes it,

Rather than taking nature apart and simplifying ecosystems . . .
restorationists are actively putting it back together. Rather than analyzing nature for the sake of dominating and controlling it, restorationists are synthesizing it for the sake of living symbiotically within
the whole. (*Revolutions* 268)

In the West, Restoration would involve returning the arid lands to their
predam, preagribusiness condition—a presumed steady-state, ecological
economy in which the region's scant hydraulic wealth is liberated.

Despite its ecofriendly veneer, Restoration, like Reclamation, raises
serious land-use dilemmas. The realities of an urban nation, an expanding population, and an extractive economy combine with the ever-present western aridity to make Restoration seem quixotic and unproductive.
Though small-scale restoration efforts—like reforesting a clear-cut or
replanting a prairie—are often both successful and popular, it nevertheless remains true that, as a large-scale management strategy, Restoration
has little chance of success. For example, Edward Abbey's ideal of independent agrarian communities subsisting in a restored desert landscape
(discussed in chapter 4) appears unrealizable in the absence of a wholesale social and technological revolution. Some critics argue that this grail-
oriented ecology impedes a more effective, practical approach.[6]

History has also shown that in regions where irrigation fuels agriculture, hydraulic empires are virtually inevitable. If so, Restoration seems
even more untenable and Reclamation unavoidable. In many ways,
Reclamation is merely a new word for an old phenomenon—an irriga-
tion-based society run by the educationally and economically privileged.
The ancient Nile civilizations, Chinese dynasties, Mayan civilizations,
and others were dominated by elite groups capable of building and
affording water delivery mechanisms.[7] The water they provided, like the
capital they generated, flowed toward the rich and powerful. In the
United States, reclamationists used the rhetoric of Jeffersonian yeomanism to disguise the gestation of a similar hydraulic regime.

While Abbey's bioregionalist, agrarian vision of Restoration may seem
impractical, Restoration as a concept enjoys widening acceptance. This is
understandable. A philosophy that hearkens to an identifiable past (the
pre-Reclamation era) appears more inherently reasonable than one that

conjures a fictional past (West as Eden) in order to justify an untenable future. Resource managers throughout the country have also begun to ally themselves with Restoration. Around the nation a number of rivers have made incremental headway in what will undoubtedly be a long and arduous struggle against an entrenched ideology and the results of its reign.[8]

Though encouraging, these gains cannot offset the continuing degradation of rivers and arid ecosystems in the name of Reclamation and western tradition. Recovering ecosystems are local phenomena, whereas the ideology of exploitation and hydrological mismanagement is national in scope. Any long-term solution to the West's ecological dilemma must be able to differentiate effectively between local and national problems and respond accordingly.

Furthermore, though the concept of Restoration is facially more reasonable than Reclamation, it lacks internal coherence. Restoring an ecosystem means returning it to a prior state, yet there is no one premodern ecological ideal. Ecosystems are in constant flux; their resiliency depends on their responsiveness to environmental disturbance. Therefore, there can be no one ideal state. Deprived of this imagined optimal prior circumstance, the concept of Restoration loses referentiality. Attempting to return an ecosystem to an idealized static condition has more to do with human cultural preferences than with the region's ecological health. William Jordan portrays restoration as means of achieving a harmonic relationship with a particular landscape (see Wilson 114–15). Unfortunately, as the Reclamation era has made clear, a perceived harmony with one's surroundings does not necessarily dovetail with the long-term health of the region.

The central issue for those seeking an ecologically acceptable alternative to Reclamation or Restoration must be the development of a rhetoric capable of expressing a nonexploitative but realistic relationship with nature. Given Reclamation's entrenchment and its historically powerful grip on the American Puritan imagination, the task seems especially difficult. Literature has played a key role in the creation and expression of the Reclamation era, and it must, I believe, play a similarly important role in the transition to a new era of Sustainability. *Dripping Dry* represents my attempt to aid in that transition.

Few would contest that our cultural conception of nature is a linguistic construct. By the same token, few would deny that nature exists independently of language. In discussing the relationship of facts to science, Alan Gross argues that "brute facts themselves mean nothing; only statements have meaning, and of the truth of those statements we must be persuaded" (4). The same could be said of our relationship with nature. Our surroundings exist, but they gain meaning only through their connection with us. And that connection is subject to constant reevaluation and scrutiny.

Yet nature becomes accessible only through socially and culturally specific languages, codes, and disciplines. Throughout this study, I make use of a double perspective, relying both on science-based ecological history and theory, and several schools of cultural criticism, including Marxism and ecofeminism.

In the concluding two chapters I also apply systems theory to the literature and ecology of the West, using its principles to illuminate problems born of the Reclamation era, and to explore possible solutions. In the final chapter, I argue that environmentalism, which has long lacked a satisfactory definition, needs to be redefined and resituated within the context of modern electronic culture. In many ways, environmentalism resembles a colossal hypertext—disparate causes linked by cybernetic bonds that gain meaning and influence through unity. The hypertext analogy allows me to negotiate the shifting terrain of a partially constructivist, partially objectivist vision of nature while enabling environmentalism to avoid solipsism and remain flexible, practical, and accessible.

Though literary and social theory figure prominently throughout this book, the final two chapters are more overtly theoretical than those preceding. That shift occurs for several reasons. The first four chapters trace the Reclamation era from its inception through the recent past (*The Monkey Wrench Gang*, published in 1975, frames chapter 4). That emphasis on the past enables me to draw upon a rich body of history and literature to illuminate and explain the ideas advanced in those chapters. The present and future—the focus of chapters 5 and 6—allow no such luxury.[9] Attempts to contextualize the present and shape the future require a certain level of abstraction—as would any endeavor treating matters that have not yet occurred with methods that do not yet exist.

Only the future can bring the present into relief, even as the future is itself a product of the present.

American civilization, particularly in the West, stands poised on the brink of an ecologically driven paradigm shift. Though the idea of an Eden in the desert and the rhetoric of Reclamation have lost much of their luster we have yet to craft sustainable alternatives. That task must fall to theory. Theory, however, must build on history and literature, and this book's structure represents my attempt to do just that. The ideas presented in the final two chapters are the culmination of the previous four and, I believe, reward the effort expended in their reading.

Envisioning a sustainable post-Reclamation reality in the West necessitates a radical reformulation of humanity's relationship with nature. Defining and creating nature has been and remains one of the central tasks of myth, and myth is of course a product of human thought and language. Both the Reclamation and Restoration myths attempt to build a cultural conception of nature sympathetic to their respective imperatives. Reclamation posits a national need to implement the American Dream. Like Restoration and multitudinous other land-use strategies, Reclamation offers a vision of nature that is both biological and historical. This is myth not in the sense of fable, but as an interpretive system that claims value neutrality while providing cultural legitimation for an ideological agenda. The myth of the West as Eden, better known as the myth of the garden, wherein there is bounteous water to meet every human need, exemplifies this phenomenon.

There are, Roland Barthes argues, three ways of reading myth (*Mythologies* 129). If I see a picture of the Hoover Dam and decide it is a symbol of American ingenuity and technological supremacy, then I am acting as a producer. If I believe the Hoover Dam does not just represent American technological supremacy, but *is* that supremacy, then I am a reader, accepting without question the union of symbol and signifier. Lastly, if I decipher the work of the producer by divining that a human agent decided what the dam symbolized in order to further a specific agenda, then I am a mythologist. Throughout the history and literature of the West, examples of the first two ways of reading myth abound. *Dripping Dry* implements the third mode, deciphering the myths of Reclamation and Restoration and then offering an alternative, Sustainability, in their stead.

This task looms difficult, both because of the size and complexity of the region and because nature continues to evolve and create itself, a process involving language, ideology, and the land. Analyzing their interaction requires an awareness of both the ideological forces at play and of the field on which they are playing. Neither semiotics nor science alone can solve our ecological crisis. Consequently, linguistic and science-based approaches function here as complements rather than opponents. I hope that a deeper acquaintance with the history of the West and its hydrological difficulties will better enable us to construct a new rhetoric of ecology and thereby locate and sustain sources of ecological renewal.

1

The Birth of the Hydraulic Conflict

Where agriculture is dependent on an artificial supply
of water, and there is more land than can be served by
the water, values inhere in the water, not in the land;
the land without the water is without value.
—John Wesley Powell

In the eighteenth and nineteenth centuries, the American West changed
slowly from a wilderness on the nation's edge to an integral component of
the national consciousness. The journals and writings of explorers like
Lewis and Clark and Zebulon Pike gave shape to a land previously
unknown, while their descriptions led to policy decisions, migration, and
further exploration.[1] Later, with the frontier closed and the nation committed to large-scale development of the West, policies arose that
ignored ecological realities in favor of jingoistic Americana designed to
propagate the notion of the West as Eden. Wishful thinking, coupled
with a desire to remake the landscape in the image of human needs and
wants, led to what Henry Nash Smith labeled the "Myth of the Garden."
That which was not already Edenic would soon become so through
human ingenuity and American perspicacity.

Imagining the land as virgin and Edenic ignored the geographical
realities of a large indigenous population and a varied terrain and climate. Westward expansion, rather than puncturing these myths, fueled
an extraordinary campaign to remake the wilderness in the image of that
mythic landscape.[2] Ralph Waldo Emerson, echoing the national ethos of
the mid–nineteenth century, counseled "action proportioned to nature."
What nature does not yield freely, humanity should refashion to better
suit human needs. This transformative relationship with nature harmo-
nized, in Emerson's view, with nature's status as the ultimate commodity. Humans fulfill their destiny through working the land and forcing
ever-greater harvests. In a section in *Nature* aptly entitled "Commod-

ity," Emerson maintains that nature has no greater purpose than to serve "Man." And Man has no greater purpose than to work the land and take his place in the productive cycle: "A man is fed not that he may be fed but that he may work" (*Selections* 26). Emerson's views were and continue to be widely shared. The policies born of such views have led to ecosystemic catastrophe, the full implications of which are yet to be felt. The bulk of the damage occurred during the twentieth century as technological innovations permitted greater and greater short-term dominance over the land.

The Roots of Reclamation

The Bureau of Reclamation was born in 1902 to bring water wherever it was required. The impetus for reclamation lay in its ties to yeomanism, a concept whose roots lay in Thomas Jefferson's vision of the United States as an agrarian democracy. Jefferson's dream of a nation of independent farmers living off of the land captured the popular imagination. With western expansion, that dream grew more enticing still. However, implementing it in the arid West proved impossible without technological intervention. Providing water to sustain both the myth of the garden and the settlers who came West believing in that myth became the task of the Bureau of Reclamation. After a shaky beginning, the bureau quickly grew powerful, and it, possibly more than any other human contrivance, shaped the geography of the West. Consequently, the years from 1902 through the present (although the bureau's power has waned considerably in recent years) have come to be known as the Reclamation era.

The Reclamation era refers to a time of unprecedented development fueled by previously unthinkable hydraulic projects. Reclamation projects grew steadily more ambitious as the century progressed, hitting full stride between the 1930s and 1960s, but maintaining a frenetic pace into the 1980s.[3] Marc Reisner has termed the halcyon days of reclamation the "Go-Go Years." During those years, water projects sprouted like mushrooms throughout the arid lands.

Massive dams and diversion projects brought water to areas once considered irredeemably dry. Hoover, Shasta, Bonneville, and Glen Canyon Dams, among others, stand as monuments both to hydraulic engineering and to the Bureau of Reclamation's deep pockets. Enormous amounts of water suddenly became available for use, leading to the misconception that there was abundant water. The newfound ability to extract water from previously inaccessible or impractical sources was misrecognized as the ability to create a water supply.

Actually, the surge in development resulted in *less* water because the reservoirs in the desert exposed thousands of acres of increased surface area to the sun's rays, dramatically increasing evaporation. Increased agriculture also caused large amounts of water to percolate into the ground rather than return to the rivers. Nevertheless, the myth of the garden thrived, unfettered by empiricism. As Mark Seltzer observes, "Nothing typifies the American sense of identity more than the love of nature (nature's nation) except perhaps the love of technology (made in America)" (3).

The Bureau of Reclamation was a predictable outgrowth of a nation "accustomed to plenty and impatient with restrictions." Americans chose to deny aridity's existence for a while and then, when that was no longer possible, to "engineer it out of existence or to adapt to it" (Stegner, *Bluebird* 75). The latter choice was anathema, while the former strategy has ruled the West for much of its history.

In the mid–nineteenth century, advocates of western settlement insisted that "rain would follow the plow." According to this theory, Americans needed but to move west and till the land; rain would fall as a direct consequence of their labors.[4] By the 1880s, this notion had fallen into disfavor, but not before many settlers, lured by the vision of hydrological abundance, homesteaded the arid region.

The most ardent proponent of the rain-follows-the-plow credo was William Gilpin, first territorial governor of Colorado (1861–62) and indefatigable apologist for the Plains. He viewed the arid lands "through a blaze of mystical fervor," envisioning the Southwest as a bountiful paradise that awaited only the human touch to yield unimaginable bounty (Stegner, *Meridian* 2). Gilpin trumpeted manifest destiny and the boundless munificence of the West in books with grandiose titles including *The Mission of the North American People* and *The Continental Railway, Compacting and Fusing Together All the World's Continents.*

Gilpin words were buttressed by his considerable personal credibility. He had fought with the Missouri Volunteers against the Mexicans in 1846 and later joined expeditions against the Comanche and Pawnee tribes. At the time of his appointment as governor of Colorado, Gilpin had been serving as a volunteer bodyguard to President Lincoln. His reputation as an intrepid western explorer and soldier coupled with his political connections lent great weight to his words in both government and civilian circles.

In Gilpin's view, the West possessed a virtually limitless ability to sustain ever-growing numbers of immigrants in affluence and comfort. Since one needed only to turn over the soil in a western homestead for the heavens to release the requisite moisture for agriculture, the Mississippi River basin alone could, according to Gilpin, house 1,310,000,000 people. The Plains loomed even more sylvan and grandiose: "The PLAINS are not *deserts,* but the OPPOSITE," he proclaimed. They formed "the cardinal basis of [a] future empire" (*Mission* 66). In Gilpin's eyes, the western United States contained a reservoir of resources, including land, water, and precious metals (especially gold) that would readily yield to the energy and ingenuity of American pioneers. Gilpin's panegyrics of the West and his pseudoscientific explanations for the region's alleged munificence were not unique.[5] His views came to prominence in the 1860s, but they built on an already well established tradition of western self-promotion.

Thomas Hart Benton, senator from Missouri, had originally believed that the Plains could best serve the nation as a conduit to the West Coast and then to India. Later, as he became convinced of the ability of the railroads to open the region to commerce and settlement, Benton began trumpeting the region as a bucolic paradise. Speaking in Boston in 1854, Benton described Kansas as "rich like Egypt and tempting as Egypt would be if raised above the slimy flood, waved into gentle undulations, variegated with groves and meadows [and] sprinkled with streams" ("Discourse" 4).

Benton's rhetoric, coming as it did from a Southerner, was matched exclamation for exclamation by Northern free-staters like Charles Boynton and T. B. Mason. They proclaimed that the Kansas landscape contained "many scenes that can scarcely be *remembered* without tears. The soul melts in the presence of the wonderful workmanship of God" (qtd. in Emmons 14). Such paeans to the majesty and fertility of the region reflect more than simple optimism and a willingness to overlook obvious geographical traits. At the time, the North and South were locked in a high-stakes battle for social and political dominance of the Plains.

The Kansas-Nebraska Act of 1854 allowed residents of those territories to choose their status as either free or slave states. The balance of power in the nation, held uneasily in place by the Missouri Compromise (1820–21), stood ready to shift. In the North, the prospect of slavery in the Plains meant the imminent demise of the yeoman farmer. Slaveholders would occupy vast tracts and work them cheaply with slave labor. Independent yeomen would be excluded from the best land, their voices silenced by the economic might of the Southerners. Such a fate would be "a gross violation of a sacred pledge, . . . an atrocious plot" aimed at the heart of the yeoman ideal (Charles Sumner and Salmon Chase, qtd. in Emmons 12).

The enactment of the Homestead Act of 1862, which deeded 160 acres to anyone willing to settle and work the land in the West, marked an enormous victory for Lincoln's Republican party over the proslavery forces of the South. The Southern plantation system required large amounts of land, often exceeding 1,000 acres, to function profitably. Strict acreage limits on homestead properties meant that slaveholders would have great difficulty gaining a foothold in the Plains. That handicap effectively eliminated the South from further participation in American westward expansion.

The next challenge facing the Republicans lay in finding people willing to move west. Likely candidates included poor people in the eastern United States and in Europe—people who would be enticed by the promise of free land and a new start. Principal responsibility for the campaign to entice immigrants to the West fell to the railroads. While westward migration served the interests of a young nation with an expanding population and a vision of manifest destiny, it also benefited the emergent transcontinental railroad. By the mid–nineteenth century, these congruent interests formed the basis of a potent alliance.

The federal government ceded vast tracts of land to the railroads to open up the West, facilitate trade, and generally strengthen the nation. In return, the railroads marketed the land and promoted settlement. Railroad officials took to their task with an enthusiasm that bespoke the enormous profits they stood to reap from increased western settlement. Promoters (called "boomers") circulated literature proclaiming the Plains an agricultural mecca. One pamphlet even insisted that "mud in the usual sense . . . is almost wholly unknown in Nebraska" (qtd. in Baltensperger 58).[6]

The boomers' unbridled enthusiasm and their willingness to stretch the truth are reminiscent of the campaign by the Associated Farmers in the 1920s and 1930s to lure Dust Bowl refugees to California. In each instance, propagandists used the symbol of the yeoman farm and the promise of an agricultural paradise to lure people to a region that little resembled their descriptions. In the Plains, the railroads and the federal government stood to gain from increased immigration to the region but cared little what befell the immigrants once they arrived. In California, corporate growers already controlled the land and water and were merely looking for a new workforce to exploit. The common denominator in the two examples is a widespread reliance on the myth of an Edenic garden on the nation's frontier coupled with an unwavering faith in manifest destiny.

The notion of a camouflaged Eden with no historical link to European traditions permitted Americans to reincarnate themselves in a "virgin land."[7] The rugged new continent, rather than representing a continuation of European cultural hegemony, offered a singular destiny for those brave enough to seize it. Without an acknowledged history, America offered a new beginning wherein land and settler could merge into a single entity and recover—through diligence, husbandry, and mettle—the lost paradise of Eden.

Myra Jehlen argues that this vision embodied the American tendency to merge selfhood into a collective national ideal while preserving a uniqueness defined by one's own relationship to the land. Settlers inscribed their own identity on to the tabula rasa of the new continent, using its wildness as a means to self-discovery. Only through subduing the wilderness, however, could the new nation take shape and thereby confer a national identity on to its citizens. The result was a land-based Hegelian opposition; civilization and wilderness formed one thesis and antithesis, and humans and nature were another. Each half of the opposition provided the other's "cathartic," and provided the means to "the emergence of the single and unchanging truth" (82).

For nineteenth-century settlers in the West, the opposition lay in the juxtaposition of aridity with the Jeffersonian yeoman ideal. Their synthesis created the "truth" of the yeoman plains farmer. Rather than abandoning the myth of the garden in the face of looming ecological realities, Americans chose to redesign the land and carve a garden out of the desert.

In the twentieth century, the vision of the family farm transplanted to the arid lands served as the Bureau of Reclamation's raison d'être and a convenient propaganda tool for corporate capitalism, as agribusiness interests sought and gained control over much of the region's land and water. The resulting tension between societal myth and social and ecological realities infuses the regional literature. Understanding the complex interweaving of policy and fiction surrounding water and its appropriation requires that we first survey the historical underpinnings and embedded myths of the Reclamation era.

Powell and His Legacy

John Wesley Powell (1834–1902), a major in the Union army who lost an arm at Shiloh, went on to become one of the most important figures in the history of western exploration. Self-educated as both a geologist and anthropologist, Powell led a survey team through the previously unexplored Colorado River canyons in 1869. He and his eight companions were the first white people and perhaps the first of any race to successfully traverse the entire treacherous length of the Grand Canyon. Their success carried a heavy cost. Three members of the expedition died.

They also lost three of their four boats and most of their supplies. Their journey took them through previously uncharted terrain, and their courage in the face of the unknown and amid bone-crushing rapids turned them into national heroes. Powell also viewed the journey as a scientific expedition; he took measurements as carefully as he could and sought to tie his observations to a larger geological survey of the region.

During the expeditions, Powell and his crew gave names to the formations and canyons they encountered.[8] Their sense of wonder and reverence for the terrain—captured in names like Marble, Glen, and Music Canyons, Bright Angel Falls and Rainbow Bridge—gave a shape to this canyon country that most of the East Coast–based population had never seen. The fame Powell garnered from his journey, in concert with his ferocious work ethic, helped him rise through the ranks of government to wield enormous power in western land and water issues. As head of what later became the federal Irrigation Survey, Powell's efforts led to the mapping of much of the West.

After an initial rise to prominence, though, Powell's views fell into disrepute in Washington, and his reputation suffered. His fall from grace stemmed primarily from differences with powerful western senators over matters pertaining to land and water appropriations.[9] However, his reputation was rehabilitated in the early twentieth century, as conservationists selectively adopted his ideas. In a sense, the entire Reclamation era owes itself to Powell, although he probably would not have wished credit for much of it.

Powell's 1878 *Report on the Lands of the Arid Region of the United States* was a revolutionary document. Ignored at first, and then selectively implemented, the report may well be the most important document in the history of American land use. It offers the first comprehensive management strategy that acknowledges the region's ecological parameters. One of Powell's first tasks in the treatise was to debunk the notion that rain follows the plow, a theory for which he had little patience:

> [T]he operations of man on the surface of the earth are so trivial that the conditions which they produce are of minute effect, and in presence of the grand effects of nature escape discernment. Thus, the alleged causes for the increase of rainfall fail. (*Report* 91)

He further rejected the quixotic faith in technology that would supposedly create a new Eden in the desert. Instead, he proposed a system whereby the federal government would regulate the distribution of land and the construction of water projects so as to allow individual settlers to profit from the national trust. Noting that "all the great values of this territory have ultimately to be measured . . . in acre feet"[10] (qtd. in Stegner, *Meridian* 315), Powell urged that the current 160-acre homestead allotment be abandoned and that tracts be instead allocated according to their water rights.

Irrigated farms with guaranteed sources of water could produce crops even more reliably than farms in the humid regions that depended on rainfall. An arid-lands farmer with access to a reliable water source could therefore live comfortably on fewer acres. Powell proposed an 80-acre limit for irrigated quadrants. Nonirrigated tracts, depending on their location, could graze cattle or other livestock, but would need considerably more land to do so. He consequently suggested that nonirrigated pasturage farms contain 2,560 acres, that rangeland not be fenced so that livestock could graze communally, and that the vast western lands be treated as a sort of a commons (*Report* 22–23). The cumulative effect of these policies would have been dramatic. Not only would they have drastically curtailed land monopolies, but the precedent of adapting human use to ecosystemic parameters would have become a matter of law.

Perhaps more importantly, *Lands of the Arid Region* advances the idea of government control over water distribution. Yeoman farmers could not possibly finance the massive diversion projects required to bring water to many sites. Left to their own devices, they would have to either sell out or purchase water from those wealthy enough to construct delivery devices. Water monopolies would inevitably result from such an arrangement, to the impoverishment of small farmers.

> If the water rights fell into the hands of irrigating companies and the lands into the hands of individual farmers, the farmers will then be dependent upon the stock companies, and eventually the monopoly of water rights will be an intolerable burden to the people. (41)

Powell displayed an uncanny prescience in his admonition against the monopolization of water rights and in his vision of its effects on western lands and people. He anticipated the enthusiasm for unchecked development and took the unpopular stance of advocating prudence and regulation:

> [I]f in the eagerness for present development, a land and water system shall grow up in which the practical control of agriculture shall fall into the hands of water companies, evils will result therefrom that generations may not be able to correct, and the very men who are now lauded as benefactors to the country will, in the ungovernable reaction which is sure to come, be denounced as oppressors of the people. (41)

Powell was, in effect, proposing a hydraulic welfare state in the West, an idea wholly counter to the popular notions of rugged individualism and hydroabundance, as well as the designs of the hydraulic empire builders whose power and interests were already well entrenched.[11]

Virtually all of Powell's proposals died in Congress, victims of "the myth-bound West which insisted on running into the future like a streetcar on a gravel road" (Stegner, *Meridian* 338). Several decades later, at the end of the nineteenth century, a prolonged drought belatedly convinced legislators to revisit many of Powell's recommendations. Powell died in 1902, the same year that the passage of the Newlands Act paid posthumous tribute to his notion of a government-controlled hydraulic infrastructure by creating the Bureau of Reclamation. Powell, legislators admitted, was right; without government intervention, water monopolies would control what little water became available while other, larger projects would never come to pass due to lack of funding.

With the creation of reclamation districts and federal control over water distribution, legislators believed the aridity dilemma solved. They ignored Powell's warnings that the land-parceling system also badly needed reform. Without a revised system of land management, however, government subsidization of water projects during the first quarter of the twentieth century simply helped entrench corporate control of the region's water. Small farmers still could not compete with large landowners when both benefited from water subsidies. Factory farming gained strength in the West, and a mutually profitable relationship arose between the bureau and wealthy agribusinesses. The repercussions—

both human and ecological—of this relationship become glaringly apparent in the 1930s when the black blizzards and the Dust Bowl hit the Plains.

The Bureau of Reclamation justified its existence and its unprecedented power to shape the landscape by building dams and canals that generated hydroelectricity, provided nominal aid to small farmers, and watered the fields of the agribusiness giants. The incredible flurry of dam building that took place between the 1930s and the early 1980s left the country with over one hundred thousand dams. Most of the dams were built either by the bureau or by the Army Corps of Engineers. During this era, the Army Corps of Engineers and the Bureau of Reclamation pursued an expensive rivalry, attempting to one-up each other by building bigger and more expensive dams.

Whereas the Army Corps of Engineers' ostensible justification lay in its stated mission of flood control, the bureau relied on the yeoman ideal and the myth of the garden to justify its actions. The bureau's dams purported to make the desert bloom, thus enabling rugged individualists to wrest their livings from the land. That scenario was, of course, woefully inaccurate. Corporations, not individual farmers, were the primary beneficiaries of the bureau's largesse, and, despite the bureau's herculean efforts at reclamation, the total irrigated area in the West remains to this day smaller than the state of Ohio.[12]

In the 1950s, even as dam construction in the United States was reaching its zenith, a new doctrine of environmentalism, specifically the concept of Restoration, began to compete with the conservation rhetoric of the Bureau of Reclamation. In the postatomic era, faith in technology as the panacea for all of humanity's problems began to ebb. Though it continued building dams and diversion projects at a ferocious pace, the bureau also suffered several high-profile setbacks. Proposed dams in Dinosaur National Monument and the Grand Canyon met with ferocious public resistance and were shelved. Critics of reclamation projects cited human comfort as but one of many considerations in the land-use debate. The value of rivers and watersheds as something more than fodder for fields, faucets, and turbines demanded consideration. In addition, the fiction of limitless water began to fray.

The problems arose because policymakers had ignored a crucial component of Powell's management philosophy—the need to work within the region's hydrological boundaries. The Bureau of Reclamation and its allies maintained that technological advances made natural characteristics all but irrelevant to policy decisions. Powell, they claimed, would have agreed. Much of the rampant development wrought throughout the West during the twentieth century supposedly bore Powell's imprimatur. On the other side of the issue have been those who opposed the projects, also claiming Powell's posthumous approbation by pointing to his pragmatism and strident opposition to water and land monopolies.

The central symbol of the contemporary tug-of-war over Powell's postobituary blessing is Lake Powell, the massive reservoir created by the damming of the Colorado at Glen Canyon in 1963. Powell had given Glen Canyon its name during his explorations of the Colorado and had rhapsodized about the region's incredible beauty. The bureau then gave Powell's name to the reservoir that flooded the canyon, contending that Powell would have been pleased because the dam supplied hydroelectric power to a large area while also providing irrigation benefits. In addition, the dam made the unflooded parts of the canyon more accessible, thereby serving the greatest number.

Critics of the dam argue that Powell would have blanched at the tremendous waste of resources that the dam incurred as well as at the destruction of what many believe had been the most beautiful canyon system in the country. Evaporation losses from the reservoir amount to millions of acre-feet per year; irrigation benefits from the dam are comparatively minimal, and the precious silt carried by the Colorado—silt that provides fertility as well as a buttress against downstream bank erosion—backs up behind the dam, where it serves no use.

In the aggregate, Powell's writings and life's work suggest that he would have likely deemed the Glen Canyon Dam a waste of precious resources as well as a violation of the Bureau of Reclamation's stated mission. Furthermore, Powell understood better than many of his more educated descendants the importance of thinking in terms of entire watersheds rather than small sections of rivers. Glen Canyon Dam causes significant harm to downstream ecosystems, while providing incommensurate gain to its beneficiaries. For that reason also, Powell would not have endorsed it. Still, the dam's very existence, as well as the increased settlement of the Four Corners region, endorses the populist agenda that Powell championed. It would seem that Powell's vision, like the West's geography, inspires great passion while remaining eminently mutable.

Western Water Law

Over the course of its settlement, the West has variously been labeled the Great American Desert, the Promised Land, a worthless terrain, and the garden of the world. Ultimately, one's perception of the region hinges on the availability of water, which determines whether one can survive and how well. Water's primacy as both commodity and cultural sign in the Southwest arose on this foundation of scarcity and utility.[13] Its biotically privileged place in the culture predates its commodification, but the two traits have long been inseparable in the history and mythology of the American West.

The power to control water carries with it the power to control life And by "life," I refer not just to existence, but also to *quality* of life. Many of the features that define the "good life" require water and revolve around its distribution and control. In addition, since water is necessary to human biological function, in an arid region a dominant state apparatus would need to expend relatively little effort to transform water into a commodity whose scarcity privileged the water as well as its controllers. That scarcity would boost water's exchange value, leading to intensified symbolic value. Symbolic value imparts power and wealth and thereby privileges its possessor. In this sense, water becomes not just a measure of economic value, but a culturally privileged signifier as well.

Water's emergent status as commodity and signifier of wealth and expanding capabilities forced an important shift in garden mythology. The Newlands Act amounted to an implicit acknowledgment of water's scarcity as well as the limited productive capabilities of the land. Such an admission also involved conceding the limitations of the nation and its people: a prospect that remained anathema to a culture steeped in the dominant myths. Jehlen notes that "the conviction that farming brought reason and nature together (since man and nature had the same reasons)

inspired cultivation . . . but made it particularly difficult, in fact, contra-
dictory to contemplate basic changes in agrarian policy" (73). Instead of
abandoning the American Dream, the dream itself shifted focus. The
myth of the garden remained intact, but its ideal evolved from a Xanadu
to a neo-Baconian Atlantis that no longer awaited manna from heaven,
but wrested it instead from the grips of Nature.

The evolution of western water law offers an interesting perspective
on the West's adaptation to water's scarcity. Water law in the eastern
United States is based on riparian rights and evolved from the common
law of England. In general, riparian water rights allow anyone owning
property bordering a watercourse to make reasonable use of its water as
long as that use does not interfere with the reasonable uses of other riparian landowners. In the East, where water is abundant, the reasonable-use
doctrine emerged as workable and fair.[14] Twenty-nine states continue to
adhere to riparianism today.

In the West, however, riparianism proved untenable. During the
time of rapid westward expansion in the nineteenth century, demand for
water, especially for mining, far surpassed supply. Miners faced a dual
dilemma. First, the riparian system restricted water use to those who
owned land bordering streams, while the demand for water often lay
elsewhere. Second, most of the land in the West was owned by the
United States. Miners, though squatting on the land with the tacit
approval of the federal government, were technically still trespassers and
could not acquire riparian rights.

In the face of these restrictions, rules for allocating water developed
in the mining camps and gradually spread throughout the West. These
rules were similar to those for establishing and protecting mining claims.
The first user of water from a specific source held a right to that water
that was superior to all subsequent claims. As long as that claimant made
"beneficial use" of the diverted water within a reasonable time, s/he held
the water right in perpetuity.[15] The federal government recognized the
validity of this system of allocation in early mining acts and later in the
Desert Lands Act of 1877. Thus developed the doctrine of *prior appropriation* and its credo of "First in time, first in right." Prior appropriation
dominates western water law to this day.[16]

The Jeffersonian ideal could not survive unscathed in a region of intense competition for water, a region growing ever more beholden to agrocapitalism. Farmers had to seek profit rather than subsistence, a process that in turn impelled them to place more and more land under plow. They also needed to irrigate. Except for those lucky few whose acreage bordered a water source, irrigation required diversionary structures and a water right. Neither came cheap. The Homestead Act of 1862, instead of providing land for small farmers and encouraging the yeoman ideal, facilitated speculation, corporate land grabs, and water monopolies.

The Homestead Act had originally provided for 160 acres of land for all eligible applicants. In 1909, the realities of "dry farming" impelled Congress to pass the Enlarged Homestead Act, doubling the amount of land available to settlers. Neither act accomplished its goal of making small parcels available to underfinanced settlers. Nor was either parcel big enough, without an accompanying water right, to allow settlers to compete with large, well-financed agribusiness interests, many of whom had entrenched themselves in the West with the unintended aid of the earlier Homestead Act, as well as the Desert Lands Act.[17]

Technological advances in farming techniques meant greater yields, which translated to greater supply and lower-priced goods. The arrival of the tractor and the one-way disk plow in the early twentieth century ushered in an era of unprecedented agricultural productivity. In 1830, it took fifty-eight person-hours of work to bring an acre of wheat to the granary. By 1930, in parts of the Great Plains, that number had been reduced to three (Worster, *Dust Bowl* 90–91). Even as increased productivity meant greater supply and falling profit margins, the price of the machines that enabled that productivity continued to rise. Farmers found themselves putting more and more land under plow just to maintain their current income level. Many fell into debt, which in turn forced them to plant still more, ensnaring them in an increasing cycle of debt and ecological degradation that eventually led to the Dust Bowl of the 1930s. Small farmers could not compete; their debt burden soared, and more land and water fell into the hands of corporate interests, where it has since remained.

Four Visions of Water and the West

The chapters that follow divide the Reclamation era into four segments and examine each through the lens of a particular work of fiction. The four authors treated—Austin, Steinbeck, Abbey, and Kingsolver—all concern themselves deeply with ecological and human issues regarding land and water in the West.

Mary Austin found herself caught between her nascent environmentalism and love of the desert (visible throughout her canon and particularly in such works as *Land of Little Rain*), and her allegiance to conservationist dogma. *The Ford* offers an excellent look at the tensions between ecological awareness and an extractive economy. It is a roman à clef, a fictionalized version of Los Angeles's illicit appropriation of the Owens River from the Owens Valley in northeastern California, that portrays the conflict between urban and rural interpretations of conservation. Underlying the conflict is the ideological gulf separating proponents of rural agriculture from those who favored an increasingly urban western landscape.

Austin lived in the Owens Valley at the time of the controversy and decried the "theft" of the water and the disregard for the land's integrity that such a maneuver entailed. Yet she fully supported the valley inhabitants' desire to dam the river for agricultural purposes. The conflict, as Austin saw it, lay in which use of the land and water was more ethical (within the ethical system that created the myth of the garden), not whether the ecosystem ought to be left intact. The collision between Austin's protoenvironmentalism and her allegiance to the Pinchot-derived progressive agenda demonstrates the lack of coherent alternatives within an extractive relationship with nature. Her dilemma effectively exposes the inchoate glimmerings of environmentalism amid the emerging juggernaut of the Reclamation era. Those who might have resisted the Bureau of Reclamation's rise to power lacked the vocabulary with which to question its conservation rhetoric.[18]

Eventually, the bureau came to dictate who would share in the hydraulic wealth that it alone was capable of distributing. Water's utility (use value) and its status as a commodity (exchange value) became ineluctably linked as the economy of the West swelled through its newfound water wealth. When its use and exchange value merged, water truly became the region's privileged sign, thereby allowing the bureau to secure its dominance in the West.

The events depicted in *The Ford,* both historical and fictional, serve as an excellent foreground to the ensuing discussion of *The Grapes of Wrath.* By the 1930s, the Bureau of Reclamation enjoyed virtually unquestioned authority and an unlimited budget for water projects in the West. That the primary benefactors of the bureau's engineering feats were corporate interests caused little stir in Washington or in state governments. Nevertheless, the impact of the boom in settlement and cultivation in the arid regions and the trend toward ecologically harmful factory-farming techniques soon made itself felt in the form of the Dust Bowl and in the human catastrophe of the subsequent mass migration to California. *The Grapes of Wrath* uniquely captures the magnitude and scope of this tragedy.

Throughout the novel, water serves as a privileged sign whose power is directly linked to its absence. Water is visible (or rather, invisible) in the drought that led to the Dust Bowl, the Joad family's cross-country pilgrimage, and in the family's frantic laboring during California's dry season to escape the starvation and poverty that would accompany the coming rains.

Unlike *The Ford* (1917), which had little measurable impact on the controversy it depicted, *The Grapes of Wrath* (1939) became a powerful force for social change. Much as Powell's *Explorations of the Colorado River* (1875) offered Americans their first glimpse of the canyonlands, Steinbeck's novel provided many with their first glimpse of the scope of the Dust Bowl and of the mistreatment of migrant workers.

Primarily as a result of the attention focused on the situation by *The Grapes of Wrath,* as well as several other contemporary works, officials at both the state and federal levels took their first tentative steps toward land-use reform and migrant worker protection. These steps marked the first significant national stirrings of discontent about the water and land-use policies emerging from the Reclamation era.

That discontent later grows into full-scale rebellion, as evidenced by Edward Abbey's advocacy of "ecotage," or environmental sabotage, to bring the Reclamation era to an end. *The Monkey Wrench Gang* (1975) not only examines the ramifications of contemporary western water policy, but also champions its demise. To Abbey, the Glen Canyon Dam exemplifies the cycle of what I call *faux potlatch* (see chap. 4), carried on by development interests with the aid and complicity of the government. Rather than reenacting the original Native American potlatch—which involves the large-scale accumulation of resources in order that they might be ritually expended—agribusinesses enjoy a corrupted version of the potlatch that is endemic to capitalism. Southwestern faux potlatchers amass huge quantities of the region's most precious resource (water) and then waste it in a manner calculated to incur maximum personal gain. This cycle is visible in the widespread cultivation of water-intensive crops (alfalfa, cotton, rice) and cattle raising in the West accomplished with subsidized water from oversubscribed rivers.

The agribusiness consortia learned that the road to greater government subsidy lay in expending as much water as possible through maximizing their cultivation of ecologically untenable crops and livestock. Western irrigation and reclamation projects spiraled out of control, freed of any obligation to justify themselves or their cost. The irrigation program envisioned by Powell had morphed into a hydraulic juggernaut that was growing steadily more powerful and impervious to criticism.

Abbey attacks the ideology and mechanisms of the Reclamation era, offering rough-hewn solutions born of anarchist leanings. In his view, the gang's mission to destroy the Glen Canyon Dam is moral within an ethical system defined not by Reclamation ideology, but by allegiance to the principles of the land ethic: "A thing is right when it tends to preserve the integrity, stability, and beauty of the biotic community. It is wrong when it tends otherwise" (Leopold 262).[19] Out of this ethos sprang ecotage—acts of sabotage committed to prevent environmental destruction. Earth-First! (whose symbol is the monkey wrench), Greenpeace Action, and other radical environmental groups owe much to Abbey's popularizing of the notion of ecodefense.

The Monkey Wrench Gang's assault on the ideology and mechanisms of Reclamation invites a discussion of alternatives to that ideology and the feasibility of their implementation. Barbara Kingsolver's *Animal Dreams* (1990) attempts to construct just such a scenario, and the novel's successes and stumbles provide an intriguing window onto an inarticulable future. Contemporary definitions of environment derive from the communicative mechanism of a system dedicated to extraction. *Animal Dreams* presents an attempt to supplant the dominant system (and discourse) with one privileging a steady-state society. Kingsolver advocates a worldview based on organicist ecofeminism and Native American ecospirituality instead of the mechanistic, patriarchal science that has caused what Carolyn Merchant calls the "death of nature."

Systems theory posits that environmental problems do not exist until they generate communication within the system. Environmental disturbances (resonance) are relevant in direct proportion to the systemic reaction (communication) they engender. In Niklas Luhmann's view, "Fish or humans may die because swimming in the seas and rivers has become unhealthy," but so long as this "is not the subject of communication it has no special effect" (*Communication* 29). In other words, until it is articulated, a disturbance, no matter how ecologically significant, will not affect the system. It follows, then, that if communication about a disturbance can be suppressed (i.e., through lack of language to describe it), the system's functioning will continue unimpaired.

The residents of Kingsolver's fictional town of Grace, Arizona, already have little capacity for resonance because their status as a Hispanic/Native American traditional community with a strong female presence leaves them with little social or economic clout. Interestingly, while the novel's protagonist spearheads the grassroots resistance that succeeds in stopping the destruction of the all-important river running through Grace, the town's environmental victory gets subordinated to her romantic reawakening. The novel's denouement downplays the ecosystem and instead stresses the successful reproduction of community.

At novel's end we are left with a term, *environment*, without a consensus definition. Uncertainty about the meaning of environment throws notions of ecology into flux and opens the way for a new rhetoric of environmentalism more sympathetic to alternative ideological and economic systems. Creating that new lexicon is crucial; without it, environmentalists can react to new antienvironmental initiatives but cannot propose workable alternatives to the status quo. However, the status quo is not acceptable; it privileges extraction and profit over ecological and social health. Environmentalists thus find themselves in the unenviable position of having to fight to maintain an unacceptable state of affairs because they cannot articulate any satisfactory alternatives.

Dripping Dry's concluding chapter discusses the long-term implications of this linguistic gulf. I believe our current ecological dilemma offers the potential for an exciting synthesis of science-based approaches to ecological management and language-based, theoretical methods. Neither strategy functions alone; each helps shape the other. Together they create the myth system that defines social and ecological realities.

Tellingly, the three key words informing this study and pervading the western hydrological morass all lack coherent definitions. *Reclamation,* as noted earlier, implies an imaginary previous time of hydraulic wealth and human dominion. *Restoration* is equally nonreferential. Making things how they were is neither possible nor productive. The arid lands evolved from a pre-Pleistocene sea and that process of gradual change will never cease. Ecosystems are always in flux; therein lies their ability to adapt and withstand disturbance. Indeed, the stability of the desert ecosystem—as with any ecosystem—lies in its evolution. Finally, *environment,* like *nature,* remains one of the most elastic words in the language. Its definition reflects its usage, which in turn reflects the needs and ideology of the user.

Defining these terms will only become more problematic as the ordering systems we use to shape reality gain complexity. Our society's escalating reliance on cybernetics and information theory make attempts to draw boundaries around the self or language increasingly quixotic. Using an approach that might be called historicist constructivism, but which I prefer to call *linked causes,* I suggest that we abandon the losing battle against complexity and instead seek to make the language and practice of ecosystem management reflect the infinite possibilities of existence.

2

River Wars: Los Angeles, the Owens Valley, and Mary Austin's *The Ford*

> But we have yet to mention the chief blessing of arid-
> ity. This is the fact that it compels the use of irrigation.
> And irrigation is a miracle.
> —William Smythe, *The Conquest of Arid America*

Lesta V. Parker, a longtime resident of the Owens Valley, wrote the following letter to President Roosevelt around 1905 (I quote it with spelling and punctuation intact).

Pres. Theodore Roosevelt
Washington D.C.

Dear Friend:

Look on your map of California, along the Eastern boundary south of Lake Tahoe and you will find a county named "Inyo." Running onto this county from Nevada through a small corner of Mono Co. you will see the Carson and Colorado R.R. which after it enters Inyo follows along the Owens River until they both come to Owens Lake, an alkaline body of water. It is about his river that I write to you.

This river after it leaves the narrow mountain canon, runs through a broad and fertile valley for over a hundred miles. The first 20 miles of which is all or nearly so, in cultivation. . . . Indeed the people are very very proud of their little valley and what their hard labor has made it. The towns are all kept up by the surrounding farms. Alfalfa is the principle crop. . . . Cattle raising is a great industry.

There has never been any capitolist or rich people come here until lately and all the farms of the Owens Valley show the hard labor and toil of people who came here without much more than their clothes. . . . Now my real reason for writeing this is to tell you that some rich men got the government or "Uncle Sam" to hire a man named J. B. Lippancott to repersent to the people that was going to put a large damm in what is known as Long Valley. . . . Imagine the shock the people felt when they learned when Uncle Sam was paying Mr. Lippancott he was a traitor to the people and was working for a millionaire company. The real reason for so much work was because a man named Eaton and a few more equally low, sneaking rich men wanted to get controlling interest of the water by buying out a few or all of those who owned *much* water and simply "Freeze Out" those who hadn't much and tell them to "Git."

Now as President of the U.S. do you think that it is right? . . . Is there no way to keep the capitolist from forcing people to give up their water right and letting the now beautiful alfalfa fields dry up and return to a barren desert waist? . . . As you have proven to be the president for the people and not the rich I, an old resident who was raised here, appeal to you for help and *Advice* . . .

So Help The People of Owens Valley!

I apeal to you in the name of the Flag, the Glorious Stars and Stripes,

Yours Unto Eternity,
Lesta V. Parker

(Qtd. in Walton 147)

Parker emphasizes the valley residents' pioneer, yeoman traditions, their work ethic, and the progress they had made carving an Eden out of the desert. Cattle raising occupied a central, honored place in the valley's lifestyle, and the alfalfa that supported it was grown on irrigated land. Lionizing these traits despite their water-intensive character buttressed the myth of the garden. Parker's plea, as well as those of her neighbors, failed in this case to sway the state or federal government primarily because it could not subsume the perceived greater good of urban expansion. Nevertheless, allegiance to the traditional western values espoused by Parker helped fuel the engine of Reclamation that drove the West for most of the twentieth century.

This chapter examines the early collision between rural and urban values and its implications for the Reclamation era. The conflict over the

Owens River embodies many of the underlying tensions of the time. Both sides (valley residents and officials of Los Angeles) wished to divert the river's water without regard for the potential ecological consequences. Each side also claimed allegiance to the American Dream. Despite promises of unlimited water and lip service to yeoman ideals, there was, in fact, limited water and strong sympathy for urban expansion. Preaching political progressivism, cities began asserting claims to the hydraulic wealth made available through reclamation. Rural agricultural regions vehemently opposed such claims.

The Ford, as a representative literary text of the period, demonstrates how the two sides attempted to exploit the myths that had become woven into policy. Owens Valley residents portrayed themselves as quintessential yeoman pioneers who were settling the West and making the desert bloom. Los Angeles, meanwhile, viewed itself as the next phase in the West's evolution. Los Angeleños claimed that the primitive pioneers must make way for the modern city, with its growing population and burgeoning water needs. The depiction of this conflict in *The Ford* highlights not just the regional collision of rural and urban values, but also Austin's own struggle to balance fealty to "western" ideals of reclamation and irrigation with her own environmental ethics. Much of Austin's writing (including several passages in *The Ford*) suggest what later came to be known as ecofeminism. Some of the novel's structural difficulties stem from Austin's inability to align her proto-ecofeminism with the Owens Valley's wholehearted embrace of Reclamation.

The Ford, both by itself and in the context of Austin's entire canon, provides an excellent opportunity to view the ongoing tension underlying Reclamation. As Austin declared in *Cactus Thorn,* "It's really a question of water. When you have water, you can have anything you want. Anything" (5). Both sides in the Owens Valley struggle looked to utilize all available water to fuel their production-oriented local economies. Their dispute lay less in ideology than in methodology. None of the participants questioned the efficacy of a spiraling dependence on a resource already in short supply, nor did they question the ideology underlying the term *resource.*[1] That debate had to wait for the middle of the century, when ecology came of age as a science and "environmentalism" in the spirit of John Muir gained newfound political strength.

Neither the novel nor the fundamental questions it raises can be adequately studied without some familiarity with the history of the valley and its hydrology. This chapter therefore begins with an overview of the region's larger social and political history and the rise of its conflict with Los Angeles. It then turns to *The Ford,* viewing it as an avatar of the regional conflict and of the unresolved political, philosophical, and ethical issues underlying that conflict.

A Valley Gone Dry

The passage of the Newlands (Reclamation) Act in 1902 instigated an era of unprecedented hydraulic expansion in the West. The prospect of federal subsidy for irrigation projects opened up enormous possibilities for agriculture, while the likelihood of increased availability of water also brought about exponential urban growth. Shortly after the act's passage, residents of the Owens Valley began angling for the creation of a federal reclamation district that would enable them to dam the Owens River and use the stored water for agriculture. As things stood, many of the valley's crops depended on the caprice of the weather. Meanwhile, the Owens River, fed by the runoff in the High Sierra, ran unused into the sea. Periods of sparse rainfall—typical for desert ecosystems—were common, while farmers and ranchers daily gambled their livelihoods on the chance of rain.

Reclamation districts seemed the perfect poultice for this chronic threat to farmers' livelihoods. With the prospect of government subsidies for large-scale water projects, horizons for agriculture and human settlement expanded commensurately. The Owens Valley seemed an ideal candidate for federal intervention since it possessed a large, underutilized river and a growing agricultural community. Advocates of the proposed reclamation district stressed the valley's frontier conditions and their own pioneer values, thus demonstrating hardship and the need for federal aid coupled with a commitment to hard work and the American Dream. In addition, their already substantial agricultural achievements (the valley was a productive, food-growing region) indicated a solid potential return on any investment in the valley's hydraulic infrastructure. That prospect underscored the region's compatibility with the Reclamation Act's aim of efficient growth.

Owens Valley residents were naturally very excited when a man named J. B. Lippincott arrived in 1904, seemingly under the auspices of the federal government, and began surveying the valley's hydrology. Lippincott had been an engineer on John Wesley Powell's Irrigation Survey and currently worked as a survey engineer for the Bureau of Reclamation. Unbeknownst to those in the valley, however, Lippincott also worked for the Los Angeles Department of Water and Power. Coincident with Lippincott's arrival, another man, Fred Eaton, appeared and began purchasing options on local ranches at prices considerably higher than market value. Eaton, a former mayor of Los Angeles, claimed he wanted to go into cattle ranching but could not decide where. He often let options expire while purchasing others at equally high prices. Valley dwellers were delighted to be making what seemed like easy money while awaiting the creation of their reclamation district.

Their contentment was short-lived. Lippincott turned out to be acting not in his capacity as reclamation engineer, but rather as agent for Los Angeles. Eaton, meanwhile, knowing of the city's plans for the river, had been purchasing options on those ranches with the best water rights. He planned to buy the ranches cheap from valley residents and then sell the water rights to the city at inflated prices. With all this transpiring in the valley, city officials (including Lippincott) had also been quietly lobbying the federal government to table the notion of a reclamation district and support the city's plan for the water instead.

In 1905, the *Los Angeles Times* broke the story beneath a headline replete with historical irony: "TITANIC PROJECT TO GIVE CITY A RIVER." The city government soon released details of its plan to build an aqueduct that would divert the Owens River to the city's reservoirs. Lippincott's services on the city's behalf earned him a "commission" of twenty-five hundred dollars—more than half his annual salary.[2]

Los Angeles officials had argued that the water could be put to better use by the city than by residents of the Owens Valley, and the federal government eventually agreed. With the completion of the Los Angeles–Owens Valley aqueduct in 1913, the Owens River vanished, and with it went the valley's agricultural base. Formerly irrigated pasturelands reverted to desert. It was just this specter of redesertification that valley dwellers had used to lobby against the aqueduct (Walton 145). To them, allowing a "reclaimed" agricultural region to return to desert ran counter to all logic and was tantamount to lunacy. Cedric Belfrage, in a novel of the Owens Valley entitled *The Promised Land,* highlights the insanity of such a policy: "I'd like to know . . . what kind of country this is. You work all your goddamned life to make a home in a goddamned wilderness, and then a few bastards . . . can come along and turn it back into a wilderness again and call it progress" (58). In the eyes of many westerners, diverting water from agriculture to urban expansion amounted to a capitulation to nature—an admission of insufficient water to fuel infinite growth. Federal and city authorities skirted this inconsistency in the myth structure by diverting what water there was to the supposed infinite expansion of Los Angeles. Allocating federal hydrodollars to one region rather than another thus became a matter of preference rather than exigency. Indeed, optimism regarding the city's continued development was what fueled the Owens River's appropriation in the first place.

At the time of the aqueduct's construction, Los Angeles had more than enough water to meet its needs. However, its population more than tripled in the 1880s and tripled again between 1900 and 1910. The city's campaign for the aqueduct arose from "a need founded in prospect" (Hundley, *Thirst* 152).[3] Planning for L.A.'s ascendancy permitted officials to view constraints on further water projects as economic (i.e., there was not enough federal money to finance both the valley's reclamation and the city's growth) rather than hydraulic.

Owens residents, outraged at what they perceived as the city's subterfuge, campaigned vigorously to revive the now moribund reclamation district. Their protests worked to little avail. President Roosevelt declared that "this [water] is more valuable to the people as a whole if used by the city than if used by the people of the Owens Valley" (qtd. in Walton 150). This concept of the greatest good for the greatest number underlay both the Reclamation myth and the production-oriented economy.

Garrett Hardin's seminal essay "The Tragedy of the Commons" refutes the logic of the greatest good for the greatest number, arguing that simultaneously maximizing for the greatest good and the greatest number is mathematically impossible. He uses the example of an unfenced cow pasture to show that as long as the net gain to a farmer of adding a cow is larger than the net loss of others adding cows—net gain is, in this case plus one cow, while the net loss is a fraction of the commons area—farmers will always seek to maximize their gains until the commons is destroyed. In using this example, Hardin undermines a proposal of Powell's, which advocates unfenced common pasturelands as a key to judicious land management (see chapter 1).[4]

Despite its logical problems, the principle of making the best use of available resources formed the plinth of the American conservationist movement as designed by Pinchot. Pinchot's maxim, "There are two things in the world: human beings and natural resources," plainly states his allegiance to the concept of human control and domination of nature. Conservation, as designed by Pinchot and espoused by Roosevelt, aimed to "control nature and serve the material interest of humankind but with an eye to long term needs" (Nash, *Rights* 9).

The Roosevelt administration believed that diverting the Owens River to Los Angeles would serve the long-term needs of a greater number of people. John Walton argues that the change in allegiance at the federal level from pioneer communities to larger urban developments reveals an important shift in policy. That shift reflected the new realities of a nation with a closed frontier. Pioneer society had initially benefited from the federal emphasis on conquering and developing the West. During the progressive era, however, federal priorities shifted to urbanization. In the Owens Valley, "this second phase . . . was as traumatic as the first, but its victims were now its former agents" (Walton 194).

The "theft" or appropriation of the Owens River to slake Los Angeles's growing thirst signaled a clear victory for the forces of progressivism.[5] Farmers and ranchers in the Owens Valley clamored that their livelihoods were being sacrificed at the altar of urban sprawl. City officials and media, meanwhile, depicted valley dwellers as ignorant bumpkins standing in the way of progress.[6] Valley residents felt betrayed; they had believed themselves the beneficiaries of a soon-to-be declared federal reclamation district that was to have turned the valley into an agricultural paradise. Instead, city agents duped them through a series of questionable dealings.

The aqueduct went on line on November 5, 1913, despite the concerted efforts of the local populace (including acts of sabotage—arguably the first organized acts of environmental sabotage or "ecotage" in the nation's history).[7] The Owens River disappeared from the valley, flowing instead into the faucets and lawns of Los Angeleños.[8] In the Owens Valley, sagebrush displaced alfalfa. Dust storms became common because the topsoil, first anchored by desert flora and then uprooted and planted over with crops, no longer had any anchor against the driving wind. These same conditions—land reverting to desert amid dust storms and disappearing topsoil—recurred a generation later slightly further east, causing the Dust Bowl.

Whereas the Dust Bowl that tormented the Plains states resulted from decades of land abuse and the looming dominance of factory farming (see chap. 3), the Owens Valley had not been long enough under the yoke of industrial agriculture for that to have caused its ecosystemic woes. Instead, its hydrology had been sacrificed to the ecology of the city. Residents of Los Angeles, meanwhile, dwelling in a city in the desert, not only felt the biological need for water, but also sought its power and wealth-signifying allure.

It bears reiterating that neither the city nor the valley was motivated by "environmental" concerns in the sense in which that term is used today. Each side saw the valley's water as a resource and source of potential wealth. Residents of the Owens Valley had no objection to the construction of a large diversionary structure that would forever alter the course of the river. They simply wanted a share in the economic windfall such a structure would create.[9] The restorationist grail of a precapitalist Eden would not become a factor in the land-use debate until the latter half of the century. For the moment, the conflict lay in the imminent unseating of agriculture as the federal favorite son.

Despite a continued allegiance to the yeoman ideal (as evidenced by the passage of the Newlands Act), a community could not ensure its status as federal beneficiary simply by virtue of a functioning agricultural apparatus. The cultural pull of the yeoman ideal and the myth of the garden remained formidable, but reclamation decisions were ultimately matters of monetary appropriation. And monetary decisions are rarely determined by sentiment. As Raymond Williams notes, decisions concerning the fate of competing urban and rural interests are the province of a powerful minority who control capital and determine its use according to calculations of profit (295).

In the Owens Valley, as in the West in general, the locus of the decision-making process lay in the use and control of water. Its dominion dictated not just wealth, but also the prevailing geography of the region. Dams and diversionary projects changed the landscape. Where there was water, there could be food, and people, and all the concomitant changes they brought. In the valley, water also carried the power to decide who would work the land and how.

While the aqueduct's local importance involved control over the Owens River, its national significance lay in the disputants' positioning within the American myth structure. The national resonance of their respective versions of the American Dream determined access to federal largess. The spoils were, of course, hydraulic.[10]

At both the local and national levels, the struggle centered not on what constituted a resource, but rather on who controlled it and how best to use it. Any unexploited resource was "wasted," subject to claim by any one with the gumption to put it to use. This was especially true of water. To have access to water and not use it for personal gain denoted irresponsibility, making the water right subject to forfeit. This ideological underpinning for what amounted to a contest over a capital asset underscores what Jean Baudrillard, among others, cites as an egregious flaw in economic systems driven by the forces of production. To unthinkingly link humans with their capacity for production without first interrogating the motives for producing or the need to produce omits a crucial step in the socioeconomic analysis. That omission undermines both Marxism and capitalism alike.

Baudrillard believes that the Marxist ideal of "transforming nature according to human ends" shares a fundamental misassumption with capitalism. Both systems attach a perceived good to labor power. Marxism posits that workers are alienated by the sale of their labor power, whereas capitalism celebrates the benefits gained through its sale. Neither scheme allows for the more radical hypothesis that workers might be alienated *as* labor power and that transforming nature may not be a worthwhile goal (Baudrillard, *Mirror* 31). It matters little whether workers become alienated from the products of their labor and demeaned by forced participation in a system based on exchange value (as with capitalism) or are "liberated" from the wage-labor cycle yet subjugated by a system that measures human worth in productive capacity and output (as in Marxism). Under either regime, workers remain indentured to ever greater output and technological domination of nature.

This ever-worsening inequality among humans and between humans is evident in an increasing dependence on technology. Will Wright maintains that this prevailing obsession with technological domination and extractive methodology underscores a fundamental incoherence in a science-based cosmology. A society that characterizes technological advance as anything contributing to economic or personal short-term gain ignores the larger issues of sustainability and availability of supply (35). In theory, nature can always yield more. Relying on nature's unlimited productive capacity relegates concerns over ecology or supply to the realm of the technological.

It is precisely this allegiance to the exploitation of nature and to the human role as agent of production that Baudrillard cites as a central problem within the human condition. The Owens Valley conflict exemplifies the dueling agendas that characterize this mind-set. Los Angeles sought to fuel an ecologically unsustainable rate of urban development whereas the people of the Owens Valley looked to build an agricultural apparatus that would facilitate their participation in an ecologically devastating factory farm economy.[11] Both sides ignored long-term consequences, preferring to focus on the illusory surplus created by increased extraction of finite water resources.

Throughout the West, tremendous amounts of engineering know-how and capital went into maintaining the fiction that the water supply would never diminish as long as technology continued to improve the means of diversion and delivery. Fictions such as these arise from science's ability to place itself above those who would question its motives. By claiming objectivity, science appears to strip itself of ideology. Scientific actions that bolster the extant social structure attain a cloak of impartiality that immunizes them from social critique. This guise of objectivity perpetuates ecological devastation in the name of technological advance.[12]

"Good science," according to Wright, aspires to long-term ecological stability rather than short-term extractive gain: "The idea of rationality is about sustainability. . . . [I]ts inherent social criteria are the criteria of ecological coherence and reflexive evaluation, the criteria of legitimating sustainable institutions" (154). Just because technology enables the exploitation of a given resource does not necessitate or legitimate such a move. Technology is an agent of the status quo, producing tools that serve the needs of those in power. In a profit-driven economy, a project that does not enrich its sponsors is a bad investment, regardless of its ecological beneficence. As Andre Gorz notes, "Windmills . . . lost out because wind is everywhere, they couldn't be monopolized" (61).

In the West, technology permitted the proliferation of water-intensive developments despite their incompatibility with the region's hydroregime. Its scarcity combined with its biologically necessary role combined to make water the linchpin of the region's economy. Its exchange value became its defining characteristic, while the myth of water's abundance and the technology surrounding its procurement magnified the power struggle over its control.

An economic system dedicated to ever-increasing extraction makes humans and nature adversaries despite their being biologically intertwined. Such a system is illogical. According to Baudrillard, "What man gives of his body in labor is never given or lost or rendered by nature in a reciprocal way. Labor only arms to 'make' nature 'yield'" (*Mirror* 44).

This notion of a yielding (albeit indentured) landscape fits neatly with the feminization of nature that typically accompanies extractive economies and that is integral to the western myth system. Without ample water, reclamation would stall and the desert would remain "barren" and "infertile." This pejorative linking of female imagery (and, consequently, women) to land and to a subservient role in the social system forms part of a strategy of domination. Carolyn Merchant believes it forced both women and nature to become "the locus of the moral law and emotive expression," enabling a "mechanical and moral consciousness" that legitimated exploitative modes of production, reproduction, and ecology (*Revolutions* 232). Extractive technology abounds with sexual imagery, and this too is consonant with the land's dual image of mother and mate. In *The Great Gatsby*, for example, Jay Gatsby's pursuit of

Daisy maps on to the quintessentially American pursuit of "the fresh green breast of the new world." Just as Gatsby sought from Daisy to "suck on the pap of life, gulp down the incomparable milk of wonder," so too had generations of Americans attempted to possess the continent whose "vanished trees . . . had once pandered . . . to the last and greatest of all human dreams" (Fitzgerald 182).[13]

Linking women with the land and classifying both as reproductive agents and tools of the patriarchy allowed their use and abuse in the name of the common good. They become resources, and natural resources are, by definition, national assets. Managers exploit resources for the benefit of the nation. To do otherwise is wasteful. Often, the well-being of an object and the perceived national good come into conflict. Classifying the object (human or otherwise) as a resource negates this potential friction by equating its good with the well-being of those who control it. Just as women were expected to subordinate their needs and desires to the patriarchal ideal, so too did resources lose their individual identity upon becoming linked with the national good.

In the Owens Valley, the problem lay not in a failure to yield, but rather (metaphorically speaking) in a big guy muscling in on a smaller guy's girl. The region's virtue lay helpless before Washington's duplicity and L.A.'s groping embrace. A popular refrain in California opined that "the federal government held the Owens Valley while Los Angeles raped it." This phrase belies a highly important change in attitude, one that shifted the moral grammar of the conflict. Pioneers and yeomen deserved respect, but violated innocents *demanded* justice.

While the feminization of the land and the subjugation of both women and nature had been going on for much of recorded history, the struggle over the Owens River occurred at an important juncture for American geography. The Reclamation era had initiated an exponential increase in settlement west of the hundredth meridian. Shortfalls, corruption, and urban-rural conflicts were the inevitable result. Characteristically, the land, feminized by the language used to describe it, bore the blame for its supposed failure to yield. The land was deemed barren, in need of technological intervention to "restore" it to health. Without human intervention, the fickle land would revert to its previous "unproductive" state.[14]

As westerners strove to portray their respective regions as most congruent with the national vision of progress and the American tradition, Owens Valley residents found themselves hamstrung by a national swing toward urban progressivism. Though reclamation projects were legally required to benefit agriculture and irrigation, the federal government would not allow them to interfere with urban prosperity. In later years, reclamation projects came to dominate the western landscape by providing subsidized water and power to both urban and agricultural centers. These large-scale endeavors came to pass in part because state and federal governments learned from the example of the Owens Valley.

Austin's Ambivalence

Because of its pivotal place in American hydrological development and in California's history, the Owens Valley's tribulations have spawned a number of books, essays, and films (the most popular being the movie *China-town*). I focus here on Mary Austin's *The Ford* for several reasons. The novel sprang from the pen of one of the foremost nature-writers of the time as well as one of the country's first "environmentalists" and "feminists" (though neither term attained its current definition during Austin's lifetime).[15] Austin also lived in the Owens Valley during the period when Los Angeles began its quest for the region's water. In fact, her then-husband, Wallace Austin,[16] donated a water right worth over five thousand dollars to the ad hoc committee in the valley that had organized to fight the aqueduct. His action appears in barely disguised form in *The Ford* (387).

Austin had made her reputation as a "desert rat" and writer of western landscapes. Her earlier and most successful work, *Land of Little Rain* (1903), was a collection of vignettes about the California desert and those who dwell within it. Its evocative descriptions of the landscape and its inhabitants offered an early paean to the notions of environmental protection and limits to growth. Even the book's title suggests nature-imposed parameters on human activity in an arid climate. According to Lois Rudnick, Austin was one of the first to advocate a nonexploitative, harmonious relationship with the land:

Austin . . . opposed the concept of the land as virgin and the Judeo-Christian imprimatur that man must rule, tame and reform "her." . . . That no one had mastered it—indeed that it could not be mastered—was attractive to [someone] seeking to make [an] impact on American literature. . . . Even when envision[ing] the land in specifically female terms, "she" is not typically exploited or exploitable. (11–12)

By the time of *The Ford* (1917), Austin's outlook had changed. Part of the text's forced happy ending involves the victory of Kenneth Brent, protagonist and displaced agrarian, over Old Man Rickart, venture capitalist. The valley's salvation lies, Austin suggests, in the ascendancy of Brent's view that those who work the land have the right to use it however they see fit and are entitled to whatever yield they can coax from it (*Ford* 436). To Austin, the valley's expanding agricultural aspirations were both natural and salubrious to the region's ecology, even if they did not jibe with her overall vision of land use.

The novel opens at the Arroyo Verde [Owens] River with a symbolic baptismal scene involving Kenneth Brent. The landscape is pastoral and, while dangerous (young Kenneth nearly drowns), strongly evokes the bucolic splendor that drew the Brents to the region. Nevertheless, Kenneth's father, Stephen, knows well that the agricultural community of Tierra Longa cannot survive without a dam to divert the river to their fields. To him, a dam is not only necessary, but natural. "Wasting" precious water flouts common sense and nature's will. According to the narrator in *The Ford,* "It was a little river, but swift and full, beginning with the best intentions of turning mills or whirring dynamos, with the happiest possibilities of watering fields and nursing orchards, but discouraged at last by the neglect of man, becoming like all wasted things, a mere pest of mud and malaria" (34). The narrator's claim that rivers (and all other things as well) require human intervention to avoid a sordid and ugly uselessness goes unchallenged despite its apparent incongruity with Austin's oft-stated reverence for nature.

While Austin was able to admonish in *The Land of Little Rain,* "The land will not be lived except in its own fashion" (33), and later (in *Stories from the Country of Lost Borders*) to note, "It takes man to leave unsightly scars upon the face of the earth" (88), she nevertheless felt that certain human uses could and should shape the land. In *Lost Borders* Austin contends,

> It is the proper destiny of every considerable stream in the west to become an irrigating ditch. It would seem that the streams are willing. They go as far as they can, or dare, toward the tillable lands in their own boulder-fenced gullies—but how much farther in the man-made waterways. It is difficult to come into intimate relations with appropriated waters; like very busy people they have no time to reveal themselves. One needs to have known an irrigating ditch when it was a brook and to have lived by it. (123)

Here, Austin displays a marked ambivalence toward the channelization of rivers even while acknowledging it as their destiny. One cannot become familiar with a channelized stream—one needs to have lived by it in its previous incarnation. Yet if the streams' telos is fulfilled, no one will know them. For a desert rat like Austin, such a fate is usually unthinkable. Again, Austin's reluctant progressive bent collides with her nascent ecological worldview.

The result, at least in *The Ford,* is a clear victory for progressivism. Stephen Brent, depicted in the novel as a gentle man of the earth, is also the father of the valley's reclamation project. He adds rhetorical force to his vision by linking it to history and the destiny of the region's inhabitants:

> "Fifty years ago, when my father drove over the Pass, there was this house here and hacienda at Agua Caliente. . . . Even in those days they dreamed of a dam at Indian Gate. . . . Water," he said, "water and power . . . and farms . . . farms, not cities." (361)

Brent's willingness to exploit the land to suit human desires is evident throughout the novel and nowhere more obvious than in the following: "Wherever the land flings a handful of corn we run and scramble for it like beggars in the street. And she laughs—she laughs. I tell you, Burke, we've got to master her—we've got to compel her" (62). This overtly adversarial stance belies Brent's gentle agrarian exterior. "Mastering" and "compelling" the land form the basis of an extractive economy dedicated to development irrespective of ecological parameters—precisely the offenses for which Los Angeles stood accused.

Austin nevertheless characterizes the dispute as one between a business proposition and a way of life (367). She ignores the fact that the
region's desire for a reclamation district stemmed from its residents'
vision of the valley's becoming, through agriculture, a more productive
participant in the nation's extractive economy. Even as Tierra Longa's
inhabitants attempt to distinguish themselves from the faceless capitalist
invasion by trumpeting their traditional values and land use, their
rhetoric betrays them. They envision themselves as true yeomen living
close to, and off of, the land, but they participate in the same extractive
economy as the city they fight.[17]

Their behavior buttresses Baudrillard's contention that the "mirror
of production" allows no other conception of nature than as the dominated other (*Mirror* 58). He argues that humanity is incapable of imagining nature as anything other than a vehicle for human needs. We are
trapped by the constraints of economy and language—neither of which
has the flexibility to shape another way of seeing the nonhuman environment. "Nature is the concept of a dominated essence and nothing else.
. . . And it is by being sublimated and repressed that Nature becomes a
metaphor of freedom and totality. . . . Everything that invokes Nature
invokes the domination of Nature" (55–56). Similarly, even while cele-
brating the unconquerability of the desert, Austin advocates its subjugation and development. She appears to half agree with Powell that human
activity can do no lasting damage to a planet that is so vast and apparently
impervious to harm. Yet in other contexts, Austin decries the "scarring"
that humans wreak upon the earth.

This dichotomy may be a product of its time. In 1878 in *Report on
the Lands of the Arid Region,* Powell could not imagine any human activity that could cause terrestrial harm of any significance. However, by the
time Austin published *The Ford* in 1917, human capacity to cause harm
had grown exponentially. The era of total war had arrived, bringing with
it trench warfare, mustard gas, the machine gun, and aerial bombard-
ment. Technology's capacity to destroy both people and the land was
starkly and permanently revealed.

Austin recognized the revolutionary implications of recent technological breakthroughs but retained a strong allegiance to an earlier time
when the land's permanence provided comfort and certainty. The myth

of the garden played off that ambivalence, offering a seductive fiction that humans could redesign nature and bring the desert to bloom while allowing adherents to believe that their actions did no lasting harm. Thus could Austin advocate the channelization of rivers, secure in the knowledge that the changes were for the good and that the land was too vast and the region too dry for humans to alter it in any significant way.

By contrast, Los Angeles's appropriation of the Owens River qualified, in Austin's view, as wanton environmental destruction and a human tragedy. Late in the novel, when the loss of the river seems a fait accompli, the narrator laments the seeming inevitability of the valley's defeat. Elwood, the fictionalized Fred Eaton character, and the conniving urban capitalism that he represents will ultimately defeat the people of the valley because Elwood represents "progress": "The difference between what they fancied lay behind Elwood's schemes and what . . . was Elwood's likeliest motive, gave to inevitable defeat the quality of ancient tragedy; the tragedy of men defeated, not squalidly by other men, but by forces within themselves which had the form and dignity of gods" (*Ford* 290). Austin implies that the valley residents cannot win because their opponents spring from within some inherently more powerful part of themselves. This is a telling passage; it acknowledges that the same mentality that created the concept of Reclamation created the propensity to urban sprawl as well. The two phenomena are intertwined. Demand for crops comes from those who do not grow them. Nonfarmers tend to live in urban areas, and it is they who provide the market for the crops grown in reclamation districts. The symbiosis would be beneficial for all parties but for the inevitable competition for the region's scarce water. The disparity in water wealth inevitably leads to an inequality in capital accumulation as well.

Earlier in the novel, Austin ironically notes the irresistible allure of "Capital" on the valley dwellers and their steadfast belief that if they too had it, their rural vision would hold sway. The irony, she suggests, lies in their ignorance of the true nature of capital. They cannot control it because capital, like water in the West, flows toward the rich and powerful. One acquires capital by participating in precisely that economic system currently driving the valley to ruin. One cannot be a rich yeoman because one becomes rich on the backs of yeomen.

Austin describes with little sympathy the futile quest for wealth of the men of the valley:

> They must have Capital; and if they did, such was their deep conviction Capital in the end would have them. Capital went about seeking whom it might devour, yet such was their strange illusion about it that they believed that if once they could lay hands on it, Capital could be made to run in their harness, breed in their pastures. To those who owned Capital . . . it ate out of their hand, but its proper nutriment was the contents of poor men's pockets. (*Ford* 95)

The people of the valley believe that they can make capital join nature as a slave to human ambition. Yet Austin harbingers Baudrillard by suggesting that no economic system driven by exchange value can function as anything but an engine of production that will ultimately impoverish the vast majority of its functionaries, including nature. Nonetheless, she makes an impassioned plea not just for the valley's rescue, but also for the establishment of a reclamation district. Austin's dilemma embodies the contradiction at the heart of early-twentieth-century environmentalism. Suspicious though she was of "conservation" as espoused by Pinchot and Roosevelt, Austin could not escape its grasp.

The Ford also draws an interesting parallel between the water war and the petroleum boom that took place roughly conterminously in California at around the turn of the century. As depicted in the novel, venture capitalists first invaded the valley for its oil, making a healthy profit for themselves at the expense of local inhabitants. Then, just as the community began to rally around the notion of a community-based irrigation system, the capitalists reinvaded, seeking to co-opt that resource, too. Water and oil are linked capital assets—commodities whose control carries the power to shape the local geography.[18]

In an economic system designed to allow those with capital to continue amassing more, control over important commodities naturally falls to those in power. Yet, such is the case with the valley's petroleum, with its water soon to follow. Yet, despite the dismal fate suffered by the actual valley, the novel, like most modeled on the Owens Valley, has a happy ending. This dogged optimism, persisting despite the actual loss of the

Owens River, illustrates both the bullish enthusiasm of the Reclamation era and the potency of its accompanying myth system.

In most ways, *The Ford* is a typical melodrama. The Brent family and their neighbors live a debt-ridden but happy existence in the Inyo (Owens) Valley. The only discordant note comes from Marcia Brent, the woman of the house. She longs for the culture and clean floors of city life and considers every day spent in Tierra Longa as another step toward martyrdom. Eventually, after pressuring her husband into an ill-fated oil venture and seeing it fail, Marcia Brent falls ill and dies. Husband and wife share a moment of redemptive bonding right before she goes to her reward. With his wife's death, Stephen Brent's zest for living dies as well. He becomes lethargic and all but unable to care for his two children.

The children mature rapidly. Soon, they are the caregivers. The family continues to scrape a meager living from ranching while gazing covetously at the Arroyo Verde (Owens River) and longing for a dam to divert its waters to their fields. They fantasize about the beautiful landscape that the dam will reclaim for the valley: "Once the gate was shut again by a concrete dam, Tierra Rondo would resume its ancient use as a lake bed for the stored waters of the river, which now ran all at large in a wide shallow forge far seaward, and in wet years mingled its freshness with the tide" (298). The dam is the particular dream of Stephen Brent. His fantasy of a dam in the valley coincides with what Austin suggests is nature's original intent. Building a dam becomes a natural act that will fulfill the thwarted designs of nature. This reasoning allows Austin to skirt the issue of human defilement of the land and instead construct a scenario wherein yeomen like Brent "restore" the land to its intended use. "Restore" thus becomes conflated with "reclaim."

The telos of Reclamation required large-scale dam-building and expenditure of capital and resources to support the fiction of a terrain and climate conducive to agriculture. Austin's attempt to link the concepts of restoration and reclamation indicates a need to rationalize the subjugation of nature. Even she, who loved the desert and its aridity (she wrote lovingly of Death Valley, among other places, in *The Land of Little Rain*), harbored the notion that the West could and should support expanded cattle ranching and agriculture. But, as the true-life Owens Valley example shows, that vision of western life had to contend with the looming specters of the city and venture capitalists. Urban capitalists sought to extract surplus value while ignoring entrenched cultural traditions. Rural people formed easy prey for false promises of wealth and devised schemes to enrich themselves without regard for yeoman traditions.

In Austin's Tierra Longa, the first temptation lies in oil. The petroleum venture fails because Stephen Brent and his partners attempt to lock horns with Old Man Rickart, symbol of corporate capital. Kenneth Brent would later understand the magnitude of his father's error: "He would see in a flash, Rickart and his kind as a work of nature, gigantic, inevitable, like the epoch which stored the oil under Petrolia" (*Ford* 245). Portraying a venture capitalist as a "work of nature" even as he seeks to destroy the valley demonstrates the depth of Austin's ambivalence regarding humanity's role in the biotic economy. Her ambivalence echoes that of Frederick Jackson Turner, whose seminal essay of 1892, "The Significance of the Frontier in American History," sought to situate western expansion within the larger fabric of American culture. Turner argued that the wilderness was necessary to the formation of the American consciousness. Pioneers settled the wilderness, and civilization followed on their heels. The newly civilized society then marginalized pioneer values, causing the pioneers to move west and the cycle to begin anew. In this vision of American culture, pioneers are simultaneously the cutting edge of culture and an anachronism. In many ways, Rickart is a metaphor for Turner's vision of the West's evolution. As a venture capitalist born in Tierra Longo but now allied with the city, Rickart embodies Turner's thesis that pioneers simultaneously represent the apotheosis of the human condition and an intermediate stage in the progression toward an urban existence.

Rickart seems to have an interest in every profit-oriented venture and no compunction about ruining anyone—even friends and neighbors—who interferes with him.

> Lands, water and minerals, he took them up and laid them down again, wholly uninformed of the severances and readjustments made necessary by that temporary possession. . . . [H]e did not know that men are warped by these things and that women died of

them. It was as if a huge bite had been taken out of the round of his capacity, and left him forever and profitably unaware of the human remainder. (176)

Rickart's business savvy and his unconcern for others earn him the grudging admiration of those in the valley. They want to be like him even as he tramples them underfoot. Opposing him in a business venture is the commercial equivalent of defending the Alamo. The valley's population learns this again through Brent's dream of irrigating the area.

Young Kenneth Brent, hoping to learn how to survive in the business world, goes to work for Rickart, while his sister Anne, by far the most intelligent and interesting character in the novel, becomes a real estate broker in the valley. Anne plans to develop the region in the image of her father's dream even as Rickart mounts an underhanded campaign (using Elwood) to garner the valley's water and sell it to Los Angeles. At this point, the novel's plot roughly follows the real-life struggle between the city and the valley. In the novel, Kenneth Brent quits his position with Rickart and dedicates himself to saving the valley. He had inherited his father's passion for reclamation, and the shared commitment between father and son forges an almost transcendental bond between them. Austin suggests it forms a similar bond between them and the land: "the figure of the watery waste spelled much to his father, that in the moments when they faced it together . . . seemed wondrously shared between them" (34).

Kenneth Brent has an epiphany when he realizes that the Rickarts of the world do not share his feeling for the land. The father-son bond of the Brents contrasts with that of the senior and junior Rickarts. The younger Rickart and Kenneth have been friends since childhood, but their respective conceptions of Tierra Longa mirror the differences between yeoman traditions and corporate commerce: "[T]he long, lion-like valley which still held for Kenneth the only sense of home, of the continuity of existence, was to his friend one of the pieces of the game. The river with its fruitful possibilities he would have wound up like a scarf and tossed to one side or the other as the play went" (165). Even in this brief passage, the balance of power is clear. Brent's worldview and happiness pivot upon the caprice of Rickart and other venture capitalists. Rickart and his allies own much of the valley and have no compunctions about desiccating it for profit. This mercenary outlook gains them a great deal of leverage, leaving Brent with no reciprocal purchase.

The plot of *The Ford* then veers from true-life events. Anne Brent's plan to wrest the valley's water back from Rickart and the looming urban monolith succeeds, thanks to Kenneth Brent's labors. Los Angeles, in the guise of Rickart, decides to get its water elsewhere, ostensibly because Rickart "didn't really want the water of Arroyo Verde" and was "sore at having his plans interfered with" (422). Anne professes a love she does not feel for Rickart's already betrothed son in order to heal the rift between Kenneth and the elder Rickart. Kenneth marries the woman Anne had chosen for him while she (Anne) retreats into a sage and sanguine spinsterhood. The valley is saved; water will flow into local irrigation ditches rather than the city's faucets. The yeoman forces of reclamation have stymied the urban armies of progressivism, enabling the river to once again serve the needs of agriculture rather than those of the city.

Of course, the Owens Valley's actual history differs starkly from Austin's version. Over the more than eighty years since the completion of the aqueduct, the valley has evolved into a national symbol and rallying force against urban imperialism. Ironically, the loss of its water meant that the valley was never developed. Rather than turning into an agribusiness hub like the Imperial Valley, the Owens Valley gained local renown as an uncrowded wilderness area. But in the 1970s, Los Angeles began massive groundwater pumping in the valley, destroying the natural vegetation and drying up remaining springs and artesian wells. Valley dwellers and environmentalists joined forces for a series of court battles. There were also once again sporadic acts of ecotage and property damage, including the shooting of an arrow attached to a stick of dynamite into the William Mulholland Memorial Fountain in Los Angeles.

By the early 1980s, when it became clear that Los Angeles was losing in both the courts of law and public opinion, the city began negotiating in earnest for a mutually acceptable settlement. Negotiations continued throughout the 1980s, and in 1991 the parties reached a settlement. The agreement required Los Angeles to rewater fifty-three miles of the "dry channel" of the Owens River, establish off-stream ponds and wetlands, and undertake other environmental projects. The city also had to pay Inyo County $2 million annually to offset the county's reduced tax base stemming from Los Angeles's ownership of its land. The agreement also made the city's groundwater pumping subject to environmental considerations. While substantial, the Owens Valley's victory was not complete. Among other problems, residents remained unsatisfied that the city did not have to rectify its desiccation of the Owens Lake. The dust from the dry lake bed continues to generate choking dust storms that sometimes carry all the way to Bakersfield, a distance of roughly seventy miles.

Austin's fictional solution to the valley's water crisis concerns itself more with catharsis than with the situation's actual complexity. However, *The Ford* does anticipate ecofeminism by linking the subjugation of women with that of the land and merging the two into a potent force for social change. Anne's role in the valley's salvation offers an excellent view of Austin's early feminism as well as her proto-ecofeminism. For example, Kenneth Brent is essentially a dolt. Without Anne's maneuvering and prodding, he never could have kept Rickart from the valley's water. Anne, for her part, understands that the preeminence of the patriarchy relegates her to a supporting role despite her superior business sense and intelligence. Even Kenneth realizes (with Anne's help) the congruence between the current system of land use and women's role in society: "Anne had called it a man-made world, and all he had seen of it went to show that men had made it badly. But what could men do in a world which land, waters, the worth of women, had no measure but a man's personal reaction (373). This passage groups land, water, and women— three potent signifiers in the western value-system. It also underscores their subjectivity. The exchange values of all three are, according to Austin, determined by the dominant ideology—in this case, capitalist patriarchy. That act of valuation has become involuntary, a rote practice descended from the original arranging of the signs in such a way as to perpetuate the (de)valuation of women and nature.

Anne recognizes the impossibility of openly flouting the power structure and chooses instead to subvert from within. She refuses to recognize the legitimacy of an economy organized around an arbitrary grouping of signs.

Anne was not troubled by any incubus of a System. "There isn't any such animal," she insisted. "It's the way we look at things. . . . Society is a sort of mirage, a false appearance due to refraction . . . because we have an androcentric culture." (233)

Her philosophy contains much that would later become ecofeminism. She labels extant reality "man-made" while noting alternative ways of seeing that do not privilege men and invite the ascension of women.[19] She further contends that the male way of seeing the world, based as it is on an elaborate, constructed vision designed to gratify male impulses, is less realistic than the female perspective, since women see from the point of view of the subjugated: "Take marriage, for instance; a woman will marry a man because he is clean and honest and will make a good father . . . but a man won't marry a woman unless she makes him feel a certain way . . . unless there's a—mirage" (233). In Austin's view, women look for qualities that will facilitate healthy relationships and propagate the species. Men insist that women become accomplices in their fantasies.

Here too, Austin presages many ecofeminist concepts. According to many ecofeminists, women, like the land, serve as pleasure vehicles in a male-constructed Xanadu. Because land has traditionally been feminized, just as women have been objectified, the link between women and nature is stronger than that between men and nature.[20] Indeed, men have consciously alienated themselves from nature, choosing instead to link themselves with culture. The resulting dualisms of women/nature, men/culture, while traditionally serving to subjugate women and nature, can potentially empower women and provide the means for constructing a nonandrocentric society.[21]

Unfortunately, Austin's early ecofeminist awareness collides with her strong allegiance to Reclamation ideology and its gospel of terrestrial and hydrological domination. Her entire oeuvre demonstrates a continuing struggle to accommodate Reclamation with environmentalism. *The Ford* provides perhaps the best example of their incompatibility.

Austin believed that Los Angeles's appropriation of the water affronted the region's terrestrial integrity even as she endorsed the valley's plan to dam the river and force the water into irrigation ditches and fields that had been shorn of their native flora. She somehow managed to accommodate this land use with a belief that the land should not be lived "except in its own fashion" and with her smoldering anger over human scarring of the landscape. In *The Ford,* it is Anne who engineers the valley's victory over the city. She, who had decried the male-dominated world that constructed "mirages" that measured the worth of women and land solely in terms of their ability to offer gratification, uses her femininity to trap the younger Rickart into backing off the city's project. Her goal is to permit her father and brother to "master" and "compel" the river.

The conflicts within Austin's protoenvironmentalism exemplify the inherent tension infusing the myth of the garden. The land was supposedly Edenic, capable of supporting millions in bucolic splendor yet simultaneously in need of technological intervention to subdue it and force it to yield. Reclamation offered a compromise between these two poles. By "reclaiming" the land from aridity and "unproductivity," American diligence would revive a previous era of Edenic abundance. The land's health was tied to a commitment to its cultivation. Reclamation thus legitimated large-scale agriculture through its linkage with yeoman principles of land use and the biotic integrity of the ecosystem.

One of the final passages of *The Ford* offers an excellent encapsulation of Austin's outlook and a clear view of its close connection with the myth of the garden. In explaining to Rickart why he had flouted Rickart's authority and saved the valley, Kenneth Brent "make[s] clear his conviction that the earth was the right and property of those who worked it, and that its values should accrue to them if to anybody" (436). Thus, even Austin, one of the nation's most ecologically minded citizens, could not separate herself from the commodification of nature inherent to productive economies. As Anne says in the novel,

> Look at the land . . . the first thing to learn is that you can absolutely
> find out what land is good for, and in time we'll find that, no matter
> what you feel about it, it only belongs to the people who can do
> those things. . . . I can make a Socialist out of a prune man . . . by
> keeping him six years on a piece of ground that was meant to grow
> potatoes. (234)

Austin recognized that all visions of the land were ineluctably linked with production, and, despite misgivings about the ramifications of such a tie, she embraced it for lack of a better option. Of the two alternatives—yeoman husbandry and urban sprawl—Austin allied herself enthusiastically with the former.

This faith in the right of yeomen to shape and subdue the land, while at the same time condemning those qualities when evinced by others, portends the conflicts in *The Grapes of Wrath*. The Okies in Steinbeck's story also claim allegiance to traditional yeoman values while at the same time participating in ecologically disastrous factory farming. As in *The Ford*, water forms the privileged sign; its control determines who will work the land and in what manner.

Colorado River, looking upstream toward Boulder Canyon, future site of the Hoover Dam, circa 1928. (Courtesy of the Henry J. Kaiser Collection, Bancroft Library, University of California, Berkeley.)

Hoover Dam, construction in progress, circa 1933. (Courtesy of the Henry J. Kaiser Collection, Bancroft Library, University of California, Berkeley.)

Sharecropper entering California, circa 1935–45. (Farm Security Administration photograph, courtesy of Bancroft Library, University of California, Berkeley.)

Hoover Dam, Arizona-Nevada border. (Photograph by Robert Dawson.)

Owens Valley water leaving Owens Valley and entering
Los Angeles. (Photograph by Robert Dawson.)

Drying Rye Patch Reservoir, Nevada. (Photograph by
Robert Dawson.)

Spillway, Lake Berrysea, California. (Photograph by
Robert Dawson.)

Dry Arkansas River used as a wheatfield, Dodge City, Kansas.
(Photograph by Robert Dawson.)

3

Turning Wine into Water: Water's Crucial Absence in *The Grapes of Wrath*

Eastward I go only by force; but westward I go free.
—Henry David Thoreau

The Old Testament describes wilderness as "a thirsty ground where there was no water." When the Lord wished to punish, he threatened to "turn the rivers into islands and dry up the pools and . . . command the clouds that they rain no rain upon it." When granting redemption in Isaiah, God promises instead that "waters shall break forth in the wilderness and streams in the desert" and that "the desert and dry land shall be glad" (Deut. 8:7, 15, Isa. 5:6, 35:1, 6, 43:20).[1] The Garden of Eden provided the antithesis of desert wilderness, a place where water flowed freely and manna of all sorts lay ready to spring out of the ground. This is the imagery that spawned the myth of the garden. It is also one of the many biblical cross-currents running through John Steinbeck's canon. At the dawn of the common era, John offers Jesus his baptism in the river Jordan. Two millennia later, Jim Casy baptizes Tom Joad in an irrigation ditch.

The Grapes of Wrath represents an indictment of the Myth of the Garden and its accompanying myth of the frontier. The lever with which Steinbeck pries apart and ultimately dismantles these fictions is a critique of the agricultural practices that created the Dust Bowl and then metamorphosed into a new set of norms that continued to victimize both the land and its inhabitants. Both nineteenth-century homesteading (based on the Homestead Act of 1862) and agribusiness, its twentieth-century descendant (born from the failure of the Homestead Act), relied on the (mis)use of water to accomplish their respective goals. And both policies resulted in ecological disaster.

The Plains were called upon to supply grain for the international war effort in 1914 and to feed a hungry nation whose population continued to multiply exponentially. Throughout the nation, industrialization held sway as the isolationism of the nineteenth century gave way to the globalism of the twentieth. These transitions required great expenditures of resources and, in the Grain Belt, the resource most in demand was water. As farmers poured their short-term profits back into land and seed, their fates became ever more dependent on the availability of water. This era of expansionism coincided with a period of greater than average rainfall in the region. When the climatic pendulum swung back toward aridity, Plains farmers had to declare hydrological bankruptcy. Still, neither the farmers nor the federal government would abandon the myth of the garden. As the government scrambled to dam rivers and force water into the arid lands, farmers clung fast to their vision of uncountable abundance amid a green world.[2]

The class stratification depicted in *The Grapes of Wrath* arose from corporate control over water. However, the region's aridity made water an absent signifier. Both in the novel and in the desert itself, water's conspicuous absence is what makes it so powerful. The flooding that climaxes the novel is thematically situated to provide maximum counterpoint to the drought that originally forced the Joads to migrate west. Disenfranchised and dehumanized, the Joads can only curse the rising floodwaters even as they once prayed for a deluge to feed their parched crops.

By the end of the novel, the cycle of alienation is complete; people whose humanity was once integrally tied to the land and the weather now care nothing for the growing season or the health of the earth. Their survival has come to depend on shelter from the elements rather than the elements themselves. They have become components of the factory-farming process, economically distant from the corporate growers who oppress them, but closely tied to the industrial ethos that rewards the subjugation of nature. The primary difference between the growers and the migrants now lies in their respective relationships with water, the privileged sign. The growers, owners of the irrigation channels, centrifugal pumps, and watertight mansions, control it, while the Okies, starving and drenched, are at its mercy.[3]

In *The Grapes of Wrath*, Steinbeck presents an archetypal Plains family caught in the modernization of the American dream. Adapting to the realities of a closed frontier and a desert in the country's midsection involved retrofitting the dominant myths to encompass corporate capitalism as well as accepting water's scarcity and preeminence as commodity in the West. This shift in ideology completed the antiquation of the Joads' way of life. Ecological realities had long ago proven their lifestyle quixotic, but it took the coincidence of the Dust Bowl and corporate agribusiness to dislodge the Okies from their land and homes.

Steinbeck acknowledges water's primacy in the West by documenting the social ramifications of the ideology that permitted its monopolization and waste. The ecological decimation of the Plains, the preeminence of agribusiness, and the migrants' brutal poverty in California are all attributable to this hybrid of yeomanism and hydrocapitalism. Steinbeck's abiding affection for the yeoman agricultural ideal also appears throughout the novel. Donald Worster believes that this nostalgia comes at the expense of a coherent critique of the water-based oligarchy primarily responsible for the ecological degradation of the Southwest and its accompanying human suffering (*Rivers* 229). While Worster's criticism has substantial merit, it fails to address the symbolic power attached to water that pervades the novel. That in *The Grapes of Wrath* Steinbeck chose to stress his affection for the yeoman tradition rather than explicitly condemn modern hydraulic society does not detract from the book's success in subverting the hydroindustrial paradigm. From the drought in Oklahoma, to Noah's refusal to leave the river in Arizona, to the raging floodwaters that climax the text, Steinbeck weaves water into the novel's structure and also into virtually every thematically significant event in the novel.[4]

The reactions of the state and federal governments to the book's publication as well as that of the oligarchy-controlled California media demonstrate the novel's effectiveness. The migrants' struggle became a national cause célèbre, and the novel's verisimilitude was debated at the highest levels of government.[5] Vehement condemnations of the book and its author followed shortly after publication in 1939 and continued for years. The most vociferous denunciations came from the water barons and their political allies, suggesting that, contrary to Worster's contention, Steinbeck did indeed understand the politics of water use and that his novel attacked it successfully.

One of the most effective techniques used by the press to discredit the novel involved letters to the editor from supposed "Okies" protesting that the conditions depicted in the novel did not really exist. The letters told of friendly treatment by the growers, clean living conditions, and enough work for everybody. The papers also spread rumors of Okies wanting to kill Steinbeck for telling lies about them. Little information defending Steinbeck's version of events reached the public at large until a number of other exposés (most notably Carey McWilliams's *Factories in the Field*) were released and photographs documenting the migrants' conditions gained widespread notoriety.[6]

The first part of this chapter examines the complicated history of the region, offering *The Grapes of Wrath* as a lens through which to view the ecological, hydrological, and social factors that caused the Dust Bowl and the subsequent mass migration of the "exodusters" to California. The second section examines water's role as absent signifier more closely within the novel and relates it to contemporary difficulties stemming from water's use and control in the Southwest.

Creating the Dust Bowl

Not just in the Hebrew Bible but throughout history, the habitability of any region has been determined by the availability and accessibility of its water. The Spanish explorers who first traversed the Southwest deemed it an inhospitable wasteland, unfit for human settlement except by savages content to scrape their existences from the unforgiving rock. American trailblazers including Lewis and Clark and Zebulon Pike also held little hope that the arid region could sustain American settlements. Such criticism, however, quickly disappeared in the storm of patriotism that surged through the new United States. Parallel visions of world dominance and transcendental bonding with nature created a unique blend of ideologies that sought to sustain simultaneously an extractive economy and an unspoiled, untrammeled frontier. Not till near the turn of the twentieth century did the inexorable collision of these visions loom close enough to draw the notice of the nation's policymakers. This collision resulted in what Carolyn Merchant calls an "ecological revolution." Ecological revolutions are caused by increasing tension between ecosystemic requirements and the modes of production that drive the economy. When this tension reaches unsustainable levels, it generates "transformations in consciousness and legitimating worldviews" (*Revolutions* 5). The Newlands Act, with its implicit recognition of the hydrological parameters of the West, represented one such transformation.

In the Owens Valley, the tension that spurred the transformation took the form of a clash between urban progressivism and rural populism, with both sides asserting entitlement to the region's water. Urban forces prevailed in the valley, but elsewhere, in the agribusiness-controlled regions of California, agriculture remained dominant. The growers' control over water gave them virtually unlimited power. Later, when the exodusters flooded into the region, they quickly learned the scope and implications of the growers' primacy. The hydrological basis for the growers' power probably did not surprise the migrants, who were themselves intimately familiar with water's power to shape lives. Their very presence in California stemmed directly from a cyclical shortfall of water in the nation's midsection.

American history shows that people traditionally migrated to the Plains during periods of high rainfall. When the rains subsided to typical levels, people retreated or pressed on. But, by the 1920s, the frontier was closed and Americans had bought into the notion that technology and God would see to it that the Great Plains became the world's agricultural capital. They clung to this notion despite the fact that meeting the grain demands of a global economy in a region where annual rainfall fluctuated between seven and twenty inches made little ecological sense. When they could not meet their goals, Plains dwellers lashed out at the weather, believing it caused their woes. There was not enough water, they complained; the weather had failed them.

This argument is analogous to blaming a gravel pit for yielding no gold. That is not to belittle the very real human tragedy of the Dust Bowl nor to deny the nobility of many of those who suffered through it. Nevertheless, the Dust Bowl's ecosystemic catastrophe was both avoidable and remediable, though not by means that were palatable to the region's residents. They remained unwilling or unable to face the ecological realities of the region. According to Worster, typical Plains farmers of the time can be expected to "fail to anticipate drought, underestimate its duration when it comes, expect rain momentarily, deny that they are as hard hit as outsiders believe . . . admit that some help would be useful, demand that the government act and act quickly . . . without strings . . . pooh-pooh the need for major reform . . . eagerly await the return of 'normalcy'" (*Dust Bowl* 28). When New Dealers attempted to innovate, they met with entrenched hostility. Plains farmers believed that Providence would see to the fate of the region and "Providence, not Washington, would see them come out all right" (28). It is precisely this stubborn adhering to traditional values while implementing ecologically pernicious agricultural methods that brought on the "dirty thirties."

The values themselves have their genesis in the dual myths of the garden and the frontier. The Joads' saga in *The Grapes of Wrath* offers a fictional version of the consequences of those myths. Both derive from a perceived superabundance of resources, a national fantasy that prodded the Joads toward Oklahoma and then later to California. Belief in an infinite national trust fueled dreams of individual wealth and national dominance amid a rugged land that would never cease testing all those attempting to wrest an existence from it.[7] West of the ninety-ninth meridian, water's perennial scarcity threatened to undermine this popular vision. Rather than subvert the prevailing value system, Americans bought the notion of hydroabundance promulgated by ideologues like William Gilpin. Their insistence that rain followed the plow and their boasts that the West contained infinite supplies of minerals and timber convinced people like Grampa and Gramma Joad to move west, settle in the arid region, and take up the Jeffersonian yeoman ideal.

Jefferson, however, lived in Virginia. His philosophy stemmed from his intimacy with farming practices in the humid region. He was profoundly ignorant of agricultural techniques west of the Mississippi, and his ideas did not adapt well to the arid West. A century after Jefferson's time, Powell labored for close to thirty years to bring western land-use policies closer to western terrestrial and hydrological realities. By the turn of the twentieth century, the regional and federal governments acknowledged that agricultural practices in the arid lands required severe retooling. By then, however, powerful corporate interests domi-

nated the region's economy. The conflict between misguided government policies, yeoman land-use ideals, and geographical realities had
been exacerbated by the profit-centered tactics of agribusiness concerns.

Early in the novel, Steinbeck establishes the fundamental conflict
between yeoman farmers and the banks over title to the land. According
to a nameless tenant farmer speaking early in the novel,

> Grampa took up the land, and he had to kill the Indians and drive
> them away. And Pa was born here, and he killed weeds and snakes.
> Then a bad year came and he had to borrow a little money. An' we
> was born here . . . our children born here. And Pa had to borrow
> money. The bank owned the land then. . . . Sure cried the tenant
> men, but it's our land. We measured it and broke it up. We were
> even born on it, and we got killed on it, died on it. Even if it's no
> good, it's still ours. . . . That makes ownership, not a paper with
> numbers on it. (*Grapes* 34–35)

This passage reveals several of the guiding principles governing life in the
Plains. First, the term "bad year" refers to inadequate rainfall and an
accompanying water shortage, a cyclical reality of Plains life that formed
one of the bases for the collapse of the yeoman life. Second, right of ownership was established through displacing Native peoples. That act, in
and of itself, constituted (in the farmer's eyes) a right of title. Last,
birthing and dying on the land created a blood-right of succession that no
financial transaction could negate. The quotation reveals the teller's sadness that the laws of the country conflict with the laws of the land.

For Plains farmers, working the land was the litmus test of possession. Agrarian ideology held that only those who work and love the land
can truly own it: "If a man owns a little property, that property is him, it's
part of him and it's like him. If he owns property only so he can walk on
it and handle it and be sad when it isn't doing well, and feel fine when the
rain falls on it, that property is him. . . . Even if he isn't successful he's big
with his property" (*Grapes* 39). Such feelings descend directly from the
dual myths of the frontier and the garden. The frontier myth posited that
land in the West was not inhabited by anybody with legal rights and that
the strength of the nation lay in its boundless and unsettled western frontier. The myth of the garden held that the land would yield bountiful har-

vests to any American willing to work it. Any failure in these natural laws was necessarily transitory and had no lasting relevance. Unfortunately, these precepts were disproved by the Okies' experiences in both Oklahoma and California. After a prolonged drought revealed the unsustainability of their farming methods and drove them from their homes, the wet-dry cycle in California nearly caused their demise.

Not only did meteorological laws conflict with their yeoman belief system, the Okies also found their way of life colliding with the policies of a nation committed to corporate capitalism. Empiricism and a bottom-line mentality created rigid parameters for decision making. For agrarians, land constituted a part of themselves and their culture, but banks and corporations translated it into assets on a balance sheet. Where the Okies spoke of "bad years," account managers acknowledged the reality of sparse rainfall and a semiarid climate. Historical climatic patterns decreed that "bad years" for rainfall were the norm for the Plains, a fact that made tenant farmers a poor investment. In addition, years of drought and overreliance on nutrient-draining cash crops devastated the land. Those keeping accounts looked to squeeze out every vestige of production before abandoning it for more lucrative investments:

> But you'll kill the land with cotton.
> We know. We've got to take cotton quick before the land dies. Then we'll sell the land. Lots of families in the East would like to own a piece of land. (*Grapes* 34)

For banks, it became a matter of short-term profit at any cost—extracting the land's limited value and then discarding it for more lucrative investments. But for the tenants, faceless corporate "monsters" intentionally destroying the land's fertility through overcultivation of cotton, a nutrient-draining crop, provoked violent, if futile resistance (*Grapes* 35). Paradoxically, however, the Joads and their neighbors had often planted cotton and, at the time the novel opens, are sharecropping frenziedly in order to build up a stake to take west: "The whole bunch of us chopped cotton, even Grampa" (*Grapes* 90). The differences between the Okies and the banks lay more in scale and philosophy than methodology and eventual result. Both sides participated in the capitalist mechanism, but the banks were better adapted to thrive within it.

Treating the nation's breadbasket as an expendable resource assumed an infinite reservoir from which to replace it. Short-term profiteering posits that the future will take care of itself. It depends on a telos of inexhaustible plenty, a concept central to the frontier and garden myths. These myths have shown remarkable durability: the onset of the Industrial Age and accompanying supremacy of corporate capitalism did not eradicate them, but simply adapted them to the twentieth century.

Richard Slotkin offers an intriguing explanation for this transition. He argues that the systems of myth and ideology that developed in the United States depended on a positive valuation of physical migration, which revolved around two geographical poles: the "metropolis" and the "frontier." The metropolis must have negative associations, or no one would want to leave, while the frontier has to offer riches enough to satisfy our dreams. Emigrants suffer in the wilderness while temporarily regressing to a more primitive state. The results, though, more than compensate for the ephemeral loss of civilization's comforts: "The completed American was therefore one who remade his fortune and his character by an emigration, a setting forth for newer and richer lands; by isolation and regression to a more primitive manner of life; and by establishing his political position" (*Environment* 35).

This description offers striking parallels to the Joads' saga. Slotkin's analysis takes the city, or the metropolis, as the emigrant's point of departure, but substituting the Dust Bowl region does not interfere with the argument. Since the trappings of the Industrial Revolution came late to the Plains, the region lacked the large, mechanized urban areas that posed such an effective antipode to the wilderness frontier. Instead, mechanization and factory farming—both consequences of industrialization—provided the major impetus that drove families like the Joads from the Plains. In the Dust Bowl, wage-slavery and the specter of starvation resulting from technological and economic displacement offered the negative contrast to the frontier. The Okies' choices, in Steinbeck's view, were either to serve the enemy by driving a tractor through their neighbors' homes and raping the land with machinery and cash crops, or to leave.

When the Joads first came to Sallisaw, Oklahoma, they endured isolation and primitive conditions while homesteading their land and seeking to fulfill yeoman ideals. Aridity and untenable agricultural practices caused the dream's collapse, forcing thousands of people like the Joads to again move west. This time they settled in California, geographical border of the once limitless frontier and now a privatized corporate fiefdom. Once more, the Okies suffered primitive, dehumanizing conditions while attempting to exercise their supposedly inalienable human rights. But the growers' cartel had disenfranchised them even before they arrived, forcing them into a nomadic existence designed to destroy the homesteading instinct so central to the frontier myth.

Despite uncountable acres lying fallow, no land was available for the Okies. Their dreams of subsistence farming proved fundamentally incompatible with a system designed to allow a select few to grow vastly wealthy on the toil of disenfranchised adherents to an old American Dream. What ultimately kills Jim Casy and exiles Tom Joad is—as in Slotkin's paradigm—an urgent desire to participate in the political process. They do not succeed because the growers' control over water rights allows them complete dominion over the local government and media as well. I will discuss this phenomenon at greater length shortly. Its relevance here stems from water's role in the third major cause (in addition to aridity and unsustainable agricultural practices) for the Okies' westward migration: inadequate irrigation and a perceived drought.

Steinbeck and Water

Steinbeck's humanistic bent impelled him to focus on the human dimension of the agricultural calamity that drove the Okies west. However, the underlying motivation for both the Okies' behavior and that of the agribusiness concerns can be analyzed in hydrological terms.

Drought did not cause the Dust Bowl. Rainfall in the Southwest in the 1930s fell well within historical norms; cycles of drought are more common than periods of heavy rain.[8] An accurate account of the region's troubles should focus on the depression and local agricultural mismanagement. The depression, though, did not seriously affect the Great Plains until the onset of the Dust Bowl in the early 1930s. If local farmers had continued planting and harvesting cash crops at the rate they had in previous decades, the Plains might have escaped the worst of the depression. Unfortunately, by the end of the 1920s, they had borrowed heavily and expanded their acreage to maximize yields. When the crops failed and the "black blizzards" came, the national plague of poverty and joblessness infected the Plains as well.

By the 1930s, Plains farmers had plowed under virtually all the region's grasslands. Without sod or other vegetation to hold the topsoil in place, the land became highly vulnerable to ecological disturbance. When the drought hit, the land had no natural defenses with which to anchor that topsoil. The resulting dust storms stripped the land bare. Steinbeck offers this lyrical description of one such storm:

> The air and the sky darkened and through them the sun shone redly, and there was a raw sting in the air. During the night the wind raced faster over the land, dug cunningly among the rootlets of the corn, and the corn fought the wind with its weakened leaves until the roots were freed by the prying wind and then each stalk settled wearily sideways toward the earth and pointed the direction of the wind. . . . Now the dust was evenly mixed with the air, an emulsion of dust and air. Houses were shut tight, and cloth wedged around doors and windows, but the dust came in . . . [and] settled like pollen on the chairs and tables, on the dishes. The people brushed it from their shoulders. Little lines of dust lay at their door sills. (*Grapes* 2–3)

Those famous storms did not savage the entire Plains. The most severe wind erosion took place primarily in eastern Colorado, western Kansas, and the Oklahoma and Texas panhandles.[9] Yet if even the most drought-afflicted region had retained its indigenous vegetation, the dust storms would have been much less powerful and their damage drastically reduced. Instead, profit-oriented agriculture and ecological ignorance turned a cyclical shortfall of water into a catastrophe.

High-yield, single-crop agriculture is a dubious ecological proposition even in humid regions, but in the Southwest it becomes disastrous. Barring a shortfall of precipitation, the average homestead usually proved adequate for subsistence farming. The region could not, however, sustain the rigors of a market-driven agriculture, a task that agriculture's metamorphosis into an industry soon demanded.

Steinbeck condemns what he saw as a dissolution of the values so cherished by the people who settled the region—connectedness to the land coupled with love and gratitude for its sustaining them. Such reverence became obsolete with the ascension of factory farming.

> The driver sat in his iron seat and he was proud of the straight lines he did not will, proud of the tractor he did not own or love, proud of the power he could not control. And when that crop grew, and was harvested, no man had crumbled a hot clod in his fingers and let the earth sift past his fingertips. No man had touched the seed, or lusted for the growth. Men ate what they had not raised, had no connection with the bread. The land bore under iron, and under iron gradually died. (*Grapes* 38)

Steinbeck mourned this change in values but offered no viable solutions. Even as they cursed the technology that drove them west, Steinbeck's characters traveled in cars bought through the trade of their mules and watched with sadness as tractors did the mules' work in a fraction of the time.

The Okies formed the pivot point for the western land's transition from earth mother to degraded resource. As the yeoman ideal gave way to the demands of a market economy, the Okies adapted their methods to meet the new reality. Even while clinging tenaciously to a preindustrial, agricultural vision, the Okies grudgingly acknowledged the new dominance of the capitalist shift and the technology that accompanied it.

Muley Graves, unable to relinquish his ties to the land, did not go with his family when they moved west. Rooted to the place where he was born, Muley's rage against the dual inequity of bad land and evil bankers is steeped in the populist tradition:

> 'Cause what'd they take when they tractored the folks off the lan'? What'd they get so their margin a profit was safe? . . . God knows the lan' ain't no good. Nobody been able to make a crop for years. But them sons-a-bitches at their desks, they just chopped folks in two. . . . Place where folks live is them folks. They ain't whole, out lonely on the road in a piled-up car. Them sons-a-bitches killed them. (*Grapes* 55)

For Muley, the link with the land still stained with his father's blood is stronger than his ties to wife and family. He cannot leave even as he acknowledges that he is a living anachronism. Sharing a meal with Tom Joad and Jim Casy of rabbits he snared while roaming through deserted farms, Muley repeatedly asks, "You fellas think I'm touched?" (*Grapes* 53, 54).[10]

Muley's protests held little weight with a population caught up in the fervor born of technological advance. It did not matter if the land was poor because human ingenuity would transform it. No longer need the land yield forth its bounty; it would instead be mined and harvested. Modern agriculture provided the means to merge Henry Adams's classic juxtaposition of the dynamo and the virgin.[11] Through this synthesis, the earth ceased to be a virgin and became a wife.

In *To a God Unknown,* Steinbeck openly acknowledges the sexual bond between men and the land. After Joseph, the story's protagonist, literally makes love to the earth, the narrator matter-of-factly notes, "For a moment, the land had been his wife" (11).[12] Later, as Joseph gradually merges his life force with the earth, his epiphany and death come with the realization that rain is the lifeblood of the land and that without a reintegration of humans and the land, both will die. In *Grapes,* written a decade after *To a God Unknown,* Steinbeck again acknowledges the sexual link— this time in the form of rape: "Behind the harrows, the long seeders— twelve curved iron penes erected in the foundry, orgasms set by gears, raping methodically, raping without passion" (37). The hopeful synthesis portrayed in *To a God Unknown* has given way to violent sexual assault.[13]

As industrialism began to dominate the West, the accompanying mind-set fit a unique niche in the American dream of rugged individualism and merit-based achievement. Myra Jehlen argues convincingly that the uniquely American bond with the land and nature makes Americans believe anything they choose to do is right and natural: "The settlers' implementation of the continent's permanent contours and conditions . . . vivifying the land from inside . . . places the emerging social structures beyond debate, in the realm of nature. Those who assist the emergence of those structures, moreover, wield the power of nature itself" (57). One way Americans cast the conquest of land within the current political climate involved classifying irrigation as a struggle between the forces of good and godless communists. In 1960, Robert Kerr, former governor of Oklahoma and head of the Senate's Select Committee on Water

Resources as well as cofounder of the Kerr-McGee Corporation, summed up a widely held philosophy of the arid lands when he rhetorically asked, "Can a pagan Communist nation . . . make more efficient use of soil and water resources than the most advanced and enlightened nation in the world? Can ruthless atheists mobilize and harness their treasures of God-given wealth to defeat and stifle freedom-loving peoples everywhere?" (323–24).

Westerners could restore Eden, but doing so involved "reclaiming" their place in paradise through diligence and industry. Men would finish what nature had begun. Eden, ideologues hastened to point out, was an irrigated garden. Adam fell, but Americans would stand tall. By the time of the Dust Bowl, the Bureau of Reclamation had already emerged as a potent force in the shaping of the western landscape, intending to fulfill Powell's credo of "rescuing" and "redeeming" the land from aridity.

The true meaning of the word *reclamation* lost all significance in the technological assault on the region's hydrology. The verb *to reclaim* implies prior ownership; those seeking to irrigate the desert could make no such claim. Nevertheless, they would do whatever needed to be done to get water to the land and restore it to its imagined, bountiful state.[14] Any water that ran into the sea without serving some agricultural purpose was a providential oversight correctable through human diligence.

Denying the hydrological realities of the Southwest permitted westerners some fanciful notions about American ingenuity. Henry Luce's *Time* trumpeted the rediscovered limitlessness that irrigation technology brought to the frontier: "Irrigation experts are now convinced that the rapidly growing U.S. can expand indefinitely within its present boundaries" (qtd. in Worster, *Rivers* 266). This quotation is pregnant with contradiction. Indefinite expansion within acknowledged boundaries is, of course, self-contradictory. Attributing this ability to accomplish the impossible to the calculations of irrigation experts beautifully underscores the incongruities within western water policy.

Western land barons relied on irrigation to accomplish the impossible and ignored or destroyed anyone or anything that might interfere with the attempt. The Joads and their contemporaries were ill equipped to cope with the growers' zeal. They clung to traditional yeoman values even while participating in the market economy that was rendering them obsolete. Caught between two worlds, they could not linger in Oklahoma and set out instead for the land where word of mouth from previous migrants combined with a propaganda campaign by the corporate growers to entice exodusters westward.

As they traversed the migrant highway, the Joads met many who, like themselves, had readily believed the leaflets spread by agents of the California growers.

> Why, I seen han'bills how they need folks to pick fruit, an' good wages. Why, jus' think how it's gonna be, under them shady trees a-pickin' fruit an' takin' a bite ever' once in a while. . . . An' with them good wages, maybe a fella can get hisself a piece a land an' work out for extra cash. Why, hell, in a couple a years I bet a fella could have a place of his own. (*Grapes* 160)

Those handbills stood in sharp contrast to the misery that gripped the Plains.[15] There, families faced wrenching poverty and slow starvation while signs in shop windows ironically proclaimed things like: "Great Bargains in Real Estate. Bring Your Own Container."

That the Plains could no longer sustain the yeoman ideal did not necessarily spell the death of the American Dream for a dispossessed people, barely literate and ready to jump at any hope of salvation. The California growers cartel, already profiting from a cycle of wage-slavery based on the exploitation of Mexican workers, believed that additional workers could only increase their profit margins.[16] When the supply of cheap immigrant labor was drastically cut back by immigration restrictions, the growers recruited Dust Bowl refugees instead, luring them with promises of a vast, temperate paradise wherein they might re-create the homesteads they had been forced to leave.

This new myth of the garden presented an even more seductive exterior than the Plains. It adapted the Jeffersonian ideal to a region where husbandry was allegedly secondary to the munificence of nature. Grampa, before becoming overwhelmed by his attachment to the land he cleared and raised his family on, fantasized about bathing in a washtub full of grapes where he would "scrooge aroun' an' let the juice run down my pants" (*Grapes* 100). But this vision of unchecked abundance was a calculated product of the growers' propaganda mills. California agriculture owed less to nature's bounty than to human engineering. The landscape was "a forced plant—the product of irrigation. [T]he great farm valleys were [once] wastelands and deserts into whose reclamation has gone untold human suffering" (McWilliams 5–6). Agribusiness consortia dangled visions of their own wealth and massive landholdings before the Okies in order to fuel their (the cartel's) hegemony. And the irony of that vision, as Steinbeck depicts it, is that the growers were as alienated from their land wealth as they forced the Okies to be: "And it came about that the owners no longer worked their farms. . . . [T]hey forgot the land, the smell and the feel of it, and remembered only that they owned it. . . . And the owners not only did not work the farms any more, many of them had never seen the farms they owned" (*Grapes* 257). In the landowners' view, alienation from the land was an ingredient for success and profit. They considered themselves businessmen, not farmers, who packaged a product for sale.[17]

The California growers had grown immensely wealthy and powerful as the result of an uneasy but mutually profitable alliance with the Bureau of Reclamation. They had managed to consolidate the dual definitions of *garden* into one highly profitable vision of production and wealth. No longer could *garden* signify either a region of natural, providential splendor or an area of human-created agrarian abundance; the Edenic garden propounded by Gilpin and his nineteenth-century allies was completely replaced by the Baconian vision of a human-engineered paradise achieved through work and intellect. Humans—specifically men—had invented the tools necessary to subjugate nature. Those tools had brought water to the desert via centrifugal pumping and, more importantly, through the diversion of rivers.

Shaping the perceived objectivity of science to fit the needs of western agriculture enabled an elite group to gain control over the dissemination of knowledge, leading to their dominion over the region's geography.[18] Literally overnight, worthless land became incredibly valuable through shady, often illicit dealings that brought subsidized water to the region. The men whose schemes created this technological garden stood to profit most from its enactment, and it was they who formed the powerful growers' cartel that enslaved the migrants. Those who controlled the water controlled the entire regional economy, and that domination bled into every other facet of life.

Californian agribusiness's command over nature and drive for ever greater wealth required large, transient labor forces who would work for very low pay. The growers had traditionally indentured immigrants and other disenfranchised groups since little public outcry arose from their mistreatment. The arrival of the Okies, a large, skilled, English-speaking labor force whose migrant status left them bereft of governmental protection, appeared to be a tremendous windfall. In the novel, however, the latent power of the oppressed becomes the looming threat to the water-based oligarchy.

The Okies come to embody Marx's concept of alienated labor.[19] Their corporate oppressors force them to work ever harder and faster in order to eke out a subsistence, yet each hour worked and each piece of fruit harvested brings them closer to unemployment and starvation. They must also compete against each other by underbidding fellow workers in a futile attempt to participate in an exclusionary economic system. The growers, meanwhile, must dehumanize the workers, degrading them as they do the land so that their acts of subjugation can be perpetrated on objects beneath contempt.[20]

Steinbeck's *In Dubious Battle* treats the worker-grower relationship in terms of class struggle. In *The Grapes of Wrath*, he elevates it to the realm of epistemology, viewing the schism between workers and land barons as symptomatic of the larger issue of human alienation from the earth and as a catalyst for the synthesis of humans and their surroundings into an all-encompassing organismic one: "Three hundred thousand, hungry and miserable; if ever they know themselves, the land will be theirs. . . . And the great owners, who had become through their holdings both more and less than men, ran to their destruction, and used every means that in the long run would destroy them" (*Grapes* 263). The combination of the growers' self-destructive behavior and the unendurable conditions imposed on the Okies will lead eventually (Steinbeck suggests) to a radical reordering of California's agricultural class structure.

The cycle of poverty imposed on the Okies in California contained a seasonal period of starvation during the rainy season. Water again, this time through superabundance, became the immediate threat to the Okies' survival. When Rose of Sharon goes into labor, the men outside struggle frantically to erect a dam to keep the boxcar shelters dry. Water, priceless commodity and building block of life, now endangers the birthing process and threatens to starve an entire class of people. Both attempts— the birth and the dam—prove unsuccessful. As the floodwaters force the Joads to flee, Uncle John is assigned the task of burying the stillborn child. Instead, he co-opts the water, using it and the dead child to spread his message of despair and defiance.

Setting the infant corpse adrift on the floodwaters, Uncle John tells it to: "Go down an' tell 'em. Go down in the street an' rot an' tell em that way. That's the way you can talk. . . . Go on down now an' lay in the street. Maybe they'll know then" (*Grapes* 494). Driven from Oklahoma, where widespread refusal to acknowledge water's scarcity resulted in an unsustainable way of life, the Okies found themselves in a new region where water's seasonal abundance and scarcity were integrated into a sophisticated capitalist infrastructure with water at its base. As a disenfranchised and powerless class, the migrants had no opportunity to gain control over water and consequently could not participate in the dominant discourse. Uncle John's act represents an ephemeral yet powerful appropriation of the preeminent unit of capital. He uses water to convey a message of worker defiance aimed at the heart of the power structure.

The dual hopes for the migrants, according to Steinbeck, are class alliance and worker control over the tools of domination. When Tom Joad takes over the task of organizing the Okies from the martyred Casy, the class struggle takes a symbolic step forward. When Uncle John symbolically seizes control over the waters that enslave his people and threaten their lives, he takes another step toward toppling the ruling class.

Shortly after Uncle John's act of defiance, Rose of Sharon's gift of her maternal milk to another starving Okie demonstrates that Tom's, Casy's, and John's acts will eventually show result. Sheltered from the water by a barn, itself a potent symbol of the yeoman agricultural ideal, Rose of Sharon's offering of her breast to a fellow migrant demonstrates a class cohesion that remains powerfully intact. While her stillborn infant rots in the town below, Rose of Sharon breast-feeds an old man whose advanced state of starvation has caused him to regress to a prelingual state. Her act

and the old man's condition represent the succoring of the infant movement toward social change.

Each act, while primarily symbolic, is also genuinely subversive. In
these small acts of defiance and hope, suggests Steinbeck, lie the restoration of traditional ties between people and between people and the land.
Despite their socialization into a culture in which water is both hoarded
and feared, the Okies have not completely acquiesced to their role in the
factory-farm mechanism. They retain their dreams of an idyllic land
where the family farm reigns supreme and water and land are distributed
according to need and connectedness to the land rather than amassed
corporate capital and political dominance.

In the final analysis, however, the migrant dream of resurgent family
farms reclaiming their place as the preeminent agricultural ideal cannot
work in the arid lands. Water reclamation projects, because of their
expense and complexity, require the participation of an elite, educated
class. The projects inevitably become political pawns. The family farmer,
loyal to a subsistence ideology and unwilling to exploit the land past its
carrying capacity, cannot compete with wealthy, powerful, corporate
interests that have no similar ethical constraints. For this reason, the
novel, though hopeful, does not offer any quantifiable hope.

Worster takes this lack of an attainable goal to be the novel's major
failing. Decrying the system of land distribution without explicitly condemning the accompanying hydrological autocracy leads to the specious
notion that simply putting the land in the hands of the migrants will solve
the region's problems. In a section of *Rivers of Empire* entitled "The
Grapes of Wealth," Worster argues that Steinbeck never explicitly draws
attention to the "elaborate hydraulic apparatus" that enabled agriculture
in California. Succulent fruit and luxuriant cotton seem to spring from
nature's goodness rather than from "the contrivances of advanced water
engineering and the social organization it has required" (229). Since
Steinbeck failed to acknowledge the inherent oligarchic nature of irriga-
tion-based societies, he creates the false impression that equitable land
distribution and a classless society will return the region to ecological stability. Unfortunately, there are no historical precedents for this vision.

Furthermore, in Worster's view, returning the family farm to the arid region without altering the national capitalist infrastructure will, given the Plains example, cause devastating ecological harm.

Worster's critique raises the problematic issue of Steinbeck's unrepentant affection for the family farm but does not, as I mentioned earlier, address the powerful critique of hydraulic society implicit in the novel's structure. That Steinbeck used water throughout the novel as an absent signifier suggests that he was well aware of its power and complicity in the region's power hierarchy. When, at the novel's end, Steinbeck suddenly introduces water as a tangible presence and powerful symbolic force, it empowers the migrants by allowing them to demonstrate their class cohesion and latent strength.

Structuring the novel in this manner permitted Steinbeck to criticize the extant hydraulic society more effectively than he could through overt polemics. Indeed, the novel's reception, both locally and nationally, bears witness to its power. That power underscores the most crucial flaw in Worster's argument. If the novel caused both the government and the nation at large to reevaluate federal irrigation subsidies for corporate growers, it must have effectively criticized the inequity and corruption infusing California's water-appropriation methods. The Hearst-Chandler-Copley broadsheets pilloried the novel and its author throughout California. Only after a *Life* magazine exposé and Eleanor Roosevelt's endorsement of the book's veracity did the tide of public opinion begin to turn in Steinbeck's favor.[21]

The rage and furor from the agribusiness conglomerates and their allies arose because *The Grapes of Wrath* shook the very foundations of the water-based oligarchy. Worster himself acknowledges this:

> Up to the very end of the decade, both the Bureau [of Reclamation] and the Department of the Interior were placidly moving forward . . . avoiding any cause for alarm on the part of the growers in California. . . . What changed all of that undoubtedly was . . . *The Grapes of Wrath.* . . . Suddenly, it became rather difficult for a liberal government in Washington to give subsidized, unrestricted water to groups like the reactionary Associated Farmers, to underwrite their labor policies and their concentration of wealth. (*Rivers* 245)

It appeared that the fundamental principles underlying reclamation could no longer escape critical scrutiny and reform.

Nevertheless, despite a temporary surge in popular and governmental concern, neither the novel nor the reform movement it generated achieved any significant, lasting change in western water policy. Pork-barrel appropriations bills continued to subsidize corporate growers who continued to behave as if they lived in a technologically controlled Eden. The migrants' struggle faded into the background with the outbreak of World War II, when the nation turned to the West once again to fuel the American war machine.

The Okies benefited from the wartime surge in production, finding work in munitions factories and other war-related industries. Relieved, the growers turned once again to immigrant labor, a class of people they could be relatively certain of keeping disenfranchised and powerless. So the cycle of exploitation resumed after only a brief hiatus. Public interest in the issue peaked again two decades later in the 1960s, when Cesar Chavez briefly managed to organize the Migrant Farm Workers Union into an effective national lobby. Nevertheless, both the dam building and worker exploitation continued.[22]

Only in the 1990s, after a prolonged drought and numerous aborted attempts at reform, did the Californian agricultural machine begun to sputter. Years of drought and insupportable agriculture in an arid land are on the verge of accomplishing what neither Powell nor Steinbeck nor any individual person could accomplish alone: decanonization of the myth of the garden and its accompanying myth of the frontier. These myths, dominant since the birth of the nation, eventually ran headlong into the realities of a closed frontier and a finite hydrology. In 1992, Steven Goldstein, spokesman for former interior secretary Manuel Lujan, aptly summed up the situation when announcing the curtailment of further water subsidies to California growers, saying: "We recognize . . . what a hardship this will be. But we cannot make it rain."[23] The progression in consciousness that preceded Goldstein's statement was neither smooth nor uncomplicated. It involved a fundamental shift in how Americans viewed the land, a shift redolent with controversy and conflict.

4

Waging Water: Hydrology versus Mythology in *The Monkey Wrench Gang*

> Whiskey is for drinkin': Water is for fightin'.
> —Mark Twain

> "The dam?"
> "Yes sir."
> "Not the dam."
> "Yes sir, we have reason to think so."
> "*Not* Glen Canyon *Dam!*"
> "I know it sounds crazy. But that's what they're after."
> —*The Monkey Wrench Gang*

Whereas Steinbeck's lingering nostalgia for the Jeffersonian yeoman ideal in *The Grapes of Wrath* arguably diverts his attention from the true nature of the southwestern agricultural and hydrological crisis, Edward Abbey focuses his energy in *The Monkey Wrench Gang* on documenting the ramifications of western water policy and vociferously advocating its demise. *The Monkey Wrench Gang* offers a prescription for grassroots action to restore beleaguered western lands and give the canyon country back its heart: the Colorado River. The Glen Canyon Dam, in Abbey's view, killed a living river and sounded the death knell for the entire Southwest.

The Monkey Wrench Gang was published in 1975 but, according to Abbey's epigraph, relies on historical events that occurred "just one year from today." It depicts a world where the myth of the garden has evolved into uncontrolled, government-subsidized growth-mania that has flooded much of the garden and poisoned the rest. Part of the novel's implicit irony stems from the forces of subversion having come full circle. In the Owens Valley during the early part of the century, residents dynamited dams as acts of defiance against the Los Angeles Department of Water and Power. The city's appropriation of water rights had destroyed the valley's once-rich agricultural infrastructure, leaving the region barren and sere. Later in the century, Steinbeck depicts starving Okies enjoined by agribusiness and absentee owners from planting subsistence crops on land purposely kept fallow. That land that they did plant was sown with high-yield, nutrient-draining cash crops that destroyed the soil's ability to support life. By Abbey's era, a lush, green desert was neither the ideal, nor commonly perceived as attainable. With agribusiness and other ill-conceived ecological practices causing the western United States to suffer a faster rate of desertification than sub-Saharan Africa, Abbey chose not to portray frustrated farmers unable to reap nature's bounty from a technologically controlled Eden. Instead he created heroes committed to destroying the apparatus that engineered the garden in the first place. Rather than commit sabotage in support of the agrarian ideal—as Owens Valley residents did and as the Okies conspired to do—Abbey's characters subvert that ideal through acts of "ecotage."[1] As in the Owens Valley, Abbey's characters look to dynamite a dam, but for vastly different motives. They hope to drastically reduce western agriculture by restoring the land to its naturally arid, "unproductive" state.

The opposition between "productive" in an extractive economy and "productive" in a steady-state economy is stark. In an extractive system, production means depleting nonrenewable resources in order to generate energy and goods. By contrast, a productive steady-state economy emphasizes renewable resources and expending no more energy than the system can replace. This range of meaning within the term *productive* underscores its malleability and the consequent power of economic systems to shape the discourse.

To Abbey, the Glen Canyon Dam embodies a cycle of *faux potlatch* carried on by development interests with the aid and complicity of the government. Rather than following the traditional potlatch scheme, involving large-scale accumulation of resources that are then given away or destroyed in a wholesale display and redistribution of wealth, practitioners of the southwestern faux potlatch amass huge amounts of the region's most precious resource (water) behind incredibly expensive dams and then waste that water in a manner calculated to maximize personal gain.

The aim is not to redistribute wealth, but to hoard it through manipulation of the nation's ideological biases and economic apparatus. Abbey underscores this in the following passage from *The Monkey Wrench Gang:* "Beneath the superstructure the dynamo purred on, murmuring the basic message: Power . . . profit . . . prestige . . . pleasure . . . profit . . . prestige . . . pleasure . . . power . . ." (234). The dam may store water and generate hydroelectricity, but its true purpose, in Abbey's view, is to enrich a select few.

An edifice designed to hoard wealth for the elite runs counter to the central tenets of potlatch. Among the Oweekano Kwakiutl tribe, for example, chiefs always died poor because they potlatched so frequently. "The idea of hoarding or accumulating wealth for any other purpose would have been regarded as abnormal, unthinkable, even shameful. . . . Paradoxically, to give away wealth was to be wealthy" (Cole and Chaikin 11–12). Throughout this chapter, my use of the term *potlatch* refers to the ceremonial expenditure of wealth practiced primarily by Native American communities in the Northwest until the early part of this century.[2]

Potlatch is a generic term referring to the feast and dance rituals of northwestern tribes involving large-scale giving of gifts by the host. The lavishness of the gathering and the extravagance of the attendant gifts awarded prestige to the host while obligating guests to reply in kind at a future potlatch. Often, a potlatch left a prominent member of the community all but destitute. This poverty further enhanced his status. "After the food is consumed, the dishes are given to those who ate from them. After the potlatch ends the host gives away the planks of his house and is said to have 'gone all the way.' The host is then left with nothing but his great prestige and renown to clothe him" (Rosman and Rubel 179–80). Wealth among these tribes was amassed for the sole purpose of giving it away. A host who potlatched knew that he compelled attendees to do the same. In this way, wealth never stayed static, but instead constantly circulated among communities.[3]

Within this complex marriage of prestige and poverty lay an economic system entirely foreign to capitalism. Rather than a spiraling economy dedicated to maximizing personal gain, the potlatch mandated periodic redistribution of resources among the community. Currency had no value unless it remained in circulation. Therefore, accumulated wealth in a potlatch economy was an oxymoron; possessions gained value only through their distribution. Not surprisingly, the encroaching ideology and economic system of European-descended settlers showed little tolerance for the potlatch. Missionaries and Canadian and American legislators all but eradicated it by the middle of the twentieth century.[4] In place of the potlatch rose a corrupted, water-oriented faux potlatch that was endemic rather than alien to capitalism and could not function outside its economic borders.

While maintaining a facade of profitless expenditure, faux potlatch actually greatly enriches its practitioners. For example, diversionary structures carry Colorado River water into the desert, where it is used to cultivate alfalfa and cotton, though nonarid regions of the country produce more than enough of these crops. In fact, producing cotton and alfalfa in the West via subsidized water and corporate tax incentives actually drives down world prices and increases the financial burden on farmers who do not receive such subsidies. However, the farmers who grow the alfalfa and cotton in the desert prosper. This type of agriculture increases water's scarcity while offering little tangible benefit to the majority of the citizenry. Demand for water, already in short supply, heightens, and the resulting scarcity boosts its exchange value.

In a traditional potlatch, the expenditures of the growers and the government would cause a widespread redistribution of wealth among all members of the community while enhancing their own status as givers. The givers would then start reaccumulating assets while waiting for others to potlatch, thereby continuing the circulation process that precluded the monopolization of wealth. However, since the faux potlatch is a closed system, the growers' expenditures benefit no one but themselves. Their waste acts as a trigger mechanism, causing the leviathan state to demonstrate that it retains the power to enrich and thereby placate its powerful citizenry.

The state expends also, but to little obvious gain. Its actions serve as preventative maintenance—rearguard actions aimed at maintaining political dominance. Only the growers benefit. The grower's behavior is, of course, calculated to achieve just such an aim. Even though the faux potlatch involves orgiastic expenditure and profligate waste, it offers no community gain or resource redistribution.

The term *faux potlatch* draws on Georges Bataille's description of the bourgeois appropriation and retooling of the potlatch ritual for purposes of power consolidation and capital gain.

> As a game, potlatch is the opposite of a principle of conservation. . . . In the market economy, the processes of exchange have an acquisitive sense. Fortunes are no longer placed on a gambling table. . . . It is only to the extent that stability is assured and can no longer be compromised by even considerable losses that these losses are submitted to the regime of unproductive expenditure. (122–23)

Allan Stoekl argues that, in Bataille's view, bourgeois methodology bears only a superficial resemblance to potlatch, just as potlatch itself only slightly resembles Thorstein Veblen's vision of "conspicuous consumption." To Bataille, conspicuous consumption does not embody hedonism or economic inefficiency but is rather a perversion of the human need to destroy. The ability to destroy fungible assets without causing oneself harm or suffering any diminution in power reaffirms one's place in the power structure (xvi). This redefining of "destruction" as an inherently profitable, risk-free enterprise forms the essence of southwestern hydraulic capitalism.

Abbey asks that we trade in the ecologically pernicious faux potlatch and myth of the garden for the environmentally sound, steady-state economy implicit in true potlatch. As Bataille illustrates through the "Icarian Complex," humanity accumulates in order to expend—we rise in order to fall. Our species seeks the base.[5] Risk and fall are inherent predicates of the true potlatch ritual. Bataille compares the human condition to a "deliriously formed ritual poker. But the players can never leave the game. . . . At no time does a fortune serve to shelter its owner from need. To the contrary, it functionally remains—as does the possessor—at the mercy of a need for limitless loss" (122–23). In Bataille's view, the risk of loss permeates and enriches the potlatch. Likewise for Abbey, risk greatly enhances life in the desert: "Because freedom, not safety, is the highest good" (*Gang* 26).

In Abbey's world, blowing up Glen Canyon Dam is the ultimate potlatch. Even as it represents the quintessential act of profligacy—an apparent squandering of the region's most precious resource, the dam's demolition is appositionally a supreme act of conservation. This paradox reflects what Bataille argues is not a conflict between the exalted and the base, reason and unreason, but their synthesis. Just as ingestion cannot exist without excretion, just as death and life coexist conterminously, so too is expenditure linked with accumulation. Any disruption of the natural order of things represents unsustainable "Icarian Revolt."[6]

In the true potlatch system, dispersion and destruction of wealth provide the only justification for its accumulation. Destroying Glen Canyon Dam would entail demolishing a massively expensive edifice and releasing millions of acre-feet of water for no discernible profit. However, the land as well as those residents who lack water rights would benefit enormously from the reallocation of the region's water wealth. In this sense, the dam's demise would constitute symbolic potlatch. It would also undermine the commodity value of water, emphasizing its utility instead. Use value would thereby replace exchange value as the dominant mode of valuation, and the riverine ecosystem would be restored.

In addition, just as potlatch restores balance by destroying and reallocating wealth, so too would destroying Glen Canyon Dam begin the process of reestablishing ecological equilibrium in the canyonlands. With ecosystemic balance restored, the cyclical process of accumulation and expenditure could begin again without any predetermined advantage for agribusiness.

Reclamation, as noted earlier, implies that the region once yielded abundant water and crops to all who asked as well as prior ownership and domain. This vision, steeped though it is in the myth of the garden, runs counter to history. On the other hand, *restore,* as used by Abbey in *The Monkey Wrench Gang* and other writings, has a referent in the recent past. It advocates the return of the Colorado River ecosystem as well as that of the arid lands in the river basin to their predam states, a steady-state ecological economy wherein the wealth of the river, captured behind a dam and forced to enrich a powerful minority, is liberated and redistributed to the land and people at large.

Unfortunately, the Colorado's ecosystem can no more return to its predam state than the American auto industry can return to the days

before the arrival of Japanese cars. Rivers flow unceasingly; they epito-
mize constant change. There is no static past, frozen in time, to which
they can return. Dams irrevocably altered the river and the land and the
habits of those who live in their shadow. One can no more "restore" a
dammed river than unfertilize an egg.

"Reclamation" represents the ritualized hoarding and sham expenditure practiced by agribusiness, with wealth remaining in the hands of a
privileged few. Reclamation ideology, as we have seen in Austin and
Steinbeck, exploits the potent but nevertheless specious myth that the
Southwest will bloom into a new Eden under the stewardship of American expansionism. It promotes venture capitalism cloaked in a Jeffersonian yeoman, pioneer mask. The region's ecology and natural beauty are
acceptable casualties in the conquest of nature.[7]

Abbey confronts the ecological ramifications of this cycle and
attempts to explode the myth of the garden providing its ideological
justification. His characters conduct a fictional struggle against what
Worster calls the "hydraulic empire," a "hydraulic society of the West,
increasingly a coercive, monolithic and hierarchical system, ruled by a
power elite based on ownership of capital and expertise [with people]
organized and induced to run, as the water in a canal does, in a straight
line toward maximum yield, maximum profit" (*Rivers* 5). Ann Ronald
argues that Abbey's vilification of dams and dam builders lampoons the
ideology of superabundance that enslaves rivers to the forces of corporate greed, advocating an insurrection that will "dismantle the dynamo"
(139). While urging his vision of an agrarian anarchist steady-state economy, Abbey also champions "inhumanism," a term coined by Robinson
Jeffers to describe people who reject the notion that human endeavor is
the central aim of life and that all other life is of inherently lesser value.[8]

Within both economic systems—faux potlatch and the agroanarchist
steady state—water forms the privileged sign; its control determines the
power structure. The machinations of corporate capitalism work to
negate water's use value. Because profligacy implies vast resources at
one's disposal, wasting without concern for loss demonstrates control.
Hence, water barons flaunt their hegemony and wealth while simultaneously creating a perceived need for ever-increasing subsidy and water

infusion. This cycle is "faux" potlatch because it redistributes only upward—it has no beneficiaries beyond those who called it.

Those who do benefit profit handsomely from the transference of hydraulic capital. Creating an artificial surplus of water-intensive crops like cotton and alfalfa increases the scarcity and hence the price of water. This expanding shortage causes the state to divert more water to the growers' use. Water's exchange value increases even as agribusiness enjoys larger hydraulic subsidies. Since water resources remain finite, a larger share to agribusiness means a smaller share for everything else (including the desert ecosystem). Furthermore, elevated exchange value means that those not enjoying government subsidies must pay more for their water.

The Monkey Wrench Gang represents a rebellion against the continued faux potlatch carried on by western water interests with the aid and complicity of the Bureau of Reclamation. The gang's mission to blow up Glen Canyon Dam is embellished by numerous guerrilla actions on behalf of the desert and its human and nonhuman inhabitants. They aim to subvert the myth of plenty that simultaneously drives the corporate capital machine and destroys the land and hydrology of the very garden it purports to create. In Abbey's world, "If so-called civilization can violate the land, as it did in Glen Canyon . . . then so-called violence can be used to stop it" (Ronald 195).

George Hayduke and company look to replace systemic land abuse with a system of land use more aligned with Powell's original prescription for the region. Abbey views the dam as the height of hydrological hypocrisy and an insult to Powell's vision (the fact that the reservoir behind the dam is named Lake Powell exacerbates the insult). *The Monkey Wrench Gang* portrays human victims of the faux-potlatch cycle banding together to restore an ecologically stable society in keeping with Abbey's philosophy of "agrarian anarchy." "Resist Much, Obey Little"; the epigram from Walt Whitman that begins the novel aptly encapsulates Abbey's proposed solution to the southwestern ecological crisis. He advocates removing the self-perpetuating cycle of wage/gain profligacy and replacing it with a system based on ecological continuity and community-based government (*One Life* 25–28).

Among the region's principal villains, in Abbey's view, are the corporate growers for whom the vestiges of the agrarian myth have themselves become exploitable commodities in the pursuit of tangible wealth (water, capital). Trading on the enculturated national reverence for the farmer (a perquisite that small farmers had themselves long exploited), agribusiness increases its control over the privileged sign. As early as 1955, Richard Hofstadter argued, "In reality, the rest of us support the farmer; for industrial and urban America, sentimentally and morally committed to the ideal of the family farm, has undertaken . . . to support more farm-owners on the farm than it really needs under modern agricultural technology. It is in part because of the persistence of our agrarian traditions that this concession to the farmers arouses less universal antagonism than do the efforts of other groups menaced by technological changes" (8) In the American West, massive agricultural subsidies (primarily in the form of artificially low water prices) support the beef cattle industry (alfalfa and hay comprise two of the region's primary crops). Yet despite huge expenditures of water, grain, and topsoil, the seven Colorado River basin states produce only 23 percent of the nation's cattle value. The expenditures continue due to the preeminence of the cattle and agroindustrial lobbying complex. The power of the western agricultural lobby has grown even as the number of farmers has dwindled. A well-run, vocal organization, the agriculture lobby has used the national affection for the historic role of the farmer to consolidate a great deal of power, money, land, and water in the hands of an elite.[9] Abbey descries this phenomenon, labeling western cattlemen "nothing more than welfare parasites." In an essay entitled "Free Speech: The Cowboy and His Cow," Abbey turns his barbed wit on the American penchant for romanticizing cowboys. He maintains that both cowboys and their profession are greatly overrated and that altogether too much honor is heaped on people who spend their lives "contemplating the hind end of a cow" (*One Life* 18).

Since growing alfalfa and cotton in the desert requires massive infusions of water, their cultivation in an arid region makes little ecological sense. The justification for the production of enormous quantities of these crops in the arid West must therefore be social rather than scientific. It arises from a sense of entitlement buttressed by technology. Wasting water in the desert while spending immense sums to "reclaim" the land from aridity theoretically demonstrates that even the ecologically impossible yields to American ingenuity. Nature became another tool for the ascendancy of the chosen people. In the words of Emerson, "Nature is thoroughly mediate. It is made to serve. It receives the dominion of man as meekly as the ass on which the savior rode" (*Works* 45).

Fulfilling the American destiny handed down from the Almighty required that humans make a green world out of an arid land. This ethos exemplifies the uniquely American combination of technological ascendancy and perceived divine right. God and technology theoretically would provide the means through which humanity would dominate and then achieve independence from nature.[10] The settlement of the West owed much to this conjoining of human industry with the presumed will of the Deity. It allowed humans to co-opt God's will and turn it into human destiny and then use that notion of human destiny to expand the fortunes of a select few. The state would subsidize this process.

By 1975, when *The Monkey Wrench Gang* was published, the ideological mechanism underlying a self-perpetuating cycle of expenditure and subsidy had long been in place. Those who would waste water had learned to turn to the Bureau of Reclamation and cry poverty. They found a sympathetic and powerful audience. The bureau responded by building dams and diversions that provided water to raise more crops and cattle, which in turn required more water, ad infinitum.[11]

Bernard DeVoto expressed the western attitude toward the federal government as, "Get out and give us more money." The phrase reflects the schism between the pioneer myth whose accompanying animus toward external authority continues to influence western ideology and the realities of the Reclamation era. None of the monumental reclamation projects that pepper the West could have been built without federal subsidy. Meanwhile, very few of the enormous ranches and farms that supposedly embody the western way of life could exist without these reclamation projects. This leads to an ironic counterpoint wherein westerners fiercely assert their independence while loudly demanding increased federal aid.

In essence, the powerful members of the community ritually expend vast amounts of water in a way that vaguely recalls the American tradition of yeoman husbandry and infinite ambition. While their methods and ideology bear little resemblance to the Jeffersonian notion of family farms and subsistence agriculture, they do purport to subdue the forces of nature to the needs of humans and thus, in some sense, embody the dual notions of American ingenuity and manifest destiny. Their propaganda seized on this shared goal and successfully conflated agribusiness and the mythic western figure. Both claimed as their symbol a man who is independent, one with the land, and dedicated to the perpetuation of the "American" way of life. This yeoman facade struck and continues to strike a resonant chord within the government, engendering an almost Pavlovian political response.

The state, that is, the Bureau of Reclamation, affirms the national ideology and its own entitlement to govern by helping corporate growers waste water under the guise of taming nature. The state also participates in the cycle through massive federal spending and wasteful hydroexpenditures of its own. The most obvious and arguably the most ecologically repugnant of these expenditures are the huge federal dams festooning the West.[12]

Glen Canyon Dam, object of the monkeywrenchers' animus, went on line in 1964 at a final cost of $300 million.[13] It had a 27 million acre-foot storage capacity at the time of its completion, though it annually forfeits 70,000 acre-feet of storage space to siltation. It also suffers annual evaporation losses of 450,000 acre-feet.

Meanwhile, the Colorado River is vastly oversubscribed. Even without calculating the massive evaporation losses of Glen Canyon and the many other reservoirs constructed along its length, the Colorado's annual flow almost never reaches the figure ascribed to it by the various states, courts, and federal agencies when they divided its water among the basin states and Mexico. For example, the Bureau of Reclamation originally apportioned 16.8 million acre-feet of Colorado River water despite the river's average flow of 13.9 million acre-feet. This led to the Colorado being called a "deficit river," meaning that more water was appropriated from the river than it actually had. Labeling the river as deficient permitted the river's managers to blame the water for not being sufficiently plentiful. It allowed people in the West to continue behaving "as if the river, not the plans and works of those who used its waters, were to blame for its shortcomings" (Fradkin 15).

Those shortcomings have become glaringly obvious. It has been over a generation since the Colorado reached its mouth in the Gulf of California. When the little water that remains after dams and diversions reaches the delta in Mexico, it is three times as saline as ocean water and flows so weakly that it disappears into the sand long before reaching the Gulf.

Acknowledging the impossibility of attaining hydrological equilibrium under the current scheme requires accepting limitations on growth. And that concept, until very recently, remained something that neither the government nor regional agrointerests could entertain. Building dams affirmed—at least for the short term—state dominance over water and the accompanying right of its distribution. Dams also created reservoirs, which generated the illusion of an ample supply of water. But the very acts aimed at demonstrating control and abundance instead revealed a critical shortage. And in times of shortage, the rich generally become richer while the poor grow poorer still.

Such are the consequences of the agrarian myth in the Southwest. Over the years, both sides of the debate regarding development in the arid regions have co-opted Powell's doctrine for their own ideological gain. Whereas Abbey quoted Powell to commemorate Abbey's last trip through Glen Canyon (*Desert* 192), the Bureau of Reclamation attaches Powell's name to the reservoir that flooded the canyon and published a book entitled *Lake Powell, Jewel of the Colorado.* Abbey is all too aware of this irony and excoriates those responsible: "The impounded waters form an artificial lake named Powell, supposedly to honor but actually to dishonor the memory, spirit and vision of Major John Wesley Powell. . . . Where he and his brave men once lined the rapids and glided through the silent canyons . . . the motorboats now whine, scumming the water with cigarette butts, beer cans and oil, dragging the water skiers on their endless rounds, clockwise" (*Desert* 173–74). Viewing the dam and reservoir as blights on the landscape and as a desecration of the canyon provides an easy justification to the plan to destroy them.

In *The Monkey Wrench Gang,* the people Abbey places on the front lines of the struggle against the despoliation of the western landscape have varying motivations for their shared ideals. Doc Sarvis and Bonnie are indignant ecovandals. Doc destroys road signs because they interfere with his serenity, while Bonnie, in the beginning, acts mostly out of com-

panionship for Doc. She later develops her own sense of outrage, especially when confronted with the ravaged landscape of a mountain clear-
cut (*Gang* 209–12).[14] Doc participates reluctantly and with abject
pacifism. He is the humanist of the gang, acting out of a love for humanity as well as for the landscape. His actions manifest a quixotic desire to
resist the fatalism that otherwise infuses his outlook.

> "The reason there are so many people on the river these days is
> because there are too many people everywhere else. . . . The wilder-
> ness once offered men a plausible way of life," the doctor said.
> "Now it functions as a psychiatric refuge. Soon there will be no
> wilderness. . . . Soon there will be no place to go. Then the madness
> will be universal. . . . And the universe goes mad." (*Gang* 60)

Rebelling against what he sees as inevitable, yet also dedicated to serving
the very people responsible, Doc lumbers gregariously into the breach.
At tale's end, he and Bonnie even sacrifice their freedom to go to the aid
of Bishop Love, their chief antagonist.

Nevertheless, Doc's role in the gang's ecotage should not be under-
estimated. As resident sage, his imprimatur lends dignity to their exploits,
and his checkbook enables them. Despite deriving his wealth from the
technologically enhanced ability of medicine to treat the needs of an
expanding population, Doc good-naturedly funds a guerrilla war against
the source of his creature comforts. He is in effect redistributing his
wealth in a manner that will, if successful, force widespread emulation.
The novel's conclusion validates the depth of Doc's commitment as he
gives up his lucrative practice to tend to a small, remote community.

Seldom Seen Smith and George Hayduke represent homegrown victims of the technocracy. Smith, a river guide, has seen his livelihood
defaced and his place of business drowned. His official address remains
Hite, Utah, though that town now lies beneath tons of silt and water.
Slow to anger but deceptively fanatical, Smith is the one who suggests
destroying the dam, a telos that soon infects the gang's entire existence.
His quest is quasi-religious:

> "Dear old God," he prayed, "you know and I know what it was like
> here before them bastards from Washington moved in and ruined it
> all. You remember the river, how fat and golden it was . . . Remem-

ber the deer on the sandbars . . . and the catfish so big and tasty and
how they'd bite on spoiled salami? . . . Remember the cataracts in
Forty-Mile Canyon? Well, they flooded out about half of them too.
. . . Listen . . . There's something you can do for me, God. How
about a little old *pre*-cision earthquake right under this dam? . . .
Okay, God, I see you don't want to do it just now. Well all right, suit
yourself, you're the boss, but we ain't got a hell of a lot of time.
Make it pretty soon, goddammit. A-men." (*Gang* 32–33)

Smith cannot decide whether to pray or to chastise God. As a Mormon,
he is obligated by church dogma to have as many children as he can
(Bishop Love, his nemesis, has eleven).[15] He is polygamous, a lifestyle
that runs counter to modern church teachings and that only the most traditional Mormons continue to embrace. Smith, though, is childless, a
renegade "jack" Mormon. He is uncomfortable with the teachings of his
church but cannot renounce them entirely. Even his name, "Joseph 'Seldom Seen' Smith" suggests an inherent ambivalence about Mormonism.
Though a namesake of the church's founder, Smith's nickname suggests
an incongruity between his lifestyle and the tenets of the Latter-day
Saints.

In a sense, Smith's theological quandary mirrors the dilemma of the
expanding Southwest. As a river guide, he makes his living taking tourists
into the canyonlands. His welfare thus depends on a constant influx of
people into the region. Despite this apparent need for population expansion, Smith makes it as difficult as he can for people to visit or settle in the
Southwest. He blows up bridges, destroys surveying equipment and
power stations, and commits various other acts of ecotage. His dilemma
resembles Doc's, and both men display similar reluctance at the start of
every operation. The only anchor for Smith's worldview is the need to
destroy Glen Canyon Dam:

> The blue death, Smith called it [Lake Powell]. Like Hayduke, his
> heart was full of a healthy hatred. . . . He remembered the golden
> river flowing to the sea. He remembered canyons called Hidden
> Passage and Salvation and Last Chance and . . . some that never had
> a name. . . . All of these things now lay beneath the dead water of the
> reservoir, slowly disappearing under layers of descending silt. How
> could he forget? He had seen too much. (*Gang* 31)

The theological overtones of the canyons chosen are no accident. Smith's religious association with the dam's demise recurs throughout the novel. Monkeywrenching provides him with a kind of theological walkabout—a quest for the presence of a righteous God. He believes in right and wrong but remains uncertain as to the existence of a just and merciful God:

> "All we need is to make one little crack in it, Doc. One crack in that dam and nature, she'll take care of the rest. Nature and God."
> "Whose side is God on?"
> "That's something I aim to find out." (*Gang* 258)

While Smith's fervor remains low-key and resonates with his own brand of theology, Hayduke evinces the hard-core fanaticism that drives the gang.

> Hayduke thought. Finally the idea arrived. He said, "My job is to save the fucking wilderness. I don't know anything else worth saving." (*Gang* 211)

As a Vietnam veteran, former POW and Green Beret medic, Hayduke brings his own brand of post-traumatic stress disorder to the war to save the West.

> I get a pension too. Twenty-five percent disability. Head case. One quarter lunatic. I must have a dozen checks waiting for me at the old man's place. . . . They really wanted to court-martial me but Mom wouldn't stand for it. Anyhow, when I finally got free of those jail-hospitals and found out they were trying to do the same thing to the West that they did to that little country over there, I got mad all over again. (*Gang* 330)

Hayduke often finds himself flashing back to his days in the jungle fleeing the helicopters that were supposedly on his side. A former POW half-brainwashed into a Vietcong, George Washington Hayduke lived in terror of American forces. His return to the States offers little respite. He is again pursued (the novel's structure suggests) by those same forces that drove the United States into an unwinnable, resource-draining war.

Hayduke is a caricature—a monomaniacal force of nature with a taste for Schlitz. His brute determination and survivalist tactics, coupled with an almost suicidal bent, enable him and his cohorts to successfully carry out much grander operations than they otherwise could. Even his colleagues worry about his sanity and then, because of their association with him, question their own.

Because of his quixotic drive, it seems only right that Hayduke should meet and bond with Jack Burns, the mythic Quixote-figure of several other Abbey novels. Burns is the "Brave Cowboy" of the novel by the same name, an anachronism who refuses to die and whose lifestyle and sense of loyalty have no place in a West dedicated to personal gain and terrestrial degradation. In *The Monkey Wrench Gang*, Burns is transformed into an ecowarrior—a vagabond like Hayduke except that he rides a horse instead of driving a jeep. Together they symbolize the past and future of the West.

Burns has come from the past to help Hayduke re-create a world where independence and a land-based value system will once again hold sway.[16] Burns also represents Hayduke's lone-wolf trait carried to an extreme. As a mythic figure who comes out of the night and refuses to give his name (until the novel's sequel, *Hayduke Lives*), Burns symbolizes what Hayduke will soon become—a ghostlike figure, more legend than man. Interestingly, Burns also represents what even Hayduke knows is the dangerous world of solipsism and make-believe: "For even Hayduke sensed, when he faced the thing directly, that the total loner would go insane. Was insane. Somewhere in the depths of solitude, beyond wildness and freedom, lay the trap of madness" (*Gang* 106). Abbey extricates Hayduke and Burns from their seemingly inevitable madness by bonding the two together at book's end. As their existence fades into legend and society assumes them dead (Burns by the side of the road in *The Brave Cowboy* and Hayduke in a fusillade of bullets at the end of *The Monkey Wrench Gang*), they somehow find each other and that bonding saves them from the otherwise inevitable madness.

Abbey does not dispute Hayduke's instability, but he does suggest that Hayduke is a product of his time and that the status quo also contains a form of madness that will require a certain amount of fanaticism to dislodge it: "Viewing it this way, we can see that the religion of endless growth—like any religion based on blind faith rather than reason—is a kind of mania . . . indeed a disease. . . . Growth for the sake of growth is the ideology of the cancer cell. Cancer has no purpose but growth; but it does have another result—the death of the host" (*One Life* 21). Throughout his oeuvre, Abbey advocates desperate measures to contravene the rampant destruction that the corporate-state monolith hungry for water and land wreaks on the landscape.

In prior times, writers of the West created scenarios where characters drew their strength from their unending battles to carve a life from the majestic yet merciless land.[17] Abbey turns this formulation around. The land's survival depends, in the case of Hayduke, on his resourcefulness and his power to inspire others to restore the ecosystem's balance. In *Desert Solitaire,* Abbey draws an important distinction between civilization and culture, calling civilization "the vital force in human history" and culture "that inert mass of institutions and organizations which . . . drag[s] down the advance of life." Civilization, he claims, is "the wild river" and culture "592,000 tons of cement" (277).[18] It is up to Hayduke to rescue the West from culture. Hayduke embodies Abbey's oft-stated desire to replace our current, highly integrated social system with a loose knit series of autonomous societies living in harmony with their surroundings.[19] While Hayduke himself is not so thoughtful, his goal of "sav[ing] the fucking wilderness" and his blows against the faux-potlatch system breathe behavioral life into Abbey's polemical ideas.

In *Abbey's Road,* Abbey declares, "If we can draw the line against the industrial machine in America, and make it hold, then perhaps . . . we can gradually force industrialism underground, where it belongs, and restore to all citizens of our nation their rightful heritage of breathable air, drinkable water, open space, family-farm agriculture, a truly democratic political economy" (137). This argument recalls Bataille's recipe for the dissolution of the bourgeois state. Abbey contends that industrialism forms an autocratic monolith that usurps the basic human rights and needs of the world's inhabitants. Potlatch (though Abbey does not use the term), as a socially encoded redistribution of ecological wealth (water, air, open space, etc.), must replace the faux potlatch practiced by the industrial oligarchy, or the biotic economy will implode.[20]

According to Bataille (and Abbey), industrialism's capacity to cause vast ecosystemic harm stems from the ascension of science to the seat of highest authority within the technoindustrial paradigm: "It is possible in all freedom to be a plaything of evil if evil itself does not have to answer before God" (Bataille 49).[21] Science and the machine displace natural theology, allowing technology to remake the earth in the image of human ingenuity. In the United States "Americans saw themselves as building their civilization out of nature itself, as neither the analogue nor the translation of Natural Law but its direct expression" (Jehlen 3). Rather than interpreting Original Sin as the necessity to remake human behavioral norms, it signaled the need to remake the earth through scientific advance into a facsimile of the original Eden.

In the Southwest, this renovation revolved by necessity around the manipulation of water and its diversion for use in irrigation, hydroelectricity, and urban sprawl. For Bataille, the myth of the garden may be seen as Icarian revolt—a denial of the cyclical rise and fall of all things. He acknowledges Nietzsche's notion of the simultaneous ascension-martyrdom of Christ as the ultimate expression of *ressentiment* power and imputes similar motivations to his own formulation of "imperative heterogeneity"—a pious materialism obviating all impulsions but the pursuit of power. Attempting to remake Eden in our own/God's image denotes a continued refusal to recognize the cycle of rise and fall and the ascension of the base (as represented by Hayduke as well as by the desert itself) inherent in the health of the economic system as well as the ecosystem.[22]

Bataille sees no easy solution to this cyclic hoarding of power. Any attempt at subversion must border on the fanatical if it is to succeed. His description of such a fanatic recalls Abbey's Hayduke: "[T]he introduction of a lawless intellectual . . . into the world of legitimate thought defines itself at the outset as the most arduous and audacious operation. And it is evident that if it were not practiced without equivocation, with a resolution and a rigor rarely attained in other cases, it would be the most vain operation" (80). Obviously, Hayduke is not an intellectual. Rather than injecting a renegade theoretician into an extant philosophical framework, Abbey inserted an action-oriented individual into a functioning state apparatus.

The results of the gang's efforts are hopeful but inconclusive. Initially, things go well as the gang successfully carries out a number of monkeywrench operations. Eventually, however, they are tracked down and cornered by Bishop Love and the Search and Rescue Team. During a standoff in a box canyon, Bishop Love suffers a heart attack and Doc and Bonnie go to his aid and their arrest. Smith, half-starved and unable to run any farther, is captured in a public campground, while Hayduke appears to get shot to pieces and fall five hundred feet to his death.

Slowly, the outlook improves. Doc and Bonnie's humanitarian acts lead to the partial conversion of Bishop Love (a conversion he repudiates in the novel's sequel). The surviving three members of the gang stand trial for, and publicly repent of, their actions. Doc even converts to Mormonism. They retire from monkeywrenching and become law-abiding members of society living under the watchful eye of their parole officer. Glen Canyon Dam remains intact, and the faux-potlatch cycle seems destined to continue.

Into this supposedly peaceful status quo steps Hayduke, unrepentant and more dangerous than ever. After staging his death in the canyon, he goes into hiding and then reemerges having metamorphosed into a pure force of nature. No longer is he distracted by erotic need (for Bonnie) or even the standard appurtenances of twentieth-century existence. He has become a legend (Rudolf the Red) and an untraceable warrior for the canyonlands. Having landed a job in the bowels of the hated dam, he has every intention of fulfilling the gang's mission.

Furthermore, as the prolegomenon of the novel suggests (part of which is quoted at the beginning of this chapter), the movement has gained adherents, becoming larger than the actors themselves. So despite their forced diaspora, the gang's work continues even as its members fulfill their parole. Abbey suggests that though the time may not be right for the demise of faux potlatch, seeds have been planted that will eventually choke the hydraulically illegitimate state apparatus. Corporate control over the privileged sign is no longer assured. The forces of ecological stability will use whatever means are necessary to restore hydrological equilibrium to "the heart of the heart of the canyonlands."

> Somewhere under the heavy burden of water going nowhere, under the silence, the old rocks of the river channel waited for the promised resurrection. Promised by whom? Promised by Capt. Joseph "Seldom Seen" Smith; by Sgt. George Washington Hayduke; by Doc Sarvis and Ms. Bonnie Abzug, that's whom. (*Gang* 112–13)

In an odd postscript wherein life imitates art, EarthFirst!, a radical environmental group that advocates ecotage and whose symbol is the monkey wrench, took up the gang's mission as their own. In 1981, they unfurled a huge canvas crack on the face of the Glen Canyon Dam, announcing to all their goal, its total demise. Abbey, for his part, wrote the introduction to *Ecodefense,* the manual of ecotage drafted by Dave Foreman, the founder of EarthFirst!. Abbey also incorporated Earth-First! and other radical environmental actors into *Hayduke Lives,* the posthumously published sequel to *The Monkey Wrench Gang.* Having created a new myth of the ecowarrior that, like the myth of the garden, spawned real-life progeny, Abbey weaves a new story containing characters from fact and fiction. In doing so he simultaneously acknowledges both the potency of myth and the irony of its predominance.

5

The Environmental System: *Animal Dreams* and the Rhetoric of Environment

A river is more than an amenity; it is a treasure.
—Oliver Wendell Holmes

At the beginning of the twentieth century, Mary Austin believed in spite of herself that Reclamation would work to the good of both humans and the land. In the 1930s, John Steinbeck portrayed Reclamation's horrific social and ecological effects while still hoping that it could be retailored to benefit yeoman farmers. The 1970s find Edward Abbey raging against the desecration of the canyonlands and advocating the forcible destruction of Reclamation and all its trappings. By 1990, Barbara Kingsolver seeks to articulate a vision of a post-Reclamation American West. The problem she faces also plagued her forebears; it is extraordinarily difficult to articulate a vision for change in a language designed to resist it.

In *Animal Dreams,* Kingsolver attempts to describe a new western reality, predicated on an organicist, ecofeminist vision. She does not succeed. That does not mean, however, that the novel is a failure. Read as an ambitious effort to rethink social and ecological mores, *Animal Dreams* gains richness, offering a disturbing glimpse at the difficulties inherent in the construction of a post-Reclamation era.

Many of those difficulties are communication-based, and for that reason my analysis of the novel adopts a systems-theoretical approach. Systems theory provides a means for studying communication within complex systems. A system is an organization of components functioning as a unit to perpetuate the survival of the whole. A human, for example, is a biological system comprised of many function systems (digestive system, nervous system, etc.). Humans are themselves components of a larger social system, which in turn forms part of an ecosystem, and so on.

Systems are formed and maintained through communication among components. That communication constructs meaning. Meaning is not *transferred* through communication; it is *created* through communication. There must be mutual comprehension by both parties before meaning becomes realized. Without mutual comprehension, attempts at communication create only noise. If, for example, I am training a dog to sit, I may have to repeat the command over and over. The dog may roll over, heel, shake hands, or lie down in an attempt to find meaning in my words. Eventually, it will glean that I wish it to sit and at that moment—when the dog and I understand each other—my command ceases to be noise and becomes communication.

Animal Dreams tackles a problem far more complicated than dog training. The concepts Kingsolver wishes to communicate (and therethrough give meaning) have not been articulated before. There are no words to describe a post-Reclamation society. In fact, the language Kingsolver must use resists such ideas because, if actualized, the ideas will topple the current power structure. Kingsolver thus faces the dual challenge of formulating a coherent alternative to Reclamation using language that hinders her at every turn, and then communicating that vision to her readers. This chapter analyzes the efficacy of her attempt and places it in the context of the late Reclamation era.

Literature has historically provided a potent medium through which to stretch and prod language. Layers of meaning and the elastic divisions between fiction and nonfiction as well as among other literary genres have probed the form and function of text as text and as discourse. Environmental literature has done this out of necessity, since the amorphousness of both the genre and the term *(environment)* means that their respective meanings require constant reworking.

This lack of consensus triggers repercussions, especially with regard to the environment. Though most people can agree on the need for environmental reform in the West, there is much less agreement as to the meanings of *environment* or *reform.* Consequently, communication stalls and attempts at "environmental protection" break down. In this way, linguistic inertia protects the status quo. This centrality of communication to social change combined with the lack of a static definition of environment forms an imposing barrier to an ecologically viable society.

We have seen that the etiology of Reclamation lay in a national allegiance to the American Dream, not in an empirical, science-based cosmology. Restoration dogma, meanwhile, mirrors a growing disenchantment with the ecological destruction wrought by an extraction-based social system, and is an effort to address the conservation movement's inability to craft alternatives. Yet any alternatives to the present system, including Restoration, can only come about through language, and language poses a formidable obstacle indeed.

Reclassifying Resources

When parties communicate, each party represents an external perturbation to the other. For example, suppose I engage you in conversation as you lie lost in reverie, dreaming of the previous evening's romance. You wish to return to your thoughts and, so, gently disengage yourself from further conversation. You use language (both verbal and body) to facilitate your return to equilibrium. I disturbed you (an external perturbation), and you responded through language in a manner designed to eliminate the disturbance.

Whenever two or more parties communicate, that interaction represents a departure from the status quo. At times, the discourse may describe a perturbation of great magnitude (perhaps a war requiring delicate diplomacy to subdue) or a pleasurable situation that it would be beneficial to prolong (such as the previous evening's romance). In both instances, language provides the mediating force that enables coexistence. I will discuss this facet of language in more detail shortly. For now, it suffices to realize that language facilitates homeostasis while discouraging radical change. This seems only logical; language is an invention of the system it maintains and is shaped by those in power as a means of retaining dominance. It has evolved as a tool for maintaining the status quo.

Discourse is possible because function systems share the goal of the larger system's autopoiesis, the process by which systems maintain and reproduce themselves.[1] That common goal of all the system components creates a shared context through which to construct meaning. In the human body, the continued survival of the particular human provides the common context. Like all complex systems, humans contain many function systems for handling particular facets of their autopoiesis. The nervous, circulatory, and digestive systems fulfill different functions dedicated to the maintenance and continued viability of each human being. The same diversification and delegation takes place in social systems dedicated to the reproduction and maintenance of society. The legal, political, educational, and economic systems function independently, while remaining dedicated to the good of the whole.

Discord within a system becomes inevitable as complexity increases. Function systems can have distinct, competing goals even while sharing the larger imperative of maintaining the unity. Teachers and parents may differ on how best to educate a child, two developers may disagree on how best to build on a tract of land, and so on. While the disputants disagree, they share a common medium through which to mediate their conflict. Without that common context, communication devolves into noise.[2]

In a social system, a conundrum arises when people perceive the system's operation as flawed yet cannot conceive of the means to correct that flaw. This is a phenomenon distinct from the self-regulatory activities of different function systems, as when the judicial and political branches differ over the interpretation of a particular statute. Radical reform would involve instigating fundamental changes in the structure and boundaries of a system. Language offers the only means through which to effect these changes, even as its mission constrains its vocabulary to prevent such radical shifts.[3] As a result, system opponents must work within a medium designed to subvert their agenda. This paradox has serious implications for those wishing to depose the Reclamation era and install a more (hydro)logical regime in the West.

The prevailing definition of environment was produced by a system that views its surroundings through a lens dedicated to economic expansion. It evaluates all things according to their potential value, which then determines their use. Even before technology reduces its matter and energy to products, Timothy Luke observes, "Nature already is transformed discursively into 'natural resources'" ("Environmentality" 58).

The system's validation and perpetuation lie in linguistically configuring its surroundings to reflect its aims.

Animal Dreams underscores the flexibility of the term *resource*. Classifying an object as a resource confers value. A natural resource conjures images of an asset ripe for exploitation. Designation as a resource removes an object from the shadowy realm of "environment" and tosses it into the swift-flowing stream of transactive capitalism, where its value becomes a product of discursive maneuvering. In Kingsolver's fictional town of Grace, Arizona, land and water are vital resources for the disenfranchised indigenous community. By contrast, the privileged members of the economic system (the Black Mountain Mining Company) measure the region's resource potential by its subterranean ore content. Once the ore is extracted, the land becomes permanently devalued.

Because water is ancillary to the mining process, the company gauges water's worth by measuring its exchange value in a market economy, a value that increases with scarcity. For the inhabitants of Grace, however, scarce water means less food. Consequently, for the townspeople, water's worth appreciates in direct relation to availability and use value. Though they would pay more for water during times of scarcity, that is a function of exchange value, not a measure of water's functional worth in a subsistence economy. The differing methods of valuation of the mining company and the Grace townsfolk stem from divergent notions of environment and are fundamentally incompatible.

In systems-theoretical terms, *environment* refers to everything that is *not* the system. It includes everything with which the system cannot communicate. Yet the environment is not merely chaos lurking outside the system's boundaries; it is itself a network of systems for which our system comprises *its* environment. The two sides, system and environment, share a dynamic border that shifts and flows in response to perturbation. A system responds and adapts to environmental perturbation in a manner designed to ensure its survival (autopoiesis). If the system survives, it will have gained complexity, enabling it to better cope with similar perturbations in the future. In other words, it will have evolved.[4]

The environment (i.e., whatever lies outside a system's boundaries) cannot be articulated because it lies, by definition, outside the realm of communication. As the sum total of everything not the system, the environment is necessarily far more complex than the system itself. Meaning lies in the relationship between the system's components, while the system's stability depends on its ability to reproduce and function despite and because of ongoing environmental disturbance. *Animal Dreams* represents an attempt to replace the dominant system (and discourse) with one that privileges a steady-state economic apparatus.

Kingsolver advocates replacing atomized, patriarchal science with an organicist worldview predicated on ecofeminism and Native American ecospirituality. In this new reality, land-based values would enjoy a higher status expressed through a language designed to perpetuate those values.[5] Seventy-three years earlier, Mary Austin encountered problems when attempting to manipulate the newly formed Reclamation rhetoric to fit a nascent environmental agenda. By 1990, nine decades of linguistic evolution allow Kingsolver more flexibility, though the obstacles remain enormous. A closer examination of *Animal Dreams* reveals the scope and nature of many of these barriers.

Systems Theory and *Animal Dreams*

Codi Noline, the novel's protagonist, has no link with her past. Her traumatic childhood in Grace—characterized by her mother's death; emotional neglect by her father, Doc Homer; and her own miscarriage or abortion at age fifteen—leaves her disconnected from the passionate environmentalism of her youth, and prone to listlessness. Though smart and capable, Codi feels unfit for any employment more meaningful than late-night Slurpee duty at a Tucson 7–11. When Doc Homer's deteriorating mental state leads Codi back to Grace to care for him and to teach high school biology, she feels terrified despite her extensive background in science and an all but completed medical degree.

Hallie, the other Noline sister, offers a stark contrast. Though the two sisters were inseparable as children and well into adulthood, they followed vastly different life trajectories. Codi, once the youthful firebrand, now drifts, bereft of ambition and passion. Hallie, who as a child had dutifully followed Codi on her missions to rescue coyotes and otherwise save the planet, has become the leader who dares to go wherever her beliefs take her. Hallie's itinerant idealism eventually leads her on a quixotic and ultimately fatal mission to aid Nicaraguan peasants under attack by American-funded Contras. The novel's treatment of Hallie's behavior is markedly ambivalent. Though brave, her actions seem neither productive nor wise. Rather than address the problem—American unwillingness to tolerate an alternative economic system to the south—Hallie treats the symptom, with predictable results. She dies a martyred hero, and the dirty war continues.

Codi, on the other hand, when confronted with the local mining company's poisoning of the land and water of Grace, does not follow her usual routine of abdicating responsibility and fleeing the area. Doc Homer's progressive degeneration holds her in place. Instead of leaving, she stays and attacks the problem from within. This reengagement with her surroundings and community enables a rediscovery of self. To her surprise, Codi finds her sense of self integrally tied to the health of the society and ecosystem. The danger to Grace resulting from the mining company's actions and the silent complicity of the EPA catalyzes Codi's long dormant value system, which cannot tolerate environmental degradation.

Upon returning to Grace, Codi wanders through the local orchards, mentally comparing them to graveyards and remarking on the excessive fall of fruit. Her observation is portentous because the orchards occupy an important niche in the town's cultural tradition, and their yield provides a livelihood for the town's inhabitants. Codi's biology class later discovers that the river running through Grace verges on biotic death, its pH level akin to battery acid. Years of copper mining by the Black Mountain Mining Company (until a few years before, the major employer of the town's men) created an enormous tailings pile[6] through which the company now leaches sulfuric acid in order to recover trace amounts of valuable metals. The acid seeps into the river, poisoning it and inflicting slow death on the crops of local farmers and orchard growers. The situation is both symbolically significant, as a metaphor for the hydraulic disenfranchisement of minority cultures (in this case, the indigenous and Hispanic communities), and imminently perilous because the crops that feed the community are dying.

When Codi naively assumes that a report to the local authorities will

halt the leaching operation, Viola, the town matriarch, quickly disabuses
her:

> "Dam up the river," Viola said. "That's all they have to do to meet
> with the EPA laws. Dam it up and send it out Tortoise Canyon
> instead of down through here. . . . [I]f Black Mountain dams up the
> river, it's out of the jurisdiction of the Environmental Protection
> Agency." (*Animal* 111)

This exchange underscores a dangerous characteristic of systems that
contain multiple function systems: complexity to the point of obfusca-
tion. Because the government requires popular support to maintain its
power base, its laws must offer a veneer of equity. Yet the state also
depends on capital inflow for its autopoiesis. The challenge therefore lies
in creating laws that do not incite disfavor among the rank and file yet
buttress the corporate capital mechanism.

With water forming the arid region's privileged sign, much systemic
complexity arises from the state's double duty of appeasing the water-
poor while servicing the water-rich. To accomplish both objectives, the
state must disarm its regulatory authority. It does so by writing laws that
protect its less powerful citizenry and then legislating the means to crip-
ple those laws' enforcement. Therein lies an invidious logic: it is illegal to
poison a town's water supply but legal to desiccate the area. Similar
hydraulic subterfuges have enjoyed a long tenure in the West, dating
back to the pre-Powell era.[7]

Grace's problems also stem from its residents' prior forfeiture of their
water rights. Uneducated and ignorant of the complex field of water law,
the town's inhabitants happily sold these newly created abstractions that
had no place in their culture. They were comforted because the buyer was
the Black Mountain Mining Company, a welcomed addition to the community as its new major employer. As a result, according to Viola, "Nobody
around here's got water rights. All these families sold the water rights to
the company in 1939, for twenty-five cents an acre. We all thought we
were getting money for nothing. We had us a *fiesta*" (*Animal* 111).

Here we see clear echoes of the Owens Valley, where Fred Eaton
posed as a prospective rancher and bought options on the best water
rights in the valley. He then sold those rights to the city of Los Angeles at

a huge profit. His actions are fictionalized but wholly recognizable in *The Ford*. The theme of purloined or misappropriated water rights is common in both historical and fictional representations of the West.[8]

In *Animal Dreams,* when the mining company diverted attention from the water to the abstract field of water rights, it shifted the discourse into a realm where it held the advantage. The company is an outgrowth of the society that invented water rights; the indigenous community struggles to survive on that society's periphery. Before the Anglos came to the region, water had been apportioned according to its use value and a historic sense of community. When the state assigned water an economic value and named it a unit of exchange, it affirmed water's place as privileged sign and solidified the economic system's control over it.[9] Once control over water passed to state and corporate interests, it cast grave doubt on the long-term survival of indigenous communities.

The EPA's impotence in the face of Grace's imminent demise has multiple historical referents as well. As a regulatory arm of an apparatus designed to facilitate capital gain, the EPA must constantly renegotiate its joint allegiance to corporate ideals and environmental protection. Since the social system is driven by self-interest (autopoiesis), it strives to defend those qualities that serve its aims. However, as the system diversifies, its aims become disparate, and conflicts arise between various function systems.

An excellent illustration of the regulatory tightrope the EPA must negotiate involves the ongoing controversy over pesticide levels in food. Environmental groups and concerned citizens advocate strict limits, arguing that the pesticides are toxic and that any exposure in humans constitutes a health hazard. Agricultural interests counter that trace amounts of the chemicals do not harm humans and are essential to the business of growing food. Faced with competing demands from constituencies that are both vital to the survival of the social system, the EPA must decide what constitutes a safe level of pesticide in food. That level must appease public health advocates without crippling the food production industry.

Even among potential allies, complexity makes conflict inescapable. A rafting concern and a hydroelectric company may wish to use the same river, but their respective commercial aims clash. If the river is dammed, it loses allure to potential rafting clients. Yet, without a dam, the power company cannot generate. Both businesses seek to exploit the resource potential of the river, but their methods are incompatible. Determining how best to manage the river becomes political, a process of reconciling the multiple domains comprising the system's self-interest.[10] As societies discover or define their environment's ecological limits, they are forced to take measures to guarantee their population's continued survival in the global political economy by becoming "environmental protection agencies" (Luke, "On Environmentality" 69). They accomplish this partially through determination of system boundaries.

Boundary drawing is an inherently subjective process, infused with ideology and integral to the distribution of power. System boundaries exert a strong influence on language, which, as noted earlier, is integral to the system's autopoiesis. One of the most potent weapons that language allots to the dominant class is the power to rationalize and justify its behavior. Ethics are, after all, a mutually agreed upon set of values determined in part by the configuration of the group setting the values. If the dominator can plausibly claim that its actions are morally just and cause no harm, then the complaints of the subjugated lose legitimacy. Their indignation excites no sympathy, and their complaints fade into insignificance. Power over language also permits ecological degradation because that degradation is a boon rather than a bane for those who benefit from it. In Grace, for example, the Black Mountain Mining Company's publicist might describe the acid leaching operation as a "recycling" of the tailings to extract surplus value from already processed material in order to provide the greatest possible return on shareholders' investments.

Boundary drawing can also affect one's race, even one's humanity. Over the course of recorded American history, from the Puritans through the present day, dominant cultures have subjugated other cultures or races for their own gain through redrawing the boundaries of the human to exclude the targeted group. Slavery is perhaps the most obvious instance, but other examples abound.[11] Before turning to specific events in Kingsolver's town of Grace, it is worth considering the basis for the power that inheres in boundary drawing.

System boundaries are cognitively set, and erecting them *eo ipso* sets the environment's borders as well.[12] The environment contains the innumerable other systems that comprise reality. Defining the environment also subjectifies it; my environment must and will vary from yours because we comprise two discrete function systems (even while forming parts of the larger social system), and therefore we form parts of each other's environment. If environments vary with subjectivity, so too must the linked concepts of pollution and environmental protection. Pollution "involves questions not only of concentrations but of consequences" (Evernden, *Social Creation* 4). That fact reveals moral and empirical components to the term, as well as to the problem it describes. Identifying pollutants involves determining that a foreign presence and a potential source of harm exists within the system.[13] Making this determination requires two potentially problematic steps: designating the system's boundaries and defining harm. As might seem natural given the nature of these issues, international law has often provided the medium for their exploration.

One of the most influential pollution-related disputes in international law is the Trail Smelter Arbitration (1935–41) between the United States and Canada. The arbitration arose from a cooperative effort by the two nations to mitigate the damage caused by airborne pollutants that had crossed into the United States from Canada. A principal problem facing both the parties and the arbitrators involved the lack of consensus definitions within the international community for pollutant and damage. Every country had its own definition, and the meanings were often at odds, rendering international regulatory agreements nearly impossible. Crippled by the lack of legal precedent or a governing body of law, the arbitrators cobbled together a decision that rejected virtually all of the U.S. claims.

The Trail Smelter was built in 1896 in Trail, British Columbia. During the ensuing years, emissions from the smelter drifted across the border into Washington and fell in the form of acid rain and acid fog, causing substantial property damage. In 1931, a joint U.S.-Canadian commission concluded that the smelter had caused $350,000 worth of damage in the United States. In 1935, following complaints from residents of Washington, the settlement was deemed unsatisfactory and resubmitted for arbitration.

In 1941, the arbitration tribunal ruled that foreign emissions did not constitute pollutants unless and until they caused actual, provable, and substantial damage. If an injury could not be measured in monetary terms, there was no damage and, hence, no remedy at law. Consequently, the United States received no compensation for violation of its sovereignty (trespass across its borders) by the smelter's noxious fumes because the loss was intangible. Similarly, the tribunal refused to hold Canada liable for damage to urban property in the United States because "there [was] no proof of facts sufficient to estimate the reduction in the value . . . of such property" (*Trail Smelter Arbitration,* United States v. Canada, 3 U.N.R.I.A.A., 1908).[14]

The Trail Smelter decision is still relied upon in international law. According to its holding, harm to a nation's air is not compensable under international law. Nor can a country seek damages when foreign emissions harm wildflowers, birds, or any other resource that, while priceless, has no assigned monetary value. The rationale for the decision stems from the tribunal's ill-conceived attempt to assign fixed definitions to value-based and mutable terms like *pollutant* and *damage.*[15]

Consider again the West's hydraulic dilemma: environmentalists decry profligate expenditures of water and the degradation of habitat caused by the damming of rivers, while supporters of agribusiness and continued western development defend the expenditures as necessary and the dams as beneficial. "To the environmentalists, what is at risk is the very possibility of leading a good life. To the industrialists, what is at risk is the very possibility of leading a good life. The debate, it appears, is actually about what *constitutes a good life*" (Evernden 5). The good life, in any system, involves keeping pollutants at minimal levels. Unfortunately, as in the Trail Smelter affair, systems differ on what constitutes a pollutant.[16]

In *Animal Dreams,* Grace's inhabitants view the mine's leaching operation as pernicious to the community and to the region. Residents who were once part of the Black Mountain Mining Company have become external and superfluous. The company's new configuration has forced a redrawing of systemic and environmental boundaries.

From the company's perspective, poisoning the river with acid amounts to an insignificant side effect of a beneficial process; the river's biotic death poses no danger to the mine's viability. The towns-people, meanwhile, derive their cultural identity from the river and, following their exclusion from the economic sustenance the mine had provided, rely on it for food and livelihood. The opposing views of the mine and the townsfolk reiterate the flexibility of the term *pollutant*. The mining company considers the sulfuric acid an asset (and the river extraneous). Grace's residents, by contrast, view the acid as a pollutant (and the river as essential). If pollution means "matter out of place," or a foreign object interfering with the efficiency of a given system, both sides are correct. Even when we attach a moral component and say that pollution is an "unnatural" contaminant that could cause terrible harm to a given ecosystem, both sides remain right.[17] Terms like *unnatural* and *harm* are creations of the systems that give them meaning. Their meaning derives from the myth system into which they are integrated.[18]

From Black Mountain's perspective, the acid serves a vital purpose: aiding the continued prosperity of the local function system (the company), the larger function system (the economy), and the overarching system (society). The town advocates a policy aimed at safeguarding the viability of the land and water, as well as respect for the diverse cultural heritages that make human society unique. The strife between Black Mountain and townspeople pivots on the differing perspectives from which they attempt to facilitate autopoiesis. Each side maintains that its vision best serves the long-term needs of the system. Since both predicate their arguments on sustainability, it becomes clear that sustainability is a contested term whose meaning does not always coincide with an "environmentalist" agenda.

> Sustainability . . . cuts both ways. On the one hand, it can articulate a rationale for preserving Nature's biotic diversity in order to maintain the sustainability of the biosphere. But on the other hand, it can also represent an effort to reinforce the prevailing order of capitalistic development by transforming sustainability into an economic project. . . . Sustainability . . . becomes a discourse about exerting power over life. (Luke, "Environmentality" 28)[19]

Each system, in defining its boundaries, tacitly articulates its autopoietic requirements. When the needs of two function systems conflict, as with Grace and the mining company, the system best able to withstand the perturbation caused by the conflict will gain influence and power in subsequent interactions. This concept of realignment through conflict comprises a crucial subtheme of *Animal Dreams* as well as a seminal component of systems theory. And since the novel is set in the West, the nexus of the conflict is water.

For Black Mountain Mining, the ability to poison Grace's river bestows tremendous power. Perhaps more importantly, the company's ability to waste water in the pursuit of trace amounts of metals indicates an altered, but still potent form of faux potlatch. After wasting the water and fouling an entire aquatic ecosystem, the company turns to the EPA for permission to dam the river and permanently remove the water from circulation. The dam will increase water's exchange value, swell the worth of the company's assets by facilitating further extraction of valuable metals from the tailings, and abrogate the community whose objections to the poisoned water caused a slight catch in the company's engine of commerce.

In essence, Black Mountain seeks government assistance in constructing a dam that will solidify its cycle of lucrative hydraulic profligacy.[20] Given the circumstances—a small, minority community wriggling in the jaws of a monolithic corporation—few would gamble on Grace's chances for survival. This is particularly true in light of the EPA's silent complicity in the company's scheme.

EPA's role in the dam's approval and the town's demise is a by-product of the double bind facing government agencies. The agency's primary duty, as a regulatory arm of a system dedicated to extractive commerce, is the facilitation of that commerce. To the extent that economic growth dovetails with the nation's ecological well-being, so much the better. But when those goals conflict, capital inflow remains the system's priority.[21] Nevertheless, the EPA, as its name suggests, is also responsible for stewarding the nation's environment. The conflict within its dual mission reflects a basic incompatibility between ecological sustainability and economic growth.

According to William Ruckelshaus, who headed the EPA during the

Nixon and Bush administrations, "the strongest supporters of a forceful EPA are the industries it regulates. They want the government to set reasonable standards and they want the public to know that they are being enforced" (qtd. in Merchant, *Radical* 161). The key word in Ruckelshaus's statement is "reasonable." Reasonable standards vary with the agenda of the observer. Rational regulations, in industry's view, soothe public unease without constraining corporate growth. Environmentalists, meanwhile, advocate standards that safeguard the ecosystem, with profit margins forming an ancillary concern.

While the goals of the two sides differ fundamentally, there does exist a middle ground where a temporary compatibility becomes possible. Those in industry want to seem ecofriendly so as not to alienate their client base and to postpone fouling their own nests. A reputation for "green" behavior often benefits a corporation's bottom line. Into this mix one must factor the desire of environmental groups to appear conscientious and principled, but also their need for significant capital infusions in order to function. These corporations and advocacy groups share a primarily white, middle-class constituency. Both industry and environmental groups can satisfy (or at least pacify) their support base through cooperation and public displays of environmental conscience.

Another factor spurring the uneasy cooperation between environmental groups and corporations is money. Corporate money in large part subsidizes the environmental movement. For example, the Big Ten environmental organizations[22] draw much of their funding from corporate donors. In some cases, corporate donations comprise more than half of their budgets. Many of the largest contributors are also infamous villains of the environmental movement, including Amoco, ARCO, Dow, Dupont, Exxon, Monsanto, and Weyerhauser (Tokar 16–17). The Big Ten's corporate donor base endows them with the resources to lobby effectively and reach a wide swath of the public. However, they also become beholden to an enemy agenda, dependent upon funds earned through the very activities they condemn. Their own autopoiesis depends on the system they criticize. It is a Faustian bargain to be sure, but a commerce-driven society offers few alternatives. That lack of electives epitomizes the central dilemma of Restoration as an alternative to Reclamation, as well as that of the environmental movement as a whole. Without a workable alternative to the current system, proponents of social change must ward off the most pernicious ecological assaults without sabotaging the economy.

It would seem that in a perfectly functioning commercial society, industry could police itself. Self-regulation of this type is impossible, however, because systems cannot predict the behavior of the environment. Systems adapt/react to environmental disturbances in order to reestablish equilibrium. Prediction, by contrast, requires insight into the structure and behavior of the environment and the ability to communicate that insight. Yet the environment, by definition, is that which the system does not know. Prediction therefore has no meaning in the context of system-environment interactions.[23] The reaction of a system to a given perturbation is a function of its structure and the nature of the perturbation. Furthermore, prediction does not exist outside of language, and language does not exist outside of the system. Since the cognitive act is linguistic and therefore communicative, it constitutes interaction within the system about the environment, not communication with the environment itself.[24]

Maturana and Varela draw an intriguing parallel between the phenomenon of trophallaxis (the conveyance of signals among insects through chemical exchange, as with ants coevolving to carry out different tasks within a colony) and "linguallaxis," the human ability to conserve adaptation and preserve social unity through language: "Because we have language, there is no limit to what we can describe, imagine, and relate. It thus permeates our ontogeny as individuals: from walking to attitudes to politics" (Maturana and Varela, *Tree* 211–12).[25] This dynamic occurs within social systems because their complexity enables self-observation.

The inherent reflexivity within the communicative act cannot avoid influencing the outcome of system-environment interactions. Because the system communicates about its response to a given perturbation, that communication will inevitably affect the system's behavior. Following Heisenberg's uncertainty principle, the position of the observer affects the outcome of the experiment. In this instance, though, the observer is also an actor; the actor is observing itself.[26]

Interaction between system and environment, by contrast, is necessarily nonlingual because the environment lies outside the system's boundaries and is therefore unknown.[27] Communicating with the environment via language (rather than simply reacting to disturbance) would require a common context from which to draw metaphor and thereby enable mutual comprehension. If a common context existed, that would involve shared experience, which would in turn require familiarity—and familiarity with the unknown is oxymoronic.

The dynamics of a system's relationship to its environment is nevertheless integral to its evolution. Every unity, whether a single entity or a society, looks to facilitate its autopoiesis. Every external perturbation, so long as it does not destroy the unity, causes it to respond and adapt. Without perturbation, the unity would stagnate and evolution would cease.

Accepting the relationship between environmental disturbance and evolution leads to two intriguing conclusions. First: natural selection does not accurately describe the evolutionary process because no selection actually occurs. Response is constrained by the type of perturbation and the structure of the system. Unities that do not respond in a manner consistent with continued autopoiesis do not survive, whereas those that successfully conserve their autopoiesis produce a next generation. For each system and each disturbance, however, there is only one possible response. All other options exist only in the mind of the observer. Second: the fact that external perturbation is beneficial calls into question humanity's historic tendency toward subjugating and controlling its surroundings. Ongoing attempts to tame "nature" and the "wilderness" indicate a disturbing devolutionary trend. These concepts will be explored in more detail in the concluding chapter. First, we turn to the question of how the dynamics of system-environment interaction manifest themselves in the fictional world of *Animal Dreams*.

The Stitch and Bitch Club

In Grace, the Black Mountain Mining Company maintains that opponents of the proposed dam must be neutralized because they create unwelcome resonance within the system (with resonance defined as the communication generated in response to a perturbation). Recall that environmental problems do not exist until they generate communication.

Environmental disturbance is relevant in direct proportion to the resonance it generates (Luhmann, *Communication* 29). Black Mountain can
eliminate whatever impact and resonance Grace's citizenry might create
by simply removing the disturbance. From its perspective, however, the
disturbance is not the dam but the town.

Removing the town would serve the dual purpose of destroying the
power base of the grassroots, land-based resistance and eliminating it as
a subject of further communication. Without resonance, the river's contamination will cease, regardless of the pH of the water, because no one
will complain about it. The inhabitants of Grace must therefore fight a
two-fronted battle; they have to combat the river's contamination while
simultaneously struggling to maintain their own societal legitimacy.

Codi's coming of age and subsequent participation in the saving of
Grace stem from her liaison with Loyd Peregrina, the unknowing father
of her miscarried child, and from her bonding with the women of Grace.
The women attract her through their grassroots, activist ecofeminism,
while Loyd offers a link to Codi's past via his spiritual, land-based values
and tangible tie to her most traumatic period. Loyd's relationship with
Codi benefits both of them. He learns that his values cannot be applied
selectively and that all nature's creatures deserve to be treated with dignity.[28] She, meanwhile, learns of the spiritual power of the land and its
ability to command an allegiance unlike that formed between sentient
creatures.

> "Is there anything you know of that you'd die for?" I asked Loyd.
> He nodded without hesitation.
> "What?"
> He didn't answer right away. Then he said, "The land."
> "What land?"
> "Never mind. I can't explain it."
> "The reservation? Like defending your country?"
> "No." He sounded disgusted. "Not property. I didn't say prop-
> erty." (*Animal* 122)

Loyd explains by showing Codi places that "did not so much inspire religion as . . . seemed to be religion itself" (*Animal* 210). Loyd wishes to
integrate reverence—an unquantifiable, yet undeniably present factor

within the system—into people's everyday relationship with the land. He wants to integrate the land's sacredness into the economic and political systems, an act that would require renegotiating the boundaries of the sacred.

Viola and the other women of the "Stitch and Bitch Club" also demand a radical reordering of the system hierarchy but their methods are more immediate. Codi and Hallie's sardonic name for the coterie aptly characterizes the tension between the townswomen's traditional sex roles and their growing discomfort with them. It also describes their willingness to confront the language buttressing the status quo. The women, especially Viola, are acutely conscious that their movement's success depends on a radical reworking of their vocabulary:

> "Don't call that company the Mountain," she said curtly. "It makes it sound like something natural you can't ever move."
> "I've heard the men call it that," I said.
> Viola snorted like an old horse and started up the hill. (*Animal* 162)

Without constant vigilance, Viola knows that language can and will undermine the movement. Language is an extraordinarily powerful creative force. It builds societies and constructs ethical systems.[29] Ceding its power to an opposing social force can cause dangerous and irreparable consequences. Here, accepting the Company as a part of nature would capitulate to a vision of nature wherein acid in the water is not a pollutant and where local customs are disturbances to be quashed rather than a precious cultural heritage.

When the women meet to discuss options for saving the town, Viola makes clear that the success of the enterprise cannot depend on men (*Animal* 178). The initiative must come from women because women have shared the land's subjugation and therefore understand more intimately the necessity for action. Here, the rhetoric again recalls Mary Austin as well as the branch of ecofeminist thought that celebrates the woman-nature/man-culture juxtaposition as source of female empowerment.

One anonymous Stitch and Bitch member sums up the gulf between the male and female perspectives: "These men don't see how we got to do something *right now*. They think the trees can die and we can just go somewhere else, and as long as we fry up the bacon for them in the same old pan, they think it would be . . . *home*" (179). The trees' dying symbolizes their vanishing way of life, which, due to the narrowness of the dominant idiom, can only be described through nonlingual imagery. Nevertheless, the trees' role as metaphor endows them with significant power, particularly as the town struggles to rally support in and out of the community. The other potent symbol in the passage is the term "home," which communicates the anguish of displacement and the frustration of communicating the ineffable.

The Grace women's practical ecofeminism rejects the inculcated passivity that would permit the destruction of their homes and histories. Instead, they look to women-defined values that maintain that nonhuman nature, as the source for all life, must supplant the profit motive as society's defining characteristic. The women's activism merges with the spiritual reverence of the Native American tradition symbolized by Loyd, whose Apache heritage is both matrilineal and matrifocal. Activism and spirituality also merge in the body and mind of Codi, who uses her fluency in the rhetoric of science to further the cause. Working as a community, the women of Grace, including Codi, successfully stop the dam and the acid leaching that had all but destroyed the town.

The women save Grace through folk art. They fashion peacock piñatas and sell them to raise funds and call attention to the town's battle against the mining company. Their art creates significant resonance within the larger society, capturing the imagination of Sean Rideheart, a Tucson art dealer experienced in manipulating the system's regulatory apparatus.[30] Rideheart convinces the Stitch and Bitch club to agitate for Grace's placement on the National Register of Historic Places: "He knew all the ins and outs of becoming a historic place. He explained where to begin, and where to go after that, to see that the river would run clean and unobstructed. There was a fair amount of bureaucracy involved, but the process was reasonably speedy." Once listed as an historic site, the town need no longer fear "the onslaught of industry" nor "demolition or other negative impact" (*Animal* 277).

Invoking government regulations to protect the town offers an ironic contrast to the legislated impotence of the EPA that permitted the problem to escalate. When the town gains protection, its newly historic status is doubly ironic because it forces the system to protect the point source of its disturbance—like a lion donning a sock to protect the thorn in its paw—and because historic status implies an important role in the evolution of the social structure. Evolution, as we saw earlier, results from disturbance. Historical importance derives from a significant role in the society's evolution. It follows then, that an event's place in history is directly proportional to the severity of the disturbance it creates.

Consequently, Grace's historical importance results from its active subversion of society. This means that Grace's attempt to undermine the social system wins it official recognition as an important component of the continued evolution and preeminence of the status quo. Society retains its hegemony by co-opting Grace's victory as a means of entrenching its own power. In other words, the women win the local battle but the victory costs them the war.

The inadvertent lesson of the novel seems to be that active subversion and agitation for social change only strengthen the power structure. This seemingly unsolvable paradox subordinates Grace's successful ecofeminist/ecospiritual, grassroots revolt to Codi's reawakening, her union with Loyd, and their subsequent procreation. Kingsolver structures the novel's denouement to downplay the ecosystem and stress instead the successful reproduction of the community. In designing the novel this way, Kingsolver tacitly affirms Luhmann's hypothesis that ecological problems only become so when they generate systemwide resonance. The fight against Black Mountain Mining engendered enough disturbance to bestir the capitalist communicative apparatus and force acceptance of a less profitable alternative. But the revolt could not replace the dominant system with a new ecologically sensitive one. The struggle generated little resonance outside of Grace and therefore offers no broad alternative to the western ecological dilemma.

Grace's historic status offers no long-term implications for social reform of western land or water policy. It just spares one town a dismal fate. The social system's autopoiesis still requires short-term capital gain. Similar ecological degradation will inevitably arise elsewhere, with less palatable results. This prospect tempers the elation one might otherwise feel at Grace's salvation. Small victories in the face of larger disasters offer at best a pleasure tempered by a grim awareness of things to come.

This overarching sense of dread is an interesting and probably unanticipated by-product of manufacturing a happy ending to this environmental novel. Given the current constraints, a happy ending must involve either removing the environment from its central position within the plot, as Kingsolver does, or offering a coherent system and discourse to replace extractive capitalism. Muting the environment within the plot strips it of the ability to generate resonance and thereby force evolution. The alternative, keeping it central and articulating an ecofeminist steady-state option, remains a grail—outside the realm of effective communication.

Attempts to formulate a steady-state alternative have so far lacked specifics. For example, Herman Daly suggests that a steady-state economy is "an economy with constant stocks of people and artifacts maintained at some desired sufficient levels by low rates of maintenance 'throughput'" (qtd. in Merchant, *Radical* 37). A steady-state economy would use the lowest possible levels of materials and energy in the production phase and release the smallest possible amount of waste during the consumption phase. Terms like "desired" and "sufficient" invite a degree of subjectivity that leads to abuse and multiple definitions, much as in the earlier discussion of pollution. To further complicate matters, a steady-state economy needs a consensus definition of an optimal standard of living—a goal that smacks of utopianism.

It seems that Kingsolver had little choice but to divert readers' attention from Grace's relatively insignificant ecological victory to the personal triumph bound up in Codi's self-realization. Without a working definition of environment that does not conjure images of an extractive, ecologically pernicious economy, or an unquantifiable "not us," there can be no ecologically sanguine happy ending. Even the definition of ecology posits a barrier between organisms and their environment by semantically solidifying the schism between the two.[31] We define ecology as the science treating the interaction between organisms and their environment. Interaction contains an implicit alienation—it requires two discrete entities. The environment is therefore everything "not me."

A cybernetic approach, however, dissolves the barrier between self and other, even as systems theory dictates that the environment encompasses all that cannot be known or communicated. Mary Douglas points out that "it is not just the environment that is at risk, but the very *idea* of environment, the social ideal of proper order. The power which presents a danger for careless humans is very evidently a power inhering in the structure of ideas, a power by which the structure is expected to protect itself" (113). The destabilization of the term *environment* in turn undermines common notions of ecology. The resulting linguistic uncertainty could facilitate a new rhetoric of environmentalism more responsive to alternative ideological and economic systems.

Kingsolver's attempt in *Animal Dreams* to create an ecofeminist, organicist environmentalism does not succeed because, as yet, there exists no coherent vocabulary to describe the new regime. Without that vocabulary, combating initiatives like mines and dams must take the form of negative constructions couched in the language of the dominator. We can only say "No mine" or "No dam"; we cannot offer a coherent alternative regime. That strategy is necessarily reactive. It requires waiting for someone to suggest an act of environmental degradation before formulating a strategy designed to maintain the status quo. Yet the status quo is not satisfactory; it degrades the land and privileges extraction and profit over ecological and social health. Environmentalists thus find themselves in a vexing double bind—they must fight to safeguard a system and situation that they condemn or face an even bleaker alternative.

Environmentalism might then best be described as a passionate struggle to maintain an unacceptable state of affairs. Under the current system, change too often means serious harm. Rather than agitate for change, environmentalists must impede it in order to delay the inevitable slide into ecosystemic collapse. This mission, simultaneously both hopeless and crucial, infuses the environmental movement with a combination of urgency and despair.

Such a grim and unrewarding struggle does not easily inspire optimism. Kingsolver nevertheless wished to write an environmental novel with a happy ending. To do so she either had to create the vocabulary to describe a sustainable reality or divert readers' attention to interpersonal developments. Of necessity, she chose the latter.

6

Imagining Sustainability

> This is not the Age of Enlightenment, but the Age of
> Not Knowing What to Do.
> —Walker Percy

Restoration's undefinability renders it unattainable even as Reclamation continues its assault on the nation's hydrology and geography. It seems there is no sustainable alternative. Happily, that is not the case. The path to sustainability may be hidden and overgrown from years of disuse, and probably does not lie where the map says it should. Nevertheless, it is extant and navigable and will take us where we need to go—if we can find it.

The path does not lie where it once did because the terrain has shifted. The Reclamation era has irretrievably altered the western landscape, causing what Neil Postman calls an "ecological change." An ecological change occurs when one segment of the whole metamorphoses so dramatically that the entire society changes (18). Postman cites the printing press and television as two inventions that wrought ecological changes. On a smaller scale, the dams, channels, and reservoirs of the Reclamation era have generated a similarly irrevocable shift in both the physical and the metaphorical landscape of American society.

While driving through California's Mojave Desert recently, I passed a sign advertising "Rain for Rent." This rain could be had at the Irrigation Store, an establishment dedicated to providing farmers with the tools for trouble-free reclamation at affordable prices. Taken in the context of a century of unprecedented technological advance and national obsession with the myth of the garden, an irrigation store does not seem particularly remarkable. In the larger context of human history, however, its existence is nothing short of staggering. Empires and countries, from ancient Chinese dynasties through the current nation-states of the Middle East, have risen and fallen because irrigation technology spawned hydraulic empires in which the ability to deliver water rested in the hands of the educated, wealthy few. Today, anyone can purchase the tools of dominion at a roadside store outside of Bakersfield.

The Irrigation Store was conceived out of hubris and enabled by the ecological change wrought by the Reclamation era. The store's existence testifies to the fact that the nation's geography, for better or for worse, is forever different. Restoration's goal of remaking pristine ecosystems therefore looms as an impossible goal, comparable to unmaking glass into sand. Furthermore, if healthy ecosystems exist in a constant state of flux, which "pristine" state should they reoccupy? Inevitably, such decisions become more ideological than ecological.

In a sense, the Reclamation era represents the turbulent adolescent years dividing this nation's infancy and its maturity. In the years following its inception, the United States expanded westward, and its resources and possibilities appeared limitless. Myths like those of the garden and frontier assumed that there *should* be infinite abundance but did not investigate whether there actually *were* such riches. Visions of abundance persevered despite mounting ecological evidence to the contrary. When the frontier closed and limits to growth became impossible to ignore, the Reclamation era was born. It embodied both a reaction to and an elision of limits to growth. Reclamation became a juggernaut, wreaking havoc on the western landscape in an attempt to further a bankrupt ideology of infinite possibility.

The Reclamation era divides into five stages, with this book devoting a chapter to each. The first stage begins with John Wesley Powell's vision of a "reclaimed" West populated by family farms whose size and crops were determined by the realities of arid-lands agriculture. The next four stages are chronicled with the aid of novels, each of which reflects the social, historical, and hydrological contexts of their respective periods.

The Ford shows the heady optimism of Reclamation's early years and the clash between urban and rural constituencies even while both claimed to represent the same values. *The Grapes of Wrath* takes place during the heyday of the Reclamation era, when water, dams, and delivery mechanisms trumped all other concerns, including human rights and the health of the ecosystem. Corporate agriculture co-opted yeoman symbolism and used it to enormous personal gain. Conflict was unavoidable, as *The Monkey Wrench Gang* makes plain. Abbey's novel reflects a growing disillusionment with reclamation for its own sake and a willingness to privilege environmental concerns over economic benefit. Last, *Animal Dreams* dramatizes Reclamation's end phase. It depicts a population struggling to disrupt and replace the cycle of corporate gain, environmental degradation, and hydraulic dependency created by nine decades of Reclamation rhetoric. That brings us to the present. We must figure out what to do now.

All societies rely on common myths; we must assume that we share assumptions about the world in order for language and its embedded metaphors to function. These shared myths enable human interaction. Language is built on metaphor, and metaphor requires an assumed commonality of experience. Ludwig von Bertalanffy suggests that such "moral concepts as Freedom, God, Immortality, and Human Dignity are fictions but nonetheless of immense importance: for we have to behave 'as if' they were reality. . . . [T]he myths of tradition are fictions based on the mythical experiences of man and later invested in historical narratives" (67). Accepting this premise can prove terrifying. It suggests that the fabric of society is not made up of universally held human values, but merely illusions shared for the sake of convenience. When and if those illusions become inconvenient, and we stop behaving *as if* we share a common reality, then the societal fabric will unravel. Without a shared set of experiences and assumptions, language cannot function and communication becomes impossible.[1] And without communication, society will dissolve into chaos.

Allegiance to the notion of a shared, objective reality also has serious, negative ramifications. Attaching objectivity and incontrovertibility to a given web of myths eliminates the need to interrogate social norms. Assuming that there is one correct way of seeing the world shackles us to a particular interpretation of our environment. Freed from the need to question our behavior, we simply act, secure in the knowledge that we do the "right" thing. However, that interpretation which we accept *as if* it were true may, like Reclamation, have been designed not to advance the common good, but rather to enrich a select group.[2] In Neil Evernden's view, this ruse of objectivity is all but inevitable, as are its consequences: "[T]he tendency to practice the subterfuge of mythmaking is very understandable. In practical terms, it may very well afford us some measure of comfort by legitimating a belief in the certainty of at least a few features of existence and a few behavioral norms. But in the long run, it solves nothing, and has the added effect of drastically transforming . . . nature" (29–30).

Shared myths inevitably mutate as societies change. Returning to the examples of God, immortality, freedom, and human dignity, we see that the concepts of God and immortality have undergone radical revisions in the last 150 years, while the ongoing tragedies in Burma, Sudan, Tibet, and elsewhere demonstrate that freedom and human dignity are not universally valued. In the United States, many of our common myths revolve around the frontier, the garden, and the absence of a precolonial history. We cling tenaciously to this mixed and shifting bag of fictions that underlie the American Dream.

It is time to reconfigure those norms that we all behave *as if* were true. Societies, like ecosystems, must evolve or die. We must, in Bruno Latour's words, amend the key articles of our "discursive constitution."[3] I propose a rhetoric of Sustainability that draws on many of the mythic properties of Restoration and Reclamation while adding elements that they fail to capture.

Sustainability is less a blueprint than an organizing metaphor for environmentalism in the post-Reclamation, information age. It would operate as an autopoietic system, evolving and gaining complexity in order to ensure its survival. Using a hypertext model, Sustainability involves a radical shift away from binarism and exclusive allegiance to one paradigm. Rather than offering an ideological ur-text, Sustainability envisions a system of "linked causes" that de-emphasizes particular ways of seeing while allowing access for all. Whereas Reclamation focuses on humans (humans re-creating Eden) and Restoration concentrates on the natural (remaking the ecosystem into a pristine state), Sustainability allows conflicting views to coexist and, by deprivileging any particular one, permits all to contribute to the health of the ecosystem.

This nonbinary flexibility is crucial to surviving in a world interconnected by increasingly powerful modes of communication. One of Sustainability's strengths lies in its basis in existing social trends. Rather than proposing to overhaul human interaction, its logic is based on the concepts and rhetoric of the information age. The multiple authors and unstable narratives that characterize hypertext and information theory have already had significant impact on the world of literary criticism.[4] As the Internet enters more homes and information age concepts continue to infuse pop culture, the notion of society as a global web will become ever more bound up in cultural mythology. Even in the short time since it became popular, the Internet has demonstrated enormous potency as a cultural sign. The term *information superhighway* is already a cliché. Meanwhile, cyberpunk dominates science fiction, inspiring movies like *The Terminator, Lawnmower Man,* and *The Matrix;* presidential candidates have home pages; and MSNBC and other interactive media look to wed television and the Internet and thereby confirm hypertext's place in the cultural mainstream.

Sustainability draws on the tools and concepts of the information age, while its roots lie in the systems-theoretical concept of metabalance. Metabalance posits that a system must be fundamentally out of balance to achieve stability. If a system expends energy, it must replenish itself from external sources. Just as we eat to renew our bodies' energy reserves, so do social systems require sustenance from without for their continued survival. That means that systems are always out of balance. An in-balance system that did not expend energy would be inert and lifeless. Like any vibrant, healthy system, a sustainable society exists in a state of beneficial flux with constant inflow and outflow. It relies on disturbance and shifting perspective for its vitality and survival.

In the West, the social system feeds on food and energy produced through Reclamation. But Reclamation requires unlimited water, an ecological impossibility. As water reserves exhaust, society teeters on the verge of disaster. By contrast, a sustainable society would not become overreliant on one source of energy. Overreliance comes from privileging one particular method or way of seeing. Sustainability requires multiple perspectives, and functions through accommodation; no one constituency can subordinate opposing views indefinitely.[5]

Hypertext offers a useful analogy for visualizing the Sustainability, or linked-cause, approach to environmentalism. In a given hypertext, multiple hot links connect to other hypertexts, which then have hot links to other texts, ad infinitum. The amount of information and the possible ways of ordering it are infinite. Participants create the text out of a maelstrom of unfiltered information and give it meaning by drawing boundaries and forging links.[6] The workings of the environment can be conceptualized the same way. For example, global warming links to fossil fuel combustion, agriculture, and deforestation. Agriculture, deforestation, and industrial pollution all link to each other, and each also links to myriad other issues. Each cause has its own constituencies with competing methodologies for restoring equilibrium. Nevertheless, each cause cannot be severed from the larger matrix containing all other causes. Attempting to solve any one cause in isolation exacerbates other problems. If, for example, we isolate global warming and, for the sake of argument, limit its causes to the four mentioned above—industrial pollution, agriculture, fossil fuel combustion, and deforestation (see fig. 1)—any attempt to solve global warming without also addressing its linked causes would prove disastrous.

Let us assume that carbon dioxide is the principal greenhouse gas contributing to global warming. A large portion of the carbon dioxide released in the United States is a by-product of burning fossil fuels, which create energy that powers everything from paper mills to recycling plants. If the federal government were to attack the problem by mandating a 50 percent slash in all greenhouse emissions, the price of goods would go up, industrial production would plummet, and many businesses would close, putting millions of people out of work.

Setting aside the social and political ramifications of a large, disaffected electorate, the resulting strain on agriculture and the nation's forests would be enormous. There would likely be an urban exodus as millions of people suddenly required land on which to grow their own food. The East, with its denser population, would run into immediate problems of space. Eastern forests, only recently recovered from centuries of indiscriminate clearing and urban expansion, would again face destruction. The forest clearing would generate a feedback loop similar to the one taking place in the Amazon. The mass clearing of forests would mean fewer trees absorbing carbon dioxide even as their burning

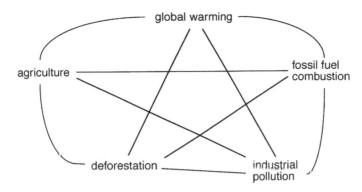

FIG. 1. An artificially closed system wherein global warming has four discrete causes, all of which link to each other and to nothing else

released more carbon dioxide into the atmosphere. Those conditions would accelerate rather than mitigate global warming.

In the West, space would pose less of a problem than water. We have already seen what resulted when legions of would-be yeomen flocked to the West and attempted to farm it. Now, with aquifers mined nearly to exhaustion and rivers oversubscribed, there would be even less water to go around. Furthermore, the sudden bulge in farmers, accompanied by a plunging GDP, would likely doom the country's existing agricultural base. Consecutive collapses of the nation's industrial and agricultural infrastructures would probably destroy the economy. Given the international community's interdependence with, and reliance on, the American economy, the resulting chaos could plunge the world into a protracted and bloody period of anarchy.

The above scenario is deliberately simplistic. A comprehensive analysis would have had to address the virtually unlimited possibilities and implications of one simple act (mandating a 50 percent cut in emissions) aimed at accomplishing one simple thing: capping greenhouse emissions in the United States. My point is this: no one cause or issue is separable from the larger web of causes to which it links. Any action at any given "website" ripples throughout the social system. Within the larger social web, however, as separate constituencies agitate for particular causes, the resulting microadjustments maintain a systemwide equilibrium. The key lies in providing access to the web.

Many of the Native American cultures that populated this continent before European settlers arrived and labeled it "virgin land" possessed a sane, forward-looking ecological perspective. Several, including the Mohawk and Iroquois, explicitly direct decisions to be made only after considering their impact on the next seven generations. In germinating our own sustainable myths, we would do well to consult and learn from those who have done it before. I am not recommending that the United States adopt Native American mythology wholesale, even if it were somehow possible to condense the hundreds of diverse Native American cultures into a how-to manual. No culture has a preexisting formula for healing the wounds of Reclamation. The solutions, like the problem, must be new.

The first step involves retooling the national mythology to incorporate the (relatively) recently acquired power to drastically alter our physical surroundings. This will entail integrating ancient perspectives of land use and history, acknowledging the much-multiplied impact of an increasingly technological and proliferating population, and developing an expanded systems-theoretical model that incorporates predictiveness as an autopoietic mechanism.

In 1872, John Wesley Powell declared that the actions of humans on the face of the earth were "trivial," and that "the conditions which they produce are of minute effect, and in presence of the grand effects of nature escape discernment" (*Report* 91). No more. In the interim 120 years, we have quintupled the world's human population (in the United States, it has sextupled), circumnavigated the planet at speeds exceeding that of sound, orbited, mapped, and so refashioned earth that we now talk in terms of "global" warming and the "end of nature."[7]

In the Middle Ages, behavior was strictly circumscribed through imprecation and allusions to the wrath of the Almighty. In the postindustrial age, we have not only lost our religious awe, we also seem unconcerned about the harm our behavior can inflict. When cruising the information superhighway, we would do well to peer out at the ravaged landscape and abandoned heavy equipment rotting on its shoulders. It has never been more important to respect and even fear our own potential and past.

We live, systems theorists believe, in a world of our own design, interacting with an environment that we can never understand. The multiplicity of perspectives that form our collective reality deters the privileging of any specific system or environment. At first, this theoretical framework appears to negate contemporary rhetoric proclaiming humans a part of the environment. But further consideration shows that systems theory does offer the possibility of commingling humans and the environment.

Systems are in constant interaction with their environments, which are themselves other systems. All exist in a continual cycle of perturbation and adjustment. Once a system learns to respond beneficially to a disturbance, that disturbance becomes integrated into the system. The system grasps how to communicate with and create meaning from the disturbance, thereby transforming it into a known quantity and removing it from the shadowy realm of environment. If you picture it in terms of a map, imagine the environment ceding a little territory to the system as a result of a border skirmish.[8] This boundary shifting occurs constantly and has important implications. Consider the following:

1. System boundaries exist only in the mind of the observer. Where, for example, does the tree root end and the soil begin? When does water cease being water and become blood? Where do I end and the bacteria in my digestive tract—organisms fully capable of existing in other media—begin? The quality of these questions suggests that no boundary between self and other or between system and environment can withstand prolonged, multivalent scrutiny.[9]

2. We are each other's environment. Even as humans are components of the larger social system, we also form autopoietic unities with discrete environments. Other unities populate those environments. One unity may form a part of many discrete systems and even more environments. The overlap between systems and environments, as well as their observer-determined status, makes

differentiating between humans and environment impossible and the attempt counterproductive. Once the artificial rigidity of these boundaries gives way to a negotiable border between environment and humanity, the environment becomes part of us and ecological conscience becomes an autopoietic imperative.

3. We cannot evolve without an ongoing relationship with the environment, including all the perturbations such a relationship entails. Consequently, the ideal of controlling nature, aptly encapsulated in the 1965 Bureau of Reclamation proclamation, "Man serves God. But Nature serves Man," is not only quixotic, but pernicious. Without unpredictable, uncontrollable perturbation, the human species would languish and die. In other words, Thoreau's overused but little understood saying, "In Wildness is the preservation of the World," continues to inform the environmental debate. We need wildness not to assuage an antiquated wilderness aesthetic, but to preserve our ability to evolve.[10]

The presence of permeable boundaries between system and environment and the need for an ecological conscience reintroduce prediction as a component of system-environment interaction. N. Katherine Hayles suggests that reality arises from an "unmediated flux" that gains pattern and form through interaction. It comes into being through mediating the flux via "self-organizing, transformative processes that include sensory, contextual, and cognitive components." Both the flux and our organizing powers are necessary to the construction of reality. The flux exists irrespective of us, but we give it coherence. Hayles labels the interactive process that shapes reality "the cusp" ("Ground" 49). "Riding the cusp" involves a healthy awareness that both the flux and constructed reality are central players in any interaction. In a reality constructed entirely through human thought, one could walk off a cliff and not fall, whereas in an objectively determined world, frogs and humans would perceive the same reality despite species-specific vantage points. Of course, neither scenario occurs in the world as we know it. The middle ground lies in what Hayles calls "constrained constructivism" (53), which acknowledges that if you jump off a cliff no amount of deconstructive posturing will prevent your fall, but also asserts that any number of culturally based explanations (gravity, God's will, etc.) could explain and give meaning to your descent.

Assigning meaning to an object plays a crucial role in that object's creation. The same principle holds true for the larger concept of environment. Since environment forms out of the flux, not wholly of it, interaction plays a crucial role in its construction. That interaction renders it partially known and therefore partially predictable as well. Hayles contrasts this vision with "Maturana's world," where the actions of autopoietic systems are determined solely through their reactions to disturbance and have no cognitive element at all ("Nature" 11).

Accepting Hayles's formulation of the subject/object, system/environment relation means that cognition plays a key role in each component's formulation. If human systems can predict or react knowledgeably to perturbation, the outlook for social change brightens. Predictive ability, combined with the enormous flexibility inherent in the multisystem approach, inspires a degree of hope for the hydraulically beleaguered southwestern United States.

Prediction requires a familiarity with history. Consequently, long-ignored Native American precepts, along with an awareness of the endemic national indifference to the repercussions of our myths and technology, can play crucial roles in devising a rhetoric of sustainability. We can and should consult our history of ill-gotten subsidy, faux potlatch, and desiccated aquifers when realigning and reaiming national environmental priorities.

Ever since the successful Sagebrush Rebellion against the ecologically sane but politically misguided policies of the Carter administration, western agricultural and political interests have ferociously resisted efforts to bring mining, grazing, and agricultural policies into step with ecological realities. During the early days of his administration, President Carter tried to institute fiscal and ecological restraints on numerous water projects. His proposals generated a tsunami of criticism in Congress and across the nation. Public Works Committee chairman Ray Roberts called Carter a captive of "environmental extremists and budget hackers" (qtd.

in Reisner 330). Nowhere was the storm of criticism more fierce than in the West, where politicians and citizens alike accused the Carter administration of attempting to destroy the western way of life.

In recent years, the rhetoric has taken a new turn that hearkens back to the halcyon days of the Reclamation era when appeals to the yeoman ideal invoked automatic federal subsidies. In 1994, Helen Chenoweth was elected to Congress, representing the state of Idaho. Congressman[11] Chenoweth is a fierce advocate of decreased federal presence in the West. She is also a founding member of the "wise use" movement, which advocates abrogating environmental laws and channeling increased power to property owners. One of Chenoweth's first acts following her election was to draft a bill she called the Civil Rights Act of 1995. The bill would have barred all federal agencies from enforcing any laws without permission of state and local officials.

Chenoweth's bill propounded a states' rights agenda that has led to armed confrontations between local militants and federal officials. The bill is neither an isolated example nor the most extreme articulation of the states' rights program. In a three-pronged political scheme whose internal contradictions are almost breathtaking, States' rights proponents advocate "returning" federal lands to the states (land that the states never owned; it was ceded to the federal government as a condition of statehood), reducing federal jurisdiction at all levels; *and* maintaining federal subsidies for mining, ranching, and irrigation so that the "western way of life" will not perish. "Get out and give us more money!" has never more accurately described this powerful component of western political consciousness.

States' rights advocates have also learned the lessons of the Reclamation era and seek to build on its legacy. Their rhetoric proclaiming the need to "reclaim" federal lands echoes the more explicitly water-based Reclamation myths that propelled the West into hydrological insolvency. Where Reclamationists looked to reclaim an imaginary garden from the desert, their ideological progeny demand the return of land they never owned from a federal government that they accuse of undermining the "American" way of life. As Chuck Cushman, a leading spokesman for the wise-use movement declared following the Republican electoral gains in

1994, "Bruce Babbitt tried to say there was a new West. The Old West voted in November [1994]" (qtd. in Blumenthal 30).

The fact that the Old West Cushman refers to never existed anywhere but in the American imagination in no way mitigates its power. Suburbia, to borrow Marshall McLuhan's phrase, "lives imaginatively in *Bonanza*-land" causing an influential segment of American culture to "march backwards into the future." Technological advances and the nation's gigantic groundwater reserves permitted Americans to spend the last century behaving *as if* the myths of the garden and the Old West conformed to the ecology of the arid lands. The rhetoric of Sustainability, by contrast, implies the possibility of a radically reorganized society even though the prospect of such a reorganization looms as all but impossible.

Still, I maintain that the task can be done. The key lies in successfully "riding the cusp" governing the interaction and construction of self and environment. This will require enhancing the system's predictive capability to offset the uncertainty that will accompany the demise of the old myths. That the human social system does not blindly respond to external perturbation, but rather constructs responses based on history and knowledge, means that autopoiesis is partly a conscious procedure and therefore subject to renovation. Language can enable that renovation process, placing social change within our reach.

History shows that we have made the reach in the past and that ecological changes have resulted. Postman observes that when evolution displaced Genesis as the myth of creation, it left a yawning epistemological void: "By calling into question the truth of [Genesis], science undermined the whole edifice of belief in sacred stories and ultimately swept away with it the source to which most humans had looked for moral authority" (160). That devastating outcome was attained almost exclusively through language. The mechanistic paradigm (which used the machine as the unifying metaphor for explaining nature)[12] through which seventeenth-century thinkers revised the myth of the garden is not yet four hundred years old, and Reclamation is only ninety-five. The biblical version of creation lasted thousands of years and until recently enjoyed the support of very powerful language and social systems. It nevertheless was successfully challenged by a language-based alternative that could not even boast the imprimatur of any central authority figure. In just a few centuries, human society unraveled a five millennia-old epistemological quilt. That is not to suggest that the Genesis myth does not retain considerable power and credibility. However, when compared to its power and authority in centuries past, Genesis has clearly lost a lot of ground to alternative explanations of creation.

Embedded within language lies unmatched power and potential to generate social change. The problem is that this potential lies fallow, allowing language's might to flow into system maintenance. Instead of trying to restore ecosystems to an imagined prior state, we might better devote our efforts to restoring language to its role as an agent of change. Re-enabling language is a central aim of Sustainability, and, given the success of the mechanistic paradigm in supplanting Genesis, it is an achievable goal for the forces of environmentalism. Nevertheless, even within the systems-theoretical definition, environmentalism continues to lack focus because of the environment's inherently subjective qualities. The term's parameters have narrowed, however, and once we accept the premise of a shared system of overlapping environments, it becomes possible to hear voices of change, even when, as in *Animal Dreams,* the voices come from the traditionally disenfranchised.

Sustainability does not require that society metamorphose into an egalitarian Kismet. Complex systems require a complex web of relations. As with hypertext, not every local component or link interacts with every other one. The map of interactions determines the global structure, which in turn determines the status of the local components. As in any observer-defined ordering system, some hierarchy is unavoidable.[13] Nevertheless, since each interaction within the system changes the global structure, all components have access to the mechanisms of change. To use another computer example: over the last twenty years, a number of myths have developed concerning how the world of computers was entirely refashioned by hackers working out of their garages. One of those early hackers was Bill Gates. Now the blue suits at IBM speak hacker lingo because it maps better onto an information age society.[14] Hacker influence migrated vertically; voices from the periphery generated enormous resonance and forced the insular world of computing to respond and adapt. Though a clear hierarchy existed and still exists, bottom-up integration proved a viable mode of access.

One of the most compelling advantages of the systems-theoretical approach lies in this redefined notion of access. With fluid boundaries, no one way of seeing harbors any more inherent legitimacy than any other.[15] Jean-François Lyotard argues that the systemic trend toward complexity has no allegiance to anything other than complexity itself: it "is not attached to an Idea. . . . It assimilates risks, memorizes their informational value and uses this as a new mediation necessary to its functioning" (7). We are simultaneously components of a large number of systems and environments, human and nonhuman, all similarly situated. Since we are each a network of systems that all form parts of other systems, it is impossible to define the boundaries of self with any certainty or permanence.

In hypertextual terms, each function system forms a hot link that takes the observer from context to context. The sequence of links and the narrative they form are entirely observer defined. As the observer's perspective changes, the system and its boundaries must also shift. What was once environment becomes system and vice versa. In light of this transitive relationship between self and other, degrading the environment is tantamount to self-destruction, while protecting it becomes an autopoietic imperative. Viewing environmental protection as self-preservation conveniently removes it from the moral realm, eliminating the need for appeals to conscience to prevent its degradation. It also does not extend human status to other life-forms—a criticism often leveled at some forms of radical environmental rhetoric.[16]

When a cause is co-opted by the status quo, as in *Animal Dreams*, it strengthens the dominance of the current paradigm. If, on the other hand, thousands of disparate causes militate for specific changes that do not necessarily dovetail with a national agenda, the system cannot co-opt them all because they often conflict, not just with the system but with each other. Paradoxically, the greater and more varied the perturbations a system experiences, the greater the likelihood of the seemingly opposing consequences of drastic upheaval and long-term health. Only through constant, unremitting flux do systems achieve metabalance.

Analyzed in these terms, and from the standpoint of both elementary logic and ecosystemic reality, Reclamation fails. First, Reclamation requires the state to provide an unlimited supply of water. Water powers the system, keeping it in metabalance. But Reclamation's existence is predicated on correcting a scarcity of water. Clearly, water cannot be both scarce and infinite. This contradiction at the base of Reclamation's existence means that the primary values or beliefs underlying the state's authority in this area are fundamentally inconsistent. Recognizing this inconsistency causes a loss of faith in the central authority, leading to what Habermas terms a "legitimation crisis." Legitimation crises are particularly problematic for modern societies because of their reliance on reason rather than religion and tradition.

Second, the ecological ramifications of this incoherence include an inevitable and worsening water shortage. This is the specter now facing the West. In addition to the Colorado River's oversubscription, the Ogallala aquifer, which underlies Texas, Kansas, Colorado, Oklahoma, New Mexico, and Nebraska, is fast depleting. Through the invention of the centrifugal pump, the Ogallala's enormous groundwater reserves pulled the Midwest out of the Dust Bowl and reestablished the region as the world's breadbasket. Unfortunately, over the last fifty years, more water has been pumped out of the Ogallala than it managed to accumulate in the last five hundred thousand. A Lake Huron's worth of nonrenewable water has vanished, never to return (Reisner 11). The shortage is both real and imminent. Reclamation fails on its own terms because there can never be enough water to fuel its indefinite autopoiesis. If we continue to ignore this ecological certainty, the system will no longer experience the beneficial flux that characterizes metabalance. It will collapse.

Luckily, Reclamation is not the linchpin of the entire social system. Though Reclamation has rhetorically wrapped itself in a cloak of indispensability over the last century, it remains but one component of a much greater whole. Entrenching itself in western iconography allowed Reclamation to withstand the many voices—from Mary Austin to Barbara Kingsolver—pressing for reform. Yet those voices, long exiled to the periphery, are vital to maintaining metabalance. Deprived of their input, the system has grown dangerously insulated and slow to change. Language has also stagnated, rendering advocates of change increasingly inarticulate. In addition, the linked issues of an incoherent hydroeconomy and a nonresponsive sociopolitical apparatus have left the nation highly vulnerable to an environmental energy crisis.

The alternative to social collapse is evolution. Systems evolve by responding to the flux born of dissonance. If dissonance is stifled, the system stagnates. Progress therefore can come from amplifying the voices of groups presently disenfranchised. Before progress can occur, though, the concept of progress must be interrogated and revised. Currently, "economic progress" links to the notion of a "high standard of living." But, as Timothy Luke argues, the crises of everyday material life over the past quarter century have unmasked this myth and shown that the perceived high standard of living is not standard, rarely high, and may not even be living (*Ecocritique* 201).

Even without a finely honed lexicon or a truly proactive ecological strategy, Sustainability's precepts can beneficially influence public policy. With the Ogallala aquifer running dry, Bureau of Land Management lands turning into parched and polluted gullies, rice sprouting under six inches of standing water in the California desert, and the Colorado basin turning saline and desiccated, pushing for an end to hydrological and other environmental inanities serves an obvious and valuable purpose.

I write these words in Los Angeles, a city in perpetual hydrocrisis whose water is almost entirely imported from other arid regions. Yet I cannot leave my building without splashing through puddles created by ubiquitous sprinklers. Pointing out the problems and peculiarities caused by disparate ecological visions has been the task of the environmental movement virtually since its birth. Landmark victories like the Clean Water Act and the Clean Air Act, the Wilderness Act, and the creation and development of the national park network testify to the movement's ability to achieve notable successes even with a reactive vocabulary. However, as the movement has grown, its rhetoric has become diluted by the conflict between maintaining the health of the environment and preserving the environmental movement. The movement continues to stave off much industry and government-sponsored harm, but its reliance on corporate funding also raises issues of credibility and diplomacy.

In recent times, the NIMBY (Not In My Back Yard) phenomenon has endured scathing criticism as a symbol of selfishness and snide unconcern with larger social issues. While much of this criticism has merit, the NIMBY phenomenon still bears scrutiny. When residents of a wealthy, gated community object to nearby low-income housing, they might deservedly stand accused of isolationism and disregarding the needs of the less well off. But when members of a Latino community objects to a toxic waste incinerator going up in their midst, are they being similarly selfish? Inversely, if the Latino neighborhood agitates for the toxic waste incinerator to be built in its midst, because the incinerator will bring needed jobs to their region, what position should the national environmental movement take on the issue? The answer, I believe, should be no position at all. In the language of Sustainability, the linked causes comprising the environmental movement do not coalesce on this issue.[17] The presence or absence of the incinerator is a local concern, requiring local expertise and passion to solve.

Even within the environmental justice movement, itself a subgroup of environmentalism, different constituencies advocate different results. In this instance, the local community may believe that the economic boon the incinerator would bring outweighs its risks. That decision does not invalidate the environmental justice movement's larger goal of shielding low-income and minority communities from environmental hazards. It merely allows the diverse voices within the movement to be heard while acknowledging that local communities have important links to other causes (education, housing, job security, etc.), and sometimes those causes take precedence.

When a gated community rallies against a housing project, its members argue from a position of wealth and systemic dominance. Their political influence guarantees them attention at the policymaking level. Therein lies the crucial distinction between them and the minority community. As Kingsolver depicted in *Animal Dreams,* for marginalized groups, systemic resonance is hard won. In the unlikely event that underrepresented people generate sufficient resonance to force systemic adaptation, it rarely creates change beyond the procedural level. In *Animal Dreams,* the town of Grace stopped the mine from further poisoning the river, but the price of victory included strengthening Reclamation's grip on the region. That victory can be considered progress, but only in the sense that battlefield triage is good medicine: both require aggressive follow-up care to enable long-term survival.

Let me here draw an important distinction between the local empowerment I advocate and the misguided rhetoric of the states' rights and wise-use movements. Sustainability through local empowerment need not mean the demise or crippling of the central authority. That central authority (in this case, the federal government) can and should be integral in the maintenance of the region's environmental integrity. John Rawls notes that "unless a definite agent is given responsibility for maintaining an asset and bears the loss for not doing so, that asset tends to deteriorate. In this case the asset is the people's integrity and . . . the agent is the people themselves as politically organized" (39). Aside from its utility as a culturally unifying force, a federal government can also play a key role in mediating local disputes.

If, for example, a Native American tribe wished to build a dam in order to garner its share of Anglo-apportioned water, the national environmental lobby would find itself in a quandary. While opposing dams on principle appears noble, it seems arrogant to deny a traditionally oppressed indigenous group access to water because European-descended settlers have already festooned the arid lands with dams in a misguided attempt to turn the West into Eden. Again, the solution lies in treating the dam not as a national matter, but as a local one where voices not usually heeded enjoy unfettered access to the decision-making process. Nevertheless, the tribe's actions would inevitably impact the surrounding region and its inhabitants. Disagreements among local communities over land and resource management might best be solved by a central governing body charged with weighing the interests of all affected parties.

Currently, the tribe would have to slog through a legal system created by a bureaucracy innately hostile to its needs and beliefs. Most matters regarding the health and welfare of Native Americans are decided by the Bureau of Indian Affairs (BIA), whose primary purpose has always been the maintenance and autopoiesis of the system that conquered and confined the Indians to begin with. In the eyes of many tribes, therefore, a helpful BIA official is like a vegetarian butcher—hard to find and cause for suspicion when you do. A sustainable alternative, by contrast, would behave *as if* the Native culture, beliefs, and needs had validity equal to the scientistic, data-oriented approach that currently guides resource management decisions. This approach would not abrogate the state but reform it by making it more responsive to formerly marginalized groups.

The set of premises presently guiding the nation enforces the pre-eminence of a Caucasian-controlled, extractive economy predicated on limitless growth and infinite resources. While the states' rights and wise-use movements seek to continue profiting from this social system, Sustainability acknowledges limits to growth and the failure of the extractive paradigm to enable long-term survival or safeguard the health of all members of the social compact. Accepting the failure of the extractive paradigm need not involve discarding transactive capitalism, however, especially since the Marxist alternative appears equally ecologically repugnant.

The reality of capitalism in the modern era is that information has replaced durable goods as the dominant commodity in the transactive economy (see Harvey). This shift to information-based transactions has potentially revolutionary implications for economic valuation because information is not a conserved quantity. If I tell you something, or sell you a piece of knowledge, you have it, but so still do I. What I am selling you then, is *access* to the same information that I have.[18] The fundamental tenet of economic transactions—the reciprocal transfer of value—must adjust to compensate for this epistemic shift. With information itself possessing no transactive value, right of access becomes the principal commodity.

Interestingly, western water rights, with their near-total transfer of assigned value from water to water rights, seem to have anticipated the information age. Water rights and water law in general occupy a special niche in the American legal system. For example, a public right in water does not usually mean that the government owns the water. It rather means that there is a common right of use. In addition, water can never be wholly privately owned. Water rights are predicated on the notion that water is a community resource that must be shared even as the intricacies of water law acknowledge that we are all part of many different communities that form an interrelated system. Despite these egalitarian precepts, however, the western water allocation system has not functioned to the benefit of all. Communitarian ideals cannot function in a system where notions of community and access are rigidly circumscribed.

The travails within the water market also demonstrate some of the pitfalls of information trading. Water rights contain an embedded entitlement guaranteeing perpetual access to water. But, with the West's water so oversubscribed, water rights lose referentiality while suffering no corresponding loss of exchange value. In other words, even though there might be no actual water over which to hold the right, the right itself does not lose value. Allocating and trading in water that does not and may never exist is constructivism without constraint, the hydraulic equivalent of walking off a cliff without any fear of falling. No matter how many dams and diversion projects get built, the hydroeconomy will still hit the ground.

Outside the hydraulic arena, *info*trepeneurs have already adjusted to the new marketplace of ideas. Communications giants reap huge profits by offering users (*not* "consumers") access to the Internet and other informational constructs, while durable goods companies diversify, seeking to do likewise. Whether capitalism can continue to thrive amid this postmodern agora remains to be determined.[19] If so, it will necessarily mutate to accommodate the realities of what Hayles calls an "informatted society." Whatever the outcome, the information age will, without question, exert a strong influence on the national geography.

Sustainability would be a logical consequence of a cultural shift to informatics. It would behave *as if* each unity and aggregation of unities merited equal access to the unmediated flux and the cusp from which we form reality. Right now, underrepresented communities must prove that their concerns resonate with an often hostile dominant system in order to merit a hearing. Despite this gauntlet built into the system, some empowered groups advocate dismantling the few safeguards for minority access that have, over time, woven their way into the societal fabric. This agenda runs precisely counter to the compelling social need. True reform would facilitate minority access instead of deterring it. A successful state is "both a relationship of domination and an invitation to protest" (Walton 307).

In a sustainable society, if a Native American tribe wished to *dis-mantle* a dam, they would merit attention and respect instead of getting classified as Luddite enviro-extremists. Many enormous Bureau of Reclamation projects were erected without considering the needs of indigenous communities or the health of the downstream ecosystem. For example, because the Glen Canyon Dam prevents silt from washing downstream to fertilize and replenish riparian lands, Native American communities who live in the Grand Canyon and the Canyon de Chelly fight a constant losing battle to keep their land and subsistence from slipping away. Erosion has diminished both the available acreage and its yield. If it seems preposterous to propose removing these enormous structures (and in many ways it is), consider how preposterous it would have been to propose building them had a wealthy Anglo community lived where the Indians do. Furthermore, not just the lives of the various riparian communities, but the life of the river itself stand imperiled. Glen Canyon Dam's enormous storage capacity increases the depth of the reservoir's water and cools it to twenty degrees below its normal temperature. The frigidity of the water released during drawdowns kills the downstream food web.[20]

In September 1997, with many of these concerns in mind, the Sierra Club proposed to drain Lake Powell and dismantle the dam. The plan found little support among the local populace who make their livings from the $500 million tourist economy or among the Navajo, whose coal plant depends on the lake water for steam and for cooling. Nevertheless, the annual water loss to evaporation, the trapped silt that fills in the lake instead of fertilizing riparian land downstream, and the fact that the dam flooded what many call the most beautiful canyon in the world generated sufficient support to merit a hearing before Congress. The plan garnered little support there, but the fact that it got a hearing at all stands as a remarkable milestone on the way to the end of the Reclamation era.

In a parallel situation, debates rage over the dams on the Columbia and Snake Rivers that have all but destroyed their once-legendary salmon runs. Of the six hundred miles of Columbia River between the Canadian border and the Pacific Ocean, only forty-seven fall into the category of river rather than reservoir. On the Snake, the Army Corps of Engineers is considering breaching four dams that together tamed the river enough to turn Lewiston, Idaho, located five hundred miles from the Pacific coast, into an inland seaport. The Corps of Engineers' proposal has galvanized some and flabbergasted others even as it has garnered considerable congressional support. In September 1999, 107 members of Congress signed a letter to President Clinton calling the preservation of the Snake's salmon and steelhead runs "a national responsibility" and urged the administration to consider breaching the dams.[21]

The complicated regional legacy of the go-go years includes electric rates 40 percent lower than the national average and a seriously degraded ecosystem. Whether or not a radical overhaul of the network of dams in the Northwest occurs, the importance of the debate lies in the evolving social status of salmon. Despite a hostile political climate, the Endangered Species Act has forced multi-billion-dollar rescue operations aimed at preserving the remaining salmon populations. On the Snake alone, the government has already spent more than $3 billion. Whatever method is finally chosen, improving the migratory environment will likely require the spending of billions more. The Bureau of Reclamation and the Army Corps of Engineers may wind up spending billions of dollars to mimic the way the river behaved before they spent billions of dollars to alter it. Among the likely consequences: decreased power generation and lakeside recreation, and significantly higher electric rates throughout the region. It is, I think, an excellent omen that the primary beneficiary of all this spending and controversy is a fish.

As the many factions sort out the situation on the Columbia, local, state and federal officials, as well as the indigenous population elsewhere in Washington, are quietly reaching consensus over the demolition of one or two dams on the Elwha River on the Olympic Peninsula. The dams, they agree, serve little purpose, disrupt the local ecosystem, and ought to be removed. With regard to a Reclamation project west of the hundredth meridian, that type of consensus is unprecedented. Whether or not the necessary funding (recent estimates put the cost at approximately seventy million dollars) will successfully navigate the federal appropriations maze remains to be seen. As with the Glen Canyon Dam, the mere fact that billion-dollar retrofits on the Columbia or demolition of structurally sound dams on the Elwha merit serious consideration seems cause for cautious but reasoned optimism.[22] Part of the reason for these limited successes stems from the grassroots involvement rather than the intercession of national environmental organizations whose plurality of views can dilute local agendas.

Without constant vigilance, "environmentalism" slips into unproductive amorphousness. The fact that former president George H. Bush and Dave Foreman (founder of EarthFirst!) both call themselves environmentalists demonstrates that the term's meaning has attenuated past the point of usefulness. An "environmental" ethic means many things to many people precisely because the complexity of interweaving systems makes specificity impossible. In the past, large environmental groups have operated under the "big tent" philosophy. Despite sporadic successes, they have not stemmed the flow of ecologically devastating policies. If the battles were instead fought at the local level by single-cause coalitions, the effect could potentially penetrate the system's rhetorical armor. The happy result might then be a change in legitimating worldview, rather than isolated local victories.

Precedent has shown that a single-issue focus can yield significant successes. Not every self-described environmentalist supports animal rights, although overlap does occur. As a result, mainstream environmental groups have not occupied the vanguard in the movement to stop animal testing and other animal abuse. Instead, People for the Ethical Treatment of Animals (PETA) and its militant ideological ally, the Animal Liberation Front, have focused exclusively on this issue, significantly reducing animal testing while crippling the fur trade. Perhaps more portentously, animal law is now being taught at a number of major law schools.

In a different ideological arena, a similarly narrow focus has enabled antiabortion groups to balkanize the issue of choice. The platform debate at the 1996 Republican Convention testified to the potency of the single-issue approach. Antichoice forces successfully forced the party to adopt a platform calling for a constitutional amendment banning abortion, over the opposition of Bob Dole, the party's standard-bearer and despite the fact that only 6 percent of the Republican electorate supported this view.

Effective as they can be individually, when interest groups link they generate a gestalt effect. This coalescence of self-interested parties undermines the supposed inevitability of the tragedy of the commons. In Garrett Hardin's scenario, individual farmers will always maximize the number of animals they graze on a common pasture because their net gain exceeds their net loss. This conflict between self and common interest applies to virtually any environmental dilemma and, according to Hardin, is tragic because it is both foreseeable and inevitable. By comparison, linked causes avert the inevitable ruination of the commons by suggesting that farmers can find separate reasons for preserving the commons and attain consensus through self-interested reasoning.

Perhaps one farmer wants more trees in order to breed a sun-sensitive cow and another finds she can get more money per cow when they are not crowded together. Still another might not want the stream fouled because it ruins the fishing. The reasons for limiting grazing are diverse, but the net result is the preservation of the commons. This nonbinary approach to conservation demonstrates the flexibility of Sustainability's conceptual framework as well as its adaptability to an increasingly complex, information-dependent world. Even in a gigantic commons filled with competing interests that do not share a common goal, the resonance generated from each linked cause will cause the system to shift and adapt as it seeks metabalance. The result may not satisfy all constituencies, but the metabalance achieved is in the common interest, and, provided the long-term health of the system is preserved, local events can and will shift with time.

This type of compromise is less likely to occur under present conditions because certain uses of the commons command greater institutional support than others. For example, a landowner who chooses not to divert water for irrigation so as to preserve the fishing would likely lose her water right because she failed to put the water to a legally "beneficial use." The right would then go to someone who demonstrated a willingness to use the water in a state-sanctioned manner like irrigation or the watering of livestock.

The mechanistic paradigm did not rise to prominence through legislative fiat; it spidered out slowly, growing stronger as the efforts of individuals in disparate fields strengthened the trend toward objectivism. In time, the rhetoric shifted and the natural theology monolith began to give way. A similar approach could yield equally powerful results for Sustainability. Linked causes, rather than common ones, offer a version of the community-based agrarian anarchy advocated by Abbey, and in a different form, by the social ecology movement.[23]

Theories already abound as to the effects the information age will exert on the nation's geography. Some scholars, like William J. Mitchell, believe that an increasingly complex and electronically linked society will bring about a demographic "renucleation," as the need to commute to work decreases. This dwindling need for travel may cause a reemergence of small-scale urban environments, even as it increases workplace isolation.[24] Whether this scenario comes to pass or gets displaced by another, it seems logical that an increasingly linked, increasingly complex world will evolve through a coalescence of local change. Perhaps with time, the NIMBY movement can evolve into NIABY (Not in Anybody's Back Yard) and eventually to NOPE (Not on Planet Earth).

In *Learning from Las Vegas,* Robert Venturi describes taking architecture students to Las Vegas and analyzing the city from the point of view of city planning. In the students' view, the solution loomed clear: raze the city and try again. That solution would not do, so Venturi suggested that the students look at the city as a system of signs and work within the given context to mend its problems.

A similar approach could prove invaluable in restoring the ecologically ravaged western United States (including Las Vegas). The infrastructure of the Reclamation era will remain for the foreseeable future; no attempt at leveling it can wholly succeed. Nevertheless, focused, reachable goals for restoring linguistic flexibility and attaining a sustainable ecological economy may prove highly effective. Each novel surveyed in this book makes an artistic attempt to reconceptualize the status quo. The results vary. Still, a quick survey of the current status of the issues these authors grappled with offers some cause for optimism. Los Angeles, faced with courtroom defeats and a surge of negative publicity, agreed to return a significant amount of water to the Owens Valley. *The Grapes of Wrath* won valuable, if inadequate protection for migrant workers and directed the public gaze upon the untenability of the myth of the garden in the Midwest. *The Monkey Wrench Gang* spawned a new form of ecointerventionism, bathed the Glen Canyon Dam in the unforgiving glare of public scrutiny, and baldly described the social and ecological ramifications of the Reclamation era. *Animal Dreams* offers a glimpse into the continuing disempowerment of indigenous communities during the late stages of Reclamation.

All four works provide useful insights into the history of the Reclamation era and the mechanics of resistance. Hope flourishes amid the knowledge that the desert still lies beneath the Los Angeles sod and that the Colorado, if unshackled, could again run silty and thick. In short, the situation is grave, the outlook tenuous, and the rhetorical tools less than cutting edge. But the cause is not hopeless and the struggle has just begun.

Notes

Introduction

1. The hundredth meridian more or less bisects the country. It runs through the middle of North Dakota, South Dakota, and Nebraska, cutting off the western third of Kansas and Oklahoma before dividing Texas in half.

2. Ironically, the word *rival* comes from the Latin *rivalis*, which refers to people on opposite banks of a river claiming the same water rights.

Throughout this study, I make dual use of the word *reclamation*. When describing the process of water diversion and delivery, I use a small *r*. When referring to Reclamation ideology, the rhetorical basis for reclamation projects, I use a capital *R*. I use the same system when distinguishing between the practice and rhetoric of restoration.

3. Maximizing both population and available goods using a finite resource base is, as Garrett Hardin demonstrates in "The Tragedy of the Commons," mathematically impossible. This ingrained structural flaw is one of several crucial problems with Reclamation ideology and is discussed in more detail in subsequent chapters.

4. Here and throughout this study I adopt Barthes's definition of the term *myth*, using it to mean not a superstitious or erroneous belief, but rather a linguistic and cultural system through which to shape reality (*Mythologies* 113–27).

5. Francis Bacon propounded his utopian vision in *New Atlantis* (1624). In his ideal world, decisions for the good of the whole were made by scientists because they alone possessed the secrets of nature. In "Salomon's House," the community depicted in *New Atlantis*, scientists use technology to manipulate nature into a more efficient medium for production.

6. For example, Martin Lewis espouses what he calls a "Promethean environmentalism" that embraces technology and the leverage it offers in order to create a sustainable economy and habitat. Lewis maintains that, absent an international return to agrarianism, the United States cannot abdicate its leadership role in the international community or in technological

research. "Even if eco-extremists were to gain power in the United States
. . . their ability to influence the evolutionary path of global society would be
nil." The ensuing power vacuum would lead to the ascendancy of Japan and
other nations whose environmental priorities differ markedly from those of
the United States (14–15).

See also Timothy Luke, who argues that a return to an "idyllic natural past
is neither likely nor necessary," and that it makes more sense to strive for
new relations of production rather than seek an apocryphal premodern per-
fection (*Ecocritique* 203).

7. I borrow both the term *hydraulic empire* and the insight from Donald
Worster's *Rivers of Empire*.

8. See also Cassuto, *Cold Running River,* an ecological biography of the
Pere Marquette River in Michigan. The river's recent history shows both the
boons and the pitfalls of restoring a river and then attempting to manage it in
a manner that exploits its rejuvenation while maintaining its biotic integrity.

9. *Animal Dreams,* the central text of chapter 5, was published in 1990.
While that is not, strictly speaking, the present, it depicts a society in the late
stages of the Reclamation era attempting to craft a new sustainable paradigm. That remains our situation today.

Chapter 1

1. Americans' ignorance about the geography of the West extended to its
leaders as well. For example, Thomas Jefferson, who assembled and funded
Lewis and Clark's expedition, had heard that one tribe of Indians was
descended from the Welsh. Part of the expedition's mission included exploring this possibility (Ambrose 154).

2. The term *wilderness* contains an inherent challenge to human civilization. *Bewilder* shares the same root and negative connotation. As Roderick Nash notes, "The image is that of a man in an alien environment where
the civilization that normally orders and controls his life is absent" (*Wilderness* 2). Wilderness also implies chaos and danger, as well as, in biblical
times, a lack of water. Eden, a well-watered garden and haven, could not
coexist with wilderness. As Nash describes it, "The story of the Garden and
its loss embedded into Western thought the idea that wilderness and paradise were both physical and spiritual opposites" (15).

3. Economist Henry Vaux points to two recurring themes characterizing
the western mind-set during the first eight decades of the twentieth century.
The first was that water's scarcity should not constrain economic growth in
the region. This was the fundamental principle and justification for the ongoing development of the region's scarce water. The second principle involved

what he calls "preemptive development," by which he meant people had to develop and use the water before someone else did (Sax, Abrams, and Thompson 682).

4. The theory that rain followed the plow drew its scientific substantiation from, among other sources, the theories of James Pollard Espy, one of the pioneers of meteorology. Espy believed that as the frontier expanded westward, the clearing of the land actually created a different weather system, warming the region and engendering precipitation for the Plains. This theory dovetailed nicely with the belief that the "'national weather' was, in effect, exactly coterminous with the ever-expanding boundary of the nation's body" (Ross 224).

5. Though his pronouncements on the climate and geography of the West drew on the writings of such nineteenth-century luminaries as Darwin and Humboldt, Gilpin's theories were his own and lacked the rigor and discipline of his eminent antecedents. That lack of rigor was a crucial failing; it led to conclusions that were "*a priori,* deduced, generalized, falsely systematized, and therefore wrong" (Bernard DeVoto, qtd. in Emmons 9).

6. For a fuller discussion of the common interests and subsequent cooperation between the federal government and the railroads, see H. N. Smith, especially chapter 2, and Emmons.

7. The sexual connotations of this term and its accompanying belief system were not lost on those men who first laid claim to the land, nor on the historians who later analyzed their actions. *Virgin Land* is the title of Henry Nash Smith's pioneering study of the mythology of the American West, answered by Annette Kolodny's ironic title, *The Lay of the Land.* The progression of the land from earth mother/maiden goddess to conjugal partner/slut has been the subject of several excellent analyses in addition to Smith's and Kolodny's, among them the works of Susan Griffin.

8. Because equipment loss prevented the accumulation of much important data, Powell led another expedition down the Colorado in 1872. His published account of those trips, *The Exploration of the Colorado River and Its Canyons,* merges the two journeys into one, primarily for literary purposes.

9. For a more encompassing view of Powell's journey, see his journals. For a more complete look at the man himself, as well as the historical climate in which he worked and lived, see Wallace Stegner's excellent biography, *Beyond the Hundredth Meridian,* as well as *The American West as Living Space.*

10. An acre-foot is 325,850 gallons, enough water to cover one acre of land to a depth of one foot. One acre-foot contains enough water to supply three average homes for one year.

11. According to Stegner, Powell's ideas ranged "so far beyond the social

and economic thinking of the period" that they "seem like the product of another land and another people" (*Meridian* 228).

12. For comparison's sake, New Mexico alone is almost three times the size of Ohio.

13. Here and throughout this book, my use of the terms *signifier*, *signified*, and *sign* follow Saussure's classifications wherein *signified* corresponds to use value, *signifier* relates to exchange value, and *sign* unites the two.

14. The reasonable-use doctrine was codified and explained in the 1827 Rhode Island court case, *Tyler v. Wilkinson*.

15. Beneficial use is a legal term of art and its definition varies from state to state. All western states, however, classify domestic, municipal, agricultural, and industrial uses as beneficial. In recent years, many have also included recreational uses. Once a user puts water to a use deemed beneficial under state law, the water right is perfected. That means the user's right to that water cannot be defeated, even in times of shortage, by other uses that might have more social value but which were asserted after that first beneficial use. Thus, in the West a farmer growing rice in the desert can prevent a city from receiving water for its residents.

16. For a good summary of western water law, as well as a comparison with riparianism, see Wehmhoefer. See also Getches.

17. The Desert Lands Act was more than merely the statutory origin of the rule of prior appropriation; it was also an incarnation of the Homestead Act. It stipulated that settlers must show "proof of irrigation" before taking title to a plot of land. Unless the land bordered a river that did not flow through a canyon (unlike most rivers in the arid region), irrigation became enormously expensive—too expensive for the average settler. The result was rampant speculation, water monopolies, and fraud.

18. John Muir had tried to construct a nonanthropocentric, "nature for nature's sake" vocabulary when he led the fight to prevent the damming of the Hetch-Hetchy Valley from 1906 to 1913. His efforts failed principally because he could not communicate his message in a manner that captured the imagination of the common American. His rhetoric was rich in spirituality and the aesthetics of the sublime. Those who loved the outdoors as Muir did readily embraced his rhapsodic descriptions, but a nation of average Americans caught up in the enthusiasm of the progressive era could not relate to it.

19. Leopold's land ethic, published in 1949 as part of *A Sand County Almanac*, has become one of the foundational principles of conservation and enormously important to the growing discipline of ecophilosophy. See, for example, Callicott.

Chapter 2

1. The term *resource,* or to "rise again," originally referred to the earth's ability to restore itself. People used resources commensurate with nature's ability to rejuvenate and replace what was lost. By the nineteenth century, however, ecosystemic needs no longer entered the equation. In *Natural History of Commerce* (1870), John Yeats wrote, "In speaking of the natural resources of any country, we refer to the ore in the mine, the stone unquarried, the timber unfelled, etc." (qtd. in Merchant, *Revolutions* 11). The result, in Annette Kolodny's view, was "the transforming of nature into wealth" (*Lay* 133).

2. The *Los Angeles Times* trumpeted Lippincott's actions as those of a hero, ignoring their obvious impropriety and focusing instead on the city's windfall: "Without Mr. Lippincott's interest and cooperation, it is declared that the plan never would have gone through. . . . Guided by the spirit of the Reclamation Act . . . he recognized that the Owens River would fulfill a greater mission in Los Angeles than if it were spread over acres of desert land. . . . Any other government engineer . . . undoubtedly would have gone ahead with nothing more than the mere reclamation of the arid lands in view" (qtd. in Reisner 70). The irony of Lippincott's supposedly being "guided by the spirit of the Reclamation Act" while actually sabotaging a potential reclamation district and destroying the agricultural capacity of a river and valley was not lost on valley residents. To those in the city, though, who saw both the Reclamation Act and the city's actions as part and parcel of a progressive agenda, no irony existed. Because the majority would benefit, the spirit of the act had been obeyed.

3. City spokesmen did not speak of future needs, however. Instead, they issued dire proclamations trumpeting the current "water famine." William Mulholland, superintendent of the Los Angeles water system and architect of the plan to divert the Owens River, did everything he could to instill the project with a sense of a terrible urgency, claiming that the city had been experiencing a severe drought since the mid-1890s. This claim may be overstated—rainfall had averaged less than three inches below normal for the years 1900–1905 (Hundley, *Thirst* 150).

4. Donald Worster notes this flaw in Powell's reasoning, observing that, while visionary, Powell's ideas offered no solution to the West's land-use dilemmas: "If there was one factor that would defeat broadly diffused democratic tenure in the region, it was precisely the demand for ever higher living standards. . . . Nothing in Powell's proposals would have stopped that process, for he had not begun to question the underlying economic values of the culture" (*Dust Bowl* 87).

5. In a strict sense, the city's actions were within the law. "Los Angeles employed chicanery, subterfuge, spies, bribery, a campaign of divide and conquer, and a strategy of lies to get the water it needed. In the end, it milked the valley bone-dry, impoverishing it, while the water made a number of prominent Los Angeleans very, very rich. There are those who would argue that if all this was legal, then something is the matter with the law" (Reisner 65).

6. The Los Angeles Board of Public Service Commissioners blamed the valley's resistance to the aqueduct on "the mental reactions of a pioneer community . . . uninformed and unaccustomed to the ways of the outside world" (qtd. in Walton 184).

7. These acts included several occupations of the pumping station (one of which turned into a weeklong town picnic) and a number of dynamite blasts to the aqueduct.

8. The *Los Angeles Herald* bragged in 1905 that the Owens River's annexation would ensure that "lawns . . . could be kept perennially as green as emerald and greater Los Angeles could go on swimmingly in its metropolitan progress" (qtd. in Hundley, *Thirst* 150). The editor's choice of the adjective "swimmingly" is particularly apt in light of the city's soon-to-be-realized status as swimming pool capital of the world.

9. As Walton notes, "The tradition-inspired revolt in the Owens Valley took place within the framework of state modernization and economic growth, not as a backward-looking attempt to restore some pre-capitalist Eden or resist the penetration of market forces. On the contrary, it sought fulfillment of the developmental promises that lured pioneers and spoke to western progressives" (194). The revolt in the valley appears less inspired by yeoman values than by a desire to modernize the region's agricultural apparatus.

10. I have provided a rudimentary outline of what was and continues to be a very complex, highly divisive issue in California's history and in national water policy. For a more thorough treatment of the regional history and the causative factors involved, see Walton; Hundley, *Thirst;* and Reisner. There are also a number of fictional treatments of the valley's struggles (other than *The Ford*), most of them melodramas, including Frances Gragg and William Putnam's *Golden Valley* (1950) and Cedric Belfrage's *The Promised Land* (1938).

11. Richard Hofstadter notes that the tendency to treat the land as a commodity rather than as a source of subsistence gradually changed the western farmer from yeoman to businessman: "The characteristic product of American rural society was not a yeoman or a villager, but a harassed little country businessman who worked very hard . . . gambled with his land, and made his way alone" (46). That transition from farmer to businessman contained the

seeds of ecological destruction for the arid western lands. A region without abundant rainfall is far more ecologically fragile than a humid zone. Factory farming, involving large-scale monoculture and intensive irrigation, destroys the soil's nutrient balance while salinating what little water the region retains. These phenomena become more apparent as the Reclamation era progresses and are discussed more thoroughly in later chapters.

12. Stephen Jay Gould has long been one of the most vocal and perceptive critics of the ruse of scientific objectivity (see *Mismeasure of Man*, especially pp. 19–29). See also Alan Gross's discussion of the need to recast scientific advances as inventions rather than discoveries. To discover, Gross argues, is to find out what already is there. Science can make no such claim, as the ongoing superannuation of scientific theories makes plain. Invention, on the other hand, "captures the historically contingent and radically uncertain character of all scientific claims, even the most successful" (7). If we treat scientific theories as rhetorical inventions, the need to explain their vulnerability to obsolescence disappears.

13. This insight is taken from Annette Kolodny's excellent discussion of the novel as illustrator of American terrestrial values (*Lay* 138).

14. Susan Griffin describes land's shifting identity: "He has made her conceive. His land is a mother . . . Again and again, in his hunger, he returns to her . . . She is his mother. Her powers are a mystery to him. Silently she works miracles for him. Yet, just as silently, she withholds from him. Without reason, she refuses to yield. She is fickle. She dries up . . . He is determined he will master her. He will make her produce at will. He will devise ways to plant what he wants in her, to make her yield more to him" (53).

15. Environmentalism at the turn of the century was known as "conservationism" and was riven with internal conflicts between "conservationists" and "preservationists." Conservationists favored judicious development of land and resources, while preservationists rejected utilitarianism in favor of safeguarding an unspoiled nature. The preservationist cause was championed by John Muir and botanist Charles Sprague Sargent among others, while the conservationists were led by Gifford Pinchot and Frederick Newell (Nash, *Wilderness* 129–40).

Feminism during Austin's time described a political position more than a philosophy. Feminists were women seeking equal rights, including the right to vote. The philosophical tenets of feminism have been around for a long time. Historians traditionally located the origin of "feminist consciousness" in the nineteenth century, coinciding with the nascency of the political women's rights movement. However, some modern historians trace it as far back as the fifteenth century and the works of French author Christine de Pizan (see Lerner 14–15).

16. The Austins were separated by the time *The Ford* was written.

17. This phenomenon crops up again in later years as those fleeing the Dust Bowl curse the banks and factory farms that drove them from their land even as they themselves rushed to adapt the same ecologically disastrous land-use strategies to their smaller farms. It was these methods more than any shortfall of water that created the Dust Bowl. See chapter 3.

18. One need only look at Texas, with its cities and communities built on oil wealth, and the fortunes of the state integrally linked to the world petroleum market, to see the tremendous impact oil can have on a region. Even with the collapse of the domestic oil market, the economy of Texas, as well as of Louisiana, Oklahoma, and several other states, remains tied to the petroleum industry.

19. Karen Warren and Jim Cheney define ecofeminism as a movement that "attempts to unite the demands of the women's movement with those of the ecological movement in order to bring about a world and worldview that are not based on conceptual structures of domination" (179). They go on to describe a methodology based on "observation set theory" that posits numerous realities while privileging none. Anne seems to be alluding to a similar concept in her suggesting that the dominance of androcentric culture lies in "the way we look at things."

20. Andrée Collard argues in *The Rape of the Wild* that female experience shares a history of oppression and abuse with nature, thus making women more sensitive to such actions and better equipped to remedy them (138). The self-imposed alienation of men from nature is inherently damaging to the biotic regime: "A culture that defines adulthood in terms of one's ability to separate from mother/nature and defines mental health according to the smoothness of this separation, is a culture that denies its life blood. Such a relationship is bound to be destructive" (28).

21. This is by no means the only view advanced by ecofeminists. While Andrée Collard, Dorothy Dinnerstein, Susan Griffin, and others advance this view, many do not. Catherine Roach, for example, rejects the notion of a closer link between women and nature, arguing persuasively that constructions such as women/nature and men/culture perpetuate a patriarchal, dualistic worldview. They also syllogistically separate nature and culture into two discrete entities. Roach believes that this alienation lies at the heart of the current ecological crisis: "This dualism is unsound because it encourages the belief that 'culture' and humanity are quite apart from 'nature' and that we humans may thus use and abuse the environment at will, without ourselves suffering from the damage we inflict. Any understanding of the world that posits an important or unbridgeable difference between the realm of the human and the nonhuman risks creating a gulf between the two in which the human, because of our inherent chauvinism or anthropocentrism, would inevitably be more valued than the nonhuman" (54). I offer this capsule view

of the diversity within the ecofeminist community in order to dissolve any boundaries I may have inadvertently drawn around the doctrine of ecofeminism. It is not my intent either in this note or in this study to do justice to the richness of ecofeminist discourse. I merely wish to point out the relevance of Mary Austin's philosophy to the ecofeminist vision that celebrates the women/nature relation.

Chapter 3

1. I am indebted to Roderick Nash for the biblical references, originally made in *Wilderness and the American Mind*, 14.

2. The trend was visible as early as 1847 to George Perkins Marsh, one of the first and most influential American ecologists and an early opponent of the myth of the garden. In a speech to the Rutland County Agricultural Society he stated that in the United States "the full energies of advanced European civilization, stimulated by its artificial wants and guided by its accumulated intelligence, were brought to bear at once on a desert continent" (qtd. in Marx, *Machine* 204).

3. Such is technology's domination over the agricultural process that growers in California's Imperial Valley do not even like it when it rains; the sun soon overheats the dampened crops and wilts the lettuce leaves (Reisner 4).

4. This tendency to privilege water, either by scarcity or surfeit, appears frequently in the Steinbeck canon. For example, *Of Mice and Men* opens and closes on the banks of a river; *The Log from the Sea of Cortez,* with its fascination with tide pools, offers the clearest presentation of Steinbeck's ecophilosophy; and *The Wayward Bus*, like *The Grapes of Wrath*, utilizes floodwaters to spur its characters to action and the acquisition of wisdom.

5. Congressman Lyle Borden of California declared *The Grapes of Wrath* to be "a lie, a black, infernal creation of a twisted, distorted mind" (qtd. in Steinbeck, *Working* xxiv). Steinbeck became the target of a whispering campaign by the growers' alliance, the Associated Farmers, one rumor being that Steinbeck was a Jew acting on behalf of a Zionist-Communist conspiracy to undermine the economy (Benson, *Adventures* 420).

6. The Associated Farmers believed the publications of *The Grapes of Wrath* and *Factories in the Field* to be evidence of a vast left-wing conspiracy, the supposed existence of which fueled their outrage at both authors. Prior to their publication in 1939, the governor of California, Culbert Olson, had also made McWilliams chief of the state's Division of Immigration and Housing. The job included enforcing the long-dormant state labor camp act. McWilliams's appointment further stoked the growers' rage and paranoia.

They labeled him "Agricultural Pest No. 1 in California, outranking pear blight and boll weevil" (McWilliams x).

7. Adherence to the doctrine of manifest destiny, even before it was so named, allowed white settlers to casually displace Native Americans without regard for history, negotiated treaty, or first right of occupancy. Completely dismissing Native claims to their homelands permitted the notion of "virgin land" to arise. Acknowledging Native claims meant dismantling an intact and seductive mythology as well as relinquishing the American right not just to continue expansion, but to exist at all.

8. That is not to say that there was not a serious drought in the Plains during the 1930s. In fact, almost the entire nation endured a terrible drought from roughly 1930 to 1936 (Hoyt 8–9, 66).

9. James N. Gregory argues that the dust storms displaced fewer people than government policies designed to bolster falling crop prices. In 1933 the federal government passed the Agricultural Adjustment Act, which paid subsidies to landowners who took their land out of production. Since the majority of farms in the Plains were operated by tenants (like the Joads), taking the land out of production effectively deprived them of their livelihood. The act compensated landowners for not planting, but left tenant farmers without food or means of earning a living (11–13).

10. Muley's unbreakable bond with his homeland offers a powerful parallel to the link between many oral cultures and the land from which their culture draws both sustenance and definition. There is, according to philosopher-ecologist David Abram, a powerful link between nonwriting cultures (many Okies, including most of the Joads and Muley, were barely literate) and the places in which their stories take place. "A particular place . . . is never, for an oral culture, just a passive and inert setting for the human events that occur there. *It is an active participant in those occurrences.* . . . [T]he place may even be felt to be the source, the primary power that expresses itself through the various events that unfold there" (162).

11. Though it does not directly treat reclamation, *The Education of Henry Adams* poignantly encapsulates the growing pains of American society as it struggled to cope with an expanded technological capacity and the new challenges presented by the twentieth century.

12. One of the fascinating aspects of this passage is that Joseph's experience is portrayed less as autoeroticism than as a sexual encounter between a man and the earth: "[T]he exultation grew to be a sharp pain of desire that ran through his body in a hot river. He flung himself face downward on the grass and pressed his cheek against the wet stems. . . . His thighs beat heavily on the earth" (*God* 11). There is no element of fantasy; he does not imagine that he is having sex with another person. He is mating with the land.

13. Kolodny argues that the progressive deterioration in cultural rever-

ence for the land was an unavoidable by-product of viewing it as feminine while seeking to settle it: "Implicit in the metaphor of the land-as-woman was both the regressive pull of maternal containment *and* the seductive invitation to sexual assertion: if the Mother demands passivity, and threatens regression, the Virgin apparently invites sexual assertion and awaits impregnation" (*Lay* 67).

14. Worster offers this account of the Plains mentality during the mid-1930s:

> "You gave us beer," they told Roosevelt, "now give us water." . . . "Every draw, arroyo [*sic*], and canyon that could be turned into a lake or lagoon," wrote a clothing store manager, "should be turned into one by dams and directed ditches & draws until there are millions of them thru these mid-western states." A Texas stockman wanted to use natural gas to pump flood waters from the Mississippi River to the Plains. . . . An old soldier from Denver penciled his ideas on ruled tablet paper: stage sham battles with 40,000 Civilian Conservation Corp boys and $20 million worth of ammunition—the noise would be sure to stir up some rain. . . . "Try it," he finished, "if it works send me a check for $5000 for services rendered." (*Dust Bowl* 39)

15. Gregory maintains that the westward migration was due less to any organized effort by the growers than by "migration chains" whereby migrants who had moved west during better times (i.e., the 1920s) and found work wrote their relatives about their success. When dust storms and the depression hit the Plains, afflicted families remembered these success stories and sought to emulate them. Hopeful songs trumpeted the splendor they hoped to find upon their arrival in the Golden State:

California, California,
Here I come too.

. . . . . .

Nothing's left in Oklahoma,
For us to eat or do.
And if apples, nuts, and oranges
And Santy Claus is real,
Come on to California,
Eat and eat till you're full.

The California government, concerned that such rosy-hued rumors would cause the state to be overwhelmed with refugees, made some token efforts to discourage migration. These efforts included posting a billboard on Route 66 outside of Tulsa that read:

No JOBS in California
IF YOU are looking for work—KEEP OUT
6 Men for Every Job
No State Relief Available for Non-Residents.

The tourist industry was also concerned about the potential effects of mass migration on the state's allure. Vacation ads featured fine print warnings like "Come to California for a glorious vacation. *Advise anyone not to come seeking employment, lest he be disappointed;* but for tourists, the attractions are unlimited" (qtd. in Gregory 22).

16. Steinbeck had already devoted an entire novel (*In Dubious Battle*) to the political implications of the worsening tensions between growers and migrants. In *The Grapes of Wrath*, he ontologizes the migrant struggle and makes the inevitability of social change even more evident. Both novels embody his "phalanx" theory, which held that the collective will of the people differs from the sum of its component parts; it is a unique entity whose force far exceeds that of its members.

17. According to one California agricultural spokesman: "We are not husbandmen; we are not farmers. We are producing a product to sell" (qtd. in Worster, *Dust Bowl* 57).

18. Foucault believes that approaching knowledge through the study of geography ("region, domain, implantation, displacement and transposition") leads to true awareness of the relationship between power and knowledge (*Power/Knowledge* 69).

19. Marx's description of worker alienation (in "Wages of Labor") is uncannily accurate when related to the migrants: "Since the worker has sunk to the level of a machine, he can be confronted by the machine as a competitor. Finally, as the amassing of capital increases the amount of industry and therefore the number of workers, it causes the same amount of industry to manufacture a *greater amount of product,* which leads to overproduction and thus either ends by throwing a large section of workers out of work or by reducing their wages to the most miserable minimum" (69). The first part of the quotation could easily be describing the situation in Oklahoma, while the second half diagrams the Okies' dilemma in California.

20. Dehumanizing other people is a complicated process. It is "fraught with deep ambivalence and anxiety" and stems from the special value we attach to human life. Groups try to objectify other groups even while admitting that the "objects" are in fact human. The victims become, in the dominators' eyes, not quite human and not quite object (L. Cassuto chap. 1).

21. After visiting a series of migrant camps in 1940, Mrs. Roosevelt told reporters, "I have never believed *The Grapes of Wrath* was exaggerated" (qtd. in Benson, *Adventures* 402).

22. In March 1950, the *New York Times* reported, "The spectre of human misery again is striking the Grapes of Wrath country. Throughout the vast and fertile San Joaquin valley . . . where the trek of the Okies made history a dozen years ago, a new cycle of destitution among farm workers is under way" (qtd. in McWilliams xii).

23. Robert Reinhold, "U.S. Says Scarce Water Supplies Won't Go to California Farmers," *New York Times*, February 15, 1992, 1+.

Chapter 4

1. Ecotage, or "monkeywrenching" (so named in honor of the novel) is, according to Dave Foreman, "non-violent resistance to the destruction of natural diversity and wilderness . . . aimed at inanimate machines and tools that are destroying life. Care is always taken to minimize any threat to people, including the monkeywrenchers themselves" (113). Abbey clarifies the term in his preface to the monkeywrencher's handbook, *Ecodefense:* "[I]f the wilderness is our true home and if it is threatened with invasion, pillage and destruction—as it certainly is—then we have the right to defend that home . . . by whatever means are necessary" (qtd. in Foreman 141).

2. Potlatch is still practiced by some Northwest tribes, but in a much altered form. It all but died out due to suppression from provincial authorities and efforts by the Canadian and United States governments, as well as by many Indians, to assimilate the Indians into the dominant culture.

3. "The hosts at one potlatch were the guests at another and in this sense potlatches are reciprocal. . . . Thus, there is an endless chain of potlatching and distributions of property between groups" (Rosman and Rubel 29).

4. For a fuller discussion of the potlatch's demise, see Cole and Chaikin's *An Iron Hand upon the People.* Ironically, contact by European settlers propelled the potlatch into far greater prominence among the tribes than it had previously enjoyed. Wealth acquired through the fur trade and later through commercial fishing and logging allowed Indians to spend far more lavishly than they could before. Precontact potlatches tended to be small affairs with handmade blankets and crafts serving as the principal gifts. Postcontact potlatches evolved into hugely expensive gatherings with commercial gifts often carrying the most value. It was only after contact that potlatches began to genuinely impoverish their participants. In this sense, capitalism sowed the seeds for the potlatch's demise before religious zeal and governmental litigiousness even entered the fray.

5. "In Bataille's view, the bourgeois individuals . . . who foster a desire to revolt by soaring 'above' are destined for a fall, and in a way, *want to fall:* thus the 'Icarian Complex,' an 'unconscious' and pathological desire to fall. Icar-

ian revolt . . . is the only pathology Bataille will condemn; it is the pathologi-cal refusal to embrace stinking decomposition" (Stoekl, in Bataille xv; emphasis added).

6. Andre Gorz integrates these arguments into an ecophilosophical con-text. In advocating bioregionally independent communities similar to those envisioned by Abbey for his agrarian anarchist society, Gorz's rhetoric overtly recalls Bataille: "All production is also destruction. This fact can be overlooked so long as production does not irreversibly deplete natural resources. . . . They regenerate themselves naturally—the grass grows back along with the weeds. The effects of destruction appear wholly productive. More precisely: this destruction is the very condition of production. It has to be repeated again and again" (20).

7. Approaches to environmental management in the United States tradi-tionally assume opposition as on a balance sheet. Environmental impact statements are, by their very nature, procedures by which environmental degradation is weighed against proposed social gain. Andrew Ross notes that "the game of winning general consent for ideas in the history of modern cap-italism has been waged on a balanced terrain of contradictions, where narra-tives about traditional values are played off against narratives of progress. Something always has to be sacrificed for progress to be made" (232).

8. Abbey recounts with pleasure Jeffers's famous advice, "Be in nothing so moderate / as in love of man" (qtd. in *Desert* 177).

9. Hofstadter observes that it is "too little realized that the farmers, who were quite impotent as a special interest when they were numerous, com-peting and unorganized, grew stronger as they grew relatively fewer, became more concerted, more tenaciously organized and self-centered" (7).

10. Leo Marx argues that Thomas Jefferson among others envisioned the machine as the agent with which to maximize the land's productive potential: "Once the machine is removed from the dark, crowded, grimy cities of Europe . . . it will blend harmoniously into the open countryside of his native land . . . turning millwheels, moving ships up rivers, and . . . helping to trans-form a wilderness into a society of the middle landscape" (*Machine* 150).

11. Phillip Fradkin points out that "cows are far and away the chief beneficiaries of water, even in the West's most populous region. . . . The Imperial Valley [of California] was the single largest user of Colorado River water; the most valuable single crop . . . was alfalfa, used for hay" (33). This is a telling statistic. The metropolitan areas of Los Angeles, Phoenix, Las Vegas, and so on, do not approach the consumption levels of corporate farms. Nonetheless, to say that cows are the beneficiaries of this water is mis-leading. Cows are grazed, fattened, and slaughtered to benefit the ledgers of agribusiness. They are no more responsible for their presence than the river is for its role in irrigation.

12. In 1975, the year *The Monkey Wrench Gang* was published, 2.3 million acre-feet evaporated from Colorado River reservoirs. That amount exceeded the total water consumption of the four upper-basin states and Nevada (Fradkin 76).

13. In 1999 dollars, the cost exceeds one billion.

14. Bonnie's relatively ancillary role in the gang's activities as well as her status as object of desire and disruptive force buttress oft-made charges of misogyny against Abbey. These charges, while perhaps justified and certainly deserving of further discussion, do not fall within the purview of this study.

15. Bishop Dudley Love is an interesting character in his own right. In many ways he is the antithesis of both Doc and Smith. Like Doc, he is wealthy and community-oriented. Yet he uses his wealth to develop the canyon lands and to fuel his own political fortunes. Love's community service consists of heading the Search and Rescue Team, a group of volunteer law-enforcers who hunt down the monkeywrenchers. And, like Smith, Love is a Mormon whose behavior does not fit with traditional standards of piety. Though a bishop in the Mormon Church, Love's religiosity is driven by cynicism and greed. As Smith tells it: "We got plenty like him in Utah. . . . They run things as best they can for God and Jesus, and what them two don't want, why fellas like Bishop Love pick up. They say it's a mighty convenient arrangement all around. Jesus Saves at eight and a half percent compounded daily" (*Gang* 109–10).

16. In Abbey's novel *Good News* (1980), Burns is the hero of a dystopian science fiction novel set in a postnuclear Southwest. Just as in *The Monkey Wrench Gang* and *Hayduke Lives* (1989), Burns is a ghostly figure from the past who rides into a skewed present and attempts to restore reverence for the land.

17. Paul Horgan, himself an accomplished writer of the West, wrote in 1964, "If there is a single pervasive theme in writing about the *west*, . . . it could be identified as the theme of man, alone, against the grand immensity of nature—the nature of the land, reflected in his own soul" ("Western Novel" 28).

18. Abbey's formulation offers an interesting parallel to John Walton's discussion of the relationship between state and culture in *Western Times and Water Wars.* Walton, paraphrasing Phillip Corrigan and Derek Sayer, notes that "state forms are cultural and cultural forms are state-regulated. The state is not an object but an 'exercise in legitimation [and] a bid to elicit support for' domination which succeeds to the extent that it constructs cultural justification" (307). For both Abbey and Walton, culture is not the celebrated product of societal advance but rather a dead weight on social evolution, an obstacle to be overcome.

19. For a concise encapsulation of Abbey's philosophy of "agrarian anar-

chy," see his essay "Theory of Anarchy" (*One Life* 25–28). For a more theoretical discussion of ecoanarchist bioregionalism see Murray Bookchin's *Remaking Society,* particularly 185–204. Abbey and Bookchin differ on many key ecological and ideological concepts, but both endorse utopian, bioregionalist visions wherein technology functions within the limits of a given ecosystem.

20. Richard Grusin maintains that the belief in the beneficialness of nature's profligacy owes much to Thoreau's formulation of nature's economy in terms of symbolic rather than market value. He points to "Wild Apples" and "Autumnal Tints" as clear indicators of Thoreau's reconfiguration of the natural economy: "Each essay takes as its subject natural objects that society thinks of as useless . . . and proceeds to show that both are invaluable. Thoreau aims to point out that his contemporaries misvalue nature not because they insist on seeing it in economic terms but because they insist on understanding its economy in terms of market exchange rather than symbolic expenditure" (38). Nature's profligacy, according to Thoreau, is something to emulate rather than criticize. In his journals, he praises the system that "can afford to let so many moons burn all the day as well as the night— though no man stands in need of the light. . . . Nature would not appear so rich . . . if we knew a use for everything. . . . Her motive is not economy but satisfaction" (qtd. in Grusin 36). This Thoreauvian system of natural theology stood in stark contrast to the technocentric paradigm that was fast taking hold of the nation.

21. I do not claim that Abbey attempted to integrate Bataille's formulations into his fiction or that Abbey had even read Bataille. However, Abbey did hold an M.A. in philosophy from the University of New Mexico, and his oeuvre suggests a familiarity with a number of philosophical schools. Furthermore, the fact that *The Monkey Wrench Gang* is dedicated to Ned Ludd, godfather of the Luddite movement, certainly indicates Abbey's sympathy for such a view.

22. In *Desert Solitaire,* Abbey quotes Bakunin to make a similar point. Bakunin states, "There are times when creation can be achieved only through destruction. The urge to destroy is then a creative urge" (*Desert* 185).

Chapter 5

1. Biologist Francisco Varela defines an autopoietic system as one that is both autonomous and continually self-producing (13). In *Ecological Communication,* Niklas Luhmann adapts Varela's concept to social systems, arguing that when system elements are conceived of as communicative acts

rather than bioenergetic entities, the concept of autopoiesis extends to the social domain. For an excellent summary of the way the biological notion of autopoiesis maps onto social systems, see Paulsen 121–27.

2. "Unlike the concept of meaning, that of information is always to be understood relative to an actually given, constantly changing state of knowledge and individually structured preparedness to process information. The very same meaning complex can thus result in quite different information, depending on when and by whom it was actualized in experience" (Luhmann, *Essays* 31). Or, to adapt William Paulsen's analogy, one person's lucid intelligent conversation on one phone line becomes mere random noise when it bleeds into another conversation on another line (67).

3. Paulsen argues that language is itself both an autopoietic system, "one that has defined and continues to define itself in the course of the recursive interactions that are its use," and also an allonomous system, one that serves a purpose outside itself (129–30). This characterization is very close to the idea of language as a function system in the maintenance of the larger unity. It does, however, help explain language's centrality within each function system that makes up the unity. It further illuminates why language is sometimes ineffective as the communicative medium for the unity: "[I]t has its own internal self-referential laws . . . the features of an autonomous system that is the accretion of all the other messages that have been sent within it" (130).

4. Luhmann observes that "evolution is only possible on the basis of deviant reproduction of systems" (*Theory* xii). For a good discussion of complexity as a beneficial adaptive mechanism, see La Porte.

5. This contrasts with the mechanistic worldview that "arose simultaneously and in support of early capitalism. . . . Mechanism and its ethic of domination legitimates the use of nature as commodity, a central tenet of industrial capitalism" (Merchant, *Radical* 11).

6. Tailings are the waste product created by the mining and refining process. They often contain heavy metals and other toxic materials.

7. For example, the Homestead Act's requirement that settlers display an "erected domicile" on their land to show that they meant to live on the property created a boom in the sales of birdhouses. Speculators placed the birdhouses on their property in order to comply with the letter, if not the spirit of the law.

Another famous example of quasi-legal fraud involves Henry Miller's acquisition of his 1,090,000-acre ranch in California's Central Valley. The Swamp and Overflow Act stated that any federal land that overflowed enough to allow traversing in a flat-bottomed boat could belong to anyone who promised to drain and reclaim it. According to legend, Miller bought a boat, hitched it to a horse-drawn wagon, and dry-land boated across several counties (Reisner 46).

8. For variations on this same theme that specifically treat native New Mexicans, John Nichols's *The Milagro Beanfield War* (1974) provides a fictional account, while Stanley Crawford's *Mayordomo* (1986) offers a compelling first-person narrative of the author's experiences as ditch boss on an *acequia* (irrigation ditch).

9. Ivan Illich describes the resulting schism between traditional and contemporary visions of water: "H_2O and water have become opposites. . . . H_2O is a social creation of modern times, a resource that is scarce and that calls for technical management. It is an observed fluid that has lost the ability to mirror the water of dreams" (76).

10. Politics is the shifting arena in which contested processes inevitably land. When function systems cannot agree on who retains regulatory authority for a given process, the arbitration of the dispute is political: "The third value that is excluded from the code of legal and illegal, i.e., what for the time being is neither legal nor illegal, appears in the legal system as politics. Thus the legal legitimization of political decision-making leads to the reintroduction of the excluded third value into the system" (Luhmann, *Communication* 73).

11. There are many such examples. The most topical is perhaps that of the Mexican migrant workers in California. Prior to the arrival of the exodusters, Mexican migrant workers had been brutally exploited with little thought given to their welfare or even their survival. The growers justified their treatment of the Mexicans by reasoning that the Mexicans were just "living as they normally do, making themselves available to serve whites in their quest to make the desert a garden" (Mitchell 109).

In *White by Law*, Ian Haney-López describes the strained reasoning process used to determine "legal" whiteness for purposes of American citizenship. Racial classifications for immigration served the dual purpose of defining the nation's borders and the borders between races. Haney-López uses several landmark court cases from the first two decades of the twentieth century to demonstrate the value of whiteness to whites and the accompanying need to define it in such a way as to further rarify the status of white people.

For another discussion of dehumanization through boundary drawing, see Andrew Light's essay "Urban Wilderness." Light argues that in a world where the frontier has long since dissolved, the heart of darkness now beats in the inner city, a place where middle-class fears combine with racism and difficult living conditions to create an urban "jungle" of the type first depicted by Upton Sinclair.

Light points to the film *Falling Down*, where an L.A. defense worker played by Michael Douglas decides he cannot take it anymore and attempts to clear out the jungle by force. The filmmakers claimed the film was a critique of racism and simplistic attitudes about the inner city. Unfortunately, film audiences saw it instead as an accurate portrayal of the urban wilderness, and audiences identified with its portrayal of a righteous inner-city crusader. In Light's view, absent a prevailing notion that the inner city is the only truly uncivilized place remaining, films like *Falling Down* would not be possible.

12. Luhmann comments that "systems define their own boundaries. They differentiate themselves and thereby constitute the environment as whatever lies outside the boundary" (*Communication* 6). It is worth noting that the act of drawing boundaries and defining environment is a self-interested act. The system will designate boundaries conducive to its autopoietic potential.

13. Mary Douglas observes that "pollution behavior is the reaction which condemns any object or idea likely to confuse or contradict cherished classifications" (36).

14. The Trail Smelter Arbitration has been the subject of a great deal of scholarly interest both in and outside of the international legal community. For a history of the smelter and the region, see Turnbull. For concise and readable discussion of the legal side of the smelter's history, see Rubin.

15. An ironic coda to the Trail Smelter story further interrogates the concept of damage. Since 1906, the Trail Smelter has been owned by the Cominco Corporation, a multinational mining concern with mines and interests all over the world. Some of Cominco's holdings are in Madagascar, where mining companies are currently viewed by some as ecofriendly because the mines cause less harm to the local environment than the rampant deforestation taking place elsewhere on the island.

16. See Mary Douglas's discussion of dirt and pollution as windows through which to view a system's ordering methods. Dirt, according to Douglas, is never an isolated event. "Where there is dirt there is a system" (35).

17. "This linkage of human to human is, in the final analysis, the groundwork of all ethics as a reflection on the legitimacy of the presence of others" (Maturana and Varela, *Tree* 247). A group can, if it wishes, exclude those with differing views. The result will be two or more independent ethical frameworks and infinite potential for moral posturing during conflicts. One need not look far to see this theory borne out by current events.

18. Following Barthes, I use myth within the Saussurean signification system wherein the union of the signifier and signified yields a sign, imbued with meaning through the communicative act. Barthes uses the example of a black pebble as potential signifier. When used as the indicator of a death sentence (the signified), the black pebble, as the union of signifier and signified, becomes a sign. But the sign is only valid within the specific context (myth) that gives it meaning (*Mythologies* 111). And myth, as Barthes repeatedly stresses, is a "type of speech," or language (109).

19. See chapter 6 for an extended discussion of sustainability as I envision it defining a post-Reclamation reality. While I do not disagree with Luke, my definition of sustainability requires multiple perspectives and would not permit one dominant interest to transform it into an "economic project."

20. Both the dam and the cycle form signature features of faux potlatch. Systems theory presupposes a form of potlatch that recalls Bataille: "All structures of social systems have to be based on this fundamental fact of vanishing events . . . or words that are dying away. . . . The events themselves cannot be saved; their loss is the condition of their regeneration. . . . Disintegration and reintegration, disordering and reordering require each other, and reproduction comes about only by a recurring integration of disintegration and reintegration" (Luhmann, *Essays* 9). Since faux potlatch displaces the normal acquisition/expenditure cycle, it is not surprising to find it at work in a system dedicated to limitless growth.

21. Systems are not capable of long-range planning. Hence they are always concerned with short-term autopoiesis. Other matters become relevant once survival is assured. "[O]nce the essential ontogenic requisite of reproduction is fulfilled, everything is made possible. Reproduction is a necessity; otherwise there is extinction" (Maturana and Varela, *Tree* 107). Capital is necessary to the system's short-term survival, whereas the system can sustain a great deal of ecological damage and still endure. Therefore, capital acquisition takes precedence.

22. Big 10 members include Environmental Defense Fund, Environmental Policy Institute, Friends of the Earth, Izaak Walton League of America, National Audubon Society, National Parks and Conservation Association, National Wildlife Federation, Natural Resources Defense Council, Sierra Club, and the Wilderness Society.

23. In an early essay applying systems theory to ecology and the notion of environment, Bernard Patten recognizes and rejects the notion of prediction in system-environment interaction: "[T]he [system] cannot anticipate its future environment; it is *nonanticipatory*. . . . [T]he only way it could [predict] (since it is determinate) would be based on information about the future. This possibility is precluded for the causal object" (259).

24. Observing environmental interaction requires an ongoing calculus that strives to integrate entropic variations. Yet the calculus is an elaborate fiction; only one outcome can result from a given perturbation—the one that actually occurs. As Luhmann observes, "The theory of self-referential systems . . . has realized that the classical instruments of the acquisition of knowledge, namely deduction (logic) and causality (experience), are merely forms of simplifying the observation of observations. . . . Methodologically, this means that the point of departure has to be the observation of self-observing systems and not the assumed logic of causal-

ity" (*Communication* 9). Calculating probabilities is a second-order organizational device (i.e., derived from a system's ability to observe itself) and an implicit admission that though only one possibility exists, we cannot know it.

25. Maturana and Varela do distinguish, however, between language as acquired behavior and the innate behavior seen in the insects. They note that acquired communicative behaviors depend on an organism's ontogeny as well as its particular history of social interactions. Innate behavior, by contrast, can characterize an entire class of organisms and is independent of ontogeny and social history (*Tree* 207).

26. The principle of the actor as observer is integral to second-order cybernetics and essential to the application of systems-theoretical principles to human social systems. See Rasch and Wolfe, especially 7–13.

27. As Luhmann succinctly notes, "A system can see only what it can see. It cannot see what it cannot. Moreover, it cannot see that it cannot see this" (*Communication* 23). Interestingly, defining the unknown simultaneously demarcates the known. It therefore constitutes an act of self-definition (*Essays* 7).

28. See, for example, Loyd's decision to give up cockfighting after Codi persuades him that animals suffering for human amusement is incongruent with the dignity of life (*Animal* 185–91).

29. Maturana and Varela see language as the fundamental constitutive force defining the human condition. As such, it is virtually all-powerful: "Every human act takes place in language. Every act in language brings forth a world created with others in the act of coexistence which gives rise to what is human. Thus every human act has an ethical meaning because it is an act of constitution of the human world" (*Tree* 247).

30. It is an often-remarked-upon phenomenon that the most powerful art tends to come from society's margins. From a systems-theoretical perspective, that trend is entirely logical; art objects are communicative devices and communication arises in response to disturbance. Disturbance will not likely come from components of a function system thriving within the current equilibrium. It will rather be generated by those segments of society whose needs and goals conflict in some capacity with those of the unity. Art upsets equilibrium through interrogating the known and offering new ways of seeing. In other words, it disturbs various societal function systems, generating resonance and forcing them to adapt and evolve. *Animal Dreams* is an example of one such self-conscious attempt to force beneficial adaptation in the social system currently governing the West.

31. As Evernden notes, "Ecology cannot be presumed to be the exclusive ally of the environmental movement, for it provides information that can just as well be used to manipulate nature as to defend it" (10).

Chapter 6

1. Nicholas Wade comments, "Given that consciousness, the one thing that we feel absolutely sure about, is in fact an illusion, it is not surprising that we lack the vocabulary to describe this embarrassing state of affairs" (22).

2. This phenomenon extends to the legal realm as well. Robin West, among others, notes that the legal system's control over the means of normative discourse creates "clusters of beliefs" in the legitimacy of the social structures that buttress the society:

> One part of those clusters of beliefs is the moral perspective . . . from which particular laws are criticized or celebrated. For example, while we may feel free to criticize a particular legal rule as inefficient, or a proposed bill as nonrepresentative of the public will, or a criminal statute as overintrusive into our privacy, we find it much harder to criticize our moral commitment to efficiency, or representation, or privacy against which these laws are evaluated. . . . The result is that the vast bulk of the particular rules and the process of the extant system that govern our behavior are seen as morally legitimate—as in accord with our moral beliefs. Meaningful criticism of the law against truly independent moral standards is thereby frustrated. (5–6)

As with environmentalism, critics of the legal system have consequently been frustrated in their attempts to articulate "a credible basis for the moral criticism of law that would be other than complicit in the legitimation of the law's fundamental authority" (6).

3. Latour defines the discursive constitution as the set of practical and theoretical principles that "defines humans and nonhumans, their properties and their relations, their abilities and their groupings" (15).

4. See for example, Porush; Landow; and Paulsen.

5. Speaking of the inevitable conflicts of multiculturalism, Stanley Fish notes that substantial numbers of citizens of one country are finding themselves also members of a culture that calls into question that country's "philosophical boundaries." This collision of values means that there may never exist any permanent formula for resolving conflicts between and among citizens. What is needed, Fish argues, citing Charles Taylor, is some "inspired adhoccery" (63). This notion of "inspired adhoccery" aptly captures the essence of Sustainability as I envision it.

6. There is some debate among theorists as to whether hypertext can properly be considered nonlinear. It is certainly true that many if not most hypertext users often follow highly linear paths, screening out information that is not already identified and defined. Martin Rosenberg argues that

hypertext is, for this reason, better labeled "multilinear." While Rosenberg is correct that hypertext, at least for the moment, does retain significant vestiges of linearity, it clearly offers an exponentially larger number of narrative possibilities.

7. No one has summed up our ecological dilemma more concisely than the framers of the Endangered Species Act. The 1973 House report accompanying the bill declared, "Man's . . . effective domination over the world's support systems has taken place within a few short generations. Our ability to destroy, or almost destroy, all intelligent life on the planet became apparent only in this generation. A certain humility, and a sense of urgency, seem indicated" (United States Congress).

8. The map analogy is not wholly accurate because the system and environment are not finite. Even as the system grows more complex and gains a little territory from the environment, so too does the environment grow more complex and regain its previous size. A more accurate analogy might be a three-dimensional map with the system and environment sharing one border but having nothing limiting their expansion on any other side.

9. Donna Haraway's "Cyborg Manifesto" provides a fascinating and provocative discussion of the boundaries between humans and technology. See also Jim Tarter, "Collective Subjectivity and Postmodern Ecology," for an interesting analysis of the impact of fluid boundaries on the discipline of ecology.

10. Wallace Stegner describes humanity's dilemma beautifully: "We are a wild species, as Darwin pointed out. Nobody ever tamed or domesticated or scientifically bred us. But for at least three millennia we have been engaged in a cumulative and ambitious race to modify and gain control of our environment, and in the process we have come close to domesticating ourselves. . . . Just as surely as it has brought us increased comfort and more material goods, [progress] has brought us spiritual losses, and now threatens to become the Frankenstein that will destroy us" (*Sound* 145).

11. Chenoweth insists upon being addressed as "Congress*man*" because she believes it is the only form of the title that commands respect. She was reelected in 1996 and 1998.

12. The mechanistic paradigm was developed in the 1620s and 1630s by a group of French thinkers including Descartes, Mersenne, and Gassendi. They drew on the Baconian principle of dominion over nature to redefine contemporary notions of order. Instead of picturing the world as an organic whole, functioning according to the will of nature, they pictured it mechanically, wherein each part functioned according to a rational and determinable set of laws. Once the machine replaced the infinite cosmos as the metaphor for nature, it became possible to imagine tinkering with the mechanism and reshaping the world according to principles of human rationality. For a fas-

cinating discussion of the development and subsequent dominance of the mechanistic paradigm, see Merchant, *Death* 192–235.

13. There is considerable disagreement among scholars as to the democratizing properties of hypermedia. See Charles Ess, "The Political Computer," especially pages 230–32, for a survey of the differing views. For my purposes, the debate is not relevant. Whether hypertext truly democratizes or merely creates a new hierarchy, Sustainability's efficacy remains unimpaired.

14. According to *Wired* magazine, even corporate CEOs have signed on. The October 1996 issue features an interview with author and former Citicorp/Citibank CEO Walter Wriston. While Wriston "used to be the most powerful banker in the world," according to the interviewer, "now he's talking like a cyberpunk" (Bass). These types of linked linguistic and social shifts lend credence to Richard Rorty's contention that cultural change is more about changing vocabularies than unearthing truths (*Philosophy* 352).

15. This development proves especially important because both ends of the ideological spectrum are prone to appropriating the mantle of objectivity. Mechanistic science has long assumed itself to be ideology-free, while feminist philosophers of science like Sandra Harding oppose traditional models by arguing for a "strong objectivity" capable of culling disruptive (anti) social interests from research data. See Wolfe 40–41.

16. Deep ecologists, for example, are often accused of misanthropy because one of the movement's principal tenets is that of biocentric equality—that "all things in the biosphere have an equal right to live and blossom and . . . that all organisms and entities in the ecosphere are . . . equal in intrinsic worth" (Devall and Sessions 67). Allegiance to this view can lead to troublesome ontological questions about the relative value of the malaria mosquito or the living virus that causes AIDS, compared to the value of human life.

The deep ecological perspective has come under withering criticism even from within the environmental movement. See, for example, Murray Bookchin's critique in *Remaking Society,* 9–13.

17. Among the linked causes of environmentalism that might wind up on opposite sides of the incinerator issue are groups that support incineration over burying wastes and their counterparts who support ground storage; indigenous rights groups versus advocates of environmental justice; wilderness preservationists (if the alternative to incineration involves storing the waste in a remote area) versus proponents of urban renewal; and so on. The incinerator, like many issues that theoretically should galvanize the environmental movement, might polarize it instead.

18. Walter Wriston argues that the basis for wealth has evolved from land to labor to information. In a famous remark now inscribed in the lobby of the

lobby of New York's Library of Science, Industry, and Business, Wriston declared, "Information about money has become almost as important as money itself." Since information cannot actually be sold, this thought might more accurately be expressed as "*Access to* information about money has become almost as important as money itself."

19. Fredric Jameson addresses the dilemma of capitalism in an information society, claiming that the distillation of living entities into bodies of information actually increases commodification rather than complicating or diminishing it.

20. According to Jack Stanford, director of the University of Montana's Flathead Lake Biological Station, "The river is essentially dead. You can put a drift net in the river for fifteen minutes and catch one or two insects" (qtd. in Devine 72–73).

21. Sam Howe Verhovek, "Returning River to Salmon and Man to the Drawing Board," *New York Times*, September 25, 1999, 28.

22. There have been other noteworthy developments in the realm of dam demolition. In the summer of 1999, a hydroelectric dam on Maine's Kennebec River was demolished, per federal order, in order to open the river to salmon and sturgeon migration. In addition, Pacificorp, a northwestern utility company, recently announced that it would take down the Condit Dam on Washington's White Salmon River by the year 2006 rather than pay $30 million to retrofit it to enable salmon migration. The Condit, at 125 feet high, is the tallest dam ever slated for demolition in the United States (Verhovek, 28).

23. Timothy Luke offers an analogous blueprint for reform that he calls "ecological populism." Luke's formulation, grounded in a critique of the ecopolitics of Bookchin, Marcuse, and Soleri, offers a vision of "communities . . . united by new narratives of their own historical consciousness, beyond and behind the nationalist myths of new class bureaucrats nor the progress discourses of corporate public relations, and by more concretely articulated social, ecological, and cultural interests grounded in immediate environmental and political conditions" (*Ecocritique* 200).

24. I adapt these ideas from a talk Mitchell delivered at the 1995 Digital Dialectic Conference in Pasadena, California. See also *City of Bits*, a book that appears in traditional print form from MIT Press, or in hypertext at http://www.mitpress.mit.edu/City_of_Bits/index.html.

Bibliography

Abbey, Edward. *Abbey's Road*. New York: Penguin, 1991.

———. *Beyond the Wall*. New York: Holt, Rinehart and Winston, 1984.

———. *Black Sun*. New York: Simon and Schuster, 1971.

———. *The Brave Cowboy*. New York: Avon, 1992.

———. *Desert Solitaire: A Season in the Wilderness*. New York: Ballantine, 1978.

———. *Down the River*. New York: E. P. Dutton, 1982.

———. *Fire on the Mountain*. New York: Avon, 1992.

———. *The Fool's Progress: An Honest Novel*. New York: Avon, 1990.

———. *Good News*. New York: Plume, 1991.

———. *Hayduke Lives!* Boston: Little, Brown, 1990.

———. *The Journey Home*. New York: E. P. Dutton, 1977.

———. *The Monkey Wrench Gang*. New York: Avon, 1976.

———. *One Life at a Time, Please*. New York: Henry Holt, 1988.

Abram, David. *The Spell of the Sensuous*. New York: Vintage, 1997.

Adams, Henry. *The Education of Henry Adams*. New York: Random House, 1931.

Allen, John L. "The Garden-Desert Continuum: Competing Views of the Great Plains in the Nineteenth Century." *Great Plains Quarterly* 5.4 (fall 1985): 207–20.

Ambrose, Stephen. *Undaunted Courage: Meriwether Lewis, Thomas Jefferson, and the Opening of the American West*. New York: Simon and Schuster, 1996.

Austin, Mary. *Cactus Thorn: A Novella*. Reno: University of Nevada Press, 1988.

———. *Earth Horizon*. Boston: Houghton Mifflin, 1932.

———. *Stories from the Country of Lost Borders*. New Brunswick: Rutgers University Press, 1987.

———. *The Ford*. Berkeley and Los Angeles: University of California Press, 1997.

———. *The Land of Journey's Ending*. New York: Century, 1924.

———. *The Land of Little Rain.* New York: Penguin, 1988.

Bacon, Francis. *Essays and New Atlantis.* London: Walter J. Black, 1942.

Baltensperger, Bradley H. *Nebraska: A Geography.* Boulder, Colo.: Westview Press, 1985.

Barthes, Roland. *A Barthes Reader.* Ed. Susan Sontag. New York: Hill and Wang, 1983.

———. *Mythologies.* Trans. Jonathan Cape. New York: Hill and Wang, 1982.

Bass, Thomas A. "The Future of Money." *Wired* 4.10 (October 1996). www.wired.com/wired/archive/4.10.

Bataille, Georges. *Visions of Excess: Selected Writings, 1927–1939.* Ed. and trans. Allan Stoekl with Carl R. Lovitt and Donald M. Lesle Jr. Minneapolis: University of Minnesota Press, 1985.

Bateson, Gregory. *Steps to an Ecology of Mind.* New York: Ballantine, 1990.

Baudrillard, Jean. *America.* Trans. Chris Turner. New York: Verso, 1988.

———. *The Ecstasy of Communication.* Ed. Slyveree Lotringer, trans. Bernard Schutze and Caroline Schutze. New York: Autonomedia, 1988.

———. *The Mirror of Production.* Trans. Mark Poster. St. Louis: Telos Press, 1975.

———. *Selected Writings.* Ed. and trans. Mark Poster. Stanford: Stanford University Press, 1988.

Beegel, Susan F., Susan Shillinglaw, and Wesley N. Tiffney Jr., eds. *Steinbeck and the Environment: Interdisciplinary Approaches.* Tuscaloosa: University of Alabama Press, 1997.

Belfrage, Cedric. *The Promised Land.* New York: Garland, 1978.

Benson, Jackson. "Hemingway the Hunter and Steinbeck the Farmer." *Michigan Quarterly Review* 24.3 (summer 1985): 441–60.

———. "Through a Political Glass, Darkly: The Example of John Steinbeck." *Studies in American Fiction* 12.1 (spring 1984): 45–59.

———. *The True Adventures of John Steinbeck, Writer.* New York: Viking, 1984.

Benton, Thomas Hart. "Discourse of Mr. Benton of Missouri before the Boston Mercantile Library Association on the Physical Geography of the Country between the States of Missouri and California." Tremont Temple, Boston, December 20, 1854.

Berkman, Richard L., and W. Kip Viscusi. *Damming the West.* New York: Grossman Press, 1973.

Berry, Wendell. *What Are People For?* San Francisco: North Point, 1990.

Bertalanffy, Ludwig von. *Perspectives on General System Theory.* Ed. Edgar Taschdjian. New York: George Braziller, 1975.

Billington, Ray Allen. *Westward Expansion: A History of the American Frontier.* 4th ed. New York: Macmillan, 1974.

Bishop, James, Jr. *Epitaph for a Desert Anarchist: The Life and Legacy of Edward Abbey.* New York: Atheneum, 1994.

Blumenthal, Sidney. "Her Own Private Idaho." *New Yorker* July 10, 1995: 27–33.

Bookchin, Murray. *Remaking Society: Pathways to a Green Future.* Boston: South End Press, 1990.

Bookchin, Murray, and Dave Foreman. *Defending the Earth: A Dialogue between Murray Bookchin and Dave Foreman.* Boston: South End Press, 1991.

Bramwell, Anna. *Ecology and the Twentieth Century: A History.* New Haven: Yale University Press, 1989.

Bryant, Paul L. "Edward Abbey and Environmental Quixoticism." *Western American Literature* 24.1 (May 1989): 37–43.

Callicott, J. Baird. *In Defense of the Land Ethic: Essays in Environmental Philosophy.* Albany: State University of New York Press, 1989.

Carson, Rachel. *Silent Spring.* Boston: Houghton Mifflin, 1987.

Cassuto, David N. *Cold Running River.* Ann Arbor: University of Michigan Press, 1994.

Cassuto, Leonard. *The Inhuman Race.* New York: Columbia University Press, 1997.

Cole, Douglas, and Ira Chaikin. *An Iron Hand upon the People: The Law against Potlatch on the Northwest Coast.* Seattle: University of Washington Press, 1990.

Collard, Andrée, and Joyce Contrucci. *Rape of the Wild: Man's Violence against Animals and the Earth.* Bloomington: Indiana University Press, 1989.

Crawford, John F., and Annie O. Eysturoy, eds. *This Is about Vision: Interviews with Southwestern Writers.* Albuquerque: University of New Mexico Press, 1990.

Crawford, Stanley. *Mayordomo: Chronicle of an Acequia in Northern New Mexico.* Albuquerque: University of New Mexico Press, 1993.

Cronon, William, ed. *Uncommon Ground: Towards Reinventing Nature.* New York: Norton, 1995.

Darwin, Charles. *The Descent of Man.* Princeton: Princeton University Press, 1981.

———. *On the Origin of Species.* Cambridge: Harvard University Press, 1964.

Davis, Robert Con, ed. *The Grapes of Wrath: A Collection of Critical Essays.* Englewood Cliffs, N.J.: Prentice-Hall, 1982.

Devall, Bill, and George Sessions, eds. *Deep Ecology: Living As If Nature Mattered.* Salt Lake City: Gibbs Smith, 1985.

Devine, Robert S. "The Trouble with Dams." *Atlantic Monthly* (August 1995): 64–74.

Ditsky, John, ed. *Critical Essays on Steinbeck's "The Grapes of Wrath."* Boston: Hall, 1989.

Douglas, Mary. *Purity and Danger.* London: Routledge and Kegan Paul, 1966.

Eagleton, Terry. *The Ideology of the Aesthetic.* Cambridge, Mass.: Basil Blackwell, 1990.

Eco, Umberto. *Semiotics and the Philosophy of Language.* Bloomington: Indiana University Press, 1986.

Emerson, Ralph Waldo. *Essays and Lectures.* New York: Library of America, 1983.

————. *Selections from Ralph Waldo Emerson.* Ed. Stephen E. Whicher. Boston: Houghton Mifflin, 1957.

————. *The Works of Ralph Waldo Emerson.* Vol. 1. Boston: Houghton and Mifflin, 1876.

Emmons, David M. *Garden in the Grasslands: Boomer Literature of the Central Great Plains.* Lincoln: University of Nebraska Press, 1972.

Ess, Charles. "The Political Computer." *Hypertext Theory.* Ed. George P. Landow. Baltimore: Johns Hopkins University Press, 1994.

Evernden, Neil. *The Social Creation of Nature.* Baltimore: Johns Hopkins University Press, 1992.

Fink, Augusta. *I-Mary: A Biography of Mary Austin.* Tucson: University of Arizona Press, 1983.

Fish, Stanley. *The Trouble with Principle.* Cambridge: Harvard University Press, 1999.

Fitzgerald, F. Scott. *The Great Gatsby.* New York: Scribner and Sons, 1925.

Flader, Susan. *Thinking Like a Mountain.* Columbia: University of Missouri Press, 1984.

Foreman, Dave. *Confessions of an Eco-Warrior.* New York: Harmony, 1991.

Foreman, Dave, and Bill Haywood, eds. *Ecodefense: A Field Guide to Monkey Wrenching.* Tucson: N. Ludd Press, 1988.

Foucault, Michel. *The Order of Things: An Archeology of the Human Sciences.* Trans. Alan Sherdan-Smith. New York: Vintage, 1970.

————. *Power/Knowledge: Selected Interviews and Other Writings, 1972–1977.* Ed. Colin Gordon. New York: Pantheon, 1980.

Fradkin, Philip L. *A River No More.* New York: Knopf, 1981.

Fritzell, Peter A. *Nature Writing and America.* Ames: Iowa State University Press, 1990.

Habermas, Jürgen. *Legitimation Crisis.* Trans. Thomas McCarthy. Boston: Beacon Press, 1975.

Getches, David. *Water Law.* 3d ed. St. Paul: West, 1997.

Gilpin, William. *The Cosmopolitan Railway, Compacting and Fusing Together All the World's Continents.* San Francisco: History Co., 1890.

———. *The Grain, Pastoral, and Gold Regions of North America.* Philadelphia: Sower Barnes and Co., 1860.

———. *The Mission of the North American People: Geographical, Social, and Political.* 2d ed. Philadelphia: J. B. Lippincott, 1874.

Glotfelty, Cheryll, and Harold Fromm, eds. *The Ecocriticism Reader.* Athens: University of Georgia Press, 1996.

Gore, Al. *Earth in the Balance: Ecology and the Human Spirit.* New York: Houghton Mifflin, 1992.

Gorz, Andre. *Ecology as Politics.* Trans. Patsy Vigderman and Jonathan Cloud. Boston: South End Press, 1980.

Gould, Stephen Jay. *The Mismeasure of Man.* New York: Norton, 1981.

Gragg, Frances, and William Putnam. *The Golden Valley: A Novel of California.* New York: Duell, Sloan and Peoree, 1950.

Gregory, James N. *American Exodus: The Dust Bowl Migration and Okie Culture in California.* New York: Oxford University Press, 1989.

Greiner, Patricia. "Radical Environmentalism in Recent Literature concerning the American West." *Rendezvous* 19.1 (fall 1983): 8–15.

Griffin, Susan. *Woman and Nature: The Roaring Inside Her.* New York: Harper, 1978.

Gross, Alan. *The Rhetoric of Science.* Cambridge: Harvard University Press, 1990.

Grusin, Richard. "Thoreau, Extravagance, and the Economy of Nature." *American Literary History* 5.1 (spring 1993): 30–50.

Haney-López, Ian F. *White by Law: The Legal Construction of Race.* New York: New York University Press, 1996.

Haraway, Donna J. "Cyborg Manifesto." *Simians, Cyborgs, and Women: The Reinvention of Nature.* New York: Routledge, 1991.

Hardin, Garrett, assembler. *Population, Evolution, and Birth Control: A Collage of Controversial Ideas.* 2d ed. San Francisco: W. H. Freeman, 1969.

Harvey, David. *The Condition of Postmodernity: An Inquiry into the Origins of Cultural Change.* Cambridge: Blackwell, 1989.

Hayles, Katherine. "Searching for Common Ground." *Reinventing Nature: Responses to Postmodern Deconstruction.* Ed. Michael E. Soulé and Gary Lease. Washington, D.C.: Island, 1995.

———. "Simulated Nature and Natural Simulations: Rethinking the Relation between the Beholder and the Natural World." *Uncommon Ground: Towards Reinventing Nature.* Ed. William Cronon. New York: Norton, 1995.

————. "Virtual Bodies and Flickering Signifiers." *October* 66 (fall 1993): 69–91.

Hepworth, James, and Gregory McNamee, eds. *Resist Much, Obey Little: Some Notes on Edward Abbey.* Salt Lake City: Dream Garden, 1989.

Horgan, Paul. *Of America East and West.* New York: Farrar, Straus and Giroux, 1984.

————. "The Western Novel—a Symposium." *South Dakota Review* autumn 1964.

Hofstadter, Richard. *The Age of Reform from Bryan to FDR.* New York: Knopf, 1972.

Hoyt, John. *Drought of 1930–34.* U.S. Geological Survey, Water Supply Paper 680. Washington, D.C., 1936.

Hundley, Norris, Jr. *The Great Thirst: Californians and Water, 1770s–1990s.* Berkeley and Los Angeles: University of California Press, 1992.

————. *Water and the West: The Colorado River Compact and the Politics of Water in the American West.* Berkeley and Los Angeles: University of California Press, 1975.

Illich, Ivan. *H₂O and the Water of Forgetfulness.* Berkeley, Calif.: Heyday Press, 1985.

Jameson, Fredric. *The Political Unconscious: Narrative as a Socially Symbolic Act.* Ithaca, N.Y.: Cornell University Press, 1981.

————. *Postmodernism; or, The Cultural Logic of Late Capitalism.* Durham: Duke University Press, 1991.

Jay, Gregory. *America the Scrivener: Deconstruction and the Subject of Literary History.* Ithaca, N.Y.: Cornell University Press, 1990.

Jehlen, Myra. *American Incarnation: The Individual, the Nation, and the Continent.* Cambridge: Harvard University Press, 1986.

Kerr, Robert S. *Land, Wood, and Water.* New York: Fleet, 1960.

Kingsolver, Barbara. *Animal Dreams.* New York: Harper Perennial, 1991.

————. *The Bean Trees.* New York: Harper and Row, 1988.

————. *High Tide in Tucson: Essays from Now or Never.* New York: HarperCollins, 1995.

————. *Holding the Line: Women in the Great Arizona Mine Strike of 1983.* Ithaca, N.Y.: ILR Press, 1989.

————. *Homeland and Other Stories.* New York: Harper and Row, 1989.

————. *Pigs in Heaven.* New York: HarperCollins, 1983.

Kolodny, Annette. *The Land before Her: Fantasy and Experience of the American Frontiers, 1630–1860.* Chapel Hill: University of North Carolina Press, 1984.

————. *The Lay of the Land.* Chapel Hill: University of North Carolina Press, 1975.

Krutch, Joseph Wood. *The Desert Year.* New York: William Sloane, 1952.

Kupperman, Karen Ordahl. "Fear of Hot Climates in the Anglo-American Colonial Experience." *William and Mary Quarterly* 41.2 (1984): 213–40.

————. "The Puzzle of the American Climate in the Early Historical Period." *American Historical Review* 87.5 (December 1982): 1262–89.

La Porte, Todd R. "Organized Social Complexity: Explication of a Concept." *Organized Social Complexity: Challenge to Politics and Policy.* Ed. Todd La Porte. Princeton: Princeton University Press, 1975.

Landow, George P. *Hypertext: The Convergence of Contemporary Critical Theory and Technology.* Baltimore: Johns Hopkins University Press, 1992.

Lange, Dorothea, and Paul Schuster Taylor. *An American Exodus: A Record of Human Erosion in the Thirties.* New Haven: Yale University Press, 1969.

Lanham, Richard A. *The Electronic Word: Democracy, Technology, and the Arts.* Chicago: University of Chicago Press, 1993.

Latour, Bruno. *We Have Never Been Modern.* London: Harvester Wheatsheaf, 1993.

Leopold, Aldo. *A Sand County Almanac.* New York: Ballantine, 1988.

Lerner, Gerda. *The Creation of Feminist Consciousness.* New York: Oxford University Press, 1993.

Levine, George, ed. *One Culture: Essays in Science and Literature.* Madison: University of Wisconsin Press, 1987.

Lewis, Martin W. *Green Delusions: An Environmentalist Critique of Radical Environmentalism.* Durham: Duke University Press, 1992.

Lewis, Meriwether, and William Clark. *The Journals of the Lewis and Clark Expedition.* Lincoln: University of Nebraska Press, 1983.

Light, Andrew. "Urban Wilderness." *Wild Ideas.* Ed. David Rothenberg. Minneapolis: University of Minnesota Press, 1995.

Lopez, Barry. *Crossing Open Ground.* New York: Scribner, 1988.

Luhmann, Niklas. *Ecological Communication.* Trans. John Bednarz Jr. Chicago: University of Chicago Press, 1986.

————. *Essays on Self-Reference.* New York: Columbia University Press, 1990.

————. *A Sociological Theory of Law.* Trans. Elizabeth King and Martin Albrow. Boston: Routledge and Kegan Paul, 1985.

Luke, Timothy W. *Ecocritique: Contesting the Politics of Nature, Economy, and Culture.* Minneapolis: University of Minnesota Press, 1997.

————. "On Environmentality: Geo-power and Eco-knowledge in the Discourses of Contemporary Environmentalism." *Cultural Critique* 30 (spring 1995): 57–82.

Lyotard, Jean-François. *The Inhuman: Reflections on Time.* Trans. Geoffrey Bennington and Rachel Bowlby. Stanford: Stanford University Press, 1991.

Manes, Christopher. *Green Rage: Radical Environmentalism and the Unmaking of Civilization.* Boston: Little, Brown, 1990.

Marsh, George Perkins. *Man and Nature; or, Physical Geography as Modified by Human Action.* Cambridge: Harvard University Press, 1965.

Marx, Karl. *The Economic and Philosophic Manuscripts of 1844.* Ed. Dirk J. Struik, trans. Martin Milligan. New York: International, 1964.

Marx, Leo. *The Machine in the Garden.* New York: Oxford University Press, 1964.

———. "Pastoralism in America." *Ideology and Classic American Literature.* Ed. Sacvan Bercovitch and Myra Jehlen. New York: Cambridge University Press, 1986.

Maturana, Humberto R. "Science and Daily Life: The Ontology of Scientific Explanation." *Research and Reflexivity.* Ed. Frederick Steier. London: Sage, 1991.

Maturana, Humberto R., and Francisco J. Varela. *Autopoeisis and Cognition: The Realization of the Living.* Dordrecht: D. Reidel, 1985.

———. *The Tree of Knowledge: The Biological Roots of Human Understanding.* Trans. Robert Paolucci. Boston: Shambhala, 1992.

McKibben, Bill. *The End of Nature.* New York: Random House, 1989.

McClintock, James I. "Edward Abbey's 'Antidotes to Despair.'" *Studies in Contemporary Fiction* 31.1 (fall 1989): 41–54.

McPhee, John. *The Control of Nature.* New York: Farrar, Straus and Giroux, 1989.

———. *Encounters with the Archdruid.* New York: Farrar, Straus and Giroux, 1971.

McWilliams, Carey. *Factories in the Field: The Story of Migratory Farm Labor in California.* Santa Barbara: Peregrine Press, 1971.

Merchant, Carolyn. *The Death of Nature: Women, Ecology, and the Scientific Revolution.* San Francisco: Harper and Row, 1983.

———. *Ecological Revolutions: Nature, Gender, and Science in New England.* Chapel Hill: University of North Carolina Press, 1989.

———. *Radical Ecology: The Search for a Livable World.* New York: Routledge, 1992.

Mitchell, Don. *The Lie of the Land: Migrant Workers and the California Landscape.* Minneapolis: University of Minnesota Press, 1996.

Muir, John. *My First Summer in the Sierra.* New York: Penguin, 1987.

———. *The Yosemite.* Garden City: Doubleday, 1962.

Murray, John A. "The Hill beyond the City: Elements of the Jeremiad in Edward Abbey's 'Down the River with Henry Thoreau.'" *Western American Literature* 22.4 (February 1988): 301–6.

Nash, Roderick. *The Rights of Nature: A History of Environmental Ethics.* Madison: University of Wisconsin Press, 1989.

———. *Wilderness and the American Mind.* 3d ed. New Haven: Yale University Press, 1989.

———, ed. *American Environmentalism: Readings in Conservation History.* 3d ed. New York: McGraw-Hill, 1990.

National Park Foundation. *Mirror of America: Literary Encounters with National Parks.* Boulder, Colo.: Roberts Reinhart, 1989.

National Resource Council. *Restoration of Aquatic Ecosystems.* Washington, D.C.: National Academy Press, 1992.

Nichols, John. *The Magic Journey.* New York: Ballantine, 1978.

———. *The Milagro Beanfield War.* New York: Ballantine, 1974.

———. *The Nirvana Blues.* New York: Ballantine, 1981.

Norwood, Vera. *Made from This Earth: American Women and Nature.* Chapel Hill: University of North Carolina Press, 1993.

Owens, Louis. *John Steinbeck's Re-vision of America.* Athens: University of Georgia Press, 1985.

Patten, Bernard C. "Systems Approach to the Concept of Environment." *General Systems: Yearbook of the Society for General Systems Research.* Vol. 24. Ed. Brian Gaines. Louisville: Society for General Systems Research, 1979.

Paulsen, William R. *The Noise of Culture: Literary Texts in a World of Information.* Ithaca, N.Y.: Cornell University Press, 1988.

Pierce, Christine, and Donald VanDeVeer, eds. *People, Penguins, and Plastic Trees: Basic Issues in Environmental Ethics.* Belmont: Wadsworth, 1986.

Porush, David. *The Soft Machine: Cybernetic Fiction.* New York: Methuen, 1985.

Postman, Neil. *Technopoly: The Surrender of Culture to Technology.* New York: Vintage, 1992.

Potter, Loren D., and Charles L. Drake. *Lake Powell: Virgin Flow to Dynamo.* Albuquerque: University of New Mexico Press, 1989.

Powell, John Wesley. *The Exploration of the Colorado River and Its Canyons.* New York: Dover, 1961.

———. "Institutions for the Arid Lands." *Century* 39 (May 1890): 111–16.

———. "Irrigable Lands of the Arid Region." *Century* 39 (March 1890): 766–76.

————. "Non-irrigable Lands of the Arid Region." *Century* 39 (April 1890): 915–22.

————. *Report on the Lands of the Arid Region of the United States.* 2d ed. Washington, D.C.: Government Printing Office, 1879.

————. *Selected Prose of John Wesley Powell.* Ed. George Crossette. Boston: David R. Godine, 1970.

Press, Daniel. *Democratic Dilemmas in the Age of Ecology: Trees and Toxics in the American West.* Durham: Duke University Press, 1994.

Rasch, William, and Cary Wolfe. "Theory of a Different Order: A Conversation with Katherine Hayles and Niklas Luhmann." *Cultural Critique* 30 (spring 1995): 7–36.

Rawls, John. *The Law of Peoples.* Cambridge: Harvard University Press, 1999.

Reisner, Marc. *Cadillac Desert: The American West and Its Disappearing Water.* Rev. ed. New York: Penguin, 1993.

Roach, Catherine. "Loving Your Mother: On the Woman-Nature Relation." *Hypatia* 6.2 (1991): 46–59.

Rogin, Michael Paul. "Nature as Politics and Nature as Romance in America." *Political Theory* 5.1 (February 1977): 5–30.

Ronald, Ann. *The New West of Edward Abbey.* Albuquerque: University of New Mexico Press, 1982.

Rorty, Richard. *Objectivity, Relativism, and Truth.* Cambridge: Cambridge University Press, 1991.

————. *Philosophy and the Mirror of Nature.* Princeton: Princeton University Press, 1979.

Rosenberg, Martin E. "Physics and Hypertext: Liberation and Complicity in Art and Pedagogy." *Hypertext Theory.* Ed. George P. Landow. Baltimore: Johns Hopkins University Press, 1994.

Rosman, Abraham, and Paula G. Rubel. *Feasting with Mine Enemy: Rank and Exchange among Northwest Coast Societies.* New York: Columbia University Press, 1971.

Ross, Andrew. *Strange Weather: Culture, Science, and Technology in the Age of Limits.* London: Verso, 1991.

Rothenberg, David, ed. *Wild Ideas.* Minneapolis: University of Minnesota Press, 1995.

Rousseau, Jean-Jacques. *Discourse on Political Economy and the Social Contract.* Trans. Christopher Betts. New York: Oxford University Press, 1994.

Rubin, Alfred. "Pollution by Analogy: The Trail Smelter Arbitration." *Oregon Law Review* 50 (1971): 259–82.

Rudnick, Lois. "Re-naming the Land: Anglo-Expatriate Women in the Southwest." *The Desert Is No Lady: Southwestern Landscapes in*

Women's Writing and Art. Ed. Vera Norwood and Janice Monk. New Haven: Yale University Press, 1987.

Sax, Joseph L., Robert H. Abrams, and Barton H. Thompson Jr. *Legal Control of Water Resources: Cases and Materials.* 2d. ed. St. Paul: West, 1991.

Sears, John F. *Sacred Places: American Tourist Attractions in the Nineteenth Century.* New York: Oxford University Press, 1989.

Seltzer, Mark. *Bodies and Machines.* New York: Routledge, 1992.

Slotkin, Richard. *The Fatal Environment: The Myth of the Frontier in the Age of Industrialization, 1800–1890.* New York: Atheneum, 1985.

———. *Regeneration through Violence: The Mythology of the American Frontier, 1600–1860.* Middletown, Conn.: Wesleyan University Press, 1973.

Smith, Henry Nash. *Virgin Land: The American West as Symbol and Myth.* New York: Vintage Books, 1950.

Smith, Zachary, ed. *Water and the Future of the Southwest.* Albuquerque: University of New Mexico Press, 1989.

Stegner, Wallace. *The American West as Living Space.* Ann Arbor: University of Michigan Press, 1987.

———. *Beyond the Hundredth Meridian: John Wesley Powell and the Second Opening of the American West.* Lincoln: University of Nebraska Press, 1982.

———. *The Sound of Mountain Water: The Changing American West.* New York: E. P. Dutton, 1980.

———. *Where the Bluebird Sings to the Lemonade Springs: Living and Writing in the West.* New York: Penguin, 1992.

Steinbeck, John. *America and Americans.* New York: Viking, 1966.

———. *The Grapes of Wrath.* New York: Penguin, 1978.

———. *In Dubious Battle.* New York: Penguin, 1979.

———. *The Log from the Sea of Cortez.* New York: Penguin, 1986.

———. *The Long Valley.* New York: Penguin, 1986.

———. *Of Mice and Men.* New York: Bantam, 1978.

———. *To a God Unknown.* New York: Penguin, 1986.

———. *Tortilla Flat.* New York: Penguin, 1986.

———. *Travels with Charley.* New York: Bantam, 1962.

———. *The Wayward Bus.* New York: Penguin, 1986.

———. *Working Days: The Journals of "The Grapes of Wrath."* Ed. Robert Demott. New York: Viking, 1989.

Tarter, Jim. "Collective Subjectivity and Postmodern Ecology." *ISLE* 2.2 (winter 1996): 65–84.

Taylor, Mark. *Altarity.* Chicago: University of Chicago Press, 1987.

Thomas, Keith. *Man and the Natural World: A History of the Modern Sensibility.* New York: Pantheon, 1983.

Thoreau, Henry D. *Walden.* Princeton: Princeton University Press, 1973.

Timmerman, John H. *John Steinbeck's Fiction: The Aesthetics of the Road Taken.* Oklahoma City: University of Oklahoma Press, 1986.

Tobias, Michael, ed. *Deep Ecology.* San Marcos, CA: Avant, 1988.

Tokar, Brian. "Marketing the Environment." *Zeta* February 1990: 16–17.

Turnbull, Elsie. *Trail between Two Wars: The Story of a Smelter City.* Victoria: E. G. Turnbull, 1980.

Turner, Fredrick Jackson. *The Frontier in American History.* New York: Holt, 1947.

Udall, Stuart. *The Quiet Crisis.* New York: Holt and Rinehart, 1963.

United States Congress. *A Legislative History of the Endangered and Threatened Species Act of 1973, as Amended.* Compiled in Committee Print, Serial No. 97–6, 97th Cong., 2d sess., February 1982.

Varela, Francisco. *Principles of Biological Autonomy.* New York: Elsevier North Holland, 1979.

Venturi, Robert, Denise Scott Brown, and Steven Izenour. *Learning from Las Vegas: The Forgotten Symbolism of Architectural Form.* Cambridge: MIT Press, 1977.

von Foerster, Heinz. *Observing Systems.* Seaside: Intersystems, 1981.

Wade, Nicholas. "Software for the Brain." Review of *Toward an Understanding of Consciousness,* by Daniel C. Dennett, and *The Conscious Mind,* by David J. Chalmers. *New York Times Book Review* December 29, 1996: 22.

Walton, John. *Western Times and Water Wars: State, Culture, and Rebellion in California.* Berkeley and Los Angeles: University of California Press, 1992.

Warren, Karen, and Jim Cheney. "Ecological Feminism and Ecosystem Ecology." *Hypatia* 6.1 (1991): 178–97.

Webster, Noah. "Dissertation on the Supposed Change of Temperature in Modern Winters." *A Collection of Papers on Political, Literary, and Moral Subjects.* New York: Webster and Clark, 1843.

Wehmhoefer, Richard A. "Water Law in the Southwest." *Water and the Future of the Southwest.* Albuquerque: University of New Mexico Press, 1989.

West, Robin. *Narrative, Authority, and Law.* Ann Arbor: University of Michigan Press, 1993.

Westbrook, Max, and James H. Maguire. *A Literary History of the American West.* Fort Worth: Texas Christian University Press, 1987.

Wild, Peter. "Edward Abbey: The Middle Class Maverick." *New Mexico Humanities Review* 6.2 (summer 1983): 15–23.

Williams, Raymond. *The Country and the City*. New York: Oxford University Press, 1973.

Williams, William Carlos. *In the American Grain*. New York: New Directions, 1956.

Wilson, Alexander. *The Culture of Nature: North American Landscape from Disney to the Exxon Valdez*. Cambridge: Blackwell, 1992.

Wolfe, Cary. "In Search of Post-humanist Theory." *Cultural Critique* 30 (spring 1995): 33–70.

Work, James C. "The Moral in Austin's *The Land of Little Rain*." *Women and Western American Literature*. Ed. Helen Winter Stauffer and Susan J. Rosowski. Troy: Whitson, 1982.

Worster, Donald. *Dust Bowl: The Southern Plains in the 1930s*. New York: Oxford University Press, 1979.

———. *Nature's Economy: A History of Ecological Ideas*. Cambridge: Cambridge University Press, 1977.

———. *Rivers of Empire: Water, Aridity, and the Growth of the American West*. New York: Pantheon, 1985.

———, ed. *The Ends of the Earth: Perspectives on Modern Environmental History*. New York: Cambridge University Press, 1988.

Wright, Will. *Wild Knowledge: Science, Language, and Social Life in a Fragile Environment*. Minneapolis: University of Minnesota Press, 1992.

Wriston, Walter B. *The Twilight of Sovereignty: How the Information Revolution Is Transforming Our World*. New York: Scribner, 1992.

Index